My Moving Tent

My Moving Tent

The Diary of a Desert Rat

by A. A. Nicol, F.S.A.O.

The Pentland Press
Edinburgh – Cambridge – Durham

First published in 1994 by
The Pentland Press Ltd
1 Hutton Close
South Church
Bishop Auckland
Durham

ISBN 1-85821-180-8

Typeset by Carnegie Publishing, 18 Maynard St., Preston
Printed and bound by Antony Rowe Ltd., Chippenham

Contents

List of Illustrations

Introduction—Mobilization

O N 31ST AUGUST 1939, I was called to the colours as a driver-mechanic, in which capacity I had joined the Reserve. Five workmates went with me from the garage where we were employed, and we all had to report to Hilsea Barracks, Portsmouth.

We left Stirling, my home town, on Friday, 1st September. The train was crowded, or at least, any empty seats had large "Reserved" tickets displayed on them (probably expired) so we sat in the guard's van for 400 miles, reaching London at 10.00 p.m. The city was already completely blacked out. At Waterloo we found our connection was at midnight, so we went to the buffet for a cup of tea. We were slightly bewildered by the events of the past twenty-four hours, and everything had an aspect of unreality, a feeling that must have been shared by almost everyone in those momentous days, when the world was again being dragged into war by the fanatic from Berchtesgaden. So we sat in the dimmed light of the buffet, each with his own thoughts, while other figures, some in uniform, showed vaguely in the shadows.

Just then it seemed that everybody was quiet; that all Britain was deep in thought.

We caught the "Southern" electric train to Trafford, where we were picked up by an army lorry and taken to Hilsea Barracks. Here I had my first army meal at 2.00 a.m., served by a lad of the Boy's Service. We were then checked in, and taken to Stamshaw Road School which was to be our billet for the next few days. We slept in rows on the parquet wood floor of the main hall, and marched the mile to Hilsea Barracks and back again for each meal of the day. There was a piano in the school hall and, as is usual in a crowd, someone could play, and someone sang, which brightened things up a bit.

At the barracks we were gradually fitted out with uniform, the old service dress – as used in World War I – but with the new field service cap which folded flat. My boots were a trifle large and considerably tougher than my feet and consequently, in the tramping back and forth, six miles a day, my feet got blistered.

By this time, draftees had reported to Hilsea in their thousands, and the garrison had their hands full. We sat in groups all over the barrack square in warm sunshine, waiting to be inoculated, while the Ordnance Corps band played selections to us.

We had heard about Hitler marching into Poland, and on Sunday, 3rd September, one of the "regulars" came into the barracks and told us that Mr. Chamberlain, the Prime Minister, had announced that Britain was at war with Germany as from eleven o'clock that morning.

WAR! We had felt it was coming, but now it was an accomplished fact. Once more Germany had broken International Law; once more the nations were to be locked in a death struggle. We had no conception of the vast preparations made by Germany then, and believed that Britain and France between them could successfully deal with Germany in a matter of six months or so.

How wrong we were!

We could not foresee the long dark journey before us, the wanderings, adventures and vicissitudes, before we achieved final victory.

After five days, I was completely fitted out with my equipment and inoculated against typhoid and tetanus, after waiting in a huge queue outside the Medical Inspection room, henceforth to be known – like most things in the Army – from its initials – as the M.I. room. The inoculation made me feel slightly sick. Our civvy clothes were parcelled and sent off home. Back at the school, "details" were read out every five or ten minutes and, one by one, my friends from Stirling were posted away to different parts of the country, parting with a simple handshake and "Cheerio! Good Luck!" This was something that was to happen only too often. You made friends, often good comrades, only to lose them whenever a unit was re-formed, and it was impossible to keep in touch with them all, even by writing. Yet these friends often went through experiences together which do not occur in civilian life, experiences which bound them closer, so that they relied upon each other absolutely.

About 5.00 p.m. on Wednesday, 6th September, my name was called and I collected my kit and marched once more to the barracks, along with others bound for Catterick Camp.

My inoculated arm was now stiff and swollen, and each time we moved I had difficulty in handling my kit, which included rifle, respirator, steel helmet, greatcoat, valise, haversack, water bottle and kit bag, with cleaning kit, brushes, towels, pullover, etc. What the weight of it all was I don't know but, as I am only of average size, I felt like Atlas, carrying all the world on his back.

We were taken to the station and travelled overnight, reaching Darlington at 4.00 a.m. Here Locomotion No. 1, the first passenger railway engine, is preserved on the platform, but I was in no fit state to take much interest in it. We had to wait two hours for a connection to Richmond. The Third Class waiting room was full of sleeping figures in khaki and a policeman kept us from entering the First Class waiting room, so we sat in the buffet to wait.

Eventually, on reaching Catterick, we went to the "Piave Lines", the quarters of a section of the Royal Army Ordnance Corps. Beside a pathway, I sat on the ground and removed my boots in order to burst a huge blister on each heel. One chap gave me a couple of plaster dressings for them, out of a small tin he had. This was a cheery Yorkshireman who, on the train, had suggested we might finish up in Egypt, riding on camels. Then, he said, if we got thirsty we would only have to "... bore a hole in t'hoomp!"

Maybe he didn't know that a camel does not carry water in its hump, but the joke went down well just the same. Little did I know that I, for one, would indeed see Egypt, the Nile and the Pyramids, though not for another two years.

"But tae oor tale!" as Burns says.

Having been given breakfast, we were again split up, and some of us were sent to Bellerby, seven miles away, a desolate camp in the heart of the Yorkshire moors. The nearest village was Leyburn, two miles away.

At Bellerby, we formed the unit known as G.H.Q. Troops Workshops, consisting of Main Workshops, Main Recovery and six "Line of Communication" Recovery Sections. As we realized later, "recovery" meant getting smashed vehicles out of ditches, rivers and other awkward places; in fact general breakdown work.

Most of us had come from civilian jobs, including the officers, and only the Warrant Officers and senior N.C.O.s were regular soldiers. Behind the camp was a large vehicle park, containing everything from motor-cycles to giant Scammel tank-transporters. During the next two weeks, we learnt to handle and maintain these vehicles, and also did a certain amount of foot drill, rifle drill and gas drill.

I was in No. 3 L.O.C. Recovery Section, which consisted of one officer, one Q.M.S., one Staff Sergeant, and sixteen other ranks. Attached to us were two Gordon Highlanders, one as cook and one as G.D. (General Duty-man) sometimes called the sanitary orderly, on account of his work with latrines, but more often referred to by a name which is quite unprintable! Nevertheless, big Jock Chisholm, our easy-going Aberdonian G.D., was well liked.

I found myself in the crew of a Crossley breakdown, eight tons unladen, and with a motor-driven winch and beam crane. I had a bit of practice driving this vehicle, and reversing with a Tasker trailer behind it. Then I was given the job of painting the Unit's number and initials on some metal boxes which were intended to keep documents under lock and key. I was complimented on making a neat job so after that I got all the "sign-writing" to do, which was better than crawling under the Crossley with a grease-gun! The Crossley had over eighty grease-nipples on its chassis. I know. I had to find them all!

In the Naafi one night (I'll have to have a glossary for all these initials, unless you can work them out for yourself) we heard over the radio that the Russians had marched into Poland, meeting the Germans roughly half-way. This news caused some consternation, for at that time we were not sure whether Russia might have arranged all this with Hitler, and I think most of us got the impression that the Allies would now have Russia against them as well! We had been warned that we would soon be going overseas, and in this same N.A.A.F.I. we had our first lecture on V.D. given, strangely enough, by a naval medical officer. The canteen girls, of course, were not supposed to be present and the shutters were pulled down at the counter. The girls, however, were behind the shutters clearing up the dishes and, as our naval lecturer was using typically forthright language, it was not surprising that those nearest the counter heard an occasional girlish giggle from behind the shutters.

On the 19th September, we were told to pack ready to move next day. On the morning of Wednesday 20th, we rose before daylight and began putting our personal kit on the vehicles, which were already loaded with equipment: wooden blocks, wedges, pulley-blocks, ropes, chains, hooks, huge wooden levers, crowbars, sledge hammers, axes, spades, etc. Kit-bags were not supposed to be taken, but we managed to smuggle them aboard in the darkness. We had been told to take one blanket each and most of us took only one, though if I had known what was to come

I would have taken several. I had had my second dose of inoculations by this time, but they naturally did not affect me as badly as the first lot.

So, at 6.00 a.m. our convoy, camouflage-painted in khaki and black, took to the road. There were diesel-engined tank-transporters, A.E.C. tractor breakdowns, (13.5 tons, petrol driven). Crossleys, Morris 15 cwt. trucks (so named from their capacity) and the motor-cycles used by the dispatch riders, henceforth to be known as D.R.s, or Don-Rs.

Our arms consisted of Boyes anti-tank rifles – one to each recovery section – Bren guns, and our rifles, which we had never fired!

I sat with others in the back of our Crossley and we travelled steadily all day, stopping only for rough meals prepared on petrol cookers, which work like big blowlamps. We arrived at Lutterworth at dusk. The articulated transporters, being slower and more awkward to manoeuvre, arrived an hour later. One had knocked down a "Keep Left" pylon at a roundabout, but there were no other mishaps.

We were allowed to go to the village for a drink then we returned to the vehicles to bed down at the roadside. Some of us made a "lean-to" with a tarpaulin against the side of the Crossley, and ten men crawled into it with their one blanket and greatcoat apiece. At first it was warm, almost suffocating, but in the morning we were stiff with the cold. This was just one of the times when extra blankets would have been welcome.

The next day brought us to our destination, which was Newport, Monmouthshire. Here we got a great welcome from the local people, who came out in crowds and gave us tea, biscuits and cakes, bless them! One reverend gentleman came along the line of vehicles giving away cigarettes to all the boys, and when I said I didn't smoke, he searched in another pocket and gave me a packet of chewing-gum instead. We went on to a transit camp in Tredegar Park, Newport, and stayed there under canvas until Saturday, 23rd September.

At six o'clock on Saturday evening, we marched to the docks, where our vehicles had already been put aboard ship. For a couple of hours we sat on bales of cardboard in a warehouse but soon, as it became dark, songs began to echo through the big building. Though still "rookies", the boys were already exhibiting the soldier's propensity for keeping cheery in all circumstances, though I must say I was not feeling very bright myself.

At 8.00 p.m., we boarded the steamer *Ben My Chree* of the Isle of

Man service, now in its grey war paint. During the night we moved out on the tide to wait in the estuary till daylight. On Sunday morning, 24th September, we were joined by other small ships and an escort of two destroyers, whereupon we sailed for a secret destination, still in the first month of the war. Incidentally, I was then twenty-two years of age.

Part I
With the B.E.F. in France

CHAPTER I

Craon

THE LITTLE CONVOY sailed throughout Sunday and Monday. Our Section was crowded into a corner of the third-class saloon, where fans were whirring in a vain attempt to keep the place cool. At night, troops were sleeping all over the decks and even on the stairs. It was so stifling below that I went up on deck for fresh air. The men there could not sleep for the cold. Water was so short for the number on board that we had to queue up at certain times to fill our water bottles, and washing was out of the question.

On Monday, we seemed to be well ahead of the other ships and word came round "from the crew" (whence all "gen" originated) that two submarines had appeared in the night and had been chased by our escort, while the troopships put on full steam. We now saw land on the port side and were told it was France. To be exact it was the coast of Brittany, steep, tree-clad but rocky and dotted with little white houses with red roofs. Two French destroyers took over from our escort and brought us past Belle Île into St. Nazaire. We drew in to the quayside but did not disembark, apparently waiting for further orders. We looked curiously at the houses rising high behind the harbour. There were some civilians on the quay, and a couple of gendarmes, to say nothing of the children scrambling for pennies and yelling the one word we were to hear too often ... *"Souvenir? Souvenir?"* Someone on the top deck produced an accordion and the whole ship-load of troops joined in singing the hits of the day, *"South of the Border"* and *"Boomps-a-Daisy"*.

Later in the day, we drew out again from the quay and at dusk we began to move up the River Loire, which is about three times as long as the Thames. That evening we sailed about twenty-five miles inland on the river, a strange voyage for an Isle of Man steamer!

Strange, but very beautiful for, as we leaned on the rail, the moon came out full and clear, and a line of silver shone on the calm waters, while now and then the white hulls of the little yachts peeped out from

8

the banks. It was so serenely peaceful that the war seemed and was, in fact, remote.

Our final destination was the city of Nantes, the ancient capital of Brittany. When we did get to the quay there, it seemed that preparations to receive us were not complete, so we stayed on the ship. After the usual meal of bully beef and hard biscuits, we slept on board for the third night. We awoke next morning with mouths like flannel, and were glad to get off the ship at last.

So we set foot on French soil on 26th September.

We now marched from the docks to an empty biscuit factory, which was apparently to be our resting place. The building bore the inscription, "L.U. PETIT BEURRE. L.U." repeated in large letters across its façade and inevitably became known to the troops as the "Lulu" factory.

A sentry was immediately posted, much to the interest of the local people, who regarded his "Slope Arms" and "Order Arms" with intent curiosity. The factory was big and cold, and here I spent two of the bitterest nights of my life, lying on the concrete floor, still with one blanket, while a vicious draught blew in from the big doors. One old soldier began telling us about the First World War when he was up to his knees in mud, which didn't help us in the least. Throughout the night the floor sent a chill through our numb bodies and we were glad when daylight came and we could work the stiffness out of our limbs.

During the day, we were allowed out to see the town and we went around in small groups. Now we saw all the scenes with which we were to become familiar. Only one of the other men and myself spoke some French and we were kept busy explaining the various shop signs: *épicerie*, *charcuterie*, *confiserie*, *chevallerie*, etc.

We found our way into the Place Royale, with its ornamental fountain and joined a queue at a bank to change our money. The rate of exchange was 176 francs to the pound, so that a franc was worth roughly 1½d.

Then we thought we would sample some of the French drinks in one of the cafes. Needless to say, the boys did not think much of the raw *vin ordinaire*, which tastes something like vinegar and quinine mixed, but cognac and French beer went down better. Finally, we shared a bottle of champagne which cost only 30 francs, about 3s. 6d. The same stuff in Britain would have cost about six times as much, owing to customs duties. The mixture, of course, had some effect on us, and we proceeded on our way with a considerably brighter outlook. We could have appreciated some of that cognac in our cold billet, for there was no rum ration.

Nantes is an interesting town, with the Château des Ducs de Bretagne in its centre. This fine old castle, with its drum towers, is surrounded by a moat, partly dried up, on whose banks we saw swans and white deer. An old canal, once tidal water, had also receded, leaving a stretch of sand with several bridges over it. A local inhabitant told us the town authorities had intended turning it into gardens but now trenches were being dug in it, and air raid shelters erected.

Thus are the plans of peace frustrated by war. Yet, I suppose the First World War hastened the development of aircraft and radio and this Second World War was to give us radar and atom-power!

But that is jumping ahead.

On the second day, following another freezing night, some of us went into town again and had a steaming hot bath, after which we felt much better.

The continental method of driving on the right of the road took a little getting used to, especially as French drivers are notoriously reckless. One will often approach a crossroads at undiminished speed, his thumb pressed firmly on the button of his high-pitched horn, then scream straight across, in the unshakeable belief that no other fool should now emerge from the right or left at a similar speed. It is amazing how often they get away with it. It might be regarded as an object lesson in faith.

On Thursday, 28th September, we went back to the docks to collect our vehicles, which had now been unloaded from the ships. Soon we took the road again, driving for the first time on the right. That night we slept in bell tents which had been erected outside Savenay village, still with one blanket each. I have since learned that Savenay was the location of a base hospital in the first war, and was well known to the American troops at that time.

In the field next to us when we arrived, French cavalry horses were being trained to perform drill in response to shrill trumpet calls.

Very up to date ... if you pick an early enough date!

Next day we reached Craon, a small town in the *département* of Mayenne. Here we set up a Recovery Post. Our job was to recover smashed or broken-down vehicles over a seventy-mile radius, carry out light repairs and pass the bigger jobs back to the base workshops at Nantes.

Our billet was in a hay-loft, which we reached by climbing a twenty-foot ladder, entering by a low door. There was a small window at the far end. The French military authorities provided us with several blankets each, and we had straw on the floor, so we managed to make ourselves fairly comfortable in the cold nights. Rats would gnaw and scratch at the woodwork near our heads but we treated them with the same contempt that they apparently accorded us.

One of our first jobs, early in October, was to bring in a small truck which had run into a ferro-concrete pole carrying electric power cables. The driver had been killed, his seat being driven back into the body of the truck, which almost surrounded the pole. The concrete standard was leaning at an angle, and there was some danger that it might fall when we moved the truck, so we waited until the power was cut off, then pulled the truck out with the Crossley's winch. The winch cable on these vehicles is wound on a drum, motor-driven, and can be paid out either from the front or, by taking it round other pulleys on the chassis, it can be brought from the side or rear as required. As may be imagined, difficulties sometimes arise, if the wreck happens to be upside down in a river or in some such awkward position.

If the front axle or steering is smashed on a wreck, as often happens, it has to be suspended so that the front wheels are clear of the ground. It is raised by the crane and the forward end is then attached to the rear of the breakdown, usually by means of a triangle or "A" frame. The base side of the triangle consists of a roller (to avoid fraying of ropes) and this is lashed to the wreck.

A ring at the apex of the triangle goes on to the towing hook and the wreck is then pulled along on its rear wheels.

These details are necessary to explain what is meant by a "suspended tow", for this kind of work was regularly carried out by us throughout the whole of the war, and the phrase may recur.

We soon made ourselves at home in Craon and became well known in some of the cafés, as we were the only British troops in the town. There were exactly twenty-one of us, for the other Recovery Sections had gone further into the country to take up positions spaced out across France towards the Belgian frontier and we, No. 3 Section, were left on our own.

There were many French *poilus* about, however (some were indeed "Hairy") as this was a rest centre for a machine-gun regiment who were holding part of the far-off Maginot Line.

I still have an enamelled bracelet from Craon, bearing a picture of a Maginot gun turret and the words, *"On ne passe pas!"* This, of course, evolved from the motto of Verdun in the first war, when Petain was in command; *"Ils ne passeront pas!"* – "They shall not pass".

We were allowed to use the French troops' canteen which had several games and a wheezy old harmonium. The reading material included two copies of *Le Miroir* dating from the first war, with contemporary pictures of the front in photogravure. The harmonium may also have been used in the First World War!

One part of the canteen became our cookhouse and good food we had too. We were not on army rations, but our officer had a cash allowance with which to buy provisions in the French shops. Sometimes I went round with the cook to act as interpreter and we would purchase oatmeal, eggs, butter, milk, cheese, meat, fish, flour, potatoes, etc., all wholesome fresh food.

We maintained a night picket to guard our vehicles which were parked in an open grassy space beyond the trees which lined the road.

I shall never forget those rainy October nights on sentry duty, as I stood under the dripping plane trees and listened to the two bells of the Town Hall striking the quarters in a descending cadence ... "Ding - Dong!" ... Or the mornings, when the peace of the night was broken by the challenge of a squeaky bantam cock across the way, answered scornfully by two or more cockerels from afar off.

The last sentry roused the others at six o'clock and we tumbled down our ladder and washed under a pump marked *"pas potable"*. The water was icy cold, and brought a glow to our cheeks. One day a woman came to fill a pail at this pump and, purely as a matter of courtesy, one of our fellows offered to work the handle of the pump for her. This she absolutely refused to let him do, possibly fearing that the neighbours would get the impression she was fraternizing with the "foreigners". Or it may be that she was not used to getting any help from her menfolk!

The people were old-fashioned, religious and narrow-minded. Each Sunday morning, early, they went to Mass, dressed in funereal black. Then the children would march in procession to Sunday School, all clothed in little black smocks and led by a priest, also attired in black robes. Later everyone, women and children included, would repair to the cafés and there drink crude white wine, even the smallest child sharing in the bottle. On Sundays and on market days, all the farming people came in gigs and in deep-sided wagons to renew acquaintance. By evening, some of the men would be pleasantly inebriated, though complete drunkenness was rare in France, simply because drink can be obtained at any hour of the day.

Prominently displayed in every café is the "Law for the Repression of Public Drunkenness".

When Frenchmen play cards in a café, they use a pack of only thirty-two cards and I noticed that they played round the table in the opposite direction to us; that is, they dealt anti-clockwise.

One evening, as I walked down the street with one of the other fellows, we were stopped by a French soldier with a sandy beard and spectacles. He said there was an Englishman in the hospital and would we care to visit him? We said we would, and went with him to a small hospital attached to a convent, where we found the patient to be a D.R. who had had a spill and fractured his kneecap. He was alone in the little ward and seemed glad to have company. As we talked, a nun brought in tea, which is unusual, for the continental beverage is, of course, coffee.

Our guide, in spite of his beard, was quite a young man and was much cleaner and smarter than the average French soldier. He told us he had been training as a missionary before being called up. The usual type of *soldat* in Craon was slovenly, dressed partly in blue, partly in khaki and invariably walked about with both hands sunk deep in his pockets, even when a woman was attached to one arm.

One café in Craon was owned by an old chap who wore a peaked cap, taxi-driver style. The first time we went to his place, one of the boys tried to order some drinks in atrocious French. "Vooley-voo me ... er ... donner ... doo ... deux" (gestures to represent glasses). The old fellow listened glumly for a moment or two, then he said, "For Christ's sake, speak English!"

He had at one time worked in England and spoke fluent English, including much that was not quite "drawing-room". We became quite friendly with him and spent more time in his café than any other. It became our favourite rendezvous.

One Sunday, three of us hired out some dilapidated cycles, and set out to visit a small village called Laigne, about nine kilometres away. We had scarcely covered half a kilometre when we had a puncture. We returned to the town, exchanged our dud mount for another equally dilapidated one – I wonder if *they* were used in the first war? – and set off once more.

The road was dead straight all the way, only rising and falling with the slow undulation of the land, until it disappeared over the horizon. The main roads in many parts of France are lined with apple trees, which belong to the state. The apples fall on the verge and when they are mouldy, are gathered to be made into cider. As we discovered, these apples are much too bitter to eat and leave a furry feeling in the mouth. They are so acid that if you cut one with a penknife the blade immediately turns black.

That is one reason why the apples are allowed to lie on the verges untouched. Many were already lying at the roadside as we cycled out from Craon.

At Laigne, people came to their windows to peer at us, or looked round the edge of a door. I don't think they had ever seen a British soldier before. There was little of interest in the village itself but we had a drink in the local café, then started to cycle back as the sun went down. About three kilometres short of base, we had another puncture but, being recovery men, we were not dismayed! We evolved our own method of recovery. My two friends climbed aboard one cycle, one sitting on the top tube, while I pushed the wreck along beside my own battered mount. So we wobbled along in the dusk, back to Craon; but we had to laugh at ourselves.

In a little house near our vehicle park lived a very old lady, bent and wrinkled, with untidy white hair. She gave lessons in English and German to several of the local children and she offered to help some of us improve our French, free of charge, if we would in turn help the children by speaking to them in English. So several of us would sit in her house in the evenings and I think we did improve our knowledge of French. Each lesson began with the Lord's Prayer, which I can still recite as we did then, following her lead:

"*Notre Père,*
Qui êtes aux cieux,
Que Votre Nom soit sanctifié ..."

The experiment, however, was not quite so successful for the children for, with our various accents: Scottish, Yorkshire, etc., they got a very confused idea of English as she is spoke!

It was now near the end of October 1939 and so far we had only a moderate amount of work to do and several vehicles had been passed on to base workshops. We usually had Sundays off, unless there was a recovery job. So one Sunday, in brilliant sunshine, I went for a walk with two others, one from Honiton in Devon. We came to a farm where an old man was watering some horses and we thought we'd try to get some eggs. We could have asked in French but Devon said, "Leave un to me; I'll make 'im unnerstand!" He apparently believed that actions spoke louder than words, for he went over to the old farmer and began making signs and noises reminiscent of one of the egg-laying community. He waggled his arms, clucked and crooned in a fair imitation of a hen, while the old chap gaped at him with his jaw sagging, and we leaned helplessly on the gate. The impromptu artiste finished up on a low, moaning note that moved us to hysterics. Then, losing hope, he made signs of putting something in his mouth. Suddenly, the old fellow laughed and, taking us into the farm, he produced a large stone jug of rough cider, apparently being under the impression that we wanted a drink in return for the entertainment! When we had satisfied our thirst and regained a little of our poise, we asked for eggs in the orthodox manner and obtained a dozen for nine francs, which was cheap. The cider, of course, was on the house. Even then, I don't think the old chap tumbled to the mystic import of the pantomime, but probably thought we were all a trifle crazy.

About this time, my French-speaking mate and myself made the acquaintance of a French corporal, Lecoq, who spoke English which he had learnt from the Americans in the first war. He took us round the cafés and introduced us to those fine liqueurs, Benedictine and Cointreau. The former was originally blended by the black-robed Benedictine Monks and the latter is made from concentrated orange alcohol. In one café there was a girl called Christianne, the proprietor's daughter, who used to make rosaries for the convent. She also made necklaces, all by hand. Holding a pair of round-nosed pliers, her hands moving like lightning, she would turn a length of white metal wire into a fine chain with separate, interlocked links, yet the eye could not follow how it was done. Coloured beads, ornaments and saintly medallions were added *ad libitum*, the whole article being finished inside ten minutes. Many of us bought these necklaces to send home. On Sunday, 29th October, we played a football match against a team of French soldiers, many local supporters being present. Our own supporters (all five of them) were also on the touch-line. I was playing right-half but, in spite of this grave handicap, we won. The Frenchmen played well, moving upfield but we took our chances in front of goal and shot better, the score being 5–3. *And* we had a French referee! Continental fashion, they raised three cheers for us at the end of the game, which rather shook us.

Mail from home had taken on the importance it always has abroad, and was eagerly awaited. When it was given out, everyone gathered round the person who was shouting out the names. One by one, they went away with a treasured letter and woeful was he who waited in vain. All such mail had to be collected from Rennes, some forty miles away and once or twice I drove the unit's little Morris "8" tourer on this mail trip. To reach Rennes, you had to leave Mayenne, where all the roads seemed to be very straight and go into the next *département*, Ille et Vilaine, of which Rennes is the capital and where all roads, by contrast, twist and turn and are much more picturesque. Passing through towns and villages, I had glimpses of narrow, cobbled streets and over-hanging half-timbered houses. La Guerche de Bretagne, in particular, is a quaint and pretty town. November fogs were now common and, re-turning from Rennes in darkness, I several times met, and missed, the big square farm-carts which the French, with their usual calm disregard of road safety, brought on the roads with never a vestige of a light showing.

Soon, we learned that we were to leave Craon and, on Saturday eve-ning, 4th November, we had a farewell round of the cafés together. In one, a French radio comedian, now in uniform, obliged with a comic song, accompanied by another *poilu* on an old-type button accordion. In others, there were drinks on the house and handfuls of postcards were given to us as souvenirs. We were also saying goodbye to Bill, an interpreter from Alsace, who had latterly been attached to us. He spoke German and English, as well as his own French, and he had become one of our best friends among the local troops. As the evening wore on, and we went from here to beer, and from there to cognac, Bill got as merry as any of us. I remember him giving someone a postcard inscribed, "A Souvenir of the Craon War, from Bill". When we moved from one café to another, he insisted on shouting orders at us in English. Finally, the last café was closing, so we assembled in the street, taking arms till we stretched right across the way in one long line, with Bill somewhere in the middle. "By ze left, Quee-eek Marsh!" he yelled, and off we went, unsteadily, to our billet, singing as we went. When one swayed, we all swayed, but somehow, we managed to avoid houses, lamp-posts, trees and such like obstacles which some inconsiderate person had left lying about. Arriving at the ladder under our hay loft, we decided it was impossible for us all to go up the ladder in line abreast, so the party broke up. We said goodnight to Bill and began the perilous ascent. Now and then a foot would slip off the ladder or through the ladder or someone would be left hanging by one hand while the next man regarded the soles of his boots with mild curiosity; but in spite of these diversities, we all got into bed; though at intervals in the night, someone would stumble through the sleeping forms with the apparent intention of getting back *down* the ladder as quickly as possible.

Next day, Sunday, 5th November 1939, we left Craon, to go back to Nantes, which was to be our home until the evacuation in the following summer, about three weeks after Dunkirk.

CHAPTER 2

Nantes

O N OUR ARRIVAL at Nantes, we found we were to be attached to
No. 2 Base Ordnance Workshop, which had taken over a large
garage belonging to Drouin Frères, a local 'bus company. Our
billet was a broken-down old mansion with the grandiose name, *Le
Château de Breil*, situated in a side road off the Boulevard des Anglais
(appropriate name) and a few hundred yards from the garage, which
was in the outskirts of the city. We had two-tiered beds, made of wood
and wire netting which kept us off the stone floor, although the top
bunk was very shaky. We were given a ration of *Cerclettes*, the little
French briquettes, for the fire and, when we had filled the broken
window panes with hardboard and hung sack-cloth curtains round the
broken doors, we were fairly warm. At a later date even drinking water,
which the "Castle" lacked, was laid on for us by a tap in the "hallway".

It was still a Phoney War and neither side had made any real move.
There was only patrol activity between the Maginot and Siegfried Lines
and the British Army lay on the Belgian border with little to do. Base
Workshops, however, always had a certain amount of work in hand and
it was our job to bring in all the wrecks from the railhead at Chapelle
sur Erdre, a village station about five kilometres outside Nantes. To this
railhead came trucks, guns, searchlights and armoured cars, right across
France from the forward areas and we took them to No. 2 and several
other workshops in Nantes. The Garage Drouin dealt with tanks and
trucks, and another section in the Renault garage specialised in engine
repairs. Citroën *motor* garage was taken over for motor-cycles and trucks,
and Citroën *'bus* garage was responsible for guns and searchlights. At
first these workshops could not take all the work and we simply took
the vehicles off the railway wagons and dumped them in rows in an
adjoining field. We were also responsible for all recovery work within
a seventy-mile radius of the city and, as we might be called out in the
night, a crew of four had to stay in each night as recovery "stand-by".

This duty came round every third night and we were excused the guard duty at the workshop.

Nantes, historic capital of Brittany, is a fine city, with a population of 187,000. It is full of interesting shops which at the beginning of the war contained plenty of goods and there are several cinemas and theatres, so we had much more to do with our spare time than previously. Troops who were in Nantes will remember such cinemas as the *Olympia, Apollo, Rex, Palace* and *Katorza*. The last named was peculiar in that the seats sloped up to the screen instead of down, yet the view was quite unobstructed. All the films shown, American or English, had sub-titles in French on the screen, reminiscent of the old silent films, though the original soundtrack was retained. On Sundays, however, when most of the French cinema-goers turned out, films were shown with a synchronized French soundtrack, so that we had famous stars "speaking" in French but singing in English! Usually a completely French film would also be shown on Sunday and some of them were very good. Cinemas and other forms of entertainment are usually open till midnight on Sunday in the towns of Catholic France. What a contrast to the dreary aspect of some parts of Britain on Sunday, which gives foreigners the impression that we are a dull, miserable race.

In 1939–1940, one could still buy good food and good drinks at the cafés at reasonable prices. A light meal of eggs and chips or ham with egg omelette, French bread and fresh butter and coffee would cost only 7 or 8 francs. French beer, light or brown, was quite good and a glass of *good* cognac was only 2½ francs or fourpence. In Brussels in 1945, the price of a second-rate cognac was to rise as high as 50 francs a glass; just twenty times as much, for the Belgian franc after the liberation had the same rate of exchange as the French franc before Dunkirk. We were glad to be able to buy a supper in a café for, to tell the truth, the Army food we were now getting was atrocious. Our morning bacon had green and black lines running through it, the bread was mouldy and the tea was watery. At tea-time we had cheese one day, tinned herring or pilchard next, and jam the third day. This cycle was continually repeated so that we always knew in advance what was for tea. Nine out of ten dinners were stew, full of stringy bully-beef. Some months were to pass before an inspecting officer came round from *outside* the unit, and there was an immediate improvement. The food became really edible and there was more variety. Such items as tinned fruit, which had been scarce, began to appear fairly regularly. The men generally held the opinion that someone had been selling the food to French civilians, a transaction which would be referred to in Army slang as "flogging the rations" or "working a flanker". When things improved, we even had a jug of water and glasses on each table! The water, of course, tasted of chlorine, which was put in it to prevent the danger of typhoid fever. We dined in a draughty stine barn and here too we took our turn at cook-house fatigues. In that bitter first winter of the war, it took seven of us four hours to peel enough potatoes for one day. Our fingers and feet grew numb and the sacks of "spuds" seemed bottomless. Our ordinary work ran to fairly regular hours and we had a half-day every Sunday and Thursday unless we were on the stand-by crew for road accidents.

On these half-days, I managed to see something of the city. Tram-cars ran from near our billet along the Rue des Haut Pavés, by Place Viarme to the church of Saint Nicolas, near the centre of the town. The trams were small, single-deckers, painted yellow and usually towing one or more carriages behind them. Later, I was to see the same type of tramcar in Cairo, Naples, Brussels and Hamburg, always coloured yellow. And these French tram-drivers! Each vehicle had a bell worked by a foot-button and, as they careered along, whether anything was in the way or not the driver's foot moved rhythmically up and down on the button making a noise which, in Britain, would surely be taken as heralding the advent of a fire-engine. If anything *did* appear in front, the tram did not slow down, but the bell control speeded up to a more frantic tempo, thereby proclaiming to all and sundry that the driver, at least, was taking precautions. In the words of the song: *"Clang! Clang! Clang! went the Trolley!"*

Among other things, Nantes possessed several fine museums and an art gallery. The gallery, Le Musée des Beaux Arts, contains many interesting paintings and fine examples of sculpture. I visited it on Sunday, 12th November with another fellow and we were particularly impressed by the two huge panels on either side of the main staircase, which were each about thirty feet long. They were entitled "Mystical Brittany" and "Industrious Brittany". One rather gruesome picture showed a scene from the Siege of Nantes and depicted one of the starving garrison in the snow, cutting a slice of flesh from the body of another who was dead. Coming away from the gallery, we passed the War Memorial near the Castle of the Dukes of Brittany. A small crowd was looking at the poppy wreaths which had been laid the day before, following Allied custom. A gipsy band was playing in the open space by the Château, which is the most prominent landmark in the city.

Later we crossed the bridge over the wide old moat and, passing between two round towers, entered the Château, which dates from the fifteenth century. Within the ancient walls, we found a Museum of Decorative Arts and here were tableaux of Breton room interiors, showing figures in period costume and all the contemporary furnishings, utensils and ornaments, along with collections of swords, muskets, fusils and suits of armour.

On another Sunday, I visited the Archaeological Museum of Nantes, where hall after hall is filled with the things which delight the heart of the antiquary: guns, spears, swords, shields, crossbows, pottery, stone coffins, carvings ... and so on *ad infinitum*. One crossbow had a mechanical loading device which I had not seen before, consisting of a toothed wheel and rack, by which the cord could be wound back. The stock of this weapon was inlaid with ivory, exquisitely carved. My companion on this occasion was a Bolton man, a builder to trade, and he found some Roman roof tiles, 2,000 years old, which were identical in design with some modern ones he had used. The lid of one sarcophagus was about a foot thick, in solid stone. The builder remarked that a man who was dead in one of these would *have* to lie down! Then, looking around him, he asked if I had noticed how, throughout the ages, everything seemed to be designed for killing. I could not help but agree as I gazed at the variety of weapons, representing so many centuries of man's life on the Earth and so many lands, from the Equator to the Arctic Circle.

Lastly, in December, I went to the Natural History Museum, where I saw everything from a fly to an elephant, including a freak kitten with two heads and one with two bodies and one head. In one glass case, an Egyptian mummy was hanging, completely removed from its wrappings – black, shrunken and with a long slit from the chest down the wall of the abdomen. Next to it was a skin, a yellow human skin, taken from a French soldier who had fought in the defence of Nantes in the eighteenth century. His enemies had skinned him alive.

Such macabre exhibits are never withheld by the French. If one were to remark on this, I expect they would reply, "Well, it exists; why hide the truth?"

The display of fossils in this museum was particularly comprehensive and worthy of note, giving interesting examples of the queer things living on this planet long before the coming of man. I would hasten to assure the reader that the implication that mankind is also queer is entirely unintentional.

Our work at the railhead had become more difficult because of the recent rains. The ground where we had dumped the wrecks had become a morass and, with the movements of our heavy vehicles, it was soon churned into a sea of deep yellow mud. One of the recovery vehicles, the 13½-ton A.E.C., got bogged one day coming through a gap in the hedge and, even with all six wheels driving, it sank lower and lower till the axles were resting on the ground. We filled in the ruts till it managed to back out, then we took our axes and cut a fresh gap in the hedge and the vehicle finally extricated itself. Gradually, we removed all the wrecks to the workshops and also dealt with those still coming in by rail and for several weeks we averaged about 100 vehicles a week, most of which were the result of road accidents. Roughly half of them were so badly damaged, they had to be taken on suspended tow. When we hitched on to one truck, to pull it off the railway wagon, the chassis came right out and left the reluctant body behind. But we always expected something to fall apart, so we just looked at each other with an expression such as might have been worn by the maid with the broken vase, when she said, "It just came away in me 'ahnd, Mum!"

The wrecks were usually placed on open railway wagons with low sides, or none at all, and were roped down with one-inch ropes and had the wheels (if any) wedged by blocks. We had a crane, hand-operated, on the A.E.C., with which we lifted each vehicle, one end at a time, on to the platform. Latterly, we also had a motor-driven crane on caterpillar tracks, which was a big help, once we learned to control it properly but at first it used to swing in all directions while the driver frantically pulled and pushed at the levers and the rest of us didn't know which way to jump next.

In January we were working in greatcoats, "balaclavas", scarves and gloves, yet the wind bit through everything while we fumbled at the frozen knots where the thick ropes were tied to iron rings on the sides of the wagons. When we filled a radiator with water, the splashes froze on our greatcoats and icicles hung down under the radiator. The thermometer at that time showed thirty-four degrees of frost. We went to a place called Suce, sixteen kilometres from Nantes, to bring in a light truck on our "Tasker" trailer. The roads were covered with snow and ice, making driving a tricky business, especially with the loaded trailer behind us. The weather had made the birds very tame and I saw bullfinches, chaffinches, magpies and jays close to the road and even an owl sleeping in a tree. Later we recovered two Bren-gun carriers from Suce, with frozen radiators which should have been drained.

The Loire is a big river, yet it was completely frozen over at Nantes in that cold spell. When tugs broke up the ice, it lay in a tumbled, white mass, looking like a scene from the Arctic. Near the Haudaudine Bridge, there were some floating laundries, like big house-boats with round ends and shutters which swung up to enable the washing to be done in the water of the river. These were now tipped at all angles. As more ice came down the river, it piled up several feet thick and pushed more and more towards the banks, until it was almost as high as the boats themselves. One laundry-boat was half on the bank and half on the water. On another, a few heroic women were still trying to wash clothes in the freezing water through gaps in the ice.

At the end of January there was a sudden thaw, and the weather turned to a spring-like warmth. So the Army issued us an extra blanket each. Late, as usual.

News from home told us that conditions there had been just as bad. Wild ponies and red deer on Exmoor were found frozen to death. A group of long-distance lorry drivers, stranded at the village of Crawford, Lanarkshire, killed and ate one of the fifty sheep they were carrying. Food was dropped by parachute to a marooned Army unit in Scotland. And a letter from home brought me the news that my home town, Stirling, experienced earthquake tremors on the night of 2nd–3rd February 1940.

I must now retrace my steps a little. We had, of course, made the best of Christmas and the New Year away from home. On Christmas Eve, we had supper and a few drinks in the Café des Sports in the Boulevard des Anglais. This was the café nearest to our billet, where we regularly had supper if we were not in town, as when we were on stand-by duty. We were all well known to Madame Bonnet, the proprietrix, and many an evening of cross-talk we had with her. She made very good suppers and, during the worst weather, if one of us had a cold she would make up a hot drink of French rum and sugar for the sufferer. This was much appreciated, as we *never* had an issue of Army rum in that nine months in France; not even when we were out all night on recovery, in snow and frosty winds, as often happened. On some nights we even had two crews out at one time when icy roads caused more accidents.

On Christmas Day, we had a morning in bed for a change, rising only at 8.00 a.m. and, ignoring the Army breakfast, we had one made by Madame Bonnet in the Café des Sports. However, we all turned up for the traditional dinner at the barn. The barn was transformed with paper decorations. Each table was covered with white paper, with red and blue bands running down the middle and a varnished board at the end with the name of one of the billets, *Château de Breil, Rue de Rennes,* etc. There were bottles of beer, wine and lemonade (yes, the lemonade *was* necessary to mix with the horrible wine!). Each man had a packet of cigarettes and an autograph of the King and Queen. The dinner consisted of turkey, roast, brussels sprouts, plum duff and custard and there were plates of fruit and nuts in plenty. It was served by the sergeants and there were many cracks at their expense, taken in good part. The officers were present and the Colonel made the usual little speech of greetings. A French photographer was taking flashlight photos but, when he took a group of officers, we all began singing, *"It's only a Beautiful Picture in a Beautiful Golden Frame!"* Many favourite songs were sung then, while the old rafters quivered, but the inner thoughts of us all were, as ever, with our folks at home. This was the first of seven Christmasses I was to spend away from home, to say nothing of seven Hogmanays, so dear to the Scotsman's heart. Six of these festive seasons I spent overseas.

As we left the dining hall, we saw a crowd of people some way up the road and a fire engine in front of the small church of St. Thérèse. When we got closer, we saw that one end of the church was burnt out and priests and nuns were carrying away parts of the altar regalia. Some soldiers of the Signal Corps had been helping the firemen and one of them suddenly fainted, being apparently overcome by the effects of smoke. We ran over and loosened his neckband and a Frenchwoman threw a jug of water over his head, which might have caused choking but fortunately didn't. Two of his mates carried him away. The fire was probably caused by the candles burning in the church but a new and bigger church was already in course of construction next to our dining hall.

After Christmas, we got back to the usual daily routine. Reveille 06.30 hours; wash, shave and walk down the Avenue de la Chênaie, the long lane which led to our barn dining hall on the Vannes road. Recovery work at the railhead, then back for dinner (stew again), when we *marched* in threes, feeling like a lot of convicts, from the garage to the barn, a matter of 200 yards. Then more recovery at Chapelle sur Erdre. Our original service dress, with brass-buttoned tunic and narrow trousers, was now completely worn out and greasy from use at work but we were gradually supplied with two suits each of the new battle-dress.

In the evenings, weather permitting, we would go to a cinema or to an ENSA show in a theatre. There was also a popular fairground in an open space near the Cathedral. Perhaps we would just go round the shops buying souvenir gifts to send home. The house of Decre was the biggest general store, a three-storied building with escalators, where one could buy almost anything. Perfume, lingerie, manicure sets and embossed leatherwork were plentiful and reasonably priced. Another shop specialized in large dolls, beautifully dressed in Breton costume: velvet, lace, gold and silver thread, intricately worked, and a starched lace head-dress, just as we had seen women dressed when coming into Nantes on market day, for the country people still wear this traditional costume on all special occasions.

Incidentally, my pay then was only 2s. 9d per diem. Later, the rate of pay was increased to 3s. 9d a day but it was just as well that prices *were* reasonable in Nantes.

We often went to the Café à la Concorde for supper in town. This was a bright little place with (needless to say) good food. One of my regular companions, a North countryman, always exchanged *sonce* badinage with the prettiest of the waitresses, Jeannette. He knew no French, however, so he would get me to translate a phrase into French, explaining the pronunciation to him. After a few "rehearsals", he would beckon frantically to Jeannette to get it said before he forgot it. His atrocious accent made her giggle, but she took it all in good part, and off she'd go to serve another customer, while he laboriously learnt another sentence. This went on for some time, to the amusement of customers and waitresses alike, for the town Frenchman is truly democratic and likes a joke. After a while, Jeannette suddenly realised who was supplying the French phrases and laughed merrily at – and with – the unabashed Romeo. Blessed are they who make us laugh, for they drive away all our cares.

A party of us, including Romeo and another North countryman – who was just as daft – went to look for a roller-skating rink we had heard about, but we found it had been taken over for military use, so we began to wend our way back to the billet through the lamp-lit streets (there was only a partial black-out in Nantes). Our two light-hearted friends were apparently not discouraged at the lack of entertainment for they began to skip along the pavement, doing a burlesque edition of *"The Chestnut Tree"*, while we walked behind, chuckling at their antics. What any French passers-by thought of the crazy British, I don't know, for next they made a pretence of being "canned" and began swarming up the lamp-posts to put out the lights. We eventually got back to the billet without having attracted the attention of any of the "Gestapo", as we called the Corps of Military Police.

On the evenings when bad weather or lack of money confined us to the billet, we did our best to amuse ourselves. One man made a metal grid to keep the coal in the broken old fireplace. Another made a dart-board complete with wiring, which I painted and we also had a home-made table for ping-pong. One evening our amateur barber tried his hand at haircutting while I held a storm lantern to illuminate his work. The onlookers derived great satisfaction from the performance, which was accompanied by such cheerful remarks as, "It's all right, Jack, the towel is catching all the blood!" When the victim asked what his hair looked like, he was told it resembled a forest which had been shelled; all holes with a few stumps in between. I was next in the chair, while there were some more remarks about trimming hedges!

One night, just after we had all got into bed, one Jack was awakened by a tinkle somewhere near his bed. The tinkle was repeated, yet nobody could be seen within reach. Jack lay down again. Ten minutes later, another tinkle and Jack sat up, striking a match. Still nothing to be seen. He must have kept the matches in his hand for, at the next tinkle, the light flared immediately and Jack looked quickly around the corners of the bed. Still "nobody". Yet, even as the match died, that ghostly tinkle floated about the bed. He sat very still and again it came, not near, yet all around. Jack didn't believe in ghosts, however. "Somebody's 'avin a game 'ere!" he says. A smothered chortle from other beds indicated that some at least knew the secret of the phenomenon. The Devonian member of the section had a long piece of string leading from his own bed to the two tin lids he had fixed under the victim. The string kept the lids from making a noise when Jack moved in bed, but a jerk could produce the ghostly noise at will. A sleepy, innocent voice said, "What's the matter, Jack? Why don't you get to sleep?" More chortles, then silence ... for a while. Tinkle! Tinkle! This time, Jack wasted no more matches, but his belt whistled round the bed-posts, with no earthly or supernatural results, beyond some more spooky chuckles.

He had his revenge, though not on the actual perpetrator of the joke. Indeed, he didn't know who was responsible but, next morning, an innocent fellow at the wrong end of the room – in the bunk under mine, to be exact – found his trouser legs and pullover sleeves had been sewn up overnight! Fortunately, the floor being of stone, his boots were *not* nailed to it, as they might have been.

We were in the habit of taking odd bottles of "refreshment" to the billet and these had been accumulating for some time, so one day two of us decided to get busy and return them to "Madame" – empty of course – so we gathered them all together and walked into the café with a huge sack full of them, which we deposited before Madame. Her wonder gave way to amusement, for it was a wonderful, large and varied collection. It also represented a certain amount of Madame's capital, for she had never charged us for any of these bottles.

While bringing a vehicle in from Chapelle Sur Erdre one day, we had a slight mishap. I was steering the vehicle, being towed behind the Crossley breakdown, when an officer's car came round a bend towards us at speed. It suddenly began to skid broadside, so I steered my truck closer to the side of the road, though I had little warning. The car struck my vehicle and careered on with squealing tyres, to finish up in the ditch. Our towing cable had parted but the Crossley stopped and we got out to survey the damage. The car had struck the front wheel of the truck, but the bullet-proof tyre had taken the shock, so that was all right. The front bumper of the car had been torn off, but it was still roadworthy. There was a major with it and his driver said his brakes were binding on one wheel and had caused the car to lurch to one side. We attached a new towing cable and carried on.

Many good theatre shows were now being brought out to us by ENSA and most of these came to a small theatre called the *Salle Colbert*. One of the first in Nantes was Ralph Reader, of *Gang Show* fame. The funniest scene was where eight hefty fellows came on dressed as matronly women and all singing together, *"Where are our Wandering Boys Tonight?"* Among other performers were: Joe Loss and his band, Lloyd Shakespeare, George Formby, Herbert Younkman and the one and only Gracie Fields.I also saw two plays, *French Leave* and *Almost a Honeymoon*.

Gracie Fields, with Jack Payne's band and Peggy Cochrane, appeared at the big Municipal Theatre of Nantes, in the Place Graslin. Only one ticket was allotted to our little section and I was fortunate enough to draw it! In this theatre, smoking was strictly prohibited and a note was placed on every seat to the effect that if anyone was found smoking, the management had the power to stop the show altogether. In spite of this, a few surreptitious attempts to light up were made by fellows who could not wait even one hour till the interval gave them the chance to smoke in the corridors. However, these attempts were stopped by the M.P.s. As a consequence, the air in the theatre was clear and pleasant and there was little coughing to drown the words of the artistes. The first gallery was filled with officers and three more galleries rose to the painted roof, where cupids wheeled in an artificial sky.

The band had the first part of the programme and Peggy Cochrane gave piano and violin solos in her radio style. Then came Gracie herself, looking tired after a recent illness which had taken her to the Isle of Capri to recuperate. Her grand personality, however, carried all before it. She began with the South African *"Trek Song"*:

> *"Shall we sing a song together,*
> *Shall we sing a song?*
> *As we march along together,*
> *As we march along."*

Then followed all her old favourites: *"The Jones"*, *"The Biggest Aspidistra"*, *"The Old Violin"* and many others. She ended with what is probably her greatest song, *"Sally"*. The troops were intended to join in but there was a chorus of "Shh!" and silence fell. Gracie said, "So you're going to make me sing it myself, are you?" And you could have heard the proverbial pin drop as she sang it through. At the second chorus, we all joined in and nearly raised the roof, though Gracie's operatic voice could be heard above it all. From the pit to the lofty fourth gallery came the words:

> *"Sally, Sally, don't ever wander*
> *Away from the alley and me,*
> *Sally, Sally, marry me, Sally,*
> *And happy together we'll be.*
> *When skies are blue, you're beguiling,*
> *And when they're grey, you're still smiling – smiling*
> *Sally, Sally, pride of our alley,*
> *You're more than the whole world to me."*

A great roar of cheering broke out as the curtain fell and continued until it rose again for the anthem. Usually the *"Marseillaise"* was played before *"God Save the King"*, so we had to remain at attention throughout both anthems.

On Wednesday, 7th February, H.R.H. the Duke of Gloucester came to Nantes, on a tour of inspection. We were in the "yard" beside a No. 2 B.O.W., pulling a vehicle out of some deep mud, when a group of red-tabbed generals walked through the gate, with the Duke in the forefront. He watched a moment or two while we ploughed about in the mud, attaching a winch-cable to the bogged truck, then he went out and, a few minutes later, the little procession of cars moved off, the Duke himself driving the first one, a camouflaged Humber.

That evening, the Duke was present at the show given by Joe Loss and his band, with the Carlyle Cousins, Monte Ray and cheery Charlie Chester. As he came in, we rose and he took his seat in the middle of the front row, with generals and staff officers filling the rest of the row. This was in the *Salle Colbert*, where smoking was permitted and most of the troops consequently chain-smoked all the time. The air got very thick and both audience and artistes were coughing. Being a non-smoker myself, I could sympathize with the players, who often asked the troops in this theatre to cut down smoking during the performance, but it never made any difference. However, this was a good show and very much enjoyed, in spite of the fog. When Joe Loss announced the interval, a voice from the gallery said, "Don't drink the beer, Joe, it's lousy!"

After the interval, the proceedings became quite hilarious. Three soldiers were asked to come up on the stage to dance *"Boomps-a-Daisy"* with the Carlyle Cousins. There were cries of, "Go on, Yorkie!" and "Get up, Nobby!" and then the band struck up. One tubby little bloke almost "boomped" his blonde partner off the stage, while his mates below yelled joyful encouragement. I must say the Cousins were game and another three soldiers were soon up on the stage. Then came two trios of officers but they had to do it in fox-trot time, which meant they had to get in two "boomps" to a bar instead of one! We yelled with laughter till we were breathless.

At the end, when the Duke rose to go, three cheers were called for and, as he walked up the passage he said, "Goodnight, boys!" Some of the soldiers replied, "Goodnight, Sir!" but the irrepressible, impolite voice in the gallery said, "Cheerio, chum, stew again termorrer!"

It was bad-mannered, of course but what he was referring to was the undoubted fact that when any Very Important Person came to inspect an army unit, the men always got a specially good dinner, in order that no complaints might reach the ears of the V.I.P. Next day, cooking would revert to its usual standard which might, or might not, be good.

Arriving at our billet at 11.30 p.m., we who had been to the show found our beds – which we had thoughtfully made in advance – had been denuded of blankets by the other fellows. Naturally, we had to find our blankets so we wakened everybody up, shaking each bed thoroughly to make sure they were quite wide awake. Then, just to finish the evening off, we had a sing-song.

The time was coming round for my first leave from the Army and still nothing had happened on the "Western Front". The war of nerves was still going on, each side trying to frighten the other with propaganda. French news reels showed guns furiously banging away at nothing; parts of the Maginot Line, with its railways and elevators; ships unloading huge quantities of material; and a pair of hands pouring out francs on to a counter. They also showed pictures of huge tanks of seventy tons.

Here one of the big French tanks such as took part in the attack on the Forest of Warndt is seen. Top, it is in the open followed by infantrymen. Below, it is climbing a steep bank after making a successful crossing of a stream.
(Photos, Associated Press.)

They actually moved. And how well I remember the big French posters showing a matelot on a warship, with the inscription; *"Il Veille; – Souscrivez!"* ("He watches; – Subscribe!") Or the picture of an old woman saying *"J'ai souscrit. Et Vous?"* ("I have subscribed. And you?") They were advertising Armament Bonds.

My leave, having been postponed several times, from one "definite" date to another, was at last fixed for Wednesday, 14th February 1940, that being the day I was to leave Nantes. Before then, I took part in one of our biggest recovery jobs, on 12th February. A thirty-six-seat 'bus belonging to Drouin Brothers, whose garage we were using, had come to grief at a bridge between two bends on the Suce road. The 'bus was completely overturned at the foot of a ten-foot bank in marshy ground, beside the small river which ran sluggishly under the bridge. The passengers, some of whom had been slightly injured, had been taken away before we arrived. Normally, this would have been a civilian job, but it appeared that all local breakdown vehicles had been commandeered by the French Army and taken away towards the front, and so we were called in.

The 'bus could not be dragged to another part of the road as it would have gone into the marsh and there were other obstacles, such as trees by the roadside; so it was decided that the only way to handle it was to roll the 'bus bodily back up the bank and drag it on its own wheels obliquely through the hedge and back on to the road. We fixed a ground anchor by driving long steel spikes through the road surface and to the other anchor attached a "Trewhella" hand winch, operated by lever and ratchet. A couple of tow-chains were then rigged from the winch to the far side of the 'bus and we began the pull. We had ropes attached to the lever of the winch so that three men could pull from either side, as the lever swung, clicking from left to right. Traffic had been stopped on either side and we were watched by an interested crowd of motorists, farmers, woodcutters and children. At the first attempt, the 'bus began to rise, then a chain snapped and the wreck reverted to its former position. More tow-chains were rigged up and we began again. Meanwhile, our Crossley had been drawn up on the other side of the road but in line with the 'bus and the front end was anchored to a large tree by two-inch ropes passed round the trunk. The 'bus was now on its wheels but was still lying at a dangerous angle amidst the remains of the hedge. The ground anchor was holding, however, and now the motor winch cable from the Crossley was hooked to the front of the 'bus. The Crossley engine hummed, the cable tautened and the wreck slowly began to heave up. The winch-drum creaked under the terrific strain and now and then, as it wound the lower coils tighter and tighter, the cable slipped a little with a crack. We stood clear in case the cable snapped altogether and I noticed that the top of the tree swayed as much as three feet as the Crossley pulled against it.

At last, the 'bus was level and soon it was out on the road again, its roof crumpled and the windscreen covered with oil which had run from the inverted engine. We loosened off the cables and waved the traffic through. Altogether the job had taken three hours. Incidentally, the engine of the 'bus, which was a British Gardner Diesel, started up at the first touch of the starter and there was sufficient oil left in the sump for it to come back under its own power, without seizing up.

The following day, when drawing my leave pay from the Company Office, I was given an extra forty-five francs, a gift from the 'bus company to each member of the recovery crew.

On Wednesday, 14th February, I duly left Nantes by rail from the main station, Gare de L'État, which peculiarly enough, is situated at the Ile Beaulieu, an island in the middle of the Loire. I travelled to Cherbourg via Le Mans and Caen, the city which took such a hammering after the Normandy invasion, and also passed through Bayeux, arriving at Cherbourg on Thursday morning after a sixteen-hour journey in the uncomfortable continental carriage with its hard wooden seats. At that time we had to take full kit when on leave, including respirator, rifle and steel helmet, pack, haversack, water-bottle, *and* kit bag! Loaded thus, we marched a mile and a half to a transit camp, where we got a mug of tea and a ration bag, then another mile and a half to the quayside, where we boarded the *Scotia*. As daylight came, we sailed through the boom and reached Southampton at 2.00 p.m. Thursday, from which time our ten days' leave began.

I still had over 500 miles to travel to Stirling but my heart was light as the train carried me North; and I reached home, where my parents were expecting me, early on Friday, the 16th.

So ended my first spell overseas.

CHAPTER 3

Evacuation of St. Nazaire

"And when the last great scorer comes
To write against your name,
He marks not that you won or lost,
But how you played the game."

O N SATURDAY EVENING, 24th February 1940, my leave came to
an end, as all good things do, and I began the heartbreaking
return journey of 800 miles. I was due back at Southampton
by 2.00 p.m. Sunday and here were the usual army queues, long straggling
lines of miserable faces, each man still preoccupied with thoughts of the
home he had left and disinclined to talk. We fled through the barriers
and up the gangway of the ship but, for some unknown reason, the
vessel remained in port for nine hours after we were aboard, though the
crossing to Cherbourg itself takes only seven hours. Then again, that
awful rail journey!

I got back to Nantes on Monday night, the 26th and the first news
I got was that we now had to start work half an hour earlier in the
morning, and finish half an hour later at night. However, we also had
a fifteen minute break in the morning, which allowed us to get a cup of
tea in the N.A.A.F.I. canteen which was now established in an old garage
in the Rue des Hauts Pavés. In this canteen, one occasionally saw a long,
low and squat animal ambling about. It was a badger, his broad back
covered with coarse bristles. I believe it had been trapped by some French
people and presented to some of the troops. The poor animal was ill at
ease, however, and when I patted it, it made a half-hearted snap at me.
I don't know what became of this queer pet, for after a while it disappeared.

Besides the morning tea, it was the men's custom to have coffee after
dinner, in a café between the dining hall and the workshop. Here,

Madame was so used to being crowded out with soldiers that she made special arrangements. A certain brand of chocolate biscuit was in great demand, so she laid on extra supplies of them. She also learned that the tiny French coffee-cups were totally inadequate for the copious British thirst and only resulted in numerous repeat orders. She was unable to supply any larger cups, so eventually she provided each customer with a *bowl*, placed on a plate (saucer, in lieu of) and this became the regular custom. Whenever Tommy asked for a coffee, it was understood to be *"un grand café"* and the bowl was placed before him without question, and always at the special price of 1 franc 25 centimes. Later, the price began to creep up but this was due to international causes and beyond Madame's control, as she apologetically explained.

Life now settled down in the usual routine of recovery work and vehicle maintenance, with our usual half-days on Thursday and Sunday. One Thursday evening, I had been to a cinema show and, in the crowd coming out, I got separated from my two companions and lost them, so I began to make my own way back to the billet. Walking along a boulevard leading out of the Place Delorme, I heard a French girl saying *"Non, non, non!"* to a man in shabby civilian clothes. She seemed rather agitated but, without taking much notice, I continued on my way. However, the girl ran after me and asked in English if I would mind if she walked on with me, as this stranger was annoying her. She said he spoke bad French and seemed to be a foreigner. We moved on up the road, the fellow making no attempt to follow, while she told me she had once been with a Scottish family in Rippon, which accounted for her knowledge of English – or does that sound Irish? Turning off at the avenue where she lived, she thanked me, shook hands and said goodnight.

Our section now had another Scammel transporter in place of the one we had handed over to a Port Recovery Section in Nantes docks. Across the front of the huge cab of this articulated giant, I painted the name *"Snow-White"*. The other vehicles, of course, bore the names of the dwarfs. For a while I became a member of the crew of this transporter and our first job was to go to Rennes, now seventy miles away, with a ten-ton case of machinery, measuring about twelve feet long by eight feet high. While travelling through the countryside, I was surprised to see so many oxen in use, not only to pull carts but to pull the plough, being harnessed with the old-fashioned wooden yoke across their necks. We stopped at Derval for dinner in a little café with a notice outside expressing welcome to "Our English Friends". I took this to mean British as well and went in for, while I am indubitably British, I cannot say I am English!

The roaring, vibrating monster which was our conveyance attracted much attention from the country people. After passing through all of the six forward gears, we reached our grand top speed of a little over 15 m.p.h.. The drumming roar in the metal cab almost deafened us and, when we finally got out at our destination after five hours, our ears were ringing. The transporter was one of the earlier models, with no ramps at the rear and, when anything had to be loaded or unloaded, the great chassis had first to be lowered to the ground between the rear wheels. We did this by means of the hand-operated jacks on the rear bogie; we manhandled the bogie, with its four chest-high wheels, out of the way and eased the case down on rollers. Then we hooked up the bogie again, inserted the four-foot levers into the jacks and jacked the chassis back into position. Imagine the labour required when a twenty-ton tank is also mounted on the chassis!

After unloading the big packing case, we were supplied with blankets and put up with some "local" R.A.O.C. lads in a Nissen hut. We walked 200 yards for a meal and took it 200 yards back to the hut, by which time the tea was cold. This was at Bruz, a place about six miles from Rennes, and the men here could not get to town for amusement, as there was no 'bus service and they were not often allowed lorry transport. We went to their canteen at night and here we discovered how they provided their own entertainment. They had a piano, saxophone and drums with which to produce "music". Some were playing darts, while others sat at tables with seldom less than a full crate of beer-bottles underneath! The general atmosphere was reminiscent of a saloon in a gold-rush town of the Yukon. While the "band" ground out the ragtime, willing soloists gave renderings of the Bad Old Army Songs, the crowd joining in the choruses, some of which will never be published in their "original" form. There was *The Letter*, *The Old Monk*, *The Keyhole in the Door*, *My Love is for a Soldier Boy* and last, but surely not least of these Baleful Ballads, *One-eyed Riley's Daughter*. To these chants, the poker-faced drummer provided steady rhythm with solemn enthusiasm. Truly, a place that one might describe as "some joint".

Next day, we returned to Nantes and on Friday took the Scammel to the docks to pick up the excavator, which was so high that we caught some telephone wires and brought them down. After that I had to stand on top of the Scammel with a stick to clear low wires all through the town. Nantes looked very beautiful in the bright sunshine, though the trees lining the streets were still bare of leaves.

On Sunday, 10th March, the famous *Folies Bergères*, on tour from Paris, came to the Municipal Theatre and I saw the show from a good seat, well forward, which only cost 19¼ francs or 2s. 3d. for a variety show lasting three hours. One effective scene showed a group of convicts resting in prison as night falls. The figure of a woman in white appears beyond the bars, a figure representing someone of whom each man is thinking. She sings *"Night and Day"*, in French, of course, while the convicts, providing choral background, sit up and look towards her. As the song ends on the words, *"Nuit et Jour"*, the figure disappears, leaving the convicts gazing at the bars.

Then come the usual sketches and comedy acts. Two men in old-fashioned costume are about to fight a duel with pistols. After much argument, the seconds allocate the weapons, the contestants are placed back to back, they march the requisite number of paces, turn and fire. For a moment nothing happens; then out of a tree above falls a dead bird! Some of the jokes and gestures would not pass censorship in Britain, yet there were children of all ages in the audience with their parents. Five young ladies and a man performed a sensuous though graceful dance. All were attired only in loin-cloths. The show ended with an exotic parade of costumes so gorgeous that a murmur of awe went up from the women in the audience.

It is surprising to look back and realise that we might have been at war with Russia at this time for, in an entry in my diary for Tuesday, 12th March 1940, I mentioned a radio announcement that Britain and France had both prepared expeditionary forces to help Finland in her war with Russia, whenever Finland asked for such help. However, a few days later, peace was declared between Russia, the victor, and Finland.

Our own war, on land at any rate, was still dormant in March, though the Navy and R.A.F. were busy enough. One bright afternoon, some of us went into the Parc de Proce, a public park quite near our billet. It was a lovely place, with a stream running through leafy glades. Children were kicking a ball about on the grass, while older people sat on the seats made of tree trunks split down the middle. A soldier of the "Buffs" was taking a snapshot of a pretty French girl, as she stood at the edge of the stream where swans and ducks paddled about. We reclined, more or less gracefully, on a seat, enjoying the spring weather and decided that, so far, it hadn't been a bad war. To us and to all the people enjoying the peaceful atmosphere of the park, the war was quite remote.

One of the things we had long noticed in Nantes – and other French towns – was the almost complete lack of public lavatories. There were, however, several gents' urinals, usually placed at the side of a busy street and with no screen between them and the passer-by. We had got quite used to them and the French take no notice of such things but, on several occasions, we were slightly shaken to perceive some French couple come along, arm in arm and the man, without even releasing the girl's arm, would make use of one of these urinals. Due to the dearth of public conveniences, it has even been known for some desperate woman to enter one of the few urinals which did have screens around them.

In the last few months of our stay in France, theatre shows continued to come out to us, entertaining us in our spare time and preventing boredom. When Lloyd Shakespeare came with his band, he brought an amazing conjurer with him. While doing his tricks, he had several soldiers on the stage, with whom he mingled. Soon he began producing articles which he had taken from their pockets without arousing suspicion. Even when they were more prepared for this, he still brought forth their personal belongings and, finally, he held up a pair of braces! As they left the stage, one holding his trousers up, the sleight-of-hand expert showed a wristlet watch and a ring, which the victims had not even missed.

One of the most popular of all performers with the troops, George Formby, came to Nantes on 25th March. He gave us many of his well-known songs, playing his banjo-uke and there were many requests for favourite items, *"Window Cleaner"*, *"Leaning on a Lamp-post"* et cetera. He brought with him two performers on a spring mat, raised about two feet above the stage. A few of the boys were invited to try some tricks on the mat and found it was not so easy as it looked. One fellow came off with a rush, crashed at the edge of the stage and sprained his ankle. Another started bouncing and couldn't stop! The anxious look on his face caused quite a laugh. They were each given a packet of cigarettes and a pair of socks or gloves by Beryl, Mrs. Formby.

These shows formed a large part of our life and great credit is due to all those who made the journey out to give us entertainment. Many hard things have been said about ENSA and, as the Chinese proverb says, "Free sitters grumble most at a play!" but I have seen many fine wartime shows and those not so good were usually regarded with toleration and good humour.

The first of the A.T.S. had arrived in Nantes and a row of seats was reserved for them at the show given by Younkman's Gipsy band. When most of the troops were seated, the A.T.S. made their entrance, being immediately greeted by the storm of whistles and chirps by means of which a large section of the Army (and some civilians) display their lack of grace. Some of the girls seemed to enjoy this display but a few were shy enough to look embarrassed.

We were still carrying out recovery work and, one Sunday afternoon, I was called out with the recovery crew to St. Emilien, about thirty kilometres from Nantes. A truck was turned on its side in the middle of a stream. We waded in, pushed and levered the truck over, then attached the winch cable and dragged it out through the mud. In the process I had got my gum boots full of water. When I took them off, emptied them and put them on again, some French people standing near laughed, apparently amused at my indifference and said, *"Aw, il n'ya pas de qui hein? Ça n'fait rien!"* Or, as the troops would say, "San Fairy Ann!"

On Tuesday, 9th April, the radio announced that the Germans had invaded Denmark and landed troops in Norway. Oslo was already in German hands. So things were beginning to move! Next day, British marines were reported fighting on Norwegian soil, while naval action continued off-shore.

Another recovery job took us to St. Nazaire, where the great ship *Normandie* was built. However, we had no sooner attached the wreck in a suspended position, when a 'phone call came through telling us to go instead to La Baule, where another smash was blocking the road. So we dropped the first vehicle in the yard where we had found it and proceeded to La Baule, passing through Pornichet *en route*. Both these places, well known to peace-time visitors, are situated in a beautiful sandy bay, with bright villas, hotels and a casino or two set amid the pine trees, which gave La Baule its full name of La Baule Les Pins. Here, motor races used to be run on the broad curving sweep of yellow sand, before the eyes of wealthy holiday-makers.

We found our wreck, suspended it and hit the home trail. We had to stop once to disconnect the rear brakes of the smashed car, which were beginning to smoke, the collision having twisted the rods. We did this to the accompaniment of the rasping, ringing noise of hundreds of frogs in a nearby marsh. There was a pool behind our billet which also abounded in frogs, whose familiar noise had sometimes disturbed our sleep, as it seemed to go on all night. Whenever any of us approached the pool, the croaking would stop and all that was heard was, "Plop! Plop! Plop!" as innumerable French dinners submerged in a series of crash-dives. As we resumed our journey, the sun was going down in golden streamers and our "Q" bloke, who was driving, hit up 40 m.p.h. with the tow, which was highly irregular but darned good going.

Towards the end of April, we were suddenly allowed to walk out *without* the respirators with which we had been burdened during the previous seven months. A little later, we had our first air-raid alarm but the all-clear went an hour later. This was the first time the banshee wailing of the sirens had been heard in Nantes. We were quite interested! We stood around the doorway of our billet, listening to the eerie sound rising and falling, away over the city, but no aircraft appeared.

The countryside around Nantes was very beautiful now and, on our trips to and from Chapelle sur Erdre, we passed orchards white with apple blossom, or pink with the blossom of the peach and I also noted the lovely blue of Wistaria against a black and white half-timbered gable. At the top of our Château "garden" I heard the cuckoo, and the frogs were as busy as ever.

On Wednesday, 24th April, I saw what was to be one of the last concerts before the evacuation. In the show was Billy Merson, the little comedian who also entertained the troops in the First World War; and Ronald Gourlay, the clever blind pianist.

Among the popular songs of this period were: *"The Beer-Barrel Polka"*, *"Boomps-a-Daisy"* and a couple of songs about the Siegfried Line. They were heard everywhere. Walking along the Rue de la Fosse, near the waterfront, you heard radio-gramophones blaring out *"The Beer-Barrel Polka"* from café after café, so that you could pick up the strident melody again and again as you went along, sometimes in French, sometimes in English, usually played by an accordion band. It no sooner faded from one café, than it came with renewed vigour from the next in front. I always think that, when a person hears an old tune, it immediately calls to mind some particular place, a *place* that haunts the memory; the place where that tune was heard most of all. So I will always connect *"The Beer-Barrel Polka"* with the Rue de la Fosse.

In the Katorza Cinema, too, they had a habit of using the same tunes at the beginning and end of the programme each evening. Before the picture came a piano solo of *"Smoke Gets in Your Eyes"* and, as a send-off, we got *"Boomps-a-Daisy"*, which started the boys singing as they crowded out.

The songs about "Hanging out the Washing on the Siegfried Line" died a sudden death at the time of the Dunkirk disaster and were not to be heard for some years but I heard the records played in Belgium in 1944, as they were triumphantly revived and I have a postcard, bought in France, which shows a Scottish soldier pinning his shirt on a rope slung between two of the Siegfried guns, with the inscription below, "In the end, we hang it on the Line!"

The patter of comedians would often include jokes about the blackout although, as I have said, there was no real blackout in Nantes. One of these jokes which tickled my peculiar sense of humour concerned two little dogs, abroad in the blackout. They came to a corner where stood a man with a wooden leg. One little doggie sniffed at the wooden leg, then turned to the other little doggie with a puzzled look and said, "That's funny, I don't remember this one!"

Our round of work and entertainment was to be changed, however, and the even tenor of our way disturbed. Quite suddenly, on 10th May 1940, came news of the German invasion of Holland and Belgium. The work of years was wasted as Holland was flooded in defence. Bombing began and the Dutch brought down seventy German 'planes.

We were immediately ordered to work till eight o'clock every night, seven days a week and we could no longer visit the town, as we had to remain in the billet area in case we were required after eight o'clock. By the 14th, 2,000 tanks were said to be involved in the battle raging on the "Western Front". For the *first time*, we were given instructions on the use of the Short Lee-Enfield, loading with dummy rounds. Then we were issued with live ammunition though, as yet, many of us had never fired a service rifle! We were told to carry our steel helmets and respirators everywhere and to take our rifles when on a lorry. All this 400 miles from the front! But then, the big idea was to be ready for parachutists! In fact, we were warned that parachutists had landed seventy-five miles from Nantes. Whether any were *ever* dropped so far ahead of the German Army, I very much doubt. In Holland, however, paratroops did land in uniforms of Dutch policemen, railwaymen, postmen and even in the dress of nuns. Our Premier, Mr. Neville Chamberlain, had now resigned and the man who was to lead Britain through the dark years, Mr. Winston Churchill, took his place.

On the 15th, five days after the Blitzkrieg was launched, Holland was forced to capitulate, though some of the Dutch troops refused the order to lay down arms and guerrilla warfare continued.

On the 17th, the first refugees arrived in Nantes, all the way from Belgium. Their cars had mattresses tied on the roofs, as a doubtful protection against strafing by German aircraft, which shot up the streams of helpless civilians in order to create havoc on the roads by which the Allied forces were moving into position. Many of these cars had bullet-holes in the doors and some of the refugees had had the sad task of burying a relative by the roadside and then carrying on with the survivors. They had prams and cycles tied on the luggage grids and other precious belongings piled inside, with the passengers wedged between them. Their younger menfolk were still fighting in Belgium; or were they dead? Perhaps they would never know.

By the 21st, the Germans had reached Arras and Amiens. The French premier admitted that the French troops were not properly trained for the type of warfare in which they were involved. This, however, did not explain why bridges were not blown up behind them. Refugees were now streaming into Nantes every day. They came in lorries, cattle trucks and railway wagons. Old men and women were packed tightly, standing all the way. A long column of them was stopped along the road leading to the city and, here and there, a woman would be weeping bitterly and children would stand around, dishevelled, weary and bewildered.

Abbéville was next to fall into German hands and on the 23rd, the personnel of an Ordnance Advanced Field Workshop arrived outside our workshops from Arras. They had been shelled out, had lost all their equipment, even many of their rifles and got away on any available vehicles. Most of them had only what they stood up in.

We were still working steadily and we brought in a number of aircraft detectors, searchlights and A.A. guns which, for a change, had arrived at a railway siding in Nantes itself. These guns were all damaged in some way, having been "spiked". Some of the gunners had travelled with the guns and they told us they had been ordered to spike the guns before withdrawing from Arras. Two hours later, they were told to return to Arras to recover the guns which they had made useless and they had managed to get the guns away. So now we had to take a dozen of them to the workshop to be repaired. They were, in any case, made during the 1914–1918 war and had solid rubber tyres on their wheels. Eventually, they *were* repaired and later, on Sunday, 9th June, we helped to move them again, when they were being sent to the south of France. That was the *day before* Italy declared war on the Allies.

But to return to the month of May .... One of the gunners gave us a graphic description of the screaming bombs used by Jerry which, he said, made a noise like, "a hundred men blowing whistles!" He told us the 'planes came over in droves, 150 at a time. This seemed stupendous to us at that time, so long before our own 1,000 bomber raids were to take place.

And still the refugees poured into Nantes, while thousands more were said to be cycling and tramping out of Belgium. And where were they to go? They could not know that the Germans would overrun the whole of France. The next place to fall was Boulogne.

On Friday, 24th May 1940, we moved a 6-in. field piece (1920 model) from a gun-park to the workshop. We had to crawl along some old-fashioned cobbled streets, with the wooden wheels of the gun creaking and rumbling behind us. The iron tyres kept slipping on the steep camber of the road, so that every now and then the long muzzle swung towards the kerb, threatening to knock down any lamp-post or unwary pedestrian that came in the way.

On Saturday, the 25th, Boulogne and Amiens were re-taken by the Allies but, two days later, Boulogne was again in enemy hands. We were now getting instruction on the Bren gun.

King Leopold of the Belgians ordered his gallant little army to lay down their arms on the 29th May and the B.E.F. in Belgium were now cut off and the retreat to Dunkirk began.

Looking back, I am amazed at our lack of comprehension of the situation. On Thursday, the 30th, we were actually given a half-day off again and went to town – shopping, visiting a cinema and even discussing when we might get our next leave!

For the next few days, we carried on with routine recovery from the railhead and, on Tuesday, 4th June, we brought in two 3.7-in. anti-aircraft guns, both of which had their muzzles split wide open like a banana skin; so it seemed that they had been "spiked" too, to prevent the enemy from using them, yet they had to be brought away after all.

It is well to recall that in these dark days, when everything seemed to crumble around us and Britain stood alone, the voice of one great man alone, the voice of Winston Churchill, was raised to hurl defiance at the enemy, with these now famous words (here contracted):

"We shall fight in France, on the seas, in the air.
We shall fight on the beaches, the landing grounds,
in the fields, in the streets, in the hills.
We shall never surrender".

This was on the 4th June 1940, while the evacuation was still going on.

On Wednesday, 5th June, the evacuation of Dunkirk was completed and the harbour rendered useless. Thanks to the little ships, most of the men were miraculously saved but all the transport, many of the tanks and 1,000 guns were lost. The badly-needed equipment would be recovered by the Germans. Indeed, in 1945, the section I was then with in north Germany carried out repairs to re-captured British trucks, which Jerry had been running since 1940.

One of our fellows had been sent to Cherbourg to bring back a vehicle and, while there, he had experienced a little of the German bombing. He told us of a French sentry who was leaning on the wall of a factory (French sentries are like that) when a large portion of the wall was blown out. The sentry was still leaning on the remainder of the wall and, when someone went over to see if he was all right, he calmly waved his hand and said, in effect, "It is nothing. It is war!"

So he continued to lean on the wall.

When our friend returned, he passed once more through Craon, the first thing he heard being the bells of the Church and Town Hall, still ringing out their dreamy ding-dong! When he entered one of the cafés, he was instantly recognised and a child brought forth a badge he had left as a souvenir, months before.

On 10th June, Fascist Italy, having come to the conclusion that Hitler was doing all right in the North, decided to stab us in the back by declaring war on the Allies and attacking Southern France.

There was an alert on Wednesday, the 12th and next day we heard that St. Nazaire had been bombed. The enemy were now closing in on Paris and the French were reported to be fighting desperately to hold back 120 divisions!

One of our recovery teams was called out at midnight on Friday, the 14th and only returned at midday of Saturday, 15th June. They had picked up a field gun from a ditch near Segré, about seventy miles away, having to repair the wheel mountings before it would run on the road. It had broken away from its tractor and run over a woman refugee, breaking both her legs. One of the team was drunk when called out and he came back a sleepless, unshaven wreck. They reported Canadian troops on convoy and hordes of refugees all sleeping in the open fields.

On this same Saturday, the first warning of a move came. We went for dinner but had just started when we were told to leave our plates on the tables and return to workshops. Here we were ordered to load all the Bren gun magazines. After a while we were sent back to finish our meal and, immediately afterwards, we were told to roll up the marquee we had in the yard and load all the lorries. The men of the workshop company were employed in the same way and it was obvious that some kind of emergency message had come through.

As regards our personal kit, we were told to abandon it and take only a haversack and water-bottle. Later, this order was changed and we were allowed to bring all our kit. In any case, the lorries were carrying no more than they were when we arrived in Nantes. We took our kit-bags, etc. from the billet and some chaps burned their personal letters. The last thing I saw as I went out of the billet was our home-made dartboard beside the door, with the three darts still sticking in it. On our way back to the garage we called in to Madame Bonnet's to say goodbye. She could hardly believe that we were going away. A look of surprise and dismay passed over her face as we stood, awkwardly holding our kit. Then, as she realised we were going to *"Angleterre"*, she burst into tears and, one by one, French style, she kissed us on the cheeks in farewell.

Not until that moment, I am sure, did she comprehend the magnitude of the German threat. Never had it seemed possible that the Boche could conquer *"La Belle France"*!

That afternoon, two of us took the A.E.C. to collect the same 6-in. gun we had moved before and take it to the docks. All the machinery, lathes, etc., in the workshop were being packed into crates and, in the evening, we wound the handle of the crane on the A.E.C., lifting box after box on to various trucks. All the vehicles which could not run were being smashed. A diesel engine, used for generating electricity, had a sledgehammer driven through the crankcase. Dozens of lorry batteries were smashed while the acid ran, bubbling and hissing, over the floor. Tools and spare parts from the stores were also being destroyed, though many expensive items, such as micrometers, were kept by the men, which was better than leaving them for the enemy. Hundreds of electric bulbs were thrown in a pile and crushed by hammer blows.

Most of the workshop company moved off at dusk, leaving only the drivers of the trucks carrying the machinery, the crews of two tanks which had been in for minor repairs and our recovery section. They were making for St. Nazaire.

That night, some of us were lucky enough to find a troop-carrying A.E.C. (with no engine) which had a roof and long seats with sponge-rubber cushions. Here we prepared to sleep, the others climbing into any vehicle they could find. Scarcely had we settled down, feeling pretty weary, when the sirens began to wail. We were ordered into the air-raid shelters, with respirators at the alert and gas-capes on our shoulders. It was brilliant moonlight as we stood waiting but nothing happened and, after twenty minutes or so, we were allowed to go back to our "beds", being warned to remain at the alert. When we lay down again, I fell sound asleep with the respirator still tied to my chest.

We were up again at dawn on Sunday, 16th June and continued loading up till every vehicle was crammed. We even drained the tanks of the abandoned trucks and loaded the petrol in tins. Convoy after convoy of trucks went through all day long, carrying men of the R.A.F. and Indian troops from farther inland, all going towards St. Nazaire. Meanwhile, our own convoy remained lined up along the road, just waiting for further orders. The French population now realised that a general evacuation was taking place but there seemed to be little they could do to prepare for the coming of the Germans. Some of them, however, had descended on our deserted dining hall and removed the tables and benches for their own use!

A group of officers, including a blue-tabbed colonel, arrived at the workshop, made a brief inspection and went off again, also on the St. Nazaire road. There was an air of uncertainty about everything and, in the style of the army of that time, we, the ordinary soldiers, were left in ignorance or with only a vague idea of what was actually happening.

Next, our own captain went off somewhere in his car, telling our Q.M.S. to hang on until he came back. As it became dark again, however, our "Q" apparently began to wonder if something had happened to prevent him from returning. He went up towards the fork in the road where the convoys were still streaming past, to see if there was any sign of him, telling us to move up behind. We had just reached the fork, when along came the captain and, almost exactly at midnight, we moved off into the stream of traffic.

That journey to St. Nazaire was a nightmare. At first, the moon showed us smashed vehicles at the side of the road, some military, some civilian. Refugees were sleeping by the roadside, their cars drawn up on the grass. Later, the moon was obscured and we drove in darkness. Not a light was shown, not even the gleam of a rear-light and it became increasingly difficult to see when the vehicle in front was slowing down and, consequently, there were many bumps. The procession must have been one long line all the way from Nantes to St. Nazaire.

The A.E.C., with epicyclic gears in each huge wheel-hub, always whined when it moved and now our Devonshire driver had removed the governor which previously limited the engine speed, so the heavy vehicle simply screamed along at 35 m.p.h., thus keeping up with the lighter vehicles. Every now and then, something would halt the convoy ahead and, as the shadowy shape of the vehicle in front loomed up out of the darkness with terrifying swiftness, on would go the brakes and we would pull up just in time.

About half-way through the night, our captain asked me to drive his Morris. On we went, rushing and stopping, peering into the darkness for the moving shadow in front, which was ever growing big, then diminishing, then growing big again, like something in a horrible dream. Once someone ahead tried to overtake another vehicle; there was a jam up, the whole procession was held up for half an hour while it was cleared.

As we neared St. Nazaire, dawn began to break. The captain was sound asleep beside me and, as I drove, my own eyes were closing for seconds at a time. Suddenly, there was a lurch and, as my eyes opened, I found we were bouncing along a sloping bank. With a wrench of the wheel, I brought the car back on to the road but the captain, now awake, realised I was on the point of exhaustion and took over for the remainder of the journey.

As day broke clear on Monday, 17th June, the line of vehicles could be seen stretching all the way into St. Nazaire. We halted at an aerodrome outside the town, where hundreds of lorries were lined up in the fields and thousands of troops, including Indians, were getting some sort of breakfast ready. Here we waited till the middle of the day, making what meals we could and getting a wash at a tap near the concrete aeroplane hangars. Nearby lay a heap of kit which had been abandoned by personnel of the R.A.F. This was being sorted over by French civilians. There were socks, boots, shoes, books, some fine gramophone records of the classics and many articles of clothing, including dressing gowns. Dressing gowns! Of course, our officers were billeted in French homes and not in hay-lofts or ruinous buildings like many of the "other ranks".

I had sorted out my kit, putting the least important things in my kit-bag so that, if I had to dump anything, it would be my kit-bag that would go first. It was suddenly discovered that our vehicles and the machinery could not be loaded on board ship at St. Nazaire and we were told that we had to go all the way back to Nantes! What was actually happening, no one seemed to know and all sorts of rumours began to circulate. Trucks began to turn round, our little convoy was strung out on the road again and half of them had gone, when a D.R. on a motor-cycle was sent after them to turn them back once more. Then we got fresh orders to dump everything except our firearms and whatever else we could carry on foot.

So, on the spot, we left the vehicles, with all the equipment we had laboured so hard to salvage and the expensive recovery vehicles which had done so much work in our hands, by the roadside. I was told (by whom I don't know) that the two tanks which had been following us from Nantes were "scuttled" by their crews. They had turned the gun of each tank on the other, firing a shell into each. I also heard, later, that a party of sappers, left to carry out demolition work, drove all our vehicles into one heap, set explosive charges under them and left them blazing.

Well, we took our packs, our water-bottles and our rifles and set off along the road towards the town. Most of us had left some kit on the vehicles but we kept our greatcoats, in case we should need them at night.

It was a warm summer day, however, and in addition to the things already mentioned, we carried 100 rounds of ammunition and we had the Bren gun, anti-tank gun and two boxes of Bren magazines, fully loaded, which we took in turns, so we perspired freely as we tramped along.

We fell in with a long column of men, stretching ahead of us, but soon they all stopped, so we stopped too. The party of men immediately in front of us were in the charge of a staff-officer, a captain, if I remember rightly but wearing a red band on his cap, denoting a staff appointment. After a while our captain, becoming impatient of waiting, took us around the other party in order to go forward and find out for himself what was happening. The staff officer immediately stopped him and (rightly I suppose) began telling him off for overtaking other troops. The captain didn't take it lying down and took no pains to hide his disgust from the staff captain, who was saying something about "etiquette". However, we again drew in to the side of the road and lay down on the grass.

Suddenly, there was an outbreak of A.A. fire over St. Nazaire and we lay watching the shell-bursts for some time. There were also some objects like balls of fire floating in the sky in strings, as if they were tied together. What these were, I don't know. They may have been flares, though it was still broad daylight.

We did not know it then but, at that moment, the Cunard liner *Lancastria*, crammed full of men, was being bombed. The result was one of the greatest catastrophes that befel us throughout the war. One bomb went right down the funnel, blew the bottom out of the ship and wrecked the main stairways, leaving many hundreds of men trapped below. Later, I made the acquaintance of a fellow who had been in the *Lancastria*. He told me he was blown off the deck into the water and was picked up, semi-conscious, with shrapnel wounds in both legs. The ship turned over on her side and oil poured out on to the water. The German aircraft dropped incendiaries, which set the oil alight and many of the survivors were swimming in the midst of flames.

I saw some of these survivors, for they came aboard the ship which eventually took us from St. Nazaire. Their hands and arms were bandaged and their hair was singed. Some wore French sailors' jackets, given to them by the crews of the vessels which picked them up. What the official figures are, or whether any were ever published, I do not know but these fellows who escaped estimated that there were about 6,000 men aboard the *Lancastria*** and that *more than half* of that number were lost. I have a photo-cutting from a British magazine issued later in the war, showing part of the hull of the *Lancastria* and one propeller, sticking out of the water, with a black swarm of men clinging to it but no mention is made of the number of casualties. Incidentally, this cutting states that the ship was sunk off Brest in July, but St. Nazaire is over 100 miles to the south of Brest and the date, Monday, 17th June 1940, is one I am not likely to forget.

As I have said, we lay at the roadside, unaware of this massacre and some hours must have passed before the long column began to stir and move forward. Gradually, as we plodded down the road, the line thinned out, as those nearer the town vanished into it and we, who had further to go, struggled along with our burdens. It was late afternoon when we passed through the streets of St. Nazaire. The first couple who carried

---

* Sir Jas. Bisset (then captain of *Franconia*) has said that *Lancastria* losses were "about 3,000", i.e. twice the number of lives lost on the *Titanic*.

British troops were evacuated from France. During the last days of evacuation, British liner *Lancastria* was sunk by Nazi action off Brest, July.

the boxes of Bren magazines left them in the road for another pair to pick up and this was repeated every two or three hundred yards, leaving the last two to bring them into the docks. We were now spread out in scattered single file, sometimes with many yards between one sweating man and the next.

We were led straight on to the gangway of a cargo-boat, the *Floristan*, already packed with troops and the last straggler was no sooner on deck than the ship began to move. As she drew away from the quay, boxes of provisions, canned "bully", etc. were thrown aboard, some breaking open on the deck. A box landed on one man's rifle, splitting the butt in two. It was about 7.30 p.m. when we sailed* and we were accompanied by other ships – one was the *Baluchistan* – and two destroyers as escort. Slowly we steamed out to sea but, even in the open sea, we seemed to be travelling no faster than 8–10 knots.

---

* First German troops reached Nantes at midnight.

As night came, it grew bitterly cold on deck and, with many others, I went below, seeking room to lie down and get some sleep. Some, however, elected to suffer the cold and remain on deck, where they had a better chance of getting out of the ship if anything happened to her. Our Bren gun and two more were now mounted on their steel tripods on the after-deck and some of the R.A.F. had a Lewis gun on the bridge. Going below, I found the first hold was crammed full of Indian troops so, with some more soldiers and airmen, I went down into the bottom hold of the ship, descending a steel ladder into pitch darkness. Someone struck a match and, before it went out, I saw the hump of the propeller-shaft casing, about two feet high, running along the middle of the floor. Needless to say, I did not like it, for here we were in the bowels of the ship and *the only way out was by that narrow steel ladder*, up which only one man at a time could pass. If ever I suffered from claustrophobia, it was there in that dark hole. But fatigue conquered and I laid my greatcoat on the iron floor and slumped my weary bones upon it.

I suppose I slept for a while but it seemed just a minute later that a terrific clatter broke out like a hundred rivetting-machines, echoing through the iron-work of the ship and I heard the roar of an aeroplane engine. In a second or two the noise died away but there was a rattle in the darkness as some of the men spontaneously donned their steel helmets and moved towards the ladder. Queer how much confidence a man places in a flimsy piece of metal covering his head! I, too, moved towards the ladder but those who had reached the hold above were stopped, a voice assuring them it was, "Only a few machine-gun bullets!" and warning them not to go up on deck. As someone remarked with grim humour, it was all a question of whether the bullets were "going up, or coming down"!

One man narrowly escaped having his nose cut off by the edge of a steel helmet dropped from the top of the ladder. We were not sure what had happened up above but later, when we were once more allowed out on deck, where the moon was shining, I heard all about it. An enemy plane had come diving down on the ship from astern, with the moon behind him, lighting the vessel for him but also making a silhouette of the aircraft. The Lewis gun on the bridge fired first, with tracer, which seemed to fall short. The three Bren guns on the stern held their fire until the plane was almost on top of them, then let him have it all at once. He neither dropped any bombs nor fired his guns but banked frantically to clear the superstructure of the ship and went down towards the sea. Our (recovery) gun crew claimed the honour of hitting him and he was not seen to rise again. Everything was shadowy, of course, but all seemed convinced that the 'plane was brought down.

This incident had the effect of making everyone a bit more cheerful, for it was felt that we could at least hit back, even if it was only with a machine-gun.

Next day we made the best of our ration of bully beef and hard biscuits but we had little tea. After queuing all round the deck for a drink of tea, I was told it was all finished. Luckily, there seemed to be a plentiful supply of water, though it had coal dust and wood-splinters floating in it. Almost every part of the ship had a film of coal dust on it, so we were all in a very dirty state. There were only two small iron-walled lavatories, long overwhelmed by 3,000 men and out of order; so biscuit tins were set up in various corners as improvised latrines.

There were no more signs of German aircraft or submarines during the day, or the following night and by Wednesday morning we felt we would reach Blighty safely. Why the voyage took so long, I can't imagine, unless we did a lot of zig-zagging. It was Wednesday evening when we finally pulled in to Plymouth harbour, at the end of the worst voyage I have ever had. As our destroyer escort left us, we gave them a cheer and a wave and a bugler on our ship sounded the General Salute.

Even then, we were not allowed to land. It seemed there was no accommodation for us, so we had to spend a third night on that stinking ship. Rations were brought out to us, in the harbour; tinned sausages, tea and fresh bread. There was plenty for all, so we had our first square meal for days.

In the morning, another destroyer came in, carrying what was probably one of the last loads of humanity to come out of France. Her passengers included some nurses, a few stretcher cases, which were laid out on the deck and a number of French officers and men, who had apparently decided to become "Free French".

When finally the troops were taken off our ship, we found that we were to be last and we were to have the job of *cleaning up the ship!* This was by order of the O.C. Troops who, we were told, was the same staff-officer who had had words with our captain at St. Nazaire. We had almost forgotten him but perhaps he hadn't forgotten us, or the captain who had dared answer back!

So the Pioneer Labour Corps, who usually do this kind of work, went off before us. So did the Indians; and we, left to the last, went round the ship, sweeping up and gathering in gas capes, respirators, steel helmets and ammunition, which the men had decided to carry no further. Many of these things had been thrown overboard and some of the light stuff was floating about in the harbour, where some officials in a launch were inspecting it with the aid of a boat-hook. Then, since our improvised latrines could not stay on the ship, we heaved them over the side as well!

Finally, the tender came for us, took us off and brought us to the quayside. And here the culminating farce was enacted. A Royal Marines Band struck up and a photographer prepared to take pictures of us coming ashore, as if we were conquering heroes or something. There we were; dirty, dishevelled, tired and hungry, our main desire being to get a bath, food and sleep and instead we got martial music. The band was playing *"Colonel Bogey"*, so we began singing the Army parody, something about *"Bollocks! and the same to you!"* Then the company broke into a storm of boos, raspberries and catcalls and began yelling, "Get out of here!" The photographer looked quite shocked, and when we finally came up the gang-plank, some of the boys looked so pugnacious that I don't think he took any pictures at all.

Which just proves that, of all the things you wear, your expression is the most important!

This was really the end of the evacuation as far as we were concerned. We were given tea, cakes and fruit by girls on the quayside and we also got some Y.M.C.A. notepaper and envelopes with which to write home, postage being handled by the Association. Then we were put aboard a train and proceeded by way of Dawlish and Exeter to the camp at Perham Down, Hants. Even in my weary condition, I could still admire the lovely scenery of the Devon coast, for it was summer and the sea was blue, till it broke, foaming, on the red rocks.

At Perham Down we were allowed to rest on the grass in the sunshine, while a band played to us. This lasted a few days and we were only disturbed by a couple of air-raid alarms, both at night. The first night, we were told to get into the trenches but the second night we stayed where we were most comfortable, in bed.

Later we were moved to Leicester and here we met some of the men of the Base Workshop who had left Nantes before us. They had apparently believed they would never see us again and told us they thought we were all prisoners!

We did not wait at Leicester but went right on to Rotherham in Yorkshire, where we rejoined all the various sections of the original G.H.Q. Troops Workshops with whom we had left Bellerby for France. Some of these sections had been evacuated from Dunkirk itself and others from Boulogne and Brest. *We* were apparently "The Last of the Mucky Ones" (to parody Fenimore Cooper!)

At Rotherham we were allotted civilian billets, one or two men being placed with each family willing to take boarders. Most of us were in one street, Dean Crescent. Before we had time to make friends with the people, we were off for forty-eight hours leave to our own homes, after which we returned to Rotherham for what was to be a lengthy spell; but we were all wondering what would be the next stage of this strange war.

Interlude in Blighty

A	T ROTHERHAM, I had to learn another language new to me. *"Ah's ta ban?"* apparently meant "How are you?", *"Weers ta ban?"* was "Where are you going?" and *"Put wood in t'hoil"* meant "Close the door" ("Put wood in the hole!")

I was billeted with a Mr. and Mrs. Gill and family in Dean Crescent and a right good-hearted family they were. I am quite sure the 25s. allowance made to them by the Army never repaid them for the attention, good feeding and friendship they lavished on me. They even had a bottle of stout on the table for me with every supper. One night, when I was on guard inside the gasworks, I was told someone wanted to see me at the side entrance. One of the others took my place and, wondering who wanted me, I went along to the gateway. Here I found my host, Mr. Gill, and, guard or no guard, he hooked me off round the corner to a little pub where his good lady was sitting and on the table was the inevitable bottle of Guinness!

Most of the men were convinced that these guards were only thought up to keep us occupied. They were certainly a farce. One sergeant-major, acting as orderly-officer, came to the gasworks at midnight and turned out the guard. Because they did not turn out sharply enough for his liking, he had them doubling up and down inside the gasworks for a while. Then he found that one man had a button showing where his battle-blouse should have been buttoned on to his trousers at the back, so he ordered him to appear on first parade next morning, "properly dressed". A man finishing guard duty was usually excused early parades the following day.

Having left our vehicles in France, we were a unit without equipment and so we had little else to do but these comic-opera guards. The only useful work we did in Rotherham was shovelling sand in Corporation trucks, which was carted off to be used in making air-raid shelters. We didn't mind this job, for it *was* useful and it was healthy exercise. The Corporation, of course, were not allowed to pay us, but we got free passes to the swimming baths.

One thing I liked about Rotherham was the entertainment available on Sundays at the larger inns. Many of these in the North country have a small stage built in and my hosts would often take me to one, where we sat with our drinks at one of the tables facing the stage while singers, conjurers and other turns beguiled us, something in the manner of the early music-hall. So the "day of rest" became indeed a day of mental relaxation well gauged to take the mind off the ordinary weekly trials and tribulations and to send you more happily back to work on Monday. By contrast, the aim of my native Scotland seems to be to make the Sabbath so miserable that you are glad to *get back* to work!

We remained at Rotherham for only two months and, on 14th August, we left the good people and went to North Camp, Retford, Notts.. Here, we were under canvas for a while but soon G.H.Q. Troops Workshops were broken up and I was sent to Catterick on 30th August, along with Eddie Munt (the man from Honiton) and Q.M.S. Toms, a Channel Islander, we being the only members of the old No. 3 Recovery Section, though there were several men from other sections, notably a man from Lancaster called Gregson. I remember him particularly because he once made me a beautiful plaited leather belt with a buckle made from part of a motor piston, which I still have. I believe leather-work was his civilian occupation. He had been with No. 1 Recovery Section.

At Catterick, we settled down to barracks routine in the Piave Lines where, almost a year before, I had pricked those blisters on my feet. I was put to work in the engine bay during the day and there were occasional guard duties, fire picket, etc.

On Saturday, 7th September, I attended a performance of the play, *George and Margaret* at the garrison theatre but, before the end, the curtain was drawn across the stage and the audience of troops were warned to report immediately to their respective unit headquarters. At our lines, nobody seemed to have any instructions for us so, after a while, we went to bed.

Half an hour later, we were roused and told to parade in battle order, each man to bring his ten rounds of ammunition.

It was a full muster but no information was given to us as we stood waiting, lined up in threes. Then there was a call for all cooks to fall out and gather at one end of the line.

This looked as if we might be due for a sudden move. After waiting in line for about an hour, however, we were told to return to our quarters but to keep in readiness to be called out at a moment's notice.

I learned, much later in the war, that an enemy invasion fleet of barges was burned by the R.A.F. at the beginning of September 1940 and it seems likely that our stand-to was occasioned by some invasion alarm connected with the barges at Cherbourg. However, nothing further happened that night, no doubt because the fleet was completely destroyed.

Hitler's invasion fleet 'was burned by RAF'

Express Special Correspondent
WILLIAM DOUGLAS

CHERBOURG, Sunday.—Days when Hitler assembled a great fleet of barges and an army of 150,000 men to invade England were recalled today by Simone, the middle-aged waitress at Cherbourg's Café de Paris billiard-room.

Mr. Churchill was asked questions in Parliament when stories went round of bodies of many Germans being washed ashore on England's south coast in <u>September 1940</u>. He replied that is was a question which could wait until the war was won.

Here is the French side of the story, told by Simone:—

I was getting sort of resigned to waiting on these German pigs after Dunkirk.

The harbour was filling up with flat bottom boats of an immensity, and the soldiers were pouring in by the thousand.

The officers would clatter into my billiard-room and order drinks, heil Hitler, and sing "Tomorrow we sail for England."

The barges filled up with soliders, and the officers no longer came ashore to the billiard-room.

It was the very <u>beginning of September</u> and in the sky that night there was a furious whizzing and many battles.

While the fighting planes fought, other planes of the English dropped gallons upon gallons of oil on the barges and on the waters of the harbour; and on the oil they dropped incendiary torches.

I never saw and I never shall see such a furious fire.

The barges, tied together, burned like firewood. The screams of those Germans were like those of souls in purgatory.

For three whole days ambulance trains carried injured soliders from Cherbourg to the hospitals of Paris.

Commandant Koch was the German officer in charge of the invasion move at Cherbourg.

After thge last hospital train had left, he put on his full uniform, pinned on all his medals and shot himself.

(World copyright)

A little way down the road from the Piave Lines were the lines of the Royal Artillery, where we had noticed several big guns on railway carriages. In the first week of October, several of us were detailed for a job in these lines. I think there were two fitters and two driver-mechs.,

Eddie Munt and myself being the driver-mechs. We were taken to the biggest gun of all, which was generally shielded by a huge camouflaged tarpaulin, except when a crew was being trained on it. This was the biggest gun in Britain and, when information concerning it was later released to the press, it was referred to as, "one of the largest guns in the world". The bore was 18 in., and each shell weighed over a ton. As there was at least a foot and a half of metal at each side of the breech, the total width was almost 5 ft. The piece itself, I believe, had been on a monitor in the First World War. It was now cradled in a specially built gigantic steel carriage which ran on four bogies, each with eight wheels. The whole thing, I was told, weighed 200 tons and an artillery-man assured me that, even when the brakes on all wheels were hard on, it moved along the rails when the gun was fired! I once saw it moved on to a different line by a goods loco. It went one way all right but, when it passed the points, it had to return over a slight rising gradient. The engine shuddered and shook, puffed and panted, its driving wheels skidded round and sparks flew in showers from the rails but the mammoth hardly moved. Sand was poured on to the rails and it was slowly and with great difficulty brought to its new position.

Our job on this great gun was to fit up remote controls to one of the motor engines inside the carriage. There were two of these engines, of the Ford "V8" type, one for re-charging the recuperators and one for elevating the gun. It was required to bring the controls from the engine out through the steel side of the carriage at a point where there was a folding footplate. Here two men would stand and would be able to start the engine, "choke" it and rev. it as necessary. It was our task to design and make the arrangement of rods, levers and cables, to make this possible. It took us about a week.

During that week, we saw some of the drill carried out by the gun crews. There were two crews being trained on the big gun, one being made up of officers and one of other ranks. Each crew had over twenty members, including brakemen, engine men and loaders. There were several armoured vans behind the gun-carriage, containing the ammunition. A small derrick on the gun-carriage lifted each shell into a cradle, which ran on miniature rails towards the massive breech.

At the time, all this was secret but one day I came across a book, two inches thick, which had been left on the gun-carriage by one of the officers. It contained the whole story of the gun, with diagrams giving all mechanical details!

Britain has one of the largest guns in the world –
such a special gun that they give it a special nameplate.

Here is His Majesty's gun Boche-Buster on its special railway carriage.
The first pictures to be released.

The gun was christened *"Boche Buster"* and another of our fitters had the job to make a large nameplate about 4 ft. long with brass letters, *"H.M.G. Boche Buster"*. This plate was fixed to the hull, high up near the end where the little derrick was standing. On the middle of the hull were painted the royal coat of arms, the artillery badge and battle honours. Some time later, the gun was inspected by His late Majesty King George VI. Photographs of his visit were displayed for sale in a Catterick shop and, later still, photographs of the gun itself were released to the press. None, however, did it justice, as they were taken from strange angles, no doubt to avoid revealing details to the enemy.

Yet, if I had been an enemy agent, I could have passed on a textbook telling them all about it!

Back in our own lines, I was soon to be doing recovery work again but meantime we came in for the usual drill, to keep us occupied. I can do no better than quote from a letter I wrote home on 23rd October.

We get an hour of foot and rifle drill every morning now, sometimes with a sergeant from the Green Howards, whom I prefer to our own sergeant. It goes like this: "Squad ... 'shun; as you were! Pick your feet up and place them down. Squad ... 'shun. Slo-ope ... arms, one, two, three, one, two, three, one. Right turn, quick march ... HALT! Lead off with a full pace of thirty inches there! Quick march, left, right, left, right, left, SWING THOSE ARMS!! Abeout ... turn, abeout ... turn, abeout ... turn. I'll make you dizzy before I'm finished with you! Right wheel ... halt ... right turn ... order ... arms, one, two, three, one, two, three, one. Count the timing, shout it out loud, shout it, every one of you! And don't bang those butts on the ground!" (Was that what Shakespeare meant when he wrote ... "But me no buts"?) "Slope ... arms, one, two three ... SHOUT! I'll make you shout! I've a little sister who can shout louder than you. If I get a man not shouting, I'll have 'im out of it!" (Vague threat this.) "Present ... arms. Strike that rifle at the point of balance, with the fingers stretched upwards and the wrist on the magazine! Elbows at the sides, thumb in front of the nose!" (What did he say?) "Slope ... arms. To the front ...salute! One, two, three, four, five, down! Keep shouting the timing till I tell you to stop!"

Well, no doubt this is calculated to bewilder the enemy, or hypnotize him, so that you can walk up to him and relieve him of his

howitzer! If it really helped to bring this war to a quick finish, no
one would do it with more willingness than I."

On 26th October 1940, a Saturday, I had quite an eventful day on
recovery work. Two cars, civilian type, but commandeered for army
use, had broken down at Ripon, twenty miles away and were to be
towed back. We took two 15 cwt. trucks with us, leaving at 11.30 a.m.,
expecting to be late for dinner but not so late as circumstances made us.
First, we had trouble with the "Autovac" petrol lift in one of the trucks
and only got it going after towing it half-way round Ripon. Then we
got stuck on the way back with the same trouble on the other truck.
At the same time, one of the cars being towed got jammed in gear, so
we took the top off the gearbox and left it off. The second truck would
not start, so we had to leave it and one car, with the attendant drivers,
to be picked up later. We 'phoned Catterick to send other vehicles for
this purpose. The remaining truck took one car in tow, with myself at
the wheel of the car.

We got along quite well until we passed Leeming when, to add to
the chain of mishaps, we were involved indirectly in a road accident! A
small car overtook us and had just regained the left of the road when a
motor-cycle with a pillion passenger, coming from the opposite direction, struck the car. I did not know anything was wrong till the truck
in front of me suddenly braked hard and skidded a little sideways. I had
scant warning, being only nine or ten feet behind, on the other end of
the tow-chain but I trod hard on the brake, slid along the road and
bumped into the back of the truck.

I heard the crash of glass as my headlights fell out and, at the same
time, the motor-cycle skidded past on the opposite side of the road. My
mate and I reached the motor-cycle together. The man who had been
on the pillion sat up on the grass but the driver lay still on his face in
the road, with the machine lying across his legs. We moved the bike and
carried him to the grass verge. He began to moan. One of his rubber
boots was torn off but the foot and leg seemed all right. In ten minutes
he came round and struggled to sit up. We could not tell where he might
be hurt and he couldn't answer any questions. His face was badly marked
and his fingers bled but we could see nothing that looked serious. An
ambulance was sent for, then we began to take particulars. The occupants
of the private car were three soldiers, unhurt, and they said the motor-
cyclist was holding the crown of the road when he struck their off-side
door. The marks in the road bore this out. We had not struck either of

the first two vehicles and were only concerned with accounting for the damage to our own. When we asked the name and address of the motor-cyclist, he did not answer, though he was limping about in a rather dazed state. The pillion passenger did not know the driver's name either, as he had only been given a lift. He said, "We came from Darlington." The driver suddenly looked up.

"From where?" he asked.

The other repeated, "From Darlington; *you* were going to Birmingham."

"Were you on the back?" asked the driver.

We realised he had completely lost his memory, probably from the effects of concussion. He was led away. We continued our journey but had one more close shave at a roundabout as dusk came. A car tried to pass between the truck and the car I was steering and the driver only noticed the tow-chain at the last second.

It was quite dark when we reached Catterick and we felt very hungry. We had had nothing to eat since breakfast! The other vehicles arrived an hour later and yet another crew were out until 2.00 a.m. after that, so it seemed that recovery in Yorkshire could be as exacting as recovery in France!

Before the end of October, Q.M.S. Toms left us, to go on a draft heading for Singapore. When saying goodbye, he told us he thought it would not be long before we were all overseas again. At Catterick we were merely in a "Training Section" which held men until they were required elsewhere.

The days were getting shorter and our reveille was so early that we stood shivering on roll-call parade in the moonlight, three hours before we were due to start work.

On the last day of October, I had an unusual little job, bringing a truck load of tin ingots from a stores in the "Marne" lines to our own lines, for tinning dixies, ladles, etc.. There were thirty ingots, worth, I believe, about £150. Just one item in the equipping of an army.

There was at Catterick another A.E.C. breakdown, similar to the one we had to leave in France. It was big and powerful but, as the driving seat was open, with no windscreen, it was hardly suitable for winter weather. On Friday, 1st November, we took it up on to the moors, beyond the village of Downholme, to look for a truck. We found it, not on the road but 100 yards away, over the heather, in a bog! We got it out and, the same forenoon, we recovered another one from a deep pond near Catterick.

I don't know whether these trucks had been on manoeuvres or if this was a new, more exciting way of studying pond-life!

On Thursday, 7th November, by way of a change from recovery work, I went to the garrison theatre (the Gaiety) to see *Cavalleria Rustic-ana*, presented by the Vic Wells Opera Company.

The following Sunday, we had a trip to the North to pick up some wreck or another. We were "directed" from one unit to another, via Newcastle, Sunderland, Durham and Lanchester, before we could begin the return journey. When we got back to Catterick, we found that all except ten of the "attached" personnel in the training section had been put on a draft for overseas. I was one of the ten.

At the theatre again on Wednesday, the 13th, I saw a variety show including Peggy Desmond and the late Horace Kenney, that grand old comedian who always seemed ready to burst into tears.

On Friday, the 15th, Gregson, the leatherworker, left us, being posted away and, on Monday the 18th, Eddie Munt, who had been before a Medical Board, got his complete discharge from the Army. I began to feel like one of the "Ten Little Niggers"!

One advantage of being on recovery work was that the odd jobs you got took you out of the barracks and let you see quite a lot of the countryside. On Wednesday, 27th November, I went south to York with some rifles for repair. I entered this pleasant city by the ancient Walmgate Bar, passing inside the old city walls of white stone. Next day I was one of a crew sent north to Barnard Castle, a quaint old place on the River Tees. Travelling over the moorland roads, a large building, standing alone, was pointed out to me as Bowes Museum, which formerly belonged to the Bowes-Lyon family.

The weather up to now had been not too bad, though the trees were, of course, bare. During the following week, it became bitterly cold and on Tuesday, 3rd December, we were again called out on recovery, at eight o'clock in the evening. We were to pick up a vehicle which we were told was at Boroughbridge.

I was driving the big A.E.C. and wore a greatcoat and leather gauntlets but still the icy wind seemed to bite through them. The others sat huddled in their seats, also exposed, with their hands deep in their pockets and coat collars up round their ears. We stopped at an inn before Boroughbridge for a cup of tea (believe it or not; anyway, it was past closing time!). While we thawed out, I played a tune on the piano and the landlord and his daughter sat down to listen, apparently glad of the company.

When we got to Boroughbridge, there was no sign of the broken-down lorry, though we searched every road in the area until midnight. Our corporal-in-charge (Les Haigh, another cheery Yorkshireman) went to the police station and 'phoned Catterick. They could give no further information but ordered us to return. We got back to the depot at 1.30 a.m.. Next day we were told the missing lorry was at Wetherby, twelve miles from Boroughbridge!

A small note in my diary for 16th December 1940, reminds me that I was then issued with my first bayonet!

For the second time, I was not home for either Christmas or New Year but spent the festive season rather miserably in barracks. Our Christmas party, I remember, was highlighted only by Les Haigh giving us his version of a song about "Three Crows".

Each couplet was recited firstly by Les, then we joined in singing to the accompaniment of a big drum effect on a steel locker; Boom! Boom! Boom! Tune: as chorus of *The Quartermaster's Stores*; *"My eyes are dim, etc. ..."*

The Three Crows

There were three crows sat on a tree
As black, as black as they could be, (Repeat)
As black, as black as they could be.

"All Sing!" Boom! Boom! Boom!

One old crow said to his mate,
"Let's go and find soomthing to ate!"
They flew across an open plain,
To weer an ould fox 'ad been slain.
They perched upon 'is ould backbone,
And pecked 'is eyes out, woon by woon.
Then came a faarmer, with 'is goon
And shot them all, exceptin' woon.
And that ould crow flew oop a tree,
And said, "Tha fule, tha caan't shoot me!"
But faarmer loaded shot and shell,
And blew t'ould crow to ... Hell!

Early on Sunday morning, 5th January 1941 – about four o'clock –
we were again dragged out of bed on recovery. Once more I had to
drive the big open A.E.C. and we had to go to Wormald Green, south
of Ripon. Snow was on the ground, frozen hard. I had my greatcoat on,
woollen gloves with gauntlets on top and a balaclava, with a field-service
cap opened out over it and buttoned under the chin. In spite of all that,
the wind felt like a wall of ice as we roared along the highway. My brow
went numb with the cold, then my jaws felt as if I had lockjaw. That
passed off, then my fingers on the big steering wheel went dead and I
began to shiver all over. We stopped at a lorry-drivers' café, on the
Great North Road but it was closed, so we stuck our tingling fingers
on the radiator and stopped there for a few minutes till the circulation
came back, then carried on again. We found two trucks at the roadside
by Wormald Green railway station but there was no sign of life. Looking
into the back of the truck, we discovered a man asleep amongst the pile
of baggage. To make sure we had found the right truck, we wanted to
know the name of the unit to which it belonged, so we shook the
recumbent figure. "Who does this truck belong to?" we asked.

"Me!" murmured the drowsy one.

When he awakened properly he told us both crews were in a railway
signal-box nearby. One truck had been trying to tow the other but the
snow-chain on one wheel had snapped and was jammed around the
brake-drum. There was also a trailer. We found the rest of the men
snoring around the signal-box fire, so we thawed ourselves out for a
bit, then went back to chisel the broken chain free. We began the
journey back with one truck and a trailer on tow, while the other
truck, freed of the chain, started under its own power. However, I
think its radiator had got frozen, blocking the circulation of the water,
for, by the time we got into Ripon, it boiled itself dry and cracked
something. So we hitched it on behind as well and there we were in
the A.E.C., pulling two trucks and a trailer, coming along like a train;
and the old cement-mixer brought the whole lot in, without snow-
chains! We did get some tea on the way back, which was very welcome. Arriving at the depot we had dinner, then, as it was Sunday, we
went back to bed for a while.

There were three more recoveries that afternoon but other crews were
sent to deal with them. At 8.00 p.m. that same Sunday evening, another
draft left the barracks, supposedly for Kenya but such "destinations"
may have been intended as red herrings. This draft included just about

all that remained of the recovery sections which came out of France and I think I was the last to remain.

On 8th January, the Quartermaster took back from us the bayonets which had been issued during the previous month and also our rifles!

The next day, which happened to be my twenty-fourth birthday, I was given seven days leave. Quite a nice birthday present but I've a suspicion it was just a coincidence.

Returning from leave, I found I was at last posted. I was to join a Light Aid Detachment (L.A.D.) attached to the 2nd. Battalion King's Royal Rifle Corps. This regiment has the biggest list of battle honours in the British Army. As I discovered later, anyone attached to them is also likely to see more of the shooting than most members of the R.A.O.C. At this time the 2nd Battalion "occupied" part of Surrey. One other man left Catterick with me, Alf Askew, whose aquaintance I now made for the first time. Alf was a tall, good-natured fellow with glasses and we became good friends. When I knew him better, he told me he had left behind a fishmonger's business he owned in Darlington, to volunteer for service. Alf was never to carry on his business after the war, for he was killed in France towards the end of the war. I am sure he passed on to a brighter and far better world and a fuller life. But we know not what earthly fate awaits us and Alf and I travelled south, concerned only with finding our new unit. We had been told it was at Haslemere but, as usual, we had to be passed from one company to another and we eventually found the L.A.D. at Farncombe, near Godalming, where we arrived by truck at midnight, Saturday 18th–Sunday 19th January 1941.

The next few months were occupied in routine work, carrying out repairs to vehicles of the various companies of the regiment and recovery when necessary. We had one recovery vehicle, a stores wagon (carrying spares in steel bins) and several lighter vehicles. At the beginning of February we had two days of manoeuvres on Salisbury Plain. We spent most of the two nights getting vehicles out of bogs and ditches. In the middle of the second night, when it was snowing hard, a major and another officer came along. The major was wringing out his shirt cuffs which were soaking and seemed glad of the cup of tea we offered him, from a brew we had just made on a primus inside our truck. At 3.00 a.m. we managed to get some sleep in a nearby cellar.

We sometimes visited one company or another to do a job and occasionally to attend a company dance held in a village such as Witley or Chiddingfold. We also went to Cranleigh to see an instructional film dealing with army equipment. This film was shown in the Regal Cinema but for troops only, of course.

Once I was as far afield as Steventon in Berkshire but it was now spring and it was quite a pleasant run; the purpose being, if I remember correctly, to collect stores from a salvage depot.

One Sunday in April we had a shooting match (quite friendly) with the Home Guard. We were invited to their miniature range and we used their 0.22-in. rifles, which had no kick at all. We had no practice and we lost narrowly but I had our team's best score and also won a sweepstake by attaining a self-nominated score, so I was quite pleased. About two weeks later, we were on the range with our own service rifles and I again scored well. Whether it was because of this or because at that time I happened to be "senior soldier" I know not, but I was given charge of the one and only Tommy gun in our section; which meant I had to clean the damn' thing.

Such, then, were our activities in Surrey. We also enjoyed boating on the nearby River Wey, especially on the brighter Sundays, when the river was quite busy with skiffs and punts, filled with khaki or print frocks; or both.

There were quite a number of Canadian and French-Canadian soldiers in the area but we had little contact with them. I seem to remember some of Princess Patricia's Regiment getting themselves into trouble occasionally when out on the spree! We had our own favourite pubs wherein we enjoyed the local *Four-X*; and there was a cinema in Godalming. The Y.M.C.A. once held a musical recital in an attempt to uplift the troops. The programme, rendered by piano and 'cello, was a bit too heavy to cause much uplift. As the seats behind me became more and more empty and the people in front fell more soundly asleep, I tip-toed out.

As the weather became warmer, we enjoyed our short trips in vehicles being tested after repair. One day I was in a small armoured car when I got my first view of the Devil's Punchbowl, that perfect hollow just off the main Portsmouth road, its foliage bright beneath a brilliant sun. The armoured car, incidentally, was one of those little egg-shaped Daimlers, which run as swiftly backwards as they do forwards. The Italians would have found them useful.

Some of the boys seemed intent on killing themselves before the enemy had a chance. I remember being in a Humber staff car driven by our Staff Sergeant on the Guildford by-pass, doing eighty miles per hour. On bends, he slackened speed to a modest seventy-five!

A few of the good people of Farncombe volunteered to let us have the use of their baths, an amenity which was very much appreciated, as there was no bath in our quarters next to the garage we had taken over. We would visit some house, two at a time, have our bath and invariably the lady of the house would extend further hospitality, by producing the inevitable cup of tea to follow.

One evening, as two of us sat talking to the folks in one of these houses, the husband began trying to "sort out" my accent. He made several guesses as to where I came from but none were near the mark. I have not so noticeable an accent as some of my countrymen and, I think, during my service, my speech became a sort of happy medium; a blending of all the accents one hears in the Army. Our host finally decided that I came from Birmingham, much to the amusement of my fellow soldier. I don't know whether the Brummies or myself should feel most insulted!

We had several Londoners in our little detachment and they sometimes had visitors, since their homes were within easy reach. One family left a large parcel of delicacies which were shared among us one Sunday. We had winkles, prawns and fruit pie for tea!

One of the Londoners told us once of a dialogue overheard between some little urchins after one of the blitzes. A German airman had been shot down, and the kids had been on the scene before his remains had been removed. *"Yus, I was just-a-goin' ter tyke 'is 'ead to git the 'elmet, but they stopped me!"* *"I told yer, yer should've tyken 'is arm; look at the rings wot was on 'is fingers!"*

This story was possibly exaggerated but one wonders what effect the blitzes may have had on the upbringing and mentality of any children in the midst of such horrors.

On Friday, 16th May, I was granted forty-eight hours leave and, as Scotland was too far off, I was invited up to London by our electrician, Dave Knight, who was then at home for a week. His house was near Waterloo Station. As the station was closed following blitz damage, I had to leave the train at Vauxhall and proceed from there by 'bus.

My friend and I took a walk round Lambeth. The Lambeth Cut, a general shopping and market centre, was flattened. The Old Vic Theatre was badly damaged and some of the wreckage was still smouldering, a week after the blitz.

Water was running out of a broken pipe, in a large pool which maintained the same level all the time, so it must have drained through the rubbish somewhere.

The ruined remains of shop goods were mixed up with girders, mortar and brick.

A chalked notice erected in the middle of a wide space announced; "All are safe from the tobacconist, fish shop and tailor's."

Back at Dave's home, I was given one of the small bedrooms. The other had a hole in the ceiling, where an incendiary bomb had come through. His wife had calmly dealt with it by means of a shovel and bucket.

At one o'clock in the morning, another raid started but there did not seem to be many planes, so far as I could judge from the noise. But the guns thundered out their challenge, while bed and house shook like the cake-walk at a fair ground.

Dave's father-in-law had a bakery and next morning, Saturday, Dave decided to take over the baker's round to give his wife a break; for she usually did the job.

I gave him a hand and we went around in a little motor tricycle van, all over Westminster area. In this way I saw some parts of London I might not have seen otherwise. The round included many of the police canteens. I was twice inside Scotland Yard, which normally requires a pass and I also visited Trenchard House, Vine Street and West End Central, each time carrying a tray of cakes on my head and still dressed in khaki.

In passing, I saw the burnt-out Debating Chamber of the House of Commons and I noticed that the Clock Tower had a hole away up near the top, above the clock faces, which were also marked where panes had been broken.

In the evening we visited one of Dave's brothers at Burnt Oak, where we were pleasantly entertained. There was a radiogram and Dave's brother played the violin very well, having played on the stage. We finished the evening at the "local" before returning by the Underground to Waterloo.

In the Underground stations, I saw many people of all ages, carrying down bedding and blankets so that they could sleep in the rough bunks set up in various corners of the platforms and entrances. They would be safe from bombing but it could hardly be comfortable in these draughty, musty places. Some came down early to be sure of a place and sat rather wearily on their beds, waiting for the traffic to lessen before lying down.

On Sunday, Dave and I and the dog went for a walk. We went along Blackfriars Road where, on both sides, large buildings were gutted. An old window blind was nailed to a beam, with the words "Keep Smiling" drawn on it.

Across Blackfriars Bridge, gangs of men were pulling down houses which were unsafe. Tremendous heaps of rubble blocked the side-streets.

And on the Embankment, were there not shrapnel grooves added to the hieroglyphics on Cleopatra's Needle?

Towards Holborn Viaduct, more streets of smouldering wreckage. Huge gaunt buildings made the skyline look like a bit of a Flanders battlefield. Metal girders were twisted like sealing wax which has been heated and allowed to cool.

Tall frail-looking walls and chimneys climbed precariously to the sky while, below, great heaps of brickwork spilled out into the street. Some roads were closed, where scaffolding supported the overhanging walls, seventy or eighty feet above.

A steel railway bridge, which had been down on the road, was raised again and in position for use.

Along Holborn, we saw the burnt-out City Temple.

Near Lincoln's Inn Fields, St. Clement's Church was also a shell. Around St. Paul's was a wide open space strewn with rubble. Stairways hung in space and 'buses ran along roads which had sections roped off for repair.

The Old Bailey had a great slice out of it but the dome and the figure of Justice still stood.

Beside the G.P.O. a huge crane stood, its three giant steel legs straddling the street. Again I quote from a letter I wrote to my parents:

Everywhere there are lorries and men working in a desert of bricks, while the A.F.S. still play hoses on the smouldering ruins and steam rises in the calm air.

Yes, London has been walloped but still the people go calmly about their business in the midst of it all, though you can't go a hundred yards without seeing bomb damage.

It may be their turn next, but still they carry on.

Both the damage and the courage of these people have to be seen to be believed.

On Sunday evening, we visited another brother of Dave's out at Colindale. This one had been a pilot in the First World War, was shot down and had an artificial leg. He had some important position at an aircraft factory and met important people. He showed me a cablegram from America, passed by censor, addressed to him personally in intimate terms and signed "Rockefeller"!

He was not snobbish and we spent another grand evening, rounded off with a bottle of French white wine of 1929 vintage.

Later in the evening, I left London from Waterloo, which was again open, though the lines were damaged in parts. There was one big crater between two of the platforms.

So I returned to the unit after an interesting weekend in a city which is always interesting, even in the sad state in which I found it.

Back at Farncombe, rumours were heard about a possible move for us in the near future.

Our officer, by the way – Lieutenant Priest – was a cheerful soul and one of the easiest on discipline I have ever known. When I first met him, he gave me no time to salute, but shook hands and made me feel at home. I remember once, on pay parade, one man came in with a cigarette in his mouth. The Lieutenant looked up and calmly said, "Wrong, Cansell; go back and start again!"

On his second entry, Cansell gave him a comic salute, one of those corkscrew efforts which end with the hand quivering behind the ear, but the officer just smiled.

His humour made him well-liked and none seriously tried to take advantage of him. Any work to be done was done willingly. A sense of humour is one of the greatest assets in the British Army. But Fascists and Communists alike seem to be entirely devoid of it.

The move came off near the end of May 1941. We said goodbye to Farncombe by holding a sing-song in the Sun Inn on Tuesday, the 27th. Next morning, early, we set off for Trowbridge in Wiltshire, a distance of roughly eighty miles.

We could not, however, take the easy or obvious way of going straight there in transport. The regiment, excluding attached personnel (thank goodness) had to march the whole way. It took the best part of four days, or twenty miles per day, which is good going; perhaps as good as some of the first war troops may have done!

The K.R.R.C., of course, marched at the speed of a rifle regiment,

160 paces to the minute, while the Ordnance Corps rate was 120 paces to the minute. They also had a complete drill of their own, which differed entirely from ours. When they mounted guard, they did so on the double! We sometimes got roped in for training with them, but then it became farcical.

I once went on a short route march with a section of the regiment. At the end, when we got the order "Dismiss", I got my rifle up to the slope only to find that all the rest had only brought theirs to the vertical position at the shoulder! So my rifle stuck out away above the rest, like a Christmas tree at a party. Then they smacked the edge of the hand on the stock and turned away before I could even get in a butt salute! The officer-in-charge raised an eyebrow, but let it fall again when he saw I was not one of the Greenjackets.

The K.R.R.C., incidentally, was founded in North America in 1755 as the 62nd Royal Americans. Later, their number was changed to the 60th Rifles, the name by which they have been known since.

They served under Wolfe at Quebec and to him they owe their motto, *"Celer et Audax"* ("Swift and Bold").

They were the first rifle regiment in the Army and six Acts of Parliament were required in their formation.

The rest of their history is too full of incident for me to cover here.

To return to our journey: as the Battalion marched, so the vehicles had to be brought along behind them. Actually, we only drove for two hours of each day and the vehicles were "harboured" under trees most of the time, while we sat around, or brewed-up, or explored the surrounding lanes. We slept in our vehicles each night, or those for whom there was no room slept on the grass.

We stopped the first night at King's Somborne, a hamlet near Winchester. When passing through Winchester, I got a glimpse of the statue of King Alfred the Great, which reminded me that this ancient town was once the capital of Saxon England.

The next evening we stopped on the outskirts of Salisbury, in full view of the great cathedral spire, the tallest in Britain.

On Friday, 30th May, we were somewhere on Salisbury Plain, which was barren and shell-scarred. Many pieces of old shells, nosecaps, etc., lay about. I actually found one tree, rather stunted, and in it was a crow's nest with three young hatched out.

Finally, on Saturday, we arrived at Trowbridge. Here we gathered into one camp along with the K.R.R.s and billeted in huts. There was more regimentation now, with kit inspections and saluting being insisted upon. There were so many officers and men moving about the camp, that arms were going up and down all day long. The poor riflemen got the brunt of this discipline drive and there seemed always to be some of them on "jankers", i.e. undergoing punishment.

We took part in a battalion exercise on Thursday, 5th June, during which we covered about ninety miles. There was a collision between two D.R.s at a crossroads and one man had his arm broken.

We came along to pick up the smashed machines and, when I had time to look around, I saw a rough circle of huge stones, standing in the fields. I suddenly realised this was the Avebury Circle. There had been photographs in the press when it was discovered and excavated in 1937. It is said to be bigger than Stonehenge and there are four great "avenues" leading up to it.

A notice board erected by Morven Archaeological Society informed me that this megalithic temple was built in the nineteenth century B.C.. Place names, such as "Avebury", had been blacked out by censor.

At that time, of course, all road signposts were removed, names of railway stations were blacked out and even names above shops were hidden or altered, in case of airborne invasion.

Back at the camp, we found that the latest order put the public park at Trowbridge out of bounds to us. We, who in civilian life had strolled through dozens of parks, found that, now we were in uniform, public ground was barred to us.

The pleasure of walking out was diminished anyway, as we had to carry respirator, steel helmet, webbing and ammunition pouches. My pouches, by the way, were 1908 pattern.

Later, these arrangements were relaxed and we were allowed out without pouches and could walk in the park if we wished.

Later still, we could go out without respirator or steel helmet. Having had them so long, it felt strange without them. You kept feeling that you had forgotten something!

When there was a kit inspection, the kit had to be laid out in a particular pattern; blankets folded, valise, haversack, mess-tin, knife, fork, spoon, spare boots, brushes, etc. and the men would get the order, "Stand by your beds!" as the inspecting officer came round. Some of these inspections were so "regimental" that you were expected to have the heel and toe plates of your spare boots polished and, if you had a tin of boot-polish, the proprietary brand had to be scraped off and the lid burnished.

Once a major remarked that my spare boots were turned the wrong way. Having thus endangered the war effort, I felt constrained to observe to one of the others that where we used to be a "nation of shopkeepers", we were now a nation of window-dressers!

Each kit inspection prevented us from doing half a day's repair work to the vehicles of the battalion. We had armoured cars, motor-cycles and Bren carriers waiting for jobs to be done. A Bren carrier, of course, is one of those low-built armoured vehicles which runs on tracks and is capable of quite high speeds.

A large building, which had been a flour mill, served as a garage and workshop but, as there were iron pillars every fifteen feet or so, it was sometimes awkward to manoeuvre vehicles in or out. This building had a glass roof, which had its disadvantages. Under the radiant sunshine of June, the place became a hothouse and, as we worked, the sweat ran down our faces and dripped off our chins. This made us appreciate the chance to have a swim in the open-air Lido which Trowbridge boasted. It was a pleasant spot. The pool varied in depth from 2 ft. to 9 ft. and there was a fountain at one side and a tea-counter at the other.

I have always regretted that while I was in Trowbridge I never had the opportunity to travel to Wells or Cheddar to see the Gorge or the caverns at Wells. However, I did go on one trip which took us to the other side of the Severn.

We were running-in some new vehicles for the battalion and exchanging spares with another unit at the same time.

The vehicles were American "White" armoured cars with left-hand steering and we were the first in this country to have them. Our destination was Lydney, in Gloucestershire. The cars had open tops and we drove in shirt-sleeves, while the sun poured its rays down on us out of a clear blue sky.

We passed through Bath, an attractive town, set in a hollow and surrounded by leafy slopes. I saw one house, along whose wall the River Avon runs and on this wall is fixed a bell. The swans on the river for generations have rung this bell when they want to be fed. A bird grips the chain in its bill and pulls till the window above opens and "manna" falls!

We went on to the North by Dunkirk(!), Nailsworth and Stroud to Gloucester. Here was some of the finest scenery I had come across in England. As the road skirted the Cotswolds, there were many long climbs and as many long descents, while deep-green, tree-clad country rolled away on every side. We stopped once for a pint of cider in a little country ale-house but I can't remember where it was.

From Gloucester, we crossed the Severn and proceeded south-west to Lydney. Here we had dinner, provided by the unit we were visiting and then started out on the return journey. As we left Newnham behind us, a wonderful panorama opened out, with the Severn winding in front and wide sandy stretches standing out against a green background, where steeples and other buildings peeped out amongst slender poplars.

No wonder the railway posters say, "See the Western Country!"

About the middle of June, Lieutenant Priest left us to join another unit, so we were now awaiting the appointment of a new officer. Our detachment was not yet on its proper "war establishment", that is, it did not have the required proportion of each trade and rank that it would have in a zone of active service. The rumour-mongers were busy again, however. The Army, like some prison-camps, has its "grapevine", the "gen" usually emanating from some orderly-room N.C.O.

"We were moving again. We were going under canvas. We would have men posted to us and some posted away. And, of course, we were going abroad!"

And what of the War?

Well, in this year, 1941, the world's largest warship, H.M.S. *Hood*, was sunk when a shell hit her magazine, leaving only three survivors, surely three of the luckiest men on earth. The Navy had its revenge soon after, by hounding the *Bismarck* and sinking her in the North Atlantic.

At the time my story has reached (June 1941) Russia had not yet entered the war, though Communist and Nazi scowled at each other half-way across Poland.

Japan, too, was still sitting on the fence, like a vulture preparing to spread her wings. Crete was invaded by a large airborne force and taken by the enemy. France and the Channel Islands remained under German occupation.

Meanwhile America was still technically neutral.

In this uneasy period, we still carried on; working, waiting and wondering.

On Sunday, 22nd June, I paid a visit to the nearby small town of Melksham, the main purpose being to see an uncle of mine, then in the R.A.F. and stationed at Melksham.

As I strolled around with him, we met two girls of the W.A.A.F.

whom he knew and we were invited to the Y.W.C.A. for tea. It was one of the few times I can remember being in a ladies' club!

A few days later, I was put on a charge for the first time. An officious C.S.M. saw me coming from our garage into the camp without anklets and promptly put my name on Army Form 252 (charge sheet). If I had kept on my overalls it would have been all right but we usually left these in the garage, because they were too filthy to bring near our beds. On the other hand, as clean anklets (bright with Ordnance-Green blanco) had to be worn when walking out, we didn't put them on with our working battledress, as oil soaked right through the overalls. But I was on a charge and that was that.

The procedure is worth recalling. At a given time, I reported to the C.S.M., as did my escort, one man to march in front of me and one behind, in case the desperate criminal tried to run away. We marched in quick time, too, encouraged by the sergeant-major's, "Left–right–left–right–left!"

Outside the company commander's office we were halted and the order came, "Hat off!" And off came my hat, to be thrown on the ground, there to remain until I came out again. There are two occasions when a soldier may be hatless. One is when he goes before his C.O. on a charge; and the other is when he goes before his God in a church.

I faced the company commander at his desk, my escort now on either side of me. The charge was that of being "improperly dressed". After being questioned and giving my explanation, I was admonished.

Back outside ("Left–right–left–right–left, halt - pick up your hat; dismiss") my escort and I saluted the wall of the building which contained the holder of the King's commission and it was all over.

Soon the "grapevine" bore fruit and the fortune-tellers were proved right. We did move, to Tidworth, on 3rd July and we were under canvas. The rest was to happen in due course.

The weather was quite hot and the ground was cracked and dusty. We were fortunate in being where some Australian troops had been and we actually had a small swimming pool. I believe the Aussies had constructed it themselves but I am not sure on that point.

We now carried out our repair work under a clump of beeches in the fresh air, yet shaded from the sun.

I was given another seven days' leave on 17th July.

On the return journey, I had the company of a lad in "civvies" from Edinburgh. He had just been called up under his age group and he seemed thankful when I took him through the London Underground, which he had not seen before.

I had about 500 miles to travel and, having covered 499 by rail to Ludgershall, I had to walk the last mile to Tidworth Park Camp, as trains to Tidworth are few.

When I got to the camp, I found that one man had gone on a training course and had calmly taken my palliasse, as he had none himself. He was to be away for a month but I was quite decided that I was not going to lie on the ground for a month, so I promptly saw about getting another palliasse, even though it meant getting someone to unlock the Q.M. stores at 11.00 p.m.

This unpleasant type of person who helps himself to other people's kit, gets away with it too easily in the Army. It is one of the bad old Army games, that if a man has something stolen, he often steals a similar article from someone else, instead of reporting the first theft. One reason is that he may be held responsible for "losing" the article and be made to pay for it. The authorities no doubt feel that any man could invent a story of theft.

On Friday, 25th July, I saw the Prime Minister, Mr. Winston Churchill, at Tidworth on a tour of inspection.

He was seated in a Rolls-Royce, with his usual cigar – as I believe the American magazine *Time* described it – jutting from his face like a gun from a turret! He had a traffic escort of M.P.s (Military Police, not Members of Parliament) on motor-cycles. I was told he had promised our brigade some new equipment and tanks which had been withheld before, owing to requirements in the East.

The Germans and Russians were now locked in a deadly struggle, Hitler having decided to march East, rather than have the Russians at his back. As these totalitarian states had each grabbed one half of Poland, they could not trust one another. When thieves fall out ...

About this time, a group of men, mostly volunteers, were taken from each company of the battalion and gathered together to go overseas. At the time, we were told that the battalion would be made up to strength again, and this would delay our own possible departure but, as things turned out, these men were really an advance guard and plans were already made for us to follow.

Early in August, our brigadier came to visit us and, in a speech to the men, he revealed that we would all be going East soon.

"The Brigade," he said, "is going now and, as soon as another convoy can be made up, you will follow. It may be in anything from three weeks to three months; but when you get there I'll be waiting on the quay to welcome you!"

This started a lot of speculation as to which part of the East we would go to. Was it India, Burma, Singapore, or North Africa? Nobody seemed to know.

On Saturday, 9th August, we had another day of manoeuvres on Salisbury Plain. We drove over some very rough country. Parts of the ground were softened and undermined by ants and rabbits, so that one truck dug itself in, trying to climb a steep ridge. I went up after it and my truck was lying at such an angle that all the oil in the sump ran to one side and the oil warning light flashed on, on the dashboard.

During a quiet spell, we stopped by a clump of stunted trees, with miles of rolling plain in every direction. We took off our steel helmets (complete with green net) and under the trees we had a game of pitch and toss with our Q.M.S.!

I am afraid we "other ranks" never learned much from these manoeuvres, for we never got any information about what was supposed to happen, or what did happen.

We were twice on the range during August, once at Perham Down and once at Bulford. We took turns at firing and marking in the butts.

The "Gas" test was quite stiff. The target came up for forty seconds only, at 300 yards and, in the same time, each man had to push his tin hat back, put on his respirator, bring the helmet forward again, leaving the chin strap behind the breathing-tube, grab his rifle (with bayonet fixed) from between his knees, set sights, load, aim and fire five rounds from a kneeling position.

Next, he ran fifty yards and, as the target came up again for twenty seconds, threw himself on the ground, loaded and fired another five rounds. With the eyepieces of the respirator steaming up and the bayonet-weighted muzzle waving around as you struggled for breath, it was quite a feat to get the shots on the target at all. It was such range training, no doubt, which inspired that little wartime verse:

> *I'm not keen on musketry,*
> *For badges I'm not itchin',*
> *The only range I want to see,*
> *Is the one in Mother's kitchen!*

Anyway, this was the last time I was on the range during the war.

Things were beginning to move. We were measured for tropical kit, khaki drill, solar topee, etc. At the same time we were told we were getting another seven days leave but it was not called embarkation leave but "emergency" leave. We were also warned to leave all surplus belongings, suitcases, etc. at home. As many as twenty per cent of the battalion were to go at one time, so that the whole thing would be over in five weeks.

As it happened, I was off for Home Sweet Home even earlier than expected, before the end of August. Our allocation of leave in those last few months had been generous but most of us were not to see our homes again until early in 1944, the only exceptions being those who would be invalided home.

Long as the journey was to Scotland, it never seemed so long as the awful journey back. The last straw was the sleepy local connection from Andover. It waited in the station for twenty minutes, then crawled off, stopping and starting every few minutes on the way. At Ludgershall, it travelled some way out of the station, then decided it had got on the wrong line, or else it had forgotten the driver or something, so chuff, chuff, back we went into Ludgershall again. This was on Thursday, 4th September 1941.

I had taken farewell of my folks in the *early morning* and I finally reached camp at 11.00 p.m., tired and thirsty.

I found the camp very quiet and, in our L.A.D. at least, it seemed that more than half of the men were on leave, some of the French variety. Those who lived in the London area would go home at the weekends and it was all right so long as they returned for first parade on Monday.

Some had already been fitted out with K.D. and topees. We found that, with the shorts, we wore hose-tops (stocking-legs) on top of our ordinary socks, with old fashioned puttees on top of that. My last pair of puttees had been left in France!

The topees (cork type) were big and made everyone look smaller by comparison.

Two of my blankets were gone when I arrived but I soon acquired two more.

Everybody remarked on the rotten taste of the tea, compared with the home brew.

We now had a new officer, at last, and two other ranks as reinforcements, but neither of these two were likely to remain long with us. One was due to enter hospital for an operation; and the other had varicose veins and could neither read nor write! Some unit had been glad to get rid of them. I began to think that maybe some of our men should be posted to a different kind of army, where they could play the concertina! I wondered if they would send out the draft with bath chairs fitted with mosquito netting; soldiers, tired, for the use of!

Each man now had to sign a certificate to say he understood that, being warned for overseas, if he was absent without leave, it would be treated as desertion and would lead to court-martial.

Our new officer turned out to be a good sort. I think he was rather shaken when Lieutenant Priest came to visit us and spoke breezily about the good times we had had when he played darts with us in the local at Farncombe! Henceforth, Lieutenant Clark, our new O.C., seemed to decide he had to live up to a tradition of informality.

Like all the Clarks in the Army, he inevitably became known amongst the boys as "Nobby" but I don't think he discovered this fact until we were out in the desert!

By 13th September, we had our complete kit, including two kit-bags, one black and one white. Our glass jars of anti-gas ointment were replaced by tubes contained in a flat tin box and I had a rifle in place of the Tommy gun.

We also got a booklet on tropical diseases and how to avoid them. The rumour-mongers now had the gen that it was Egypt we were going to. We kept quiet about it outside the camp, for we knew that security was essential for the safety of the convoy when we did sail.

There had been several changes in personnel. One man came to us from Lieutenant Priest's new unit and he brought a letter from Mr. Priest, saying that he hoped we would come through "this ruddy campaign" safely and finishing, "Yours till Hell freezes!"

Of our complement, only the Q.M.S. (whose name was Pryke) and myself had been abroad before on active service but one of the newcomers, Ron Taylor, had spent a long time in lumber-camps in Western Canada. Then he and another man decided to get back to the Old Country, so they travelled as hobos to Vancouver and worked their passage on a tramp via the Pacific, Australia and South Africa. He had some interesting tales to tell of his travels.

A soldier in the tropics used to change from shorts to long trousers to protect the knees from mosquitos in the evenings but our shorts were of a new design, with a deep turn-up, which could be unbuttoned and folded down into the hose-tops, so becoming like breeches. They were soon nicknamed "Bombay Bloomers".

Up to this time, I had driven nearly every type of vehicle in the Army, except, strangely enough, the lightest of all, a motor-cycle. Thinking that in an emergency it might be useful to be able to handle one, I began to teach myself. Every time I finished a repair job on a motor-bike, I took it on a test run. Then I discovered a tank-testing track which ran straight up a steep hill over several terraces.

Soon I was taking the bikes up this track, leaping clear of the ground at the top of each bank and judging the short burst of throttle to take me over the next one. Sometimes one of the others would accompany me on another machine. It was just as difficult to get back down again for, if you braked too much, the rear end began to slide round sideways. After a week or two of this, I felt proficient enough to be able to take a motor-cycle anywhere. Not that I liked the things. I had seen too many spills on wet or icy roads for that!

In the third week of September, another fine show was brought to the troops, when John Gielgud appeared in his own production of J. M. Barrie's *Dear Brutus*, at the garrison theatre. Others taking part were Leon Quartermaine, Zena Dare, Nora Swinburne, Muriel Pavlov and Ursula Jeans, who also appeared in the film of Noel Coward's *Cavalcade*.

Such plays did nothing but good in these surroundings, not only to increase appreciation of the theatre but to influence thought; for a garrison audience, especially in wartime, contains men of every walk of life, including the best and the very worst. I have met some of the toughest and most crooked fellows I have ever known in the Army but I must say that most of the men were fundamentally decent.

"The fault, dear Brutus, is not in our stars, but in ourselves ..."

Now most of our vehicles were gone and our last job was to fit "sand" tyres on them, in place of the "mud" type. The sand tyre had a broader tread and was not so deeply cut as the other type.

We had nothing to do then but sit in our tents and read, or play chess. We had some good chess-players. One in particular, Bill Willis, nearly always beat me; but I learned a good deal that way.

When our drivers returned to camp, they told us the vehicles had been taken to Newport. They had previously been measured for height, length and breadth for shipping purposes.

When we came to this camp, we had placed a ring of sandbags around each tent, digging into solid white chalk in order to fill them. Now we emptied them all back into the trenches, the bags being salvaged.

R.M.S. "FRANCONIA"

R.M.S. "LANCASTRIA"

About 22nd or 23rd September, we had a farewell visit by two Generals, one being Sir Hereward Wake, at that time Colonel Commandant, 1st Battalion K.R.R.C. and the other Sir John Davidson, who read a message from the King. Only then were we told definitely that it was to the *Middle* East we were going.

On the last day, Wednesday, 24th September, we were confined to camp. Most of us were rather quiet, some writing a last letter home, to be left with members of the home detail, for posting. The married men were perhaps feeling the coming break with their families more than the rest of us. I noticed little Len Hartland (known as Titch) dropping a silent tear as he wrote to his wife and kiddies. No shame in that, for he no doubt felt there was a possibility that he would never return to them. As things turned out, he was one of those taken prisoner by the enemy in North Africa.

Our "establishment", so far as I can remember, was: 1 officer, 1 Q.M.S. (Warrant Officer Class II), 3 fitters, 3 driver-mechanics, 1 electrician, 1 storeman and 5 drivers. I think, however, that we were over strength for, besides the Lieutenant and "Q", I can write down the names of fourteen other ranks.

We left camp at 10.00 p.m., going in Army-commandeered 'buses to Tidworth Station and then by special train through Cheltenham and on through the night to Liverpool. Here, early on Thursday morning, 25th September, we carried our kit up the gangways and on to the 20,000 ton Cunard Liner *Franconia*.

This fine ship, although I didn't know it then, was also present off St. Nazaire when the *Lancastria* was sunk. She too suffered damage to her engine-room by underwater blast of bombs, and limped back to Liverpool on one engine. Her captain was Sir James Bisset, who later became Commodore of the *Queen Mary*.

A plate on the foremast of the *Franconia* told me that she was built in 1923, by John Brown & Co., of Clydebank. She was now in grey paint, her furnishings were removed and she was fitted throughout as a troopship, with hooks on every deck to take hammocks. In this way she carried about 3,000 troops. There were several 3-in. A.A. guns and 0.5-in. Oerlikon machine-guns on the top deck and a 6-in. gun on a special platform overlooking the stern. Soldiers of the R.A. formed the crews of these guns and travelled regularly aboard.

On this ship, then, we were to make a voyage lasting over two months; a voyage not without interest, yet unfortunately destined to begin, and end, in tragedy.

Part II

The Voyage

CHAPTER I

To Freetown

WE WERE ALLOTTED part of one of the lower decks, actually below the water-line, so that we lived under artificial light for the duration of the voyage, except when we came up on deck. Here, long tables and benches ran from the side of the ship towards the middle. Overhead, there were racks in which the hammocks were stored during the day and also our own kit, except the kit-bags, which had been put into one of the holds.

The food was good; in fact, it compared more than favourably with Army cooking. At night, the hammocks were unrolled and fixed to hooks in the steelwork above the dining-tables and the whole place became a jungle of ropes and canvas. This was the first time I had ever slept in a hammock and it was a wonder some of us didn't suffer from curvature of the spine afterwards! It was very stuffy at night, too, when we were all below together.

We were still at the quayside the day after we came aboard, Friday, 26th September. There was, I remember, an aircraft carrier in dock behind us. Some men were doing physical training in P.T. kit on the raised part of our after-deck, when there was a sudden, resounding explosion and the men were blown in all directions. A deckhand had been handling some ship's rockets, taken from a steel locker near the men, when something (possibly a cigarette) had caused them to ignite.

The deckhand and two of the soldiers were killed outright and three more died the next day. Two of the bodies were blown right over the rails and on to the deck below. I saw a pool of blood running into the scuppers, when the police came aboard to remove what was left. One body was so mangled, they had to wrap it in something like a strait jacket to hold it together. These poor relics, however, were only the earthly remains of those who had, so suddenly, passed over into a new world and a greater life.

During the next day, the ship moved out into the harbour where she anchored facing those three famous buildings which form a scene well

known to all who sail to and from Liverpool: the red Royal Liver Building, with the largest electric clock in the world and the mythical Liver
bird surmounting each of the lofty towers; the square but dignified
Cunard Building and the Mersey Docks and Harbour Board Building
with its green dome.

The landing stage, which floats, rising and falling with the tides, is
also remarkable as being the largest floating structure of its kind in the
world.

The pageant of river life, as we watched it for the next four days, was
very interesting. Busy little tugs and ferries bustled back and forward
between Liverpool and Birkenhead, occasionally whooping or tooting,
while now and then a larger ship would blare a warning, in a deeper,
more sonorous tone, and smaller craft would scuttle out of the way, like
chickens before a farm-wagon.

On a colder day, it was amusing to look down on the oval-shaped
ferries and see the whole complement of passengers, mostly business
people, office workers and typists, marching round by common consent
in a circular, endless procession, three or four abreast, to keep warm.
They rather reminded me of the bears in the zoo. I wondered what
would have happened if someone had shouted, "Abeout ... turn!"

It was on Tuesday, 30th September, that we finally sailed from Liver-
pool. At first there were only six ships in line ahead and one destroyer.
We made for the North Channel, heading roughly NNW., to pass the
Isle of Man.

At 4.00 p.m. there was a strong wind and the sea was choppy. We
were warned to sleep in our clothes, in case of any submarine action
making it necessary to abandon ship. Later there was moonlight.

By next day there were about twenty ships in the convoy, plus an
escort of five vessels; an aircraft carrier, a cruiser, two destroyers and a
corvette. The "troopers" were all big liners, some larger than the *Franconia*, some smaller, but I believe the average would be between 16,000
and 20,000 tons.

The wind was still blowing, the sea became really rough and even
these big ships were pitching, so that many of the men (and some of
the crew) were already sea-sick, though *so far* I was all right. The programme of P.T., parades and lectures, which usually took place on various parts of the decks, was cancelled.

Personally, I think I prefer the vigorous action of a smaller ship to
the slow, powerful drag which a large vessel seems to exert upon your

stomach, though perhaps the navymen would not agree with me, for at that time their destroyers were doing everything except sit up and beg!

Below decks on the *Franconia*, you could not *see* which way the ship was going to move and it was difficult to anticipate a movement before it happened. Going along a corridor, you would suddenly feel that you were struggling hard against an invisible force holding you back and the next second you would be running forward. Then, going round a corner, you were pressed against the wall, as the ship slid sideways at the top or bottom of a trough running obliquely across her path. The steep companionways were a danger, as a khaki-clad land-lubber was liable to take a header from the top step. I suppose much of the sickness was due to seeing others being sick and to auto-suggestion. For instance, some kind person would draw your attention to a piece of webbing hanging from the rack above and you would note that it was apparently thirty degrees out of perpendicular!

On Thursday, the sea was even worse and mountainous waves swept by almost to the rail. As the ship drove into these, she took water over the bows in a flurry of spray and it swept back along the deck, six inches deep. Now the majority of the 3,000 men aboard were sick; and that included yours truly. We had been sleeping below in stuffy heat, with only our under-pants on and perhaps a towel laid across the stomach. Ventilating "flues" ran above our heads, with small openings at intervals, from which came jets of cold air. One of these had been playing on my hammock and I got a chill in the tummy. This, I think, finished it, for I finally succumbed. It was the only time I ever experienced sea-sickness, for I am normally quite a good sailor. Believe me, it is like all other sicknesses rolled into one. For the next few hours I did not care whether I lived or died; or whether the ship sailed on its keel or with the funnel pointing down to Davy Jones.

In the afternoon I made an effort to get on my feet, staggered up on deck rather dizzily and forced myself to walk round and round the deck, until the fresh air had its effect and I began to feel better. Then I went to the winch-house forrard and sat on a coil of rope, watching the water foaming back from the bows. I had never expected the 20,000-ton *Franconia* to take water over the bows, for I am sure they must rise forty to forty-five feet above the water-line. Yet each time she dipped into one of those gigantic waves, it seemed she would never come up again.

But the *Franconia* had already defied the elements for eighteen years and, slowly, shudderingly, she rose again and the water poured out by the scuppers. Soon, I felt all right again (thank goodness) but many were sick for several days and some were taken to the ship's hospital because, being unable to keep food down, they were getting weaker and weaker. The wind dropped later on Thursday and the sun shone but the sea was still mountainous. We were still heading due west, so far as I could judge by the sun.

The following day, the convoy had grown to about twenty-five troop-ships and there were at least seven more destroyers added to the escort. It was difficult to count them all, as some were so far away that only parts of them showed above the horizon. The main part of the convoy was formed up in five lines, with the smaller ships at the outside of the formation. It said much for the navigators that our new arrivals could make a rendezvous at a given point in the middle of the North Atlantic and come up with us so easily. It must be remembered that, during the night, our convoy travelled without a gleam of light. There were no port or starboard lamps and not even a cigarette was allowed to glow on the open decks.

The destroyers of our escort were continually circling around us, or sweeping out to the horizon, ever watchful. On this day (Friday) one of them suddenly fired a few rounds, which burst away on the horizon. We were told later that a Heinkel had been spotted – probably a high-flying "recce" (reconnaissance plane) – and the destroyer fired at a spot beneath it to draw the attention of the rest of the escort.

This plane, of course, would call up others to the attack but, as it happened, we ran under low cloud shortly afterwards and so escaped.

On Saturday, 4th October, three of the merchant ships and two de-stroyers left us, probably making for Canada. Our convoy was now heading south-west. The days were changing though clocks were not yet altered. It was quite dark in the morning but longer clear in the evening.

On Sunday morning, after breakfast, I went on deck at 8.00 a.m. and found the stars and a full moon shining!

Later, when day broke, I saw a plane taking-off from the aircraft carrier, to go submarine spotting. Later still, there was some scattered rifle-fire from one of the destroyers. They were firing at some object in the water, possibly a floating mine, or something suspected of being a mine. Whatever it was, it was sunk without any explosion.

Our own rifles, incidentally, were in racks in the "armoury", which was none other than the swimming-pool of the *Franconia*, with boarding placed on the bottom to protect the tiles. At intervals, a fatigue party went down to see that the rifles were kept in good condition.

And now a word about our other activities.

As I have said, we had various parades, for P.T. and many lectures; each time on a different part of the deck, so that we were always moving. We also had boat-drill every day and the Captain's inspection, during which we lined up with our life-jackets fastened tightly around us. They were checked for tightness for, if loose, there would be a danger of breaking your neck if you had to jump into the water and the jacket came up under your chin. The troops also helped to man the davits. Since the number of men aboard was about double the normal complement of passengers, the boats could never have held everyone in an emergency but there were, of course, extra floats aboard and we all had life-jackets.

We occasionally took turns at scrubbing the decks, too. Those detailed for this job rose early and accompanied a member of the crew to the allotted area of deck. Here the sailor fixed up a hose and played it on the deck while we, barefoot, used coarse "stable" brooms to scrub and rubber squeegees to clear the water into the scuppers. All scraps of paper, cigarette packets and matches were thrown overboard.

The cigarettes smoked by the troops were of various South African brands, which had been picked up by the ship on a previous voyage. As soon as we had passed out of the three-mile limit, these cigarettes were sold at the canteen free of customs duty. I was not interested in the cigarettes as I have a peculiar belief that my lungs were made for fresh air, but I was interested in the cards issued in each packet depicting South African flora and fauna.

The lectures we had covered such subjects as: the situation in Libya; current affairs; ranks of the Indian Army, etc. Thus we learned about Subedars and Jemadars, Havildars and Naiks. We discovered that, although Subedars and Jemadars are officers, they have only a Viceroy's commission and are not entitled to a salute (at least this was true before India became a republic).

We were also trained in Semaphore and Morse and passed elementary examinations in these subjects and we were taught how to navigate by sun compass, a device used in conjunction with a watch. This later proved useful in the desert.

Another activity, inseparable from the leisure periods of the troops, was Housey – known to the Navy as Tombola – which appealed to the gambling propensities of many.

Sometimes three or four "schools" would be running at one time in different parts of the ship so, if you wanted to read a book, you had difficulty in finding a quiet corner away from the raucous voice of the caller. Usually there was a large school on the foredeck, where khaki figures squatted or reclined on the boards over the whole seventy-feet breadth of the deck. When the school was as large as this, the "banker" had to employ two assistants who walked about among the farthest players, repeating in a monotonous chant the caller's slang: "*Dinky-doo*, all the twos; *clickety-click*, sixty-six; *legs*, eleven; *Kelly's eye*, number one; *doctor's orders*, number nine; (House!) House called on number nine! Eyes down for the check."

One thing to be said for Housey is that at twopence a time, a man's losses are limited. That is why it is allowed in the services, to the exclusion of such games as Crown-and-Anchor.

There was a Crown-and-Anchor school on board, however. They worked with a large handkerchief printed with the necessary symbols and large sums changed hands. Whenever the ship's Master-at-Arms appeared in the offing, the handkerchief was hurriedly lifted and stuffed into a pocket, to be unrolled again later.

Of the 3,000 souls aboard, most were soldiers but there was also a detachment of the R.A.F. and about a dozen nurses.

The latter, however, were so carefully cloistered in their own part of the upper decks that they were hardly ever seen during the voyage, except when we crossed the Line, or called at a port. The story went around the ship that one officer at least saw to it that his own particular nurse was not *too* cloistered.

On Monday, 6th October, all clocks and watches were put back one hour, although we had stopped our westward movement and were now running due south. The air was getting warmer every day but on Monday evening the wind was quite strong and spray was lashed on to the decks.

At night, the atmosphere below got thicker than ever. The sweating bodies and feet in the forest of hammocks made the air positively foul, in spite of the ventilators, which now delivered warm air. When a ship's officer, accompanied by an Army officer, came down in the morning to see that we were wakened, many of the men seemed drugged by the stale air and shouting did not rouse them. Sometimes each hammock had to be shaken vigorously before any signs of consciousness appeared in its occupant.

By Tuesday, the hot sun was blazing down on a blue sea. Parts of the hatch covers were removed and extra canvas ventilators were fixed up, with long tubes going down through several decks to carry the air below. Next day, the R.A.F. were first to don K.D. We soon followed suit, bringing our kit-bags up from the hold (or rather they were hoisted by one of the ship's derricks, fifty at a time, in rope nets) and we changed from battle-dress to the lighter tropic drill. I suppose at this time we were passing the Canary Isles. Later, the sea was almost violet in colour and I find a note in my diary: "Quick twilight; from sunshine to stars in ten minutes."

On Thursday we watched with interest as a flying-boat was catapulted from the deck of the cruiser for reconnaissance. The battle-cruiser *Repulse* joined our escort about this time, too, but I am not sure if it was before or after we reached Freetown.

We were told we could write letters home during the next few days and, after being censored, they would be posted at Freetown.

The sea was as calm as the proverbial millpond now and, in the evening, we began to see the wonderful phosphorescence of the tropic waters, particularly where they broke away from the bows. It was like a million little flashing lights, with now and then a larger glow, perhaps a foot wide, sweeping along past the hull of the ship. The smaller lights are caused by myriads of minute organisms called *Noctiluca* but the larger ones must have been due to fishes or perhaps the *Pyrosoma* or fire-body, otherwise known as the sea-squirt.

I saw flying-fish for the first time on Friday, 10th October. Shoals of them kept rising as the ship approached and gliding swiftly away for fifty or 100 yards before striking the water again. There were two main types, the smaller ones being silvery blue and the larger (about ten inches long) silver-green with brown "wings". Besides the larger fins at the front, the smaller fish seemed to use two small fins near the tail to help to "keep their end up". When they jumped from the water, they actually fluttered their wings for a moment before gliding and sometimes they rose and fell a little to dodge a wave, showing that they could direct their flight.

If they touched the crest of a wave, another little wriggle saw them through to continue on their way. Entranced, I watched them for hours.

As we went further into the tropics, it grew steadily hotter and hotter. Now that we wore our light drill, it became a standing joke for a man, when he met an acquaintance, to sweep off his topee and say, "Ah! Doctor Livingstone, I presume?"

To avoid the stench below at night, some of us were now sleeping on deck. We each laid a canvas hammock on the boards, with a folded blanket to lie on, another as a cover and a life-jacket for a pillow. It was a hard bed but a sheer delight to doze off in that clean, balmy air, with the swish of the glowing waters to lull us and the bright stars seeming so near that they hung low over the ship, as if suspended from the rigging.

During the third night on deck, however (Sunday, 12th–Monday 13th) we were caught in a sudden storm. The wind roared, lightning flashed and visibility became so bad that the ship showed her navigation lights and once blew her siren. One of the canvas ventilators was ripped in shreds and, after flapping and cracking like a whip, collapsed completely. Warm rain came hissing down and I had to take up my bed and walk. Several others followed me, fast.

Inside the doorway leading to the companionways, one of our L.A.D. lay sleeping. He awoke suddenly as my foot landed in his middle and sat up. "What the Hell ...?" he began, then he lay down again just as suddenly, as the next man slapped a dripping blanket in his face. The others followed, some going round him, some over him and some apparently trying to go through him! He had no time to dodge the stampede but, after we were all inside, he rose breathlessly and tried to close the door, which had been kept open because of the heat. There was a crash, a clatter, then silence, except for the steady downpour of the rain and the moan of the wind.

"Are you all right, Bill?" said an anxious voice.

No reply ... "Bill?"

Then, as Bill got his breath back, his voice came, slowly at first but with gathering vehemence.

Bill discussed the weather. He described the ship in general and some of its present occupants in particular. His language was varied, weird and wonderful. In fact, Bill covered the subject extremely well indeed.

Through it all, we grasped the salient point that the bloody blankety-blank door had been blown off its anonymous hinges!

Next morning, the sea was as calm and innocent as if nothing had happened!

On Tuesday, 14th October, land was sighted about noon so, after fourteen days at sea, we reached Freetown, capital of Sierra Leone.

As we sailed in, in line ahead, a launch passed us flying an admiral's flag. There were natives aboard it, wearing white shorts, shirts and topees, balancing themselves very coolly along the gunwales. First, we came to a lighthouse, white with a red top, standing on a small promontory of brown rock. Behind this was a little bay where beautiful green palm fronds hung down, almost touching the bright yellow sand. Then came a small hill covered with thick green growth and something like a coastguard station on top. This was all on our right, or starboard side. Passing through the boom, we then entered the bay on the south side of which stands Freetown.

The town is situated around the foot of some dome-shaped hills, all of which have close green scrub growing right over the top. The houses showed a great variety of bright colours. There were large white houses with red roofs and small ones with green roofs. Other red or yellow buildings had black roofs and some had their verandas of yet another colour. I saw a large church and the masts of a wireless station. Further out were rows of huts with corrugated roofs and on the outskirts were single houses spaced out among the trees on the hillside. Between the rows of houses, broad spaces ran up from the shore but these were red, the colour of the soil, so did not seem to be proper streets. Nevertheless, I saw cars running across at right angles to these spaces, so the main roads were apparently parallel to the shore.

We sailed further in, almost past the town, and the anchor chain rumbled and clattered its way out through the hawse-pipe.

Later, a small oil-tanker came alongside with partly native crew and its bridge covered with green canvas awnings, on which two monkeys were playing about.

We were issued with anti-mosquito ointment and warned against sleeping on deck whilst in the anchorage because the malarial mosquitos might come as far as 200 yards from the shore.

I will quote here from a little article written at Freetown, though not published till we were again at sea. It appeared in a Battalion paper, a duplicated sheet called *The Second*. The article was entitled "Freetown – Fact and Fancy".

I expected something a lot different; dense jungle to the water's edge, mangrove swamps, clouds of insects and a cluster of mud huts or shacks in a small murky clearing. I even feared that I should see an infectious haze of visible fever creep from the shore.

The clear brilliantly coloured scene, the green hills covered with neat scrub like a nigger's head, the cool well-built houses shaded by giant cedars, are more typical of a leisurely holiday resort.

It's difficult to remember there's a war on and it's equally difficult to believe that, in reality, this is one of the most dangerous places in the world. Though most of the worst swamps have been drained in the last few years, deadly fevers are still rife and periodically epidemics break out which ravage the Settlement; the carrier insects having brought the deadly germs from far inland.

It was indeed difficult to remember there was "a war on", especially in the evening, for there was no blackout here and the lights on shore made a fairy picture as they reflected in the water and brought nostalgic memories of peace-time.

Even the ships were lit up, so that rows of port-hole lights and deck lights indicated where each ship lay and added to the general picture.

In the morning, the African shore looked even more attractive. Opposite the ship was a flat stretch of land with banks of red rock or sand sloping down to the water. There were several large huts under palms which were about fifty feet high and behind these were huge cedars, almost twice as high as the palms, with great spreading green heads and thick trunks.

Natives gathered around the huts and at 7.00 a.m. a bell rang and they began to perform some sort of labour down on the banks, which seemed to be of red sandstone.

Canoes began to appear quite early and steadily paddled their way out to the various ships. As they came nearer, we were watching from the rail, so that there was a line of topees from one end of the ship to the other. One canoe was well in front of the others and, as the black boy shipped his paddle, we wondered what language he would speak. He raised his curly head, surveyed the row of faces above and said, "Okey-doke, Okey-doke, everybody stan' easy!" and a ripple of laughter ran along the ranks. Coins were thrown into the water for him to dive for. He let them go well down, too, almost out of sight, then his supple body plunged over the side of his canoe and swam down into the green depths. As he came up again, he invariably showed the coin in his hand before climbing back into his canoe, where the money was thrown on the smooth bottom of the boat. The water ran off his close curly hair as from a duck's back and the hair never looked wet.

The natives seemed to have inflationary ideas, for they ignored copper coins and always asked for a "Glasgow tanner" or a "Liverpool shilling"! Perhaps whoever taught them these expressions had derived them from the old joke of calling a threepenny bit a "Scotch half-crown". Anyway, they dived deep and often for anything silver, until some spivs began wrapping halfpennies in silver paper. When the diver came up and found his "Liverpool shilling" a dud, he used the most unparliamentary language, which I am sure he didn't learn at the mission school.

The canoes seemed to be dug-out in one piece, judging by the smooth appearance of the bottom but they were light, only about three-quarters of an inch thick, pointed at each end and with the stern covered in behind the paddler. The paddles, too, were pointed, like big spear-blades and in the bottom of each canoe was a small wooden scoop used for bailing.

To add to the picturesque scene, some larger boats were fitted with a triangular sail, not a lateen, but with one point in the boat and the other two raised in the air, making almost the shape of the letter 'V'. There was no boom at the top, such as the lateen sail has but they reminded me rather of the rig shown in pictures of Pacific native craft, such as the *laiklolo* of New Guinea.

All the time we remained at Freetown, there was no shore-leave, except for the officers and nurses, who went ashore in a launch. It would have been impossible to disembark all the troops in that manner, even for one day but it did seem tough to have come to a place which few of us would ever reach in the normal course of events and then not be able to explore it.

However, the next few days were interesting enough and it was a change to have something to look at other than the sea. The bay was wide and I counted over ninety ships in the anchorage, excluding small craft! The ships were of various nations, of course, including the United States. The names of some of our own vessels were volunteered by different members of the crew but they were not sure of some, as they were all in "battle" grey and they could be confused with sister-ships of similar shape. Here, for what it is worth, is a list of those they mostly agreed upon:

Empress of Russia – *Duchess of Richmond* (both C.P.R.);
Samaria (a Cunard liner, like the *Franconia*);
Dominion Monarch; *Mendoza*; *Orion* (Orient Steam Navigation Co.);
one of the "Strath" ships of the P & O Line, possibly the *Strathmore*;
and one of the Union Castle ships with a squat funnel, thought to be the *Athlone Castle*.

These were all in our convoy. Many could not be identified and, of course, no "company" flags were flown, only the "Old Red Duster".

There were also several flying-boats in the bay and one day one of these, a Short Sunderland, roared past very close, almost level with the rail, while the crew waved a greeting to us.

Once, too, I saw a train coming round the foothills towards Freetown. It looked like a little toy against the natural greenery.

The heat was now terrific, as the ship lay at anchor and there was no movement to disturb the humid air. As we lined up on boat-drill, close together, with the life-jackets drawn tight around us, we felt stifled and one man almost fainted. He had to be helped to the rail and his life-jacket loosened before he recovered.

On Thursday night there was a tremendous display of lightning but with no thunder whatsoever! Out of pitch blackness, a big bank of cloud was continuously silhouetted by great blue-white flickers of light and long wriggling lines of electricity ran across the sky, such as would be accompanied normally by deafening noise but here there was not a sound. The water reflected the bluish light and ships were thrown into stark outline against it and I even saw the colour in the red bank of the shore and the green growth above it.

While I stood on deck, along with Ron Taylor, watching for twenty minutes, the display went on, still completely noiseless and without a drop of rain. We went below but others told us it was still going strong at least half an hour later.

Still no rain fell and, next day, even the clouds were gone and there was only the usual heat-haze. Next evening, the sunset had all the colours of a travel poster but was the more beautiful by reason of its glorious reality and the effect of space given by ships and palm-trees outlined against the gold, orange and blue-grey.

We weighed anchor at 3.00 p.m. on Sunday, 19th October, the engines throbbed and once more we moved out into the ocean, having been five days at Freetown. Incidentally, we heard later that one of the Battalion officers was left in Freetown to enter the local hospital.

CHAPTER 2

Crossing the Line

O N THE MORNING of Monday, 20th October, one of the officers gave us the news – which must have come by wireless – that a British ship, the British Grenadier, had been torpedoed forty miles from Freetown and about three hours' sailing behind us.

It had happened during the night and the ship was still floating two hours after the torpedo struck her.

Such are the dangers of war and the blow might as easily have been struck at our convoy. I must confess it was not a comfortable feeling at night, to hear the water swishing past the hull and to know that the surface was about seven feet above our heads. In such circumstances, if anything struck our ship, we would almost certainly be trapped by the inrush of water, even if we escaped the initial explosion. This thought, I am sure, was in the minds of all of us in our part of the ship, though we never expressed it to each other. The feeling had been there sub-consciously from the beginning and remained throughout the voyage, an uneasy something which never allowed you to relax completely.

However, we tried to lead as cheerful a life as possible and several amusements were organised, including a boxing contest and a chess tournament. The spectacle of two boxers trying to disfigure one another did not interest me, but I entered the chess tournament and won the first round, though I was later soundly beaten by the man who won the tournament.

I have already mentioned the Battalion paper, *The Second*, two editions of which I still have. Some of the short paragraphs gave amusing comment on our circumstances. For example:

Kinda interesting to have competition between friends as to how long one can stay in any one place. If you can get low down enough and disguise yourself as a bit of orange peel, you can survive the "All off this deck except P Company" or "Fall in K Company for semaphore". We have a guy who was moved twelve times in fifty-four minutes, then finished up getting swept up at the four Gs.

(Four G notes on the bugle was the call for "Sweepers" when those on fatigues appeared with brushes to clean up the mess-decks and literally swept all before them). The "Small Ads" included:

FOR SALE: Hiker's outfit, or would exchange for large family wardrobe.

VACANCY: Good sleeping accommodation may be had in the ship's ice box.

And the Editorial column remarked:

We take our hats off to:
    Little Nell Beaumont, Captain Dan Cable and French the Villain for best sketch yet. What a fine, upstanding sergeant you have, three platoon!
    Superintendent, Army P.O. 1515 for being tops in security. Told *Second* snoop: "I just burn all letters."
    Rfn. [Rifleman] who appeared on Boat Drill with towel draped round his loins due to "mislaid" kit.

As we travelled on towards the Equator, we came under a continuous pall of cloud, so that the air was actually cooler.

For one part of the ship's company, however, there was little difference. I mean the men who work down in the bowels of the ship; who are so often forgotten by those above (unless something goes wrong!). I only got an occasional glimpse of the engine-room from a narrow doorway (marked "No Admittance") from which the shining ladders descended to the inferno beneath. From that doorway issued a blast of heat as from a furnace which, of course, it was. I have been told that some parts of the metal-work in an engine room get nearly red hot. Poor "devils" below! It's a wonder they don't sprout horns and exchange their oil-cans for tridents!

On Wednesday, 22nd October, we crossed the Equator and the ceremony of Crossing the Line was duly carried out.

With so many crossing for the first time, only a representative section of the ship's company were being "initiated" but we all rolled up to see the fun and troops swarmed all over the fore-part of the ship and even thirty feet up in the rigging leading to the crow's nest!

King Neptune came aboard "out of the sea" by climbing a gangway slung over the side of the ship. Neptune Rex, his Queen and their attendants, the barbers, doctor and bears were "dressed" in colourful costume, including wigs and beards of untwisted rope, or tow, and were armed with great wooden swords, razors and two pails of concoction – one red, the other green. The judge was in full judicial costume and carried a large roll of parchment containing the "charges".

Having been received with great pomp, the "royal" entourage congregated at the forward well-deck, where a small canvas swimming pool was erected, with a tipping seat at one side of it. And now the "prisoners" were brought forth. These included the Brigadier, G.O.C. Troops; some of the nurses in bathing costume and representatives of various units of the Army and R.A.F. They were ushered in by two brawny "Sea-Cops", whose bare arms showed many tattoos.

The parchment was now unrolled and the prisoners severally charged with diverse misdemeanours, e.g.:

That you did instruct natives at Freetown in the use of foul R.A.F. language – to wit – "Good Gracious! You mess me up!."

That you did use anti-mosquito cream for hair-oil!

That you did dispose of food in an unlawful manner, namely, sea-sickness! Have you anything to say? *Don't say it!*

The charge read, each prisoner is examined by "Doc Hackem" who invariably finds it necessary to "extract" some teeth with a pair of blood-stained tongs. Next, a succession of huge pills is administered from a large spoon, until the prisoner's cheeks are bulging. Before he can close his mouth, he is thickly lathered (ladies have their hair shampooed) with red and green, shaved with a colossal blood-stained razor, tipped backwards into the water and thoroughly ducked.

Each time he comes up for air, or to chew the remaining pills, a Sea-Cop, absent-mindedly but firmly, places a hand on top of his head and the victim again submerges. If he goes to the other side, the bears are happily flapping round the edge to duck him again.

By the time the initiates are allowed to crawl out, they might be glad the world has only one Equator but they entered into the fun of the thing and were more helpless from laughter than anything else. It was as good as a circus and the members of the crew, who were the chief "clowns", obviously enjoyed it as much as anyone.

After this pleasant interlude, we got back to routine once more. We were still forging steadily south, with no alarm of any kind, though the convoy changed direction a little occasionally, as a routine precaution. If we turned to starboard, a blast of the siren gave warning, answered by a cough or a grunt from each of the ships in turn, then the whole formation went off obliquely, in much the same way that we soldiers would execute a Right Incline on the parade ground! Perhaps half an hour later, we would turn back again to port, the signal now being two short blasts, again repeated in a variety of tones, some bass, some baritone; but none of these big vessels had a voice in keeping with the feminine gender which is always given to a ship.

Meanwhile, our tireless escort was ever around us. As we came away from the pall of cloud which had been over us at the Equator, it again became very hot. For a while, we were issued with tonic mineral waters and a ration of concentrated lime juice on alternate days as a guard against heat stroke. We sometimes helped to bring up the crates of bottles and sides of meat from the big refrigerator hold.

A nice, cool job!

One day a couple of us came across a New Zealander on deck, a stoutly-built old corporal and we had a chat with him. He was a genial, kindly soul, as most New Zealanders are. He was looking forward to seeing Durban again, for he had visited it once before, when he took part in the Boer War! He had also been in the 1914–1918 War and in a dust-up with Turkey in 1929. All told, he had completed thirteen years of *active* service in both Navy and Army and here he was in uniform again! However, he was now discharged as unfit and was returning to New Zealand, to his wife and family. He had been wounded several times and once was unconscious for ten days after a tree fell on him. His discharge resulted from that injury. He said he should be getting used to war service but he wasn't and he thought more of his home now than he did in the beginning. He thought we had been too lenient with the Germans at Versailles, so that the lives lost in the 1914–1918 War were sacrificed for nothing. He hated the Germans, he said, since a certain day in July 1917 when he helped to carry away dead and wounded women from a bombed nurses' home.

They were so game, the wounded ones, that they still joked as they lay on the stretchers.

Towards the end of October, some doubtful meat and sausages were causing sickness amongst the men. We also ran into rougher seas again and on Thursday, 30th October, the ship was tossing and shuddering and taking water over the bows once more. Land was sighted about

5.30 p.m. (i.e. 17.30 hours in service parlance but, for simplicity, I will avoid using this, unless quoting orders, etc.). For the first time, I saw the albatross, several of these large birds flying along with the ship. Later, as it grew dark, lighthouse flashes were seen, coming from the Cape of Good Hope.

We rounded the Cape that night and next day ran into fog. Some trouble developed in the steering-gear on the *Franconia*, so we hove to and the convoy passed on and left us. For several hours we remained, hardly moving, in the fog, while the engineers worked down below. Finally, the fault was remedied and we once more resumed our lone course. Friday and Saturday passed, we came out of the fog into clear sunshine and on Sunday an undulating shore broke upon our view and, after passing a tree-clad headland, we came into a bay and there, set well back from the point, we saw Durban, the "Playground of South Africa".

That night, however, we spent at sea, in the outer part of the bay.

CHAPTER 3

Durban

ON THE MONDAY (3rd November), we moved into the docks and tied up at 12.25 p.m.. Natal's largest city looked very beautiful, with its miniature skyscrapers and other bright buildings with red roofs along the waterfront. Palm trees added a touch of green, while cars swept back and forth, their paintwork gleaming and windscreens flashing as they reflected the sun.

We were told we would have shore-leave as from 3.00 p.m.

Two pals of mine, the much-travelled Ron Taylor and Dick Stone-hewer, and myself went off together. We walked up on to the palm-lined Esplanade where, on the trim grass, we saw three long queues of soldiers, facing three large painted signboards. One queue was for pairs of soldiers, another for threes and the last for parties of four. Local hosts and hostesses drove up to the queues in their cars and picked up a party according to the capacity of the vehicle and took them for a drive or helped to entertain them generally. Organized hospitality!

Before we got that length, however, a big Ford 30-h.p. sedan drew alongside and we were invited to jump in by a man who turned out to be the Chief City Engineer, just going, he said, on a tour of inspection. So off we went; but before we were out of sight of the shipping, he began to ask what kind of trip we'd had and how many ships were in our convoy. Instinctively, we were vague, giving a much lower figure than the reality. Then he asked, "Which warship is that out there? Was she with your convoy?" (This was the *Repulse*.) We glanced at each other and became even more vague. We "thought" it was part of our escort, but we didn't know what ship it was. He got quite impatient at our "dumbness". "Oh, come!" he said, "surely you know the name of a big ship like that!" But we were inwardly resolved not to give any information away, even if he was the City Engineer, for we felt rather suspicious and, of course, South Africa holds a certain anti-British element. However, he dropped the subject and began to act as "guide".

He certainly took us on a very comprehensive tour of this delightful city which, he said, had a white population of 120,000 (the total population is over a quarter of a million). He had been born here and could go back fifty years into the history of the city, which was itself only a century old. He spoke of the time when only sailing ships came into the harbour.

Opposite the Cenotaph in the City Gardens, we saw a long row of rickshaws waiting, with their picturesque Zulu runners wearing fantastic headresses with horns on them. The layout of the city is clean and modern, with wide, straight streets and beautiful buildings. Big hotels towered along the Marine Parade, mostly about ten stories high, though one rose to at least fifteen stories. They were built of light-coloured material which reflected the sunlight.

As we went towards the higher ground at the back of the city (the Berea), we passed many more beautiful buildings set amongst the trees and several fine gardens and parks. Looking back down from the high ground, we had a wonderful view of the city spread out before us. Here among the trees, troupes of little grey vervet monkeys ran wild in their natural surroundings. I thought at first the name was "velvet" and, without doubt, their coats were so fine, they could easily have been taken for grey velvet. They were tame enough to feed but you had to be wary of an occasional bite, especially from a mother with young.

On we went, through the Morningside area, beyond the outskirts of the city where, laying a road foundation, there was a gang of Indians, working under a white foreman. Our guide got out and, going over to the foreman, spoke with him for a few minutes. Again we moved on and came to high ground among fields of wheat and sugar-cane. From a ridge here, we gazed on a glorious panorama. Inland, we looked over miles of verdure, stretching away into the distance in the direction of Pietermaritzburg. Below us, the Umgeni River flowed towards the sea, with fruit trees and gently waving maize on either side. The Connaught Bridge crosses the river, near the sea, and there is a road-house at the other side.

On the way back, we passed through the Indian quarter, which is rather dilapidated. Our host told us that the flow of Indian immigrants was now being restricted. He seemed to dislike them intensely and, when we saw a few copper-coloured men and women, he snorted contemptuously, "Look at them. You know what *they* are!"

Well, they were half-breeds. So what? I know that most British soldiers would rather have the Indians fighting on their flanks than the

Italians! and many an Anglo-Indian served with the forces in North Africa and fine figures of men they were, even if their skin *was* coppery. Of course, it is true that they were sometimes scorned as much by the Indians as anyone. But it is all wrong! When we pass into the next world, as we all must do, there will be no difference on account of colour; nor will there be any separate creeds, for we are all God's children.

No, we didn't like our host very much, but we politely thanked him as we parted, for the trip at least had been an education.

More material things were calling us now, for we were hungry; so we made our way to one of the canteens, where we obtained a good meal for only 10d. each. As a comparison with standards at home: for this modest sum we got two eggs, bacon, sausage and mash, coffee, bread and butter, fruit salad and ice-cream! There was plenty of sugar and home-grown fruit was so plentiful that, in most restaurants and canteens, a bowl of fruit was placed free on each table.

It was evening now but everywhere we went there were lights. Lights on cars, lights in cinema entrances, traffic lights, neon lights and flashing advertisement lights. Even when it rained, everything looked cheerful.

After a show at the King's Cinema we came out, found it dry and went to the open-air dancing at the Amphitheatre on the front, opposite the Marine Parade. The orchestra played facing a semi-circular promenade, which formed a gallery looking down on the wide paved space where the dancers moved round. There was room for 2,000 dancers!

Nearby were the Amphitheatre Gardens, nicely laid out, with covered walks, crazy paving, rockeries, a pond and thatched shelters.

As with Cinderella, our passes ended at midnight but we beat "Cinders" by one minute, arriving at the gangway at 11.59 p.m. The streets were empty long before this for, in the sub-tropical climate, people like to rise early and work in the cool of the morning. As we boarded the ship, we saw one man carrying his mate over his shoulder, completely unconscious. He went right up the gangway and past the officers collecting the passes. Apparently the South African whisky had done its work.

Next morning, our detachment were taken ashore, not exactly on leave but on a swimming parade, which was very welcome. We marched up through the streets to the open-air pool on Marine Parade. Swimmers may leave this pool if they wish and go down to the sea and their clothes are still looked after until they return. There is, however, a very strong backwash off the beach and a danger of sharks further out, so bathers are warned to stay close in.

In the afternoon, we again had passes from 1.00 p.m. and we took the opportunity of visiting the fairground, which is also on the front. We tried the scenic railway and then I won a packet of Turkish Delight by shooting down ten 'planes out of fifteen with a "machine gun" which was synchronized with a movie-screen. The aircraft dived from all angles and a line of dashes on the screen showed where your "tracers" were going! It could be handy for training service gunners – especially if the sergeant-major handed out the Turkish Delight!

But the weather was too good to waste in such amusements, so off we went to explore the city, making use of the grey-painted city buses and trams, which were entirely free to the troops, a generous gesture on the part of the city, for a soldier's pay doesn't go very far.

Traffic in Natal drives on the left, as it does at home, but a bigger proportion of the cars are American, which are preferred for the rough roads in country districts. As South Africa is bi-lingual, all street signs are in English and Afrikaans. For instance, "Cross Here" is also given as *"Stap Hier Over"*.

At a fruit stall, we ate luscious melon, while the fruit-dealer told us all about passion-fruit, oranges, mangoes, bananas and papaw, all of which grow in the province. The delicious fruit salads we had eaten were made up mostly of banana, orange and papaw (locally pronounced *'pawpaw'*). The papaw is oval, like a small melon, five or six inches long, orange coloured and the flavour is something between that of a melon and a banana. We were just too early for the mangoes, the dealer explained, they were not yet ripe. November in Durban, of course, is spring.

Next day, Wednesday, was the fifth of the month. "Remember, remember, the fifth of November!" The weather here was anything but foggy and the people seemed to make no point of remembering Guy Fawkes at all!

However, I heard a story (I don't know how true) about the Australians who had been in Durban before us and how they had supplied their own "fireworks".

A bunch of Aussies (so the story ran) had gathered some odd bits of wood and, squatting in a circle in the roadway, they built a little "campfire" in the middle and lit it, while a few people gathered round curiously. The Aussies then began singing camp songs and more people came along and stood around. Meanwhile, one of their confederates had gone to ring up the Fire Station, saying there was a fire in such-and-such a street!

Very soon, the fire engine came clanging along and firemen began unrolling hoses. By this time, quite a large crowd had gathered and people were looking out of windows in the houses above, while those in the street stood on tiptoe and craned their necks to look over the heads of those in front!

When the firemen, with their hoses, pushed a way through the crowd, sure enough, they found their fire; but not the Aussies! *They* had vanished!

Ah, well! Boys will be boys!

The Durban Publicity Association had given to each of us a printed list of places to see but one thing which did not appear on the list was the Snake Farm. We found it, though, and, on Wednesday afternoon, we spent an interesting hour or two there. It was on the north side of the city, on the way to the Umgeni and here, within a yellow-walled enclosure, we saw: black mambas, cobras, pythons, ringhals, puff adders, grass snakes and a dozen other varieties, many to be found in the bush near Durban. I believe one of the objects of the farm was to gather serum to counter snake-bite and I suppose they would also supply zoos with stock.

A Kaffir handled many of the venomous types and I saw him put a puff-adder round his neck and inside his shirt. A good job he wasn't ticklish!

During our stay in Durban, we visited several of the cinemas but the finest of all was the Playhouse. The interior decoration of this cinema is the most novel I have seen anywhere. The foyer is like the stone hall of an ancient castle with imitation oak beams and wrought iron work. All the attendants were in eighteenth-century costume. Coats, waistcoats and breeches were violet-grey in colour and the costumes were complete with wigs, white cravats and white hose. Our footman's buckled shoes preceded us up the stairway and into the cinema – or were we out in the open air again? No, the screen was there; but surely that was the sky up above …?

Luxuriously seated, I could hardly glance at the screen for looking around me. Old sandstone walls and leaded windows rose on either side and, here and there, bits of green growth peeped out of the crevices. At the top, the walls stopped suddenly, broken and ruined, with grass growing on some parts! And over all was the blue "sky" stretching away beyond the walls, which stood out in genuine three-dimensional relief. Stars twinkled and a moon began to rise slowly, imperceptibly, peeping just above the wall, while misty clouds moved silently across the sky, sometimes obscuring the moon for a brief second. On a distant hill, above the screen, stood another castle, its windows glowing with light. A breath of really cool air circulated around us, to increase the atmosphere of being in the open. Such a ventilation system would be a boon in the heat of a summer evening in Natal.

Twenty minutes later, the moon was "setting" at the far end of the wall and the clouds had cleared away, so we could concentrate on the main film, which was *Pimpernel Smith* produced, directed and acted in by the late Leslie Howard.

On our second-last day ashore, we were going along Smith Street when I walked right into two of the men who had been with G.H.Q. Troops Workshops in France and later at Catterick. They were now attached to the R.A. and in the same convoy as we were.

Our last shore leave was on Friday, 7th November. We had now seen most of the sights but, by way of a change, we visited Lever's Sunlight Soap Factory, where we were made welcome. Our guide was a young lady and, together with several other visitors, we were shown round the huge vats of liquid soap and followed the various processes from one smell to another, each a little more pleasant than the last, until finally the coloured, scented soap was pushed out in a long bar, chopped into tablets and imprinted with the necessary design.

Afterwards, they took us to a lounge and asked whether we preferred tea or beer to drink! (Wot would you do, chums?)

Then, before we went away, we were given an unexpected present of a little parcel each, containing various soaps and shaving cream! We appreciated this, for we had to buy all our soap, except for an occasional issue of coarse yellow soap for washing our clothes and scrubbing web equipment.

That evening, we had tea in the Navy League Club and later went to a sing-song by invitation of the South African W.A.A.F. At the latter club, I found a compatriot on the civilian staff, a Glasgow woman who had been many years in Durban and was enthusiastic about the fine opportunities there were in South Africa. She said she had no inclination to return to Britain.

This was our farewell to Durban and we could not help feeling sorry, as we walked back through the streets leading to the docks.

In the morning (Saturday, the 8th) at seven o'clock, tugs pulled us out from the dock. As they cast off and we began to move under our own steam, the tugs whooped farewell and other craft took up the message, while figures waved from the decks and shouted, "God-speed." Then, like a giant clearing his throat, our ship gave an acknowledgement that echoed over the city. A steam crane at the dockside piped up with a Morse signal on its whistle: dot, dot, dot, dash – V for Victory and was answered by a cheer from our decks. Yes, the thoughts of these people, going with us, were a great encouragement for the difficulties which we knew lay ahead.

On our way out, we passed the *Repulse* which again joined our escort and the streamlined Free-Dutch ship, *Nieuw Amsterdam*, which also came north later.

What memories remained (and still remain) of Durban! The lights, gold and blue tinted, throwing a glow on the little skyscrapers, themselves showing rows of lighted windows; long chains of lights marking the outline of the streets and a chaos of little lights from the villas on the outskirts, disappearing over the hill like a Milky Way; the broad streets, with a cavalcade of glittering cars, trolley-buses, trams and rickshaws; cinemas, bars, restaurants; good food, fruit salads, plenty of sugar and butter; free 'bus rides; the lovely view from the Berea, looking through a gap in the palms, down over the city, with its white, graceful buildings, interspersed with trees ...

So, after five days of shore leave, we said good-bye to delightful Durban.

We were all a trifle "browned-off" at leaving civilization behind, in view of the kind of life we expected in North Africa, but we had had our break, so there was nothing for it but to get back to parades and lectures. In order to make signalling more interesting and lifelike, Ron Taylor and I had bought some odds and ends in a bazaar at Durban and now, in our spare moments, we designed a pair of Morse "flashers" from torch bulbs, wire, strips of metal and pieces of wood. So we kept our minds occupied while the ship steamed northwards. When the flashers were finished we could sit at opposite ends of the mess-deck and send messages back and forward, writing them down and checking afterwards. This greatly improved our efficiency. The only difficulty was if someone else sat down between us. Then we had to resort to all sorts of unorthodox *semaphore* in an effort to get them to move! Usually they just waved back at us!

During the next few days, it got steadily hotter and hotter and sweat dripped from our chins and soaked our shirts. White canvas awnings and ventilators were again rigged up. The sea was calm as we passed through the Mozambique Channel. There were now eighteen ships in the convoy.

On Thursday, 13th November, H.M.S. *Repulse* took farewell of the convoy. The fine-looking battle-cruiser passed up one lane between the "troopers" and back down another, signal flags flying and the crew lining the rails, in regular rows, at attention. She made a brave sight. Each ship in the convoy flew its ensign, bugles sounded the salute and cheers echoed across the water between the ships as we said "Thanks!" for a safe voyage. The *Repulse* turned away into the expanse of the Indian Ocean.

Less than a month later, she was sunk in the Far East, along with H.M.S. *Prince of Wales*, when the Japanese launched desperate dive-bombing raids upon the two vessels. This was a couple of days after the treacherous attack on Pearl Harbour, which announced Japan's entry into the war and also brought the U.S.A. into it.

We were probably passing Mombasa when the *Repulse* left us, though no land was in sight. The following day, another warship took her place in the escort. She just came up out of the blue, lined up and carried on without fuss.

Many of us were again sleeping on the open decks while we were within the tropics.

One day I was sitting on deck reading a book, while the sun glared on the white awnings, when a phrase in the book about the sun falling through the leaves of a chestnut tree somehow took my mind back to the days of my boyhood. There, about a mile from the little village of Gargunnock, stood a favourite tree, where my chums and I used to gather chestnuts in the quiet, sunny calm of the country. The tree grew near an old grey stone bridge called the "Ghost Brig". Local legend told how, centuries ago, the victims of the plague were buried nearby, at the side of the rippling burn, this no doubt bringing about the name of the bridge. Is it not remarkable how, for thousands of years, every nation on the earth has had its tales of returning spirits? But to me the scene recalled only the happy, carefree days of youth. Strange how such nostalgic thoughts arise when *"à l'étranger"*.

Yet every soldier serving abroad must sometimes turn his thoughts to his homeland; to some particular spot with warm memories.

I wondered when we would see such days of peace again. Already there had been one "war to end war" with a terrific sacrifice of human life; a sacrifice that seemed in vain, since the same enemy had caused another world-wide upheaval.

Now we were wearing khaki once more, in an attempt to finish what our fathers began. Would the Allies make sure this time that there would never be a third world war? Would Britain keep her promises to her soldiers and provide a decent living? Would there be haggling about the pensions paid to men disabled for life? And would the people at home appreciate the peace and security when it was won or would they go on grabbing, squabbling amongst themselves, striking, instead of *serving each other*, progressing and building a happier world for all?

CHAPTER 4

Aden and the Red Sea

MAIL WAS CALLED on Monday, the 17th, which meant we were getting near port. It was still very hot and water was not too plentiful, particularly for washing but we were thankful for the salt-water baths which were available. The sea-water was heated but, of course, we had to use special soap to get any lather at all.

On Tuesday morning I saw a bird (just as Columbus did when he had almost given up hope of sighting land) and, sure enough, about 11.00 a.m., land appeared on the port side. It was a big cliff of brown rock, bulging out halfway up its face. This was Cape Guardafui, the northernmost point of Italian Somaliland. Further on, there was a sloping stretch of ground with scattered scrub. Marine life became prolific. A large shark-like fish, about seven feet long, with a brown back, lay basking just under the surface, with its dorsal fin out of the water. Two ray-fish, each five feet across, flapped lazily through the depths. Several turtles were swimming around and shoals of fish about fifteen inches long kept jumping out of the water. Flocks of little birds were flying about close to the surface and all around were hundreds of the jellyfish which are so numerous in tropic waters. Often they looked like a scattering of water-lilies on a pond.

Having rounded the cape, we sailed west, into the Gulf of Aden, passing out of sight of land once more, though the smoke of ships was to be seen away on the horizon on either side of us. We zig-zagged quite a lot and once the whole convoy turned right round and went back towards the east for two hours!

In the early daylight of Thursday, 20th November, we reached Aden. At first, we were anchored outside the harbour, from where we had our first view of the Barren Rocks of Aden. They were barren, too! Dusty red, jagged, saw-toothed hills, completely dry and without a scrap of vegetation from top to bottom. They rose layer upon layer, to sharp pinnacles, the edges of the various strata marking each level, making them look like oriental towers of Buddha.

Soon, Arab traders began to come out to us in small boats. This type of boat had provision for stepping a portable mast and they had paddles, which were simply made with a straight shaft and a round, flat blade. Sometimes the paddles were used through a rowlock, as an oar. The men themselves had golden skins and keen, intelligent faces. They were cleaner and smarter than most of the nomadic Arabs I saw later in North Africa. They wore turbans of bright colours, mostly green and sold such things as sandals, belts, cigarette-lighters and watches. The trader would throw up a rope, so that a small basket could be hauled up with the article in it and the money lowered in return.

We were still outside the next day and the *Nieuw Amsterdam* had appeared and was anchored near us.

The radio bulletins were always posted up on the ship's notice-board and, that evening, we got news of a British advance in Cyrenacia, which caused general satisfaction. We had been following these bulletins with increasing interest as we came nearer to our destination.

On Saturday, we moved into the harbour and now we saw the white and buff houses on the level ground below the hills, with here and there a little green growth. There were a few palms along an esplanade and, where this broadened into a sandy square, we got a glimpse of cars and camels side by side. The camels were of the Bactrian (two-humped) type, described by a fellow-mechanic as "twin-cylinder models"! Some of the camels, I noticed, were pulling little two-wheeled carts behind them. On the summit of one of the smaller rock hills stood a brown stone clock-tower with a red roof. Narrow roads zig-zagged up the dizzy heights of the larger hills, to look-out posts, and, in the haze around the topmost peaks, buzzards could be seen as little specks wheeling around. More of these birds were circling around the ship. One type of buzzard, the kite, is notorious amongst soldiers serving in the East for its habit of swooping suddenly to remove a titbit from the very plate held in the hand of the unwary! Because of this, the troops modified its name somewhat and perpetuated it in song. But what a song!

Well out from the shore were several buoys with little conical roofs and on a mat under each canopy sat an Indian cross-legged. This seemed a little mysterious at first, until I realised that a submarine pipe-line came from the shore to each buoy, to supply oil-fuel to the ships. The Indian was there to link up a pipe from the ship and turn on the flow.

A little way off, the *Empress of Russia* was lying, with huge doors in her side open and barges of coal alongside. A crowd of Indians were carrying the coal up on the broad ramps and into the ship's bunkers. They looked like an industrious swarm of black ants, as they disappeared into the bowels of the ship and reappeared again in a cloud of coal dust.

The *Empress of Russia*, before the war, was on the Vancouver–Yokohama run and, although a modern ship, she was fitted to burn coal, because Japan has no oil.

In the evening, a water-tanker came alongside us, with some natives aboard and, at sunset, I watched one of the men at prayer in the Moslem manner. First, he took a tin of water, no more than a pint and, pouring it on his hands, he washed his face, arms and feet with it. Then, removing his jacket, he laid it on the deck in place of a prayer-mat. He knelt upon it, facing towards Mecca (in this case to the north), murmured a prayer, not idly but thoughtfully and bent to touch his forehead twice on the mat. Unconcerned about any terrestrial audience, he continued his supplications earnestly and, I felt, with real devotion. And who is to say that because he called God by another name, his prayers would not be answered?

As darkness fell, the harbour was still full of life. Small craft scuttled about, showing their green starboard and red port lights and hooting their klaxons. Some of the Arab dhows had high, ornate sterns, like the ships of olden times. When one glided past in the dusk, it was as if a page of the past turned over.

Behind us, however, was a modern scene. British sailors, in tropic kit with white shorts, were coming down the floodlit gangway of a cruiser into liberty launches which were taking them ashore. Earlier in the day, our own officers and the nurses had also gone ashore.

One thing that excited our curiosity in the harbour was a small island near the *Franconia*. There was a small jetty and concrete pathways lined with rustic railings, which led up to a group of mud huts with thatched roofs. The wooden verandas were closed in by wire-netting, like a monkey-house. One suggestion was that it was used for quarantine purposes. We never saw any sign of life on the island, except for one poor dog wandering about alone and the buzzards which perched on the rails. Even the members of the crew could not enlighten us, though some seemed to know the port well. One sailor, who had been ashore several times, pointed out a group of café buildings at one end of the town where, he said, exhibitions of the can-can were given.

Before noon on Sunday, we moved out of the harbour again and dropped anchor in a new position outside the boom.

Three days later, we were still there and now we were in difficulties owing to scarcity of water. It was turned on at infrequent intervals and fellows queued up half an hour *before* reveille, to get a wash and shave and some even missed their dinner in order to wash clothes. Often the water would be turned off before the end of a queue reached the wash-basins. Even the salt-water taps were difficult to get at.

One good thing was that we now had a supply of juicy water-melons, of which a load had been taken on board. We had plenty for the rest of the voyage. In fact, we must have left a trail of melon pips all the way up the Red Sea!

We left Aden on Thursday, 27th November, having been there for exactly a week, and next day passed through the Straits of Bab-el-Mandeb, the Gateway of Tears.

On Saturday, I was on sentry duty at the after-hatch, one deck down, (an eighteen-hour fire-picket was maintained) when there came a terrific bang, and blast brought down chips of paint and dust from the hatch openings. The sentry's order-board clattered down from the wall and I rocked forward on my toes before regaining my balance.

I knew it must be the 6-in. gun at the stern and I wondered what they were firing at. I had visions of a submarine in the vicinity. Three more rounds were fired with an ear-splitting din and each time the concussion came down the hatch with a bump. No alarm was sounded, so I realised it was some sort of practice. A few rounds were also fired from the 3-in. A.A. guns, followed by a burst from the heavy machine-guns. Some of the fellows had been told the guns were to be tested but many, like myself, had received no warning at all.

Later, I heard that an R.A.F. corporal had collapsed and died. It was said that he had been asleep on a coil of rope underneath the platform on which the 6-in. gun was mounted. A post-mortem was being held overnight and sea burial was to be arranged for Sunday morning.

I was still on duty on Sunday morning but at a different post, on an open part of the after-deck. About a quarter to seven, they brought the body out just in front of me, sewn up in canvas and placed it on a greased chute with the Union Flag over it. A detachment of the R.A.F. paraded on deck and the body was carried to the stern rail.

The service was read, a bugler of the 2nd K.R.R.C. blew the "Last Post" and the chute was slowly tilted, till the body slid from beneath the flag. The bugler then sounded the "Reveille" to signify the awakening on the other side.

Going through the Red Sea, we had no escort, each vessel simply making its own way. We actually overtook and passed the *Empress of Russia*, which had left Aden before us, the troops yelling derisively at each other as we did so.

By Monday, we were in the narrow Gulf of Suez, with sand and rock hills on either side. On the Sinai Peninsula to our right, Mount Sinai was clearly seen, as if it were within walking distance, yet it was at least twenty-five miles away. It seemed barren too, a gaunt, sandy-red cone, with a dark cleft half-way up one side. Over 8,500 feet high, almost twice as high as Ben Nevis, it was on its lofty summit that Moses, far above the disturbances of earth, received the Ten Commandments.

We stopped at anchor for the night, close to the eastern shore, at a nameless place which the crew said was about sixty miles from Suez. There were huts and tents on shore surrounding a large vague structure like a dam without any water. Barrage-balloons were raised all round the ship, some from ashore and some from barges.

We were surprised to find the weather very cold at night.

In the morning, we continued on the last lap of our voyage, trailing one barrage-balloon behind us. We reached Suez at 10.00 a.m. and dropped anchor in the calm dead-end of the gulf. The burnt-out motor vessel *Georgic* was there too, a rusty hulk but still floating. On our left was a red and white sandstone bluff; on the right, flat sand, where the southern end of the Canal appeared, with a white monument among trees at one side of it; and ahead lay the flat town of Suez and Port Tewfik.

So we came to the end of our voyage in the *Franconia*, a voyage which had lasted over two months and during which we covered over 11,000 miles.

It was Tuesday, 2nd December, 1941.

Part III

North Africa

CHAPTER I

Egypt

WE HAD LITTLE TIME to look around us as we prepared to leave the ship. Each unit in turn collected its kit-bags – quite a long job for 3,000 men. We had dinner, our last meal on board and each mess-deck was left clean and tidy.

In the afternoon, Egyptian currency was brought aboard and we were able to exchange our accumulated pay for *piastres*. Each *piastre* was worth 2½d. and notes were printed for amounts as low as 5 *piastres*.

The various units began to disembark in long lines, down the gangway and along the quayside. Our turn came just before dark and down to the quay we went, carrying full kit plus two kitbags. We had to hang about for an hour or two, however, and Egyptian boys came around crying, *"Baksheesh, baksheesh!"* in much the same way as the French children had greeted us with, *"Souvenir, souvenir!"* two years before.

Again we felt the chill as it became dark and we began to realise that winter nights in Egypt can be very cold, in sharp contrast with the warmth of the day. A meal was laid on for us, served out by Egyptians behind a Naafi building on the quay. As we were hungry, several of us went back into the queue a second time, like Oliver Twist!

Apparently we had been waiting for a train, which eventually came in at the back of the quay. We got aboard and set off about 9.30 p.m. to travel all night, sitting on hard wooden seats.

Soon we passed a big prison-camp, surrounded by barbed wire and floodlights, with sentries patrolling around it – then we traversed mile after mile of sand. Later, we crossed a narrow waterway where there were several *feluccas* and then we were running over the black earth of the Delta. We could see little in the starlight and we did not know where we were going, for the Army in those days told you nothing.

However, we went through several towns and rumbled over a big steel bridge, which took us across water, probably one of the arms of the Nile. I could only make out the name of one town, Tanta, which I knew to be in the middle of the Delta. A faint, indescribable odour overhung the whole area. This was something with which we were to become familiar. I think anyone who has been there would recognise it blindfold, as the peculiar aroma of the Delta. It is no perfumed zephyr of exotic Egypt but a musty taint, to which the general lack of hygiene must contribute.

As daylight came we sat up, cramped and sleepless and watched a continuous panorama of: irrigated fields; water-wheels; donkeys; water-buffalo; mud houses ready to collapse, with storks' nests on the flat roofs; camels laden with produce; women carrying bundles on their heads and men washing in stagnant water without soap. The men wear the *galabia*, a sort of Victorian nightgown and the women, if married, dress in black and are veiled by the *shadour*, a black veil covering all but the eyes and "ornamented" by a brass clasp on the nose.

We duly arrived at El Amiriya, a small station on the edge of the desert, about ten miles from Alexandria. We marched a mile over sand, till we came to a tarmac road and a large military camp. Here, we began to put up tents in a cold wind, while yellow dust choked our eyes, noses, kit and rifles. The tents were not the usual Army bell-tents but were larger, oblong, with high walls and double roofs, supported on bamboo poles. They were made in India, at Cawnpore and were of doubled cotton.

We slept quite comfortably that night but we needed the four blankets issued and a greatcoat on top as well.

Our part of the camp was called Camp Adelaide and had been occupied by the "Aussies" who withstood the siege of Tobruk. We expected to be in the camp for a few weeks, until we again received our vehicles, Bren-carriers, armoured cars, etc., then we were going off across the desert to Libya. There was little of interest in the camp itself. There was a Naafi hut a mile away and a Y.M.C.A. cinema two miles away in the opposite direction. A Mohammedan cemetery lay on the way to this cinema, its clay tombs built above the ground, all facing towards Mecca but many of them were cracked, broken and mouldering.

On top of the little hill above our tents stood a newly built bungalow with Arabesque architecture, which was earmarked for the officers' mess. A windmill provided the means of raising water from a deep well. From this stony hill we could see the shallow stretch of Lake Mareotis, with the road to Alexandria running across it on a raised embankment. We watched the distant toy shapes of vehicles on the road, then the whole scene was blotted out in the tawny cloud of a sandstorm. One chap told me he had set out to walk to the lake but, after twenty-five minutes it seemed to be no nearer, so he gave up!

When the wind blew through the camp, sand permeated everything, including the food and gritted in our teeth. We had to wear our anti-gas eye-shields to protect the eyes.

Occasionally, one or two nomads would bring a mixed herd of camels, goats and fat-tailed sheep to graze on some imaginary scrub. I had noticed several of their low-set brown tents in the vicinity.

On Wednesday, 10th December, I got a pass and paid my first visit to Alexandria. The road into the city from the west passes two tanneries, which stink to high heaven; so much so that truck-drivers getting directions were sometimes facetiously told to: "take the first left, past the second smell!"

The main streets and Mohammed Ali Square were very fine but the back streets were filthy. Many of them had big military notices saying "Out of Bounds". Looking up some of the lanes, I saw lepers and people suffering from bilharzia, a disease common amongst those who work in the irrigation channels. Long before we left North Africa, we were to see too many kiddies with eyes mattering and sore, due to trachoma, while greedy flies crawled round them unhindered.

Our trucks began to arrive and at three o'clock in the morning of 13th December, I was in a party sent to Tel-el-Kebir, away back on the other side of the Delta, to collect some of the vehicles. We entrained at Alexandria and, as we entered the station at that early hour, I saw a hunched-up figure in a corner, wearing a white *galabia*. He was asleep, arms round knees, head down, sitting on cold stone, while a dim blue light gleamed above. Poor blighter! He hadn't even a tent; and nobody cared. Was it *his* fault he was born in Egypt?

Again we sat in the train as it clanked across the Delta. As dawn came, there was the same endless stream of native life. Some men sat on donkeys, persistently banging their heels into the animals' ribs as they trotted patiently along. Others led camels (the least tractable of animals) or brought the black buffalo to be harnessed to a primitive water-wheel, where for hours it would plod round and round in a circle, with a blindfold pad across its eyes to prevent its collapse through dizziness. Women carried baskets of green stuff on their heads or balanced an earthen flagon of water there. Every village had its domed mosque, usually with only one minaret beside it.

On the canals, in the absence of wind, the *feluccas* were being pulled

Feluccas on the Nile.
(Photo, Peter Hill)

by man-power. Two or three men on the tow-path leaned forward on the rope and moved the heavy boat half a step at a time. The canals themselves are used as a general lavatory by the natives. One of these "sweet water" canals, which runs out to Ismailia, originally supplied the builders of the Suez Canal with fresh water. The natives still drink from it but a European dare not even wash in it. If a soldier happened to fall in, he was given several injections to counter the effects, for a needle-like germ in the water burrows into the skin of the unlucky one.

Along the banks of the canals, I saw several *feluccas* under construction. They are built in exactly the same way as the Phoenicians built them 3,000 years ago! The timbers are fixed together by wooden pegs.

We arrived at our destination in time for dinner. Tel-el-Kebir, the scene of a battle in which British troops fought in 1882 and now a large military depot, became known to us all simply as "T.K.". We had no time to explore then but, on a later occasion, I was able to see the little cemetery of those who had died in that far-off battle and I noticed several had belonged to the King's Royal Rifle Corps. Tel-el-Kebir is one of the regiment's battle honours.

Having taken over the vehicles and checked the petrol, oil and water, we set off in a long line, along the main road towards Cairo, for our return route lay not across but round the edge of the Delta. So, after covering sixty miles, we got our first glimpse of Cairo, the largest city in Africa.

The main part of the city is modern and its broad tree-lined boulevards were busy with *gharries* and single-decked tramcars, laden with passengers who wore either the little turban, *"tazfira"*, or the red *"tarboosh"* or, by contrast, Western headgear.

As we crossed the Nile at El Gezira, I saw two of the river steamers, which looked as if they had come straight out of *Show Boat!* They were three decks high, with the funnel forward and one great paddle, the full width of the boat, at the stern.

A few miles out of Cairo we came to Mena, in the shadow of the gigantic pyramids of Giza. As we turned right, on to the Alexandria road and drove on, with these awe-inspiring mountains of stone on our left, I could just make out the tiny figures of people on the top of the Great Pyramid of Cheops. I could only hope I would have a chance some other time to explore it, as we went out on the desert road, 110 miles of desolation.

Half-way along this desert road, we stopped at a military vehicle park, where there was a Naafi. The ubiquitous Naafi! They have been much criticised for turning out watery tea but you certainly find them in the most out-of-the-way places. And after all, if the tea is weak, you can often get beer – if you have enough pay!

In the last stage of our journey, it was dark and all that was visible was a "thin red line" of rear-lights extending away in front. I was driving a three-tonner but the way was so monotonous that I could hardly keep my eyes open. The driver in front kept wandering from side to side. At least, I thought he did – but maybe I was wandering in the opposite direction! Another truck went right off the road and away across the sand but he got back into the line again, having lost only his place in the queue. We reached camp again at 3.00 a.m. – and so to bed.

Four hours later, we were up again, to get our breakfast. After breakfast, with a sudden squall of wind, the *rains* came! Tents went flat, the heavy pegs snapping on the windward like rotten carrots. Our tent stood fast but little rivulets ran in one side and out the other. Outside, men struggled with ballooning tents, while a yellow flood swept past. Deep fissures were torn in the hillside; sand and dust turned into mud; our blankets were sodden and the camp was a shambles.

We put on our gas capes and steel helmets and went out to knock in pegs. We became caked in yellow mud and our feet squelched in boots that were full of water. Ditches were dug to drain the water away but it was too late to save our kit. That night we used biscuit tins, stones, wood, anything to keep ourselves off the ground, while we slept in our clothes and the torrent still hissed down.

Next day, the rain stopped and, in a few hours, everything was bone dry again. Only the channels and the silt washed down from the hill were evidence of the deluge. It rains only on a few days of the year in Egypt but I think we got the whole annual rainfall in that one cloudburst.

However, we could say that it had laid the dust – for a while!

We each had another opportunity to visit Alexandria, where we could buy meals which were a change from Army rations. Lettuce, tomato and fruit salad were favourites, for we seldom had fresh vegetables or fruit in camp, except that tinned fruit could be bought at the Naafi. Prices in "Alex" were, however, about double what we had paid in Durban.

The cinemas showed the usual American talkies, with French sub-titles on the screen, while another small screen at one side showed the words in Arabic and Greek.

Incidentally, the street known to the troops as "Sister Street" (Rue des Soeurs) a street of dens, was the one chosen by the Egyptians to be renamed – after the victory of Alamein – Montgomery Street.

We were told we would be allowed to spend Christmas in the camp, before we set off towards the desert fighting. There was little celebration, however and, on Boxing Day, we began packing our vehicles. I was to travel on a heavy six-wheeled stores truck along with four others. We carefully packed some tins of fruit, vegetables, etc. in a locker as spare rations; a useful precaution, as it turned out.

We were due to move at 3.00 a.m., Saturday, the 27th but, after dark, H.Q. Company, to which we were attached, decided we must change a cylinder-head gasket on a truck, which had been burst at eight o'clock in the morning.

I was one of those working on the job, by lamplight and we were not finished until 2.00 a.m.. One hour to go!

The tents were gone, of course, except one with no walls. The others were asleep inside the trucks. I tried to snatch an hour's sleep under the open tent but without success, for the wind was bitterly cold.

So, at three o'clock, still sleepless, I was rather glad to join the others on the stores wagon, as we started off on our long journey to the far side of Egypt and beyond.

CHAPTER 2

The Desert and the "Jock" Columns

BEFORE CONTINUING this part of my story, it is perhaps advisable to give a rough outline of the situation as it was at the time of our arrival (December 1941).

In the earlier stages of the desert war, Wavell's small force had chased the Italians back beyond Agheila (the famous 11th Hussars even reached Marble Arch) and Agheila was in our hands.

When Rommel took charge, however, things were much tougher and his Afrika Korps advanced and surrounded Tobruk.

The siege lasted eight months but, even as we reached Egypt, the Eighth Army, as it was now called, was advancing to relieve the garrison. Our forces swept round to the south of enemy positions on the escarpment at Sollum, to Bardia, on the Libyan side of the frontier and went on by Sidi Rezegh.

"Jerry" still held Halfaya ("Hellfire") Pass, inside Egypt, where part of the Indian Division faced them.

The forces involved seemed to be two German panzer divisions and six Italian divisions. On our side were: the immortal 7th Armoured Division, the original Desert Rats, whom we were later to join; the 2nd Armoured Division; the 4th Indian Division; the New Zealand Brigade and a South African brigade.

The New Zealanders were part of the 2nd N.Z. Division, which was nowhere near full strength. The Australians had been replaced by 70th Division in Tobruk. The 50th Infantry Division was also in Africa but I think at this time was being re-organised. One of their brigades had been wiped out after facing *five* enemy divisions in the Battle of the Gap in the summer of 1941.

We ourselves were at this time part of the 1st Armoured Division and wore on our shoulders the sign of a white rhinoceros on a black ground.

To resume, then – we got on to the coast road, that lonely ribbon of tar that runs for hundreds of miles across Egypt and Libya and drove west in an extended procession.

Long after daybreak, we still moved steadily on, with few stops. We had dinner cooked by the wayside and, about three o'clock in the afternoon, halted again at El Daba, where there was another Naafi! As we continued towards Mersa Matruh, we picked up two battalion trucks which had conked out and took them on tow. This slowed our progress and we arrived at Matruh at 10.00 p.m., an hour behind the convoy. H.Q. had kept no supper for us, so we had to make do with tea, bully and hard biscuits. Feeling the effect of the previous night without sleep, I was more than tired but I slept well that night. Five of us crammed into the stores truck somehow. Ron Taylor lay on top of the steel bins near the canvas hood of the truck. My own bed was formed of two folding work-benches laid across some rows of petrol tins at the forward end and the others slept on the floor behind the bins. We had to unload some stuff, such as drums of oil, spare springs, axles, etc. to clear the floor and this became our regular routine. If we had to move quickly in the morning, we rose sharp, rolled our blankets and heaved the loose stores aboard as quickly as possible.

Mersa Matruh, in the morning sun, appeared as a small town of square white buildings, looking out on the bright blue of the Mediterranean. There seemed to be no possible reason for having a town there at all but it had been a holiday resort for the wealthier Egyptians. Inland, there was nothing but the endless, dusty waste of the Western Desert.

Starting off again (Sunday, 28th December) we left the road and went on over the desert. The surface was hard and fairly level. We drove on all day but, as we kept on attending to faults on battalion vehicles, we gradually lagged further and further behind. We had four vehicles in the L.A.D.: a 15 cwt. on which our officer travelled, a 3-ton "workshop", a Leyland recovery and the A.E.C. stores but, as time went on, we collected another eight, some of which we had got running and the rest we were towing. The convoy had long disappeared over the horizon and there was nothing but desert all round us.

Our little cavalcade carried on, however, most of the twelve vehicles either towing or being towed, and we drove into the early morning in an attempt to catch up – without success.

Our officer, "Nobby" Clark, had to navigate by compass and, in order to get a bearing in the dark, he had to drive away ahead and take a "back bearing" on a torch held by our "Q". When he was in the correct line, he flashed another torch and we drove up to him. It would have been impossible to navigate otherwise, as there was no mounting on the truck to line up the compass and, even if there had been, the dial was too small to get an accurate reading under the jerky motion of the truck. So we went on, leap-frog fashion, half a mile at a time but it was slow work and we had to give up and snatch a few hours sleep. The point was that we had to catch the battalion if we were to eat and we had a number of the K.R.R.C. with us on the extra trucks.

At five o'clock in the morning, we were moving again. The desert was still dead flat, hard and rocky. We arrived at a compass position where the battalion should have been, but they were gone. There was no landmark except a few petrol tins. We went south for a bit, then west again and came to a signpost pointing to Bir El Khamsa (The Fifth Well). Then we turned north again. We saw a mirage which looked like a lake with tall poplar trees. I climbed on top of the truck and the vision vanished. But it was still there when I came down. These images, of course, are caused by reflection and refraction through layers of air having different temperatures and we were to see many of them but we learned by experience that the "poplar tree" effect was generally caused by trucks away in the distance. The tiny black shapes were inverted and elongated by distortion until they looked like slender trees.

On we went and at midday we reached a convoy control point, where a party were encamped to direct the troops. We eventually found the battalion at 5.00 p.m.

We were now well inland and somewhere to the south-east of Halfaya Pass, which was still held by the enemy, blocking the coast road. Indeed, we heard gunfire in the distance.

We now parked with the battalion for the whole of the next day. This was supposed to be a *rest* but some of our boys were again at work on repairs, right on through the following night.

On the last day of the year, we were moving again but two trucks were abandoned on the desert, each having a broken chassis through towing over rough ground.

Such vehicles were not wasted, for they were systematically "cannibalised" by any unit travelling up or down the desert tracks. If they needed an engine, out it came; if they required a battery, off came the battery; if they had petrol pipes cut by shrapnel, they got replacements from a wreck. If it was a tyre, a wheel, a spring, or even an axle, the derelict was left perched on a pile of stones! Vehicles abandoned on the "Div. Axis" (route of travel and supply) were supposed eventually to be recovered and taken back to base but the likelihood was that by the time a recovery section came for one, they would find only an empty shell!

Leaving those trucks, however, meant that whatever they carried – stores, baggage and men – had to be put on to other trucks, with consequent overcrowding.

As we moved on, I sat in the back of the stores truck, trying to read a book. There was nothing else to look at for, now that we had left the coastal belt, even the wispy scrub had disappeared and nothing grew – *absolutely nothing!*

Reading was not very comfortable either, for dust poured into the rear of the truck in yellow-pink clouds, so that I had to keep blowing it off the book in order to see the print.

During one stop, a Scammel transporter came alongside and who should I see but Big Tim, one of the men who had been in the base workshop at Nantes! We had quite a chat about old times. The funny part of it was that he had been on the *Franconia* too, during our two-months' voyage and we had never once set eyes on each other! A big ship but a small world.

On New Year's Day, 1942, a convoy of trucks loaded with Italian prisoners passed us on the way back. There were about forty men on each truck and twenty-five trucks; that is, about 1,000 prisoners. The one guard on each truck was Indian. The trucks themselves were of Italian make.

The Italians did not seem to mind being prisoners. They had been full of zeal and "patriotism" when, in 1936, they used poison gas against the Abyssinians (a race who were Christians long before St. Augustine landed in Kent) but they didn't seem so keen now.

Mind you, maybe the *"Eyeties"* had an idea that if they all gave themselves up, perhaps that would teach Mussolini to start a war he couldn't finish!

We were still moving but, by the middle of the day, a steady wind was blowing and all around was a yellow fog of dust, through which we could only see about thirty yards. We were again lagging behind the main convoy but now we had a bigger supply of rations. Lieutenant Clark was again using the compass to check our course but, as time went on, the wind grew stronger and the dust thicker, until visibility was only five yards. We kept close behind the vehicle in front of us, or we would have lost sight of it. Eventually, we came to the barbed-wire barrier set up by the Italians along the Libyan border. We were looking for the gap at Fort Maddalena, an Italian blockhouse. While we waited, the officer's truck went off along the barrier. All of us, but especially the drivers, had faces and goggles covered with thick yellow powder and still it swirled around us.

Back came the truck. The gap was just 100 yards to the south! So we were not far out, considering the long distance we had travelled – and on we went into Libya.

Our destination was a place called Antelat, near the Gulf of Sydra, at the far side of the Barka peninsula. In other words, we were by-passing Tobruk and Benghazi, both of which were now in our hands.

We had begun to see odds and ends of enemy equipment lying about, most of it quite well made, and I was particularly struck by the first "jerrican" I picked up. The original "jerrican" was better than any of the copies produced by the Allies later. It was completely coated inside with red enamel and, even if used for water, was quite rust-proof.

Our own petrol supplies were brought forward in square four-gallon tins, known as "flimsies" because they were no stouter than biscuit tins. I have seen a truck loaded with these tins moving up in a supply column and the petrol dripping from the rear, to be sucked up by the greedy desert sand. Often when we received such a load, several tins would be empty.

"Flimsies" were, of course, expendable items and they certainly came in handy as we made basins, dixies and petrol braziers out of them.

We were swiftly learning the desert way of life and particularly how to "brew" a cup of "shay" (Arabic for tea). A brazier was made by cutting a "flimsy" in half and poking a few holes in the sides. A shovelful of sand was thrown in, soaked with petrol and set alight. This kind of fire will burn slowly for up to half an hour, with an occasional stirring of the sand to release more vapour. The "brew-can" was usually made from a petrol tin too and the taste was not too bad after the first time! The cans got sooty, of course, so instead of putting them aboard the truck beside our blankets, we made wire handles and hung them outside, usually on the towing-hook at the back.

When a convoy stopped, we watched the commander in front. If he showed a red flag and yellow flag together (the brew-up signal) there was an eruption of men. One grabbed the cans, another came with a shovel, and yet another with a "jerrican" of petrol. Fires were going in a twinkling. Such halts were of short duration but we always managed to get our *"shay"*. If the signal came to move came suddenly, we climbed aboard with the mugs of tea, balancing them carefully and drank as we moved along.

The unofficial "drill" of a brew-up was very impressive, showing a spontaneous organisation worthy of such a major operation!

Water, however, was really in short supply in those days. Our ration was half a gallon per day, and half of that went to the cooks for general use. That left us with a quart in a water-bottle for all purposes: drinking, washing, shaving and, if necessary, topping up our radiators in order to keep the trucks running!

As a man may lose up to ten pints of moisture in a day through perspiration, especially in the hot season, it is not surprising that we cut out washing and shaving for weeks on end, in order to conserve our drinking water! When we did have a wash, each man contributed a small amount from his water bottle and this was gathered in one tin basin. We then took turns at washing, perhaps six or seven of us, one after the other, until the water was black. Then, if any radiator was a bit low, it got what was left in the basin! The only way we could wash clothes was to wash them in petrol (which was red-tinted). The petrol was generally more plentiful than water and it prevented us from getting lousy and, of course, the clothes dried rapidly!

Even now, when I turn on a tap and cool, clean water gushes out, I think what a wonderful blessing it is and how little appreciated, except by those who have known what real thirst is.

Each truck carried a reserve "battle" ration of water in two-gallon tins, which was not touched except by order of an officer. It was inspected each day to ensure that it was intact. It is a sad fact that we occasionally met the kind of fellow who would drain his water-bottle without restraint and then beg a drink from others who had been more careful. The same type is to be found amongst the followers of a certain political section who say to themselves, "Oh, I haven't saved any money, but I'm entitled to some of the other fellow's."

Our journey continued over the endless wastes and, as the going was often rough, we were kept busy on repairs and were practically always well behind, so that we became resigned to driving late every night. Once I saw a wrecked Hurricane, which had had its tail shot away. Scrub began to make its appearance again and, on Monday, 5th January, we reached slightly higher ground and some flat-topped ridges. The ground had a crust of black pebbles, with soft sand beneath. Desert snails clung to the stones in large numbers. They had large white shells about two inches across and, though all around was dry, their bodies were moist and smelt salty. In fact, to my eyes they seemed just like whelks.

On several occasions during the desert campaign, our soldiers and airmen, returning from behind the enemy lines on foot, have been obliged to eat these snails to keep alive.

Soon we came within earshot of guns again and once a line of ambulances passed us, moving south. We were told that Indian troops had driven the enemy from a position ten miles south-west of us. As we came nearer to the coast again, patches of scrub appeared as much as two feet high and even an odd pheasant or gazelle would be seen, to say nothing of snakes.

We were now warned to sleep with our rifles handy.

We had caught up with the battalion once more and were parked near them in a large open echelon. As the vehicles were dispersed about 100 yards apart, in case of air-raids, the echelon stretched literally for miles, with larger gaps separating the various units of the division. At last we had a little spare time but we had to provide our own entertainment.

One day we had a hilarious game of "cricket" with iron stumps and a ball made from a stone wrapped in a rag. Steel helmets were optional. Each time the ball came down, one of the fielders slyly tossed a pebble at the wicket but the wicket-keeper said, "There's no need to do that; I've got a piece of string tied to the bails!"

Lieutenant Clark sportingly joined in the fun, took a turn at bowling and sent down some real armour-piercing missiles!

However, things were due to become a little more exciting in the near future, not by our own efforts but through those of a man called Rommel.

The first hint came from air activity over our echelon. Two brief entries in my diary are:

Tuesday – *13.1.42*
Enemy 'plane over. Four bombs.

Wednesday – *14.1.42*
Enemy 'plane down. Three shots.

Our ack-ack protection was mainly provided by Bofors guns (of Swedish design) which were extremely valuable in the desert. The shells

(40 mm.) were loaded in clips and fired in automatic repetition. The fact that our second visitor was shot down with only three rounds meant good snap-shooting. At this time we still saw quite a lot of our own planes, sometimes as many as twenty Hurricanes at once, so we were quite complacent but this turned out to be a dangerous state of mind to get into.

Our rations had a temporary boost when captured Italian stores from Benghazi came to us through the P.R.I. (President, Regimental Institute). There were Italian cigarettes, chocolate, razor-blades, tinned peas, beans and milk and Spanish sardines, which we could have if we wanted them, but we had to pay for them!

One afternoon, our big stores truck was sent to collect the ordinary rations, no lighter vehicle being available. Coming back as daylight faded, the driver became confused as he passed through the miles of scattered echelons. He completely lost his way in the dark and, after asking for directions from various units, we seemed to be going round in circles. We finished up with an anti-tank unit, who thought we were about six to eight miles out. As we had no compass, we could only wait there till dawn, when we found our way back to within a mile – then we were met by the Q.M.S., who had come out in another truck to look for us.

The following day we again moved, this time to take up battle positions. News had come through that the enemy forces in Halfaya Pass (now far to our rear) had surrendered.

We were told we were moving to outflank Rommel's forces – that we were proceeding towards *Tripoli* to get behind him! If Rommel had heard of such ambitious ideas at that time, he would have smiled.

On Monday, 19th January, we were going south towards Ajedabia, when we began to have trouble with soft sand, the wheels simply spinning round until the trucks were dug down with the axles almost on the ground. We used the "sand-channels" provided for this eventuality. These were strips of steel, about 5 ft. long, by 9 in. wide and usually perforated. The idea was to place them, one at either side, in front of the driving wheels, let the truck run along them, pick up the channels, run forward, and repeat before the wheels sank again. In practice the grids were buried deep by the weight of the vehicle and we had to plunge our hands down into the sand to find them, usually cutting our fingers on the sharp, rough edges of the holes as we dragged them up. Most times, they were badly bent, so that they stuck against something when we tried to get them under the spinning wheels. Still, we would never have got out of some spots without them. When we were finished, we would jump on them to straighten them up and fix them back on the side of the truck.

A convoy of vehicles in the desert is like a convoy of ships at sea, spread out in several lines, with the commander in front, flying a flag. If enemy aircraft were sighted, the outermost trucks turned still further out, raced as far as they had time for, stopped and everyone jumped out and scattered, taking their rifles with them. The passenger was responsible for "spotting" and later, trucks were fitted with a proper manhole in the cab roof above the passenger seat. The manhole had padded edges, so that the spotter could stand up and look around ("rubber-necking" we called it). Two bangs on the cab roof with his clenched hand was the signal for immediate dispersal.

That same Monday night, we took a turn on guard (having no repair work at the time) and we each had five rounds in the magazine. One man forgot he had one "up the spout" and there was a bang as it went off. Luckily, it struck the ground a few yards away. I think he felt like the man who coughed at the bridge party – but after a while the rattle of steel helmets died away and the disgruntled echelon returned to sleep!

On Wednesday, 21st January, the fun started.

We were parked in an area of soft sand, when a group of planes appeared high above us. Some of the boys asked me, "What are they, Nick?" (for some reason I was regarded as an expert) but to tell the truth I was busy loading stores and I gave only a careless glance up and said, "Oh, they're ours!"

Within half a minute, there was a roar and our startled eyes beheld a huge cloud of dust climbing into the sky behind us, where bombs had landed around some trucks. Nine planes rocketed past, climbing, after pulling out of their dive – and now there was no mistaking them – the characteristic "spats" on the fixed undercarriage, the anhedral–dihedral wing and, above all, the iron crosses painted on them – the Junkers 87B, better known as the *Stuka*! The unmistakable *Stuka*!

I never heard the last of that! Every time aircraft were spotted, I was "ribbed". Even in the desperate days that followed, when we ran to dodge some attack, someone would say, breathlessly, "It's all right – they're ours!"

Nevertheless, it shook us out of our complacency and we all improved our aircraft recognition from that time on.

We began to move up again, towards a steep ridge. There was more bombing somewhere ahead of us, but we kept moving forward, until suddenly we saw some of our artillery coming back in retreat! We didn't know it, but this was the start of Rommel's counter-attack. In other words, there was a "flap" on! In the ridge was a narrow gap, through which all traffic had to come. The gap and the hollow leading out of it were full of soft sand. This was the notorious "Bottle-neck Pass", somewhere near Ajedabia.

As more and more vehicles struggled back through the gap, we thought it was about time we also turned back and, when a captain of the K.R.R.C. came through in a 15-cwt. truck, we finally got the order to follow the others out. We began to turn round, got bogged in the sand and started digging like mad with shovels, heaving at the backs of trucks and running back and forth with the sand-channels. First we got the big recovery wagon out and it moved up on to firmer ground and carried on. Then the "stores" got bogged for the second time. We were almost exhausted, digging and pushing and were soaked with perspiration. Sand stuck to our bleeding fingers as we dragged at the sand-channels. One of our own tanks came out of the gap and passed us, then shells began to burst around the gap. And still we were bogged down, struggling and sweating, with a feeling of desperation in our hearts. "Q" brought back his three-tonner, we hitched a tow-chain and, with everyone pushing, we finally got out on to higher ground.

No sooner had we got moving on the level, stony ground than we stopped again. I looked out of the back of the stores and saw a Bofors pointing upwards, going "Bump-bump-bump!" That was enough, out we jumped and scattered but, of course, we had no cover – not even a slit-trench. There were about twelve planes. One after another, they peeled off in a vertical bank, then screamed down recklessly on the huddled cluster of vehicles we still formed. They ignored the shells from the Bofors and, indeed, when one Stuka dropped his nose straight towards the gun and the bombs left the racks, the crew turned and ran from the gun. I fired one puny round from my rifle, then we were scrabbling on the ground, trying to press ourselves into it. A line of bomb-bursts erupted in front, like flaming red and black fountains, accompanied by an ear-splitting noise. With a cold, desolate fear, I saw more black streaks whistling down and thought, "This lot must get us." Again the deafening eruption, closer, still in front, right amongst the trucks and the ground wobbled as if in earthquake. Shrapnel whanged past, clouds of dust rolled over and stones rattled down. A third lot of bombs burst, behind us this time, passing over our heads – and it was finished.

I pulled myself up to a sitting position and loosed off two more rounds as a parting gesture, with little hope of hitting anything. Someone said, "Gosh, fella, you've got more guts than I have!" Little did he know, it was only the kick of the rifle against my shoulder that made me feel a little better. The smell of explosive was all around us and one man beside me picked up a piece of shrapnel and dropped it again because it was nearly red hot. At the edge of the hollow, a truck was blazing and crackling. Further down, the 15-cwt. truck belonging to the battalion had stopped. When the raid started, the captain had jumped out at one side and his driver at the other side, but the driver was killed. He was buried on the spot, in a shallow, sandy grave.

Our three L.A.D. vehicles (the recovery was somewhere ahead) were undamaged except for a few shrapnel holes, so we moved on and continued until dark, stopping only once for tea and hard biscuits. We gathered a few more battalion trucks as we went along and at night we formed a little laager of our own, with a double guard. Our only Bren-gun was placed near the track we had left and several times we challenged vehicles coming along, but they were always British stragglers, still moving back. For a long time Very-light signals kept appearing in the sky, in the direction from which we had come.

As events began to speed up from this time onward, I will continue by giving the actual entries from my diary, as being more concise and simply add notes where extra detail or description is necessary. Each happening was recorded at the time, or within a few days, as circumstances allowed.

THURSDAY – 22.1.42.

More bombing. Always stop trucks, jump out and scatter. Once fifteen enemy planes flew right over us, dropping the "eggs" in front of us. We saw the iron crosses plainly as we looked up. Dick was beside me, cursing, and we saw two planes very low, machine-gunning men on the ground. Made tea with salty water, then moved again. several sections of the battalion going back too. Writing this sitting in the desert 100 yards from truck and can hear booming of bombs or guns as I write. Saw some "Jerry" 'planes a moment ago, but going past us.

(Later): We had another visit while making tea. Couldn't leave our

tea, so took our mugs to the slit-trenches. Twenty-one planes in one direction and nine bombers with six fighters in another.

We had been told that each man must dig his own slit-trench wherever we stopped and even if we stopped several times a day. A slit-trench, of course, is about 6 ft. by 2 and the depth varies according to the kind of ground you have to dig. It looks like an open grave – and often became one.

The scattered units in our area were now re-forming into mobile columns, probably by pre-arranged plan. We had failed to reach Colonel Sismey of the K.R.R.C. but we became attached to "Barren" Column, under command of an artillery colonel, who was in radio contact with "Charles" Column, commanded by Colonel Sismey, and it was thought they might get close to "Charles" Column to hand us over to them.

In the ordinary way we, as "auxiliaries", should have been with "B" Echelon, behind the fighting but no-one seemed to know where "B" Echelon was! In any case, it would be mobile too but contact had to be maintained if the forward units were to get their supplies of food and petrol, ammunition and water.

These mobile columns were called "Jock" columns after the late Major-General "Jock" Campbell, V.C., who was first to try them on a large scale. Their function was to harass the enemy and strike at his supply lines – a similar idea to Rommel's infiltration methods – but they often had to face heavier opposition than supply lines.

So far as I can recall, the column included some platoons of the K.R.R.C., four 25-pounders, four Bofors and a few anti-tank guns, which at that time were 2-pounders. Later, the columns were made bigger, with greater striking power.

On Thursday night, then, we laagered with "Barren" Column to close formation. While the column slept, we worked till early morning on a broken spring. We had no bushing to fit the shackle-pin, so we improvized by rolling a strip of brass sheet round it. As we worked, a tarpaulin was hung over us, to hide the light we were using but we heard a 'plane coming towards us. Instantly, the lamp was disconnected. The shadowy shape of the 'plane roared the whole length of the column, no more than 25 feet up, and disappeared. No shot was fired; no bombs were dropped. We could not tell whether he was friend or foe, or if he had even seen us at all in the moonlight.

FRIDAY – *23.1.42*

Moving north. Some action ahead, behind a ridge. Sounds of tank engines roaring and guns booming. Some sort of running battle is in progress. We wait, while the noise moved westwards. Beyond the ridge, the column crosses over a hundred tracks of our tanks. Nothing in sight, but the noise continues in the distance.

3.00 p.m. Some shells suddenly whistle past us, one throwing up sand twenty feet away.

(These shells didn't explode, so they were of the armour-piercing type and probably came from an enemy tank hidden in some hollow).

We move on, past where some lonely infantrymen are placing Bren-guns in defensive positions and at dusk met up with "Charles" Column, which we join.

As a column never formed its night laager on the spot where it was last seen by the enemy, we moved on again for the best part of an hour, before drawing into close column. With infiltration on both sides, you might awake to find enemy groups in any direction, even behind you! We would be moving again before dawn, to manoeuvre into a fresh position, so a man was lucky if he got five hours sleep. This night we got much less.

It was moonlight and we started to take off the four wheels of a damaged truck which was being abandoned. An officer and a few riflemen were patrolling out from the laager and I was told to be as quiet as possible, as the enemy was thought to be near. I tried to keep the wheel-brace from clanking or squeaking and the others walked on tiptoe as the wheels were lifted into another truck. Then the outposts came running in and the order was passed round, "Get aboard, quick, we're moving!"

The engines started up and, as we shot forward, there was an outburst of machine-gun and rifle fire behind us. Apparently we left two groups of the enemy firing at one another across the spot we had left!

We crawled around in circles for another two or three hours, then stopped for a little sleep. We threw ourselves down without even loosening our boots.

SATURDAY - *24.1.42*

We are in a big wadi and our 25-pounders around the rim are firing

*steadily. Can hear the orders being shouted, then a great, sighing
noise as the shells rush into the distance. Now enemy replies are
bursting near our position, two in the defile. Some of our tanks have
passed through towards the enemy.*

They were General Stuart (Honey) tanks and Crusaders with 2-pounder
guns in the turrets. They passed on the way through and we had a chat
with one of the men. He told us they were out-gunned by the German
tanks. "Jerry" could sit back and shell them from a distance, while the
little 2-pounders could not even reach him! Yet they were going calmly
into battle knowing that the bigger German guns had them at a dis-
advantage.

*More enemy shells. We are now in the open above the wadi. Planes
coming. We run to a rocky gulley. I see the "eggs" leave the planes and
know they will land close. "Whee-ee-crrrump!" We bounce on the
ground as they land in the next hollow, passing over our heads at a
slant. Shrapnel whizzes over and rattles down beside us. This time
the Bofors all open up at once and there is a smother of shell-bursts.
One truck is burning, another damaged. A man is helped away,
holding his arm across his chest – the sign of a broken collar-bone.*

For several days, the dive-bombers came over about every one and
a half hours during daylight, as regularly as a 'bus service. It became
demoralizing. We almost prayed for the sun to go down. The effect of
little sleep, strain and lack of proper meals, was beginning to tell. We
seemed to live on tea and hard biscuits with a slice of bully-beef between
them. We had not seen any R.A.F. 'planes for at least ten days but we
were told they were attacking the enemy airfields.

*(Later): Shells whine, ricochet and burst around our stores truck,
which is still on the skyline. When will we get orders to move it?
One solid A.P. shot bounces near us and makes a second cloud of
dust 100 yards away, beside an ambulance.*

We suspected our valuable stores truck was being used as a decoy but,
shells or no shells, we had to get our tea and biscuits from the truck;
though after the brew was made we went back to the wadi to drink it!

*In evening, we laager some miles away. We hear from a K.R.R.C.
back from patrol that our artillery fire (from the wadi) sent several
"Jerry" trucks up in the air. We also hear that the tail-end of "B"*

Echelon was shot to pieces by the enemy. Our mates from the missing recovery were there. One man got away in another truck but it is not known what happened to the other four. The recovery itself was lost.

That evening, we got what was to be our last ration of petrol from the column, one 4-gallon tin! We heard that some vehicles and even tanks were set on fire and abandoned, because they could get no petrol through from the "B" Echelons to enable them to run. Our division had practised manoeuvres in Blighty but they were finding it a different proposition to face the experienced Afrika Korps.

Sunday – *25.1.42*

We move early and stop with the guns taking position across our rear. I am changing a wheel on an 8 cwt. "office" truck, when shells begin bursting around us again. "All aboard!" is the shout and the punctured truck is abandoned, the two chaps from it coming on our stores. I manage to get the jack out, however, for we may yet need it ourselves. The guns are limbering up too, without firing, so the enemy must be approaching in force. We beat a hasty retreat and, as the miles are covered, more and more British trucks, Bren-carriers and armoured cars, come together from all parts of the desert, till we are one huge column, like a herd of cattle in a cloud of dust. More shells, air-bursts, about fifteen feet above the ground, spraying shrapnel downwards. Now I see the enemy tanks behind us, a row of black shapes with flashes coming from their gun-turrets. We gradually draw away from them and, further on, the column stops for a minute. Suddenly, Bill Shorter collapses beside the truck. We carry him inside the wagon, move on and then a tyre goes bang. We work feverishly to change the wheel.

(How lucky it was I had got our jack away from that other truck!)

While we jack up, the battalion M.O. comes over and gives Bill attention in the back of the truck. The jack is so stiff with the great weight of the stores above it, that I dig the ground away in order to get the wheel with the inflated tyre in position. On again. The Chevrolet with "Q" aboard is towing another and lagging behind.

This was the truck which had been damaged in the bombing at the wadi the day before. It was now carrying a swarm of men hanging all over it, stragglers from other derelicts.

*Our officer tells us to keep going, as he is going back to see "Q". We
keep going and machine-gun tracers rip across our wagon. "Jerry"
tanks are now out on our flanks. More shells as we again catch up
with the big mixed column. A Bren-carrier is blown up on its side,
then our truck becomes the target. A large brown burst appears right
behind us as we stand at the edge of the halted column. I yell to
Ron up front and he looks round, then pulls the wagon out from the
column. The shells follow us round as we go.*

Fortunately, we were moving in an oblique direction and though each
shell came a little further, they were always a few yards short. I could
only watch from the back of the truck as if hypnotized. As we again turned
parallel to the column, the last shell came and there was a clatter from a
steel bin as a piece of shrapnel struck it within an inch of my ear!

We were now very short of petrol but, by great good fortune, we
came up with a recovery section, with Scammels, at the head of the
column and they agreed to take us on tow. These were not the articulated
Scammels but the short, powerful, "tractor" type and their diesel fuel
would take them a long way. Their O.C. said he knew the way to Bir
Hacheim, some 200 miles across the desert, and that was where he was
making for. That suited us fine, though we had no choice in the matter
for we could not go much farther on our own. We didn't know it then
but Lieutenant "Nobby" Clark, "Q" and the others were prisoners,
having been cut off somewhere behind us. If "Q" had dropped the truck
on tow and taken the men on his own truck, he might have got them
away but he had to wait for orders and so they were all "in the bag".
Our stores truck was the only vehicle of the L.A.D. to escape, with five
of us aboard and two of the K.R.R.C.

There was still a little petrol left in the tank but we decided to use
our engine only to help if the Scammel had to take us over soft sand,
or other difficult ground. This proved wise, for we did strike some soft
going, where the track had been churned up and even the broad tyres
of the Scammel could hardly get a grip to pull our heavy wagon.

We went steadily on for an hour or two then had a halt on a level
stretch, near a patch of scrub. We had not been there long when a line
of aircraft was seen skimming the desert towards us. 'Damn!' I thought,
'Here we go again!' In the distance, with an end-on view, we could only
tell that they were fighters but we had learnt in any case to take cover
first and ask questions afterwards. Bill, who was still suffering severe

pains in the tummy, was helped over the tail-board and across to the scrub. Wearily, we got down. The scrub was only two feet high but I coiled myself round the bottom of one of these miniature bushes and waited, expecting a hail of machine-gun bullets.

As the planes came nearer, I saw they were Hurricanes!

They banked around us, probably puzzled by the line of "deserted" vehicles and showing the circles on their wings. I wonder what they thought as we all stood up in the scrub?

We must have appeared to them much as the clansmen appeared to Fitz-James in *The Lady of the Lake*, when they rose out of the heather! I wonder if they guessed what we had been through, to make us crawl into a miserable patch of scrub? It seemed ages since we had seen any of our own aircraft and we were so "bomb-happy" that we could only wave to them in silent relief.

Poor Bill was helped aboard again and we travelled on, well into the night, before we laagered for a few hours of precious sleep.

All next day we went steadily on, still being towed and in the evening reached the mud fort of Bir Hacheim, the "Doctor's Well", standing on a slightly higher area, with the Arabic name set out in stones bedded in the ground.

Bir Hacheim is a name known in two World Wars, for here the Turks held prisoner the crew of the British vessel *Tara* which was torpedoed off Sollum in 1915. They were rescued by an armoured car unit led by the late Duke of Westminster.

At the time when we reached the fort, it still stood alone, with none of the defences which were later placed around it when French forces defended it. At one side was a walled enclosure, used as a petrol store, and here we filled our tank and took on about sixty gallons spare in jerricans. The recovery section continued on its way, with our thanks and we stopped a few miles from Bir Hacheim for the night.

TUESDAY – *27.1.42*

Move on with mixed mob, including Indians and South Africans, towards El Adem. The same shirt has now been on my back day and night for over a month. During the last hectic week, there was a persistent rumour among the boys that we were being used as bait to draw "Jerry" into the open. I wonder! At El Adem, we are directed to a camp graced by the initials L.O.B., which are supposed to stand for "left out of battle!" Given tins of luscious peaches by Q.M.S. of the K.R.R.C., who is here on staff work. Peaches taste wonderful after weeks of bully and biscuits. The camp is full, many men of the Rifle Brigade being here but the officer in command tells us to be ready to move at 08.00 hours in the morning to join re-formed units. Bill Shorter's trouble has been diagnosed as colic and he is being left behind. Good old Bill! Sorry to lose him.

I then sat up till midnight repairing a four-inch gash in the tube of the tyre which had been changed during the "flap". As the little chemical-burning vulcanizer I used could only do a small patch at a time, I had little hope of it being a reliable job, but it might do in an emergency.

WEDNESDAY – *28.1.42*

Left El Adem via the Italian motor road to Tobruk, which is a small town with a harbour. Ah! the sea! "Water, water everywhere, nor any drop to drink!" All around are signs of the battles of both the Italian and German campaigns. Beside the roads running in from the perimeter are tons of scrap among shell-holes and bomb-craters and scattered graves with rough wooden crosses. Some old gun-posts are set in rock and the road has been blown up where it crosses a gully. Found a canteen and brought some tinned fruit for the boys, who have no money. Left Tobruk, heading west on the coast road towards T'mimi. The battalion is supposed to be at Mekhili, inland from T'mimi.

THURSDAY – *29.1.42*

Found we could not get to Mekhili as there seemed to be a general withdrawal. We were turned on the coast road and told to go back. Puncture due to picking up a round of ammo from the road. Put on our doubtful spare but burst that after two miles. Both covers shredded, so ran flat. Tyre was smoking when we got back to O.F.P. (Ordnance Field Park). Here we were lucky to obtain two covers, but no tubes of right size, so fitted an oversize. Old tyre burst into flames as soon as air got in, so made tea on it, then got going towards Tobruk once more.

From that time on, we used to say, "When in doubt – brew up!" We were due a cup of *shay* anyway, and we felt it was a pity to waste the heat from the flaming tyre. When the water was boiled, we extinguished the blaze with sand and, after the wheel had cooled, the remains of the tyre were cut away. We stopped for the night all by ourselves, just off the coast road and dined better than we had done for many weeks, on tinned sausages, beans and fruit.

Next day, we continued towards Tobruk, passing the Italian monument at Acroma road junction, where the by-pass turned inland to El Adem. This monument, with its frieze of shovels, apparently commemorated the building of the road and was inscribed *"Strada del Asse"* ("Axis Road").

But a greater axis was yet to be laid by the Desert Rats – an axis that would carry the sign of the Jerboa to the heart of Germany and play a large part in reducing the vaunted Rome-Berlin Axis to mediocrity!

When we arrived at Tobruk once more, we were not quite sure what to do next but we met a captain of the K.R.R.C., who was looking around for any spare vehicles which could be of use to the battalion. He was going to be in Tobruk for a couple of days and told us to stay and give a hand, then we could all get back to the battalion together.

This gave us the chance to get two new tubes of the right size for our tyres for, knowing that the oversize tubes we had fitted must be creased inside the covers, we expected further trouble. So off came the wheels again and, after we had them fixed, we went into Tobruk Transit Camp for the night.

SATURDAY – *31.1.42*
Still at Tobruk. Looking at the sea and the ships in the harbour, I have never felt so home-sick in all my life.

As we had neither written nor received any mail during the month we had been in Libya, I sent a 12-piastre cablegram from the Army Post Office in Tobruk, thinking this would be the quickest way of letting my folks know I was still all right. This cablegram, however, was never received.

MONDAY – *2.2.42*
Explored a church in Piazza Francesco d'Assisi. It was damaged by shell-fire but there were still some tableaux and effigies inside. The boys from the lost recovery are now at the transit camp with us but six still missing.

THURSDAY – *5.2.42*
Still at Tobruk. The enemy is now near T'mimi, to the west of Tobruk but rumours of fresh support. Bombing activity at night. One plane flew over low and machine-gunned our camp.

Most of the men in the camp were in tents, with the floor dug down below ground level, so they lay still and watched the bullet holes appearing in the walls of the tents above them! In our stores truck, we were above ground level and, when the firing began, Ron Taylor, in his usual place on top of the bins, came down like a ton of bricks on the rest of us below! He was unhurt but had wisely decided that a high altitude isn't always healthy. By the time we had sorted ourselves out in the darkness, to the accompaniment of much cussing, the plane had gone!

FRIDAY – *6.2.42*
More aerial activity. In the grub queue, there are representatives of all regiments and a dozen nationalities: Indians, Poles, South Africans, Kaffirs, Australians, French and others unknown.

SATURDAY – *7.2.42*
Sleeping in dug-out with timber roof and felt safer when we were again strafed in early morning. One dug-out had two large mess-tables in it, with empty tins still lying on them, though the dug-out had last been used during the siege. Left for El Adem, where there is a Reserve Vehicle Park. The aerodrome is a mess.

MONDAY – *9.2.42*
Tinkering up some Bren-carriers for the K.R.R.C., but they were allocated to Coldstream Guards and Poles! Dog-fights overhead, between Hurricanes and enemy aircraft. News from the battalion says about 300 lost or missing, including our officer and five other ranks. Only three N.C.O.s left in H.Q. Company!

WEDNESDAY – *11.2.42*
On way to rejoin battalion, some more strafing by enemy fighters. Found battalion thirty miles west of El Adem – but they had no mail for us.

FRIDAY – *13.2.42*
We are told that we are returning to Cairo to refit! The battalion has indeed lost 300 men and 75 per cent of its vehicles!

The same day, the depleted convoy began moving east, past El Adem again, down on to the coast road and by evening we reached Gambut.

SATURDAY – *14.2.42*
Discovered Bardia was silent and deserted. It is, or was, a lovely little place, set on cliffs high above a little bay, where I could see a sunken boat through the clear blue-green waters. Climbed to the gallery of a mosque minaret, where I had a good view of the smashed town, with its white houses and lines of meagre trees.

Passed Fort Capuzzo and came to the top of Halfaya Pass. Descended the pass by a winding, precipitous, stony track, from the great height of the escarpment overlooking Sollum Bay. There is a great amount of German equipment and guns lying about in the hollows.

I believe the escarpment here is more than 600 feet high and the view is quite impressive. It was the grandest bit of scenery we had come across so far. We were once more in Egypt and, at the foot of the pass, we came back on to the coast road. The tar road also climbed the escarpment at Sollum, but seemed to be reserved for one-way traffic only.

SUNDAY – *15.2.42*
Passed Sidi Barrani, Buk-Buk and Mersa Matruh. Road good. Sea very blue – but we were not!

MONDAY – *16.2.42*
Repairs to carrier.

TUESDAY – *17.2.42*
Night at El Daba, beside the Naafi. Had a pint (real beer!) heard the radio news and then one of the riflemen played a selection of Sullivan's music to us on the piano.

WEDNESDAY – *18.2.42*
On past the half-way house on the Alexandria–Cairo road. Arrived at military camp called Cowal Camp, near Mena and in full view of the pyramids. Our tents are pitched on hilly ground covered with shingle.

And so we came back to our base, after our short, catastrophic expedition into the desert, during which we were in contact with the enemy little more than a week!

CHAPTER 3

Cairo and the Pyramids

WHILE awaiting replacements of men and vehicles, we had a fair amount of free time and were able to visit the city, about four miles distant. There were many clubs for the forces, where we were served by Egyptian waiters, our favourite one being the New Zealand Forces Club. The cinemas were modern and well-designed, except that most of the seats were simply of polished wood, with no padding at all, possibly to avoid gathering bugs!

On our first night out, a few of us missed the truck back to camp, so we took a taxi. The taxi-driver's English was no better than our Arabic but I discovered he spoke French, so we got along quite well with that!

Our mail began to come through again fairly regularly but one letter I received on 19th February had been posted on 23rd September. Five months on the way! Fortunately, this was exceptional. The usual time was about three weeks and some of the recently introduced "Airgraphs" were even quicker.

On Sunday, 22nd February, having the half day free, Ron Taylor and I went to see the pyramids, the only surviving Wonder of the World. As we came nearer to these massive monuments, so our feeling of awe increased. It was as if the ponderous weight of countless ages hung over us. More than 4,800 years ago, many thousands of slaves had toiled under the lash, in a scorching sun, week after week, year after year, dragging the huge blocks of stone into position, to build a pharaoh's tomb.

The noise of their labour had faded with them into the dim past but, here before us, their work still stood, as it had stood for thousands of years – towering, silent, immutable.

The Great Pyramid of Cheops (or Khufu) covers an area of thirteen acres and, although from a distance the surface appears like a series of broken steps, we discovered as we approached that the "steps" were chest-high! the average weight of each stone block is two and a half

Winter sports in Cairo.
(Photo, Black Star)

tons, and they are of coarse limestone. This coarse limestone was quarried from a plateau on which the pyramid stands but originally there was a smooth coating of finer limestone, which came from the other side of the Nile. Succeeding races removed this outer casing and used it to build other structures.

We decided to climb the outside first, in case we had no energy to do so later, so round we went to the famous "Tourist's Corner", which is the easiest ascent. We went up steadily at first, heaving ourselves over the stone blocks, moving from side to side as we tried to find the smaller "steps", or pulling each other over the bigger ones – but it was warm work and our pace slackened gradually. Half way up, we stopped for a few minutes rest. We were already over 200 feet above the ground and the people below were beginning to look quite small. More than half an hour after we had started, we clambered on to the top.

We were now standing on a flat space, about twelve yards square and 450 feet up. Before the top stones were removed, the pyramid rose to a point 480 feet high. A tripod of wooden poles has been erected to show what the original height was. The view from this platform is really worth the climb.

Next to us, like a twin mountain, stood the pyramid of Khefren, with part of the polished casing still to be seen around its apex. The third pyramid, the tomb of Mankhara (Mycerinus) which is much smaller, lay behind Khefren. To the north, the dark green of the Delta stretched out, only to stop short, as if trimmed with a knife, where the sand began. And the sand continued, away to the west, as far as the eye could see, its parched monotony unbroken save by an occasional red dune.

To the east, across the Nile, we could see the ancient quarries, bitten out of the Mokattam hills, from whence came the stone used to cover the pyramids. Strange to relate, large quantities of stone were taken from Giza back across the river to these same hills, when Saladin built the Citadel, overlooking Cairo, in the twelfth century.

South, we looked along the glistening Nile, with its narrow strip of vegetation on each bank to where, fifteen miles away, stood the Step pyramid at Sakkara, the oldest large monument in the world, being about 5,000 years old. The huge corrugations or "steps" which give it its name were clearly visible from our high vantage point. The tombs of Sakkara are the cemetery of the ancient city of Memphis. For some reason, all the pyramids of Egypt have been built only on the west bank of the Nile.

Below us, near the pyramid on which we stood, was an area of smaller tombs, looking for all the world like rows of clay ovens and, a little further off, in a hollow, lay the Sphinx, its back half-turned towards us, as it gazed stonily away towards the wide river.

In the stone beneath our feet were carved hundreds of names. I saw the name of a sapper of the Royal Engineers, with the date 1917. There were many names in Greek lettering, carved by the earliest tourists to climb the pyramid, 2,000 years ago! One of these ancient Greeks had neatly engraved his name, about a yard long, with letters six inches high and deeply cut into the stone.

Surely this is the oldest "visitors' book" in the world! Unfortunately, having forgotten my chisel, I could not sign!

When we had had our fill of this absorbing scene, we began the descent, dropping or jumping from one block to another, down towards the tiny, white-clothed figures of the native guides far below.

Having reached the ground, we now wanted to go inside the pyramid. On the north side, the original entrance can be seen and, lower down, the robber's entrance, which is the one now used. With an Egyptian *dragoman*, we went up to this opening and entered a narrow, dark passage.

This was where the Turkish robbers had broken their way in during the fourteenth century, to steal the treasures of the tomb.

At one time, electric light was fitted in the Great Pyramid for the benefit of visitors but there was a fire not long before the war which, I suppose, destroyed the wiring. Anyway, our guide lit a stump of candle and, with this eerie, flickering light, we proceeded into the silent depths of the tomb itself.

After we had gone some little way, we came to a wider passage, where the candle threw our shadows, grotesquely enlarged, on the walls. Looking back, I could see no daylight, as the narrow passage was crooked. The wider passage, which was squarely built, went straight ahead but, at the left side, another gallery rose up in a steep slope, still in a forward direction. Up this sloping gallery our guide led us.

There was a wooden railing and, on the sloping stone surface, wooden planking with spars laid across to provide a foothold for visitors. As we climbed up, the *dragoman* held the candle high and gave us facts and figures as he went, his voice echoing back down the gallery.

At last the way became level again as we approached the burial chamber. The ancients had sealed the tomb by lowering three great granite slabs across the passage, forming a triple door, but these slabs had been smashed and all that could now be seen was the series of grooves in the walls of the passage, where the slabs had come down from a cavity above. Each groove was about six inches wide, but the edges were badly chipped.

So we walked forward into the inner chamber, where the candle failed to pierce the gloom at the far end. This was the King's Chamber, oblong in shape and lined with red granite which came from Aswan, 500 miles away. It was no small room, being 34 ft. long, 17 ft. wide and 19 ft. high.

In the middle of the floor lay the empty sarcophagus. It, too, is of red granite but the lid is gone and the edges are chipped and broken. The mummified remains of Cheops himself lie in the British Museum.

Now we were right in the heart of the pyramid and completely isolated from the outer world and all modern inconveniences. It was as if we ourselves had been transported back through the distant ages – as if we were again *living* in the days of Ancient Egypt and could sense its might and majesty in our environment. All around us was stone – something like six million tons of it! Yet the air was fresh and the candle still burned. Our guide showed us why.

In one wall was a small opening and the duct from this, our *dragoman* said, led a crooked path right to the outer surface of the pyramid. Its purpose was to allow the spirit of the dead Pharaoh to come and go at will.

So here was another race that believed in life after death (just as all Christians do) and also believed in spirit return.

As the candle was held near the opening, the flame leaned towards it, showing that air from the passage was going out that way.

In the floor at one end of the chamber, we were now shown a cavity: 3 ft. wide, 3 ft. deep and from 12 to 15 ft. long. This had once been filled with gold and jewellery, the king's treasure, which had been buried with him and which the robbers had sought – and found. What shouts of glee must have resounded in the pyramid as they ran their fingers through this hoard, or gazed with frenzied eyes at some glittering trinket held aloft! Even then, 600 years ago, the treasure had been undisturbed for over 4,000 years – the material treasure that no man can take beyond the grave.

The granite walls of the chamber were formed of huge slabs, one as much as 13 ft. long. In one corner, we saw that they were actually interlocked in a rough form of dove-tail! The surface of the granite was polished as flat and smooth as a sheet of glass.

The *dragoman* wanted to give us a better idea of the size of the burial chamber and, to draw our attention to the roof, which is spanned by long blocks of stone, so he now produced his *"pièce de résistance"*, a bit of magnesium wire with which (for an extra *piastre*) he proposed to illuminate our surroundings. From the folds of his *galabia* came a flat stone and, placing the magnesium on this, he lit it with the candle. As it flared and reflected from the polished walls, we had a glimpse of the full length of the chamber and noted the unsupported stretch of the roof. This massive roof of stone is estimated to weight over 100 tons – and above it rises the apex of the pyramid, which would be about 200 feet above our heads.

How such a tremendous mass was ever raised into position may well be a matter for wonder!

Still wondering, we emerged from the King's Chamber and came back down the sloping gallery. After the sudden glare of magnesium, the candle light seemed dimmer than ever. I noticed, too, that there was little more than an inch of candle left and had visions of us stumbling around in pitch blackness soon. However, as we reached the level passage below, we turned again towards the middle of the pyramid, to see the Queen's Chamber. After walking perhaps seventy yards along the passage, we reached it and found it was similar to the King's Chamber but smaller and there was another treasure cavity about the same size as the one we had seen.

Returning along the straight passage and through the narrow, crooked one, we saw daylight ahead and came out, blinking, into the sunshine. There is a third chamber, that of the High Priest, which is cut out of the rock below the Great Pyramid but our guide informed us that it was water-filled and dangerous and so had been closed.

We now went round the base of the pyramid to have a look at the other tombs, our *dragoman* leading the way with great dignity. Along one side, sand had once drifted up but this had been recently excavated, to reveal a large cavity cut down into the rock where, it is believed, the pharaoh's galley was brought to rest, so that he could use it in the next world!

The lower stones of the pyramid, now uncovered, were of a lighter, sandy colour, while the rest of the pyramid is brown.

Besides the three great pyramids, there are six smaller ones at Giza and we saw some of them – rather broken in appearance – together with other tombs of lesser royalty. We were shown hieroglyphics and pictures of stiff, conventional figures, carved in smooth limestone, with traces of pigment remaining and then we were taken to a square tomb with a roof about a foot thick, which was lying at an angle, leaving a gap of a few inches at the edge.

This, said the *dragoman*, was the tomb of one of the prime ministers of ancient Egypt. Producing another piece of candle from his *galabia* (that voluminous hold-all!) he lit it and held it to the gap under the stone roof of the tomb.

We peered into the opening and there, grinning at us, was the P.M. himself, just a skeleton lying on a stone slab!

The *dragoman* now left us to return to the Great Pyramid – having received his fee – and we continued towards the Sphinx.

As we walked round the edge of the hollow where lies this colossal sculpture, we noticed a row of openings cut in a wall of rock, the entrances to another series of tombs, but they all seemed to be empty.

We were fortunate in seeing the Sphinx completely exposed for, in past years, the sand lay around its shoulders and earlier photographs show it was once right up round the neck. The sand has now been excavated and the Sphinx sits surrounded by rock walls. There is a stone causeway in front of the paws, which are themselves 8 ft. high.

Some parts, including the paws and the tail, are built up of masonry but the greater part of the lion's body is carved from solid rock. The total height is about 60 ft. and the head is a potrait of Khefren, the pharaoh who was buried in the second pyramid. The nose is gone, believed to have been knocked off by a cannon-ball fired during Napoleon's campaign against the Mamelukes.

Between the paws is an open-air temple, where a large slab of black basalt is erected, almost against the lion's chest.

And the Riddle of the Sphinx? Well, legend says that a sphinx which lived at Thebes used to kill all who failed to solve the crucial conundrum – *"What goes on four legs, then two legs, and lastly on three legs?"*

I have never heard how many thousands of years were supposed to pass before one, Oedipus, hit on the answer, which is – *"Man"* (crawling in childhood, walking in manhood, and leaning on a stick in decrepitude!).

Which reminds me that there is also a verse, recited amongst soldiers, which professes to explain the inscrutable smile of the Sphinx.

But I'd better not quote that one!

Not far from the Sphinx stand the remains of a granite structure which used to be called the Temple of the Sphinx but which was really an elaborate gateway to the causeway which leads up to the second pyramid.

Nearby, there is a conduit built by the ancients, which still fills with water from the Nile when it rises (in September).

This finished our afternoon of sight-seeing, which we felt had been well worth while and we returned to camp.

Next day, we were granted five days' leave, Ron and I to go together, so that evening we put up at a hostel called Littoral House, just off Soliman Pasha Street, one of the main streets of Cairo. Here we revelled in clean sheets (a pleasant change from our skin-irritating blankets), clean towels, plenty of water and quite good service and meals for the rest of the week.

We were not long in continuing our sight-seeing. On our first day out we had a look at the Royal Abdin Palace of Farouk. We were not impressed. The Royal Guard looked slack and slovenly, in spite of their broad red sashes adorned with brass crescents and stars.

Then we went up towards the Citadel, the way taking us between two mosques, that of Sultan Hasan, built in the fourteenth century and the modern mosque of El Rifai (built in 1912) which stands on the opposite side of the street. This latter mosque contains the tombs of the Khedive Ismail and King Fuad.

A little way further on, we came to the Citadel, begun in 1176 by Sultan Salah el Din (Saladin), who fought against the Crusaders led by Richard I. Passing between the drum towers guarding the entrance, we walked up through this mediaeval fortress till we came to an open space before the Mohammed Ali Mosque, whose minarets tower above the Citadel. It was this mosque, known as the Alabaster Mosque, that we had come to see.

The mosque is comparatively modern, having been completed in 1867 and it was restored shortly before our arrival in Egypt.

A guide gave us large slippers to put on over our boots, because dirt from outside must never soil the floor of the house of Allah. The guide himself simply removed his sandals and proceeded in his bare feet.

Crossing the courtyard leading to the door of the mosque, I noticed that the whole area was paved with Carrara marble! The guide remarked, "Italian marble, good – but Mussolini, he's a washout!"

As we entered the mosque, the *dragoman* kept his *tazfira* on his head

The Citadel and Mohamed Ali Mosque, Cairo.

but we removed our hats, for Allah by any other name is still God, and that was *our* way of showing respect.

So we went in, perhaps in a better state than he, since we were prepared at both ends!

The interior of the mosque is very beautiful. A thousand crystal lamps hang from wide iron hoops, suspended by chains which soar away to the coloured and gilded dome. The central lamp is a huge chandelier covered with little pieces of cut crystal, like a mass of glittering icicles. These lamps are lit only during Ramadan, the Mohammedan month of fasting. Persian carpets cover the floor and there are two pulpits, one presented by King Farouk. It is made of alabaster and granite, with bronze gates decorated with gold leaf. In one corner is the tomb of Mohammed Ali, surrounded by a railing.

The walls of the mosque are panelled in alabaster, cream coloured, with a maroon grain. Each panel consists of two "slices" of alabaster placed together so that the grain forms a symmetrical design. One panel was pointed out to us as having a similarity to a map of Australia.

In the wall near the altar, one of the alabaster pillars rotates when thrust by the fingers. This lets the blind know when they have reached the altar.

Then we went outside and the guide showed us the fort built by Napoleon's orders on a nearby hill and took us into the Old Palace of Mohammed Ali, the Albanian who became Khedive of Egypt and founded the present Egyptian Royal Family.

It was Mohammed Ali who presented Cleopatra's Needle to the British Nation. His palace was used by the Red Cross during the First World War. We were shown the bath of the Khedive's ladies, which was also used by the "Tommies" with, I imagine, many facetious remarks! It was an oval of reddish marble set into the floor, little more than three feet long.

From an open space near the palace, we had a fine view of the city, old and new, sweeping away to the Nile, dotted with the domes and minarets of 400 mosques and, in between, the cracked and broken walls of the hovels where live the native people.

The guide had apparently noticed my accent, for he suddenly asked if I was Scottish and told me he had once lived in Paisley!

Then I was treated to the surprise of hearing the dusky Egyptian *dragoman* saying, "Keep yer eye on Paisley, Jock!" This is a saying which came into being in Victorian times, when Paisley was the key town in a parliamentary election. He also brought out a few other phrases, such as "Ah waant some hoat watter!" in broad Glasgow dialect!

The rest of our leave was spent in exploring the city itself and enjoying the amenities of the various Forces Clubs.

We made great use of the little yellow tramcars, touring around the outskirts to save walking. On one trip, we glimpsed El Azhar, which began as a mosque and became a university in the tenth century. It is now the largest Mohammedan university in the world.

Another thing Cairo can claim is that its Zoo is one of the three largest in the world, being about the same size as the London and Berlin Zoos. Cairo Zoo, however, has the advantage over the others, in that the climate suits the tropical animals better, so that many more of them are seen in the open. In one place, the hippos wallowed in the water and, in another, crocodiles lay like logs, basking in the sun. Nearby was exhibited another crocodile, which was mummified by the ancients, thousands of years ago. To me it looked exactly the same as its descendants lying so still below, completely indifferent to their aged ancestor up on the wall. Maybe they were saying, "Huh! He was just a reptile anyway!"

Unfortunately, the treasures of the Egyptian Museum, which include those from Tut-Ankh-Amun's tomb, had been removed to a place of safety for the duration of the war, so we were unable to see them.

One street which became a byword with the troops in Cairo was the one known as Wagh el Birket (Way of the Slaves), the home of brothels. The stone steps leading to these places were worn down in deep hollows by the feet of past generations – but how the ugly, painted women who stood in the doorways, flashing their gold teeth, could attract anyone, was beyond comprehension.

As I have said, the main streets of Cairo are beautiful and modern but, as soon as you leave them, you are in narrow, twisted lanes of dilapidated buildings which, in a more sanitary land, would be condemned wholesale. Some streets of bazaars were certainly picturesque enough in their own way. Balconies and box-like bay windows jutted out from uneven walls above the shops, while sign-boards reached into the narrow way, almost touching those which came from the other side and proclaiming their owner's superiority in a mixture of Arabic, English and French. Dirty blinds hung down outside the bazaars and beneath them moved the motley throng: black-robed women with only their eyes showing; men in white or striped *galabias*; Greeks, Jews, and a dozen other nationalities, including men and women in Western clothes; fat Egyptians in light tropical suits which seemed ready to burst; skinny Egyptians, whose clothes hung as though on a scarecrow, with a red *tarboosh* on the head; and children, scampering about as children do the world over but here with bare feet; or those too small to walk, curly-headed mites, being carried by their mothers, sitting astride one shoulder and holding on to the black-veiled head.

Sometimes, at the end of such a street, would appear one of the many mosques, somewhat more solidly built than the surrounding dwelling-houses. Once, I saw a Moslem funeral procession on its way to the cemetery. As the hired mourners chanted and howled, the bearers carried the coffin carelessly on their shoulders, at any angle at all and, when they felt tired, the coffin was simply laid on the pavement while they had a rest! The procession halted, too, but the wailing noise went on. Then after a while, the coffin would be raised again and the procession would shuffle on.

And, when the velvet dusk came swiftly down, how often we heard, from some minaret, the whining voice of the *muezzin* calling the faithful to prayer, always a nasal sing-song in a plaintive minor key, yet curiously peaceful at the end of the day.

Our leave over, we returned to duty on Sunday, 1st March and, although we could still spend our evenings in the clubs and cinemas of Cairo, we knew that in a few weeks we would be returning to the desert.

The battalion was again training, one company now being fitted out with 2-pounder anti-tank guns. Lost vehicles were being quickly replaced and in our detachment we soon had a new officer and several other ranks to take the place of those missing. Bill Shorter, cured of his colic, had come from hospital to rejoin us. Lieutenant "Nobby" Clark and his driver, Bill Willis, had been officially notified as prisoners and the others, also believed to be prisoners, were Q.M.S. Pryke, Dick Stone-hewer, little "Titch" Hartland and Alf Cansell.

Soon, we began preparing to move again. We had been transferred into the famous 7th Armoured Division, the "Desert Rats", a proud title even then, long before El Alamein. Formed at Mersa Matruh in 1938 from the Cairo Cavalry Brigade and several other units, including the 11th Hussars ("Cherry-Pickers"), the 7th Armoured Division was already a hard-bitten and experienced formation of desert fighters.

So now we too could call ourselves Desert Rats, the name taken from the *jerboa*, the little fawn-coloured animal found in the coastal areas of the desert. It is about five inches high, has big ears, short front legs and long back ones, on which it hops swiftly like a tiny kangaroo. The tail is longer than the body and ends in a black and white tuft. It was not chosen as the emblem of the division because of any fierceness for, unlike these sun-tanned "sweats", it was quite timid. Rather it was chosen because, like us, it lived in holes in the sand!

CHAPTER 4

Bir Hacheim

Towards the end of March, we were ready to return to the Libyan front, where the enemy had regained considerable ground, and the line lay somewhere near Mekhili and to the west of Bir Hacheim. We had now been supplied with little bivouacs, which made sleeping a little more comfortable. I again revert to my diary:

FRIDAY – 27.3.42
Goodbye to Cheops, Khefren and Mankhara, as we head north to Alexandria. We now carry the sign of the jerboa or desert rat on our shoulders and on the vehicles. I travel on a small Chev. truck. The big recovery has been replaced by a Dodge, built to British specification.

SATURDAY – 28.3.42
Laager near Mersa Matruh. Bivouac quite comfortable. Had real desert rat for company during the night.

SUNDAY – 29.3.42
A.E.C. has stripped a vernier coupling to the magneto. Several other repairs have already been done.

MONDAY – 30.3.42
Books available from "Regimental Library" which simply consists of two large boxes of books.

TUESDAY – 31.3.42
Reached Halfaya. Sollum Bay looks lovely from height of escarpment in sunshine as the blue Mediterranean breaks on the shore.

WEDNESDAY – 1.4.42
Laager with battalion, where we will be for some time. Digging-in bivvies, etc. parched with thirst and tasting again the dust of Libya. All very peaceful at night, with a full moon over the desert.

THURSDAY – 2.4.42
Changing tyres on Dodge recovery. Made a crude oil lamp to use in bivvy.

FRIDAY – 3.4.42
Weather very hot. Have found several limestone fossils of scallops and other shell-fish, showing that the desert has at one time been a sea-bed.

SATURDAY – 4.4.42
Took "Staff" B (whom we had given a lift from base) to his unit near Fort Capuzzo. Navigated 25 miles back across the desert alone.

SUNDAY – 5.4.42
Easter Sunday. No eggs. Darn little rations and only 12 gals. water amongst 18 men: for cooking, drinking, washing, etc. Could only half fill our water-bottles.

MONDAY – 6.4.42
More repairs. Bedford axle. Heat terrific. Sun blazing out of the blue and desert shimmering all round; waves of heat rising to distort the horizon.

TUESDAY – 7.4.42
Went to Bir Uarr to draw drinking water, then to Bir el Barrani for washing water. At the latter there is an underground cavern full of water, which contains small transparent fish, about an inch long, with the backbone clearly visible! One of the boys tried the acoustics of the cavern by yodelling. Nearby, amongst piled rocks, were several Arab graves, the grinning skulls and bones sticking out of the sand.

Most of these "wells" were just natural storage tanks, gathering drainage from a wide area of desert. Usually the only sign from a distance would be a pile of stones marking an Arab graveyard; or a mound, if digging had been necessary to reach the rock surface. At Bir el Barrani, the narrow opening had been cut down through two feet of rock in the roof of the cavern. A pile of rocks below gave foothold at the edge of the water but we hoisted the water to the surface in tins and simply had a wash-down where we stood. The water was not safe for drinking unless treated. At some wells, the sappers pumped the water up into canvas tanks, where alum was added to settle the fine, pink mud (which otherwise floated indefinitely) and then chlorine went in to make it "drinkable". However, with the two chemicals in the water, if you made tea, it often curdled! As Bir el Barrani was about thirty-five miles from the nearest part of the coast, I was greatly surprised to find those tiny fishes swimming about in it!

THURSDAY – *9.4.42*
Took some more chaps for a bath at Bir el Barrani, and filled as many spare cans as possible.

FRIDAY – *10.4.42*
Collected tea, sugar, tinned fruit, peas, beans, milk and sausages from P.R.I., to value of 40 piastres which almost wipes out my credit.

SATURDAY – *11.4.42*
On the move. Laager in close formation till dawn.

SUNDAY – *12.4.42*
Stationary south of El Adem.

MONDAY – *13.4.42*
Busy on repairs. Timing wrong on Morris wireless van.

TUESDAY – *14.4.42*
Drove to El Gubi for water. Met a French sailor who said he belonged to Dieppe!

WEDNESDAY – *15.4.42*
German Mercedes gun-tractor passed by, the first I have seen captured in running order. Wheels in front and tracks behind under armoured body.

THURSDAY – *16.4.42*
Repairs on another wireless truck. Hot Khamseen blowing, with clouds of dust. Wrecks of five Italian tanks not far off, the remains of burnt men in more than one. White metal from bearings has run out on to the sand like pools of solder.

FRIDAY – *17.4.42*
Sent to find well at Bir Duedar, eleven miles SE. Brought back eighty gallons of water, earthy but drinkable. Had a "bath" in a biscuit-tin. The Khamseen still blowing hot. No relief till sundown.

The *Khamseen* wind comes from the heart of the desert, like a blast from a furnace, drying the skin, cracking the lips and bringing with it the inevitable, gritty dust. The difficulties of working with the oily moving parts of an engine, gearbox, or wheel-bearing can be imagined, with this grit always liable to stick where least desired.

Khamseen is the Arabic word for 'fifty' and the natives say that the wind blows during a period of fifty days.

SATURDAY – *18.4.42*
Move to El Adem area. Found Italian Terni rifle, complete with bolt. Renovating same in hope of finding some ammo.

SUNDAY – *19.4.42*
Repair broken spring on Chev. (our own). Found supply of ammo. for the Italian rifle, but 75 per cent of it dud. Had some target practice at tin cans.

MONDAY – *20.4.42*
Drew water from well by the El Adem–Gambut road. Picked up a damaged Browning machine-gun, two Italian rifles, old-fashioned Terni and Brescia types and a crate of ammo. Some aerial activity overhead.

TUESDAY – *21.4.42*
More vehicle repairs. Dates on "Eyetie" rifles are 1880, 1890 and one marked "Riparato" (repaired) 1920! They are 8 in. longer than ours, heavy at the muzzle and the bore is 6.5 mm. More aerial activity. Big ack-ack barrage over Tobruk.

THURSDAY – *23.4.42*
Visit El Adem. Not far from the aerodrome is the grave of an Italian air captain, with a striking monument. A skeleton model of a 'plane in metal is built into an obelisk, so that the wings, nose and tail protrude for several feet on each side.

In the late afternoon, a great wall of dust rolled overland like a red tidal wave and a fierce sandstorm ensued.

This was indeed a tremendous sight. The approaching sand looked like a gigantic purple-red curtain, towering several hundred feet in the air and stretching as far as the eye could see on either side. It appeared to be moving slowly, until I saw a truck trying to escape it! The driver accelerated on the bumpy track until he was bouncing along at close on forty miles an hour yet, as I watched, the storm swept up behind the truck and engulfed it! We hurriedly piled stones on each peg holding down our bivouacs, tied handkerchiefs round nose and mouth, put on anti-gas eyeshields and pulled our caps down firmly on our heads. Nearer came the mass, until it seemed suddenly to be racing upon us. There was a rustle, then a swish and papers swirled up into the air higher and higher. The sun was blotted out and, with a growl, the storm tore through the camp and we were in the midst of stinging sand and dust while canvas flapped, trucks creaked and rattled and rubbish flew past. Gone was the blue sky of a moment before and we could scarcely see two yards. No work could be done and most of us were glad to creep into our bivouacs, though even in these the wind gouged a way under the walls, for the sand to stream in.

Fortunately, next day all was clear – but bare patches of ground showed where the sand had been swept away.

FRIDAY – *24.4.42*
Our officer took us to the "Med" for a swim. Traversed a tortuous track down steep wadi east of Tobruk, where we swam in a lovely cove. Two graves on the beach, with wooden crosses.

SATURDAY – *25.4.42*
Other "Eyetie" rifle now working. Stacks of ammo. Aerial activity over Tobruk. Terrific ack-ack barrage. More repairs – Chevrolet brakes.

SUNDAY – *26.4.42*
Testing Browning. Fired three rounds O.K., but the fourth burst out at the breech with a flash, bending the metal cover. Good job we pulled the trigger with a length of wire!

MONDAY – *27.4.42*
One Italian rifle barrel is blocked by a jammed round but have fitted another barrel dated 1874! This is the best of three now in working order but not one of them is accurate.

Playing around with these antiques was one way of keeping our minds occupied. Otherwise, one day was just the same as another. If I had not kept a diary, I would never have known what date to put on a letter home. Usually the others didn't know what day it was!

TUESDAY – *28.4.42*
Repairs on 2-pounder gun.

WEDNESDAY – *29.4.42*
Received Airgraph saying Uncle A. is missing, believed prisoner of the Japanese.

(This uncle eventually died of dysentery in Borneo, without proper medical attention and with only a few months to go before the Japanese capitulated.)

> *Strong wind at night, driving sand into bivouac. Put cap on to sleep, in hope of keeping hair reasonably clean.*
>
> THURSDAY – *30.4.42*
> *Pillow and blankets smothered in sand – nose and ears full – teeth gritting. Breakfast also gritty. So ends April in a land I will always associate with grit. As I write this, empty petrol tins go bowling merrily by in the howling wind, while a dim figure staggers through the dust looking like an Arctic explorer in a blizzard. When we open a tin of margarine, we can pour it on the bread as liquid. Later, the wind changes round, bringing all the sand and dust back again (as if we wanted it!).*
>
> FRIDAY – *1.5.42*
> *Visit "A" Company. One of the boys – ex 1st Battalion – has a little dog, formerly Italian owned, from Tobruk, where it was found in the first push. Has had it over a year. Goodness knows how he has managed to feed the poor little thing.*
>
> SATURDAY – *2.5.42.*
> *Found snake in bivouac. Chased it with a machete and cut off its head as it poised. About two feet long, grey with purple markings, glossy yellow underneath.*

This was probably a sand-snake and harmless but I didn't fancy having it in bed with me, nevertheless! There were some venomous types, of which we had been warned, particularly the asp. A man bitten by an asp, we were told, had about four minutes to live, unless drastic action was taken. The wound had to be slashed, the poison sucked out and crystals of soda or permanganate of potash inserted. Then the man would be rushed off in the hope of reaching one of the hospitals with the right serum before it was too late.

We always had to examine our blankets before getting between them for, besides snakes, there were other unpleasant things about, such as: scorpions, tarantulas, camel ticks and scarabs. As Shakespeare said in *The Tempest*, "Misery acquaints a man with strange bedfellows!"

Went sick with – of all things – lumbago! The M.O. said it was due to perspiring during the hot day, then being chilled in the evening.

WEDNESDAY – *6.5.42*

Back on duty, collecting springs from blacksmith's "shop" in the open air and fitting same.

THURSDAY – *7.5.42*

Go to Tobruk, getting canned milk, etc. at the Y.M.C.A. Several sunken ships in the harbour. Church in piazza now unsafe. The town must have been a picturesque sight from the other side of the harbour once, before it was smashed. There is now a large war cemetery on the outskirts.

SUNDAY – *10.5.42*

Saw big Savoia-Marchetti troop plane grounded. Now moving towards Bir Hacheim. Gave lift to French Foreign Legionnaire returning to front from hospital. He had been wounded by machine-gun fire from "Jerry" aircraft and got the Croix de Guerre for sticking to his post. He showed me the certificate of award and family photos from Nice, his home. We laager ten miles west of Bir Hacheim. Gunfire heard occasionally.

TUESDAY – *12.5.42*

Now static. Working on decarbonizing job.

WEDNESDAY – *13.5.42*

"Jerry" plane over. Two engines and twin tails. Bofors made him dodge. After firing Italian rifles at a large can, walked over to find a Primus stove inside! What a find!

What a find indeed. This meant we could now "brew-up" inside the truck in the evenings for, of course, no camp-fire could be allowed to show after dark. The amusing bit was that the can – about the shape and size of a hat-box – lay 100 yards away, where it must have fallen from some passing convoy and the Italian rifles were so inaccurate that not one bullet had struck it! If we had used our own rifles, it would have been riddled. As we approached the can, we thought it might be a booby-trap (you never knew in the desert) so we threw stones at it until it rolled over, meanwhile ducking cautiously! When there was no big bang, we opened it and *voilà*! The Primus, completely undamaged.

THURSDAY – *14.5.42*
Working only morning and evening due to intense heat.

SATURDAY – *16.5.42*
Moving back, while "Jerry" planes watch from high above. Stopped for truck which had broken down – lost the column, so took both trucks to Bir Hacheim.

This was all we could do for, as usual, we had not been given the slightest indication as to where we were going. We hoped to get some directions at the fort. And what a difference we found when we got there! It was no longer just an isolated building. Minefields and barbed wire stretched far and wide and all over the higher ground the French troops, including many of the Foreign Legion, had dug themselves in, in quite a big way. As our Staff Sergeant spoke no French, he got me to talk to the sentries, one of whom took us through the wire to his *Capitaine*, who was in a huge dug-out with maps and a telephone on the table. Having heard our story, he spoke to someone over the 'phone and then ordered a coloured D.R. to be our guide on his motor-cycle. We were led quite a distance along a winding track until we stopped at another dugout, where we found a British Liaison Officer. Now we got directions to our own Divisional H.Q., somewhere to the east of Bir Hacheim.

Emerging from the rear of the defences, we followed another track for a mile or two and reached H.Q., 7th Armoured Division. Here the Staff Sergeant was questioned, while we waited. Finally, he came back to us with one of those "escape" compasses, no larger than a sixpence, which were sometimes used when a man had to make his way over the desert alone, perhaps from behind enemy lines. We had no map but were to follow a certain compass bearing for six miles, when we should be in the battalion area. This we did and found one of the companies but we had to go another two miles in a different direction before we found the L.A.D.

SUNDAY – *17.5.42*
Woke today to find a tough little camel tick with its legs embedded in the flesh of my thigh. The legs stretched like threads as I pulled it off. I believe a better method is to hold a lighted match against the back of the insect, to make it withdraw its legs.

MONDAY – *18.5.42*
Went to Tobruk to collect stores, forty-five miles each way. Had a meal in R.A.O.C. dining hall. "Jerry" plane chased by ack-ack. Bought stamps from Army P.O. which is in the Cassa di Risparmio della Libia (Libyan Savings Bank).

TUESDAY – *19.5.42*
Going to job at H.Q., we passed the scattered remains of a plane, with the grave of an R.A.F. pilot nearby. He had been killed early in 1941, yet parts of the engine and framework of the plane lay on the dusty ground as if it had happened only a week before.

WEDNESDAY – *20.5.42*
Washing clothes – in petrol. Weather now very pleasant – sunny but breezy and cool. Some of the companies have been in action in mobile columns, this time without the L.A.D. Two wounded.

THURSDAY – *21.5.42*
Sat up till midnight listening to news and music direct from London on a radio truck on which we are working.

Then, on Friday, 22nd May, I suddenly became a casualty when a detonator burst in my hands. It happened just too simply. I had picked up the detonator from the ground, not being aware that the heat of your hand can sometimes set these things off. This one had been well baked by the desert sun before I disturbed it. When there was a sharp crack, I looked round, thinking it came from somewhere else. When I looked at my hands again, I realised they were in a mess. The top had gone from the thumb of the left hand and the first finger looked like a split banana-skin, with the bone sticking up in the middle. The right hand was also damaged.

I called to the only man within reach to bring a field dressing but he didn't know where his own was, so I told him where to find mine. This was wrapped clumsily around the left hand, then I got on a truck which was to take me to the battalion M.O.

Our officer directed that my kit be put aboard too, for it was obvious that I would not be back for some time – and off we went. My rifle, however, was left with the unit, for no arms may be carried under the sign of the Red Cross.

So now I was to get another experience I hadn't bargained for – an insight into the workings of our medical services in the field!

The truck bumped its way along the usual dusty track for a mile or so but the M.O. was apparently away on other business, so we were advised to go on to the M.O. of another regiment (I think it was the Rifle Brigade) about six miles away.

By this time, my left eye had become painful and vision was blurred and misty, so I realised it had been damaged as well and I was considerably more worried about that than my hands, in which the pain was deadened by numbness.

On we went and, after asking for directions at various groups of trucks, we spotted a motor ambulance and found the M.O. and his orderly nearby. Removing the field-dressing, the M.O. said, "Ah! Mmmmm!" just like any other doctor then set seriously to work to bandage the hands properly and put a bandage over the eye as well.

It had all happened late in the day and, as the sun was near to setting, the man who had brought me along set out on his return journey in case he lost his way in the dark – which was all too easy to do when the track consisted simply of tyre-marks in the sand! For the same reason, I could not be taken to a field-hospital that night but slept in the ambulance, after getting morphia.

Next day I reached a field hospital, where I was taken to a collapsible caravan which served as an operating theatre. I was given an injection, which I thought must be the usual heart-strengthener before a general anaesthetic but the doctors, three of them, with white masks, just stood looking at me in complete silence and I wondered, "When are they going to get busy? Why don't they give me the anaesthetic?" The 'jag', however, must have been Pentothal, for all my nerves were completely relaxed and I began to feel quite soothed and contented, without a care in the world.

I awoke in a marquee, beside other patients, all lying on stretchers and realised that it was all over and I could not even remember "passing out" on the operating table. That was the best anaesthetic I ever had (and I have experienced several other kinds) for there were no head noises and no after-effects whatsoever – not even sickness. My left arm was now in a sling, the right hand bandaged and another bandage round my head covered the left eye. I was undoubtedly very fortunate that my injuries were not worse.

Afterwards, I was moved steadily across the desert in a relay of ambulances, stopping at various field dressing-stations. I noticed several cases of dysentery. Poor blighters! They didn't get much sleep. Others had been wounded in action and some were suffering from an overdose of "desert sores", persistent, festering ulcers, which appeared wherever the skin was broken and refused to heal, in spite of the sunshine. They made admirable feeding-places for the voracious flies.

I was taken on past El Adem and into Tobruk Hospital where I arrived about 25th May. The dressings, which had now been on my hands for three days, felt a bit tight and my hands were throbbing, so I asked if the dressings could be changed. I was put on a table and a doctor began to cut away the bandages, leaving the bits which were sticking to the dried blood around the stitches on my fingers. He had noted that I was Scottish and mentioned visiting the North. He asked if I knew a certain "pub" and, having set me thinking, he suddenly jerked the remains of the bandages from both hands at once. I gasped at the sharp pain and put my head back as a small trickle of blood ran down each wrist. When they were cleaned up and re-dressed, however, vaseline was added to prevent any further adhesion of the bandages.

I spent that night in a "ward" which had not a single pane of glass in any of its windows. If there *had* been any, it would have been blown out before morning anyway! Three times during the night, enemy bombers came over and there was a tremendous din as the heavy ack-ack (3.7 in.) blasted away all around us. At this time, the nursing sisters were still in Tobruk – I believe they were evacuated soon after – and occasionally they walked calmly and quietly between the beds where lay the helpless wounded. It was peculiarly soothing to see their dim figures moving about in the shadows while the building shook and shuddered to the fall of bombs and the rage of guns outside, bellowing their defiance to the skies.

Next day, I was taken to a hospital ship, the *Llandovery Castle*, in Tobruk Harbour. The ambulance, which brought me from the hospital down to the harbour, was one of those run by a group of United States volunteers, the first Americans in the war. I chatted with the orderly who came in the ambulance and learned that he was from Denver, Colorado. As the harbour was in a mess, I was taken out to the ship in a small landing-craft. How my stretcher was hoisted aboard, I cannot remember. When all the wounded and disabled were aboard, the ship sailed out on to the dazzling blue of the Mediterranean and we had a calm and uneventful voyage to Alexandria. Here, we were put upon a Red Cross train and eventually I found myself in Number 2 General Hospital at Qassassin, near Ismailia.

Even as I arrived (on 28th May) there were rumours of an enemy push in the desert and, the next day, the radio gave official news of fierce action around Bir Hacheim and El Adem. I thought of the fellows I had left. They must be in the middle of it!

Throughout Saturday and Sunday, a terrific tank battle was fought out, north of Bir Hacheim, near Knightsbridge (the Battle of the Cauldron). And what was "Knightsbridge"? Nothing! Just an ironic name for the crossing of some tracks made by army vehicles. Like so many place names in the desert, it was no more than a point on the map. The only landmark was an army sign consisting of two posts stuck into old steel drums. Between the posts was fixed a sheet of corrugated iron, partly flattened, on which was painted the name and map-reference (to the second decimal place) KNIGHTSBRIDGE, M.R. 37984118.

I am reminded of a poem which was found on a piece of paper blowing about on the desert. It was published as "anonymous" but I believe its authorship was later traced to a Guardsman who fought at Knightsbridge.

> "Stay with me, God. The night is dark.
> The night is cold: my little spark
> of courage dims. The night is long.
> Be with me, God, and make me strong.
>
> I love a game, I love a fight,
> I hate the dark; I love the light.
> I love my child; I love my wife ...
> I am no coward ... I love life ...
>
> Life, with its change of mood and shade,
> I want to live. I'm not afraid.
> But me and mine are hard to part.
> Oh Unknown God, lift up my heart!
>
> You stilled the waters at Dunkirk,
> And saved Your servants. All your work
> Is wonderful. Dear God, You strode
> Before us down that dreadful road.
>
> We were alone, and hope had fled.
> We loved our country and our dead
> And could not shame them; so we stayed
> The course, and were not much afraid.

Dear God, that nightmare road! And then
That sea! We got there – we were men.
My eyes were blind, my feet were torn –
My soul sang like a bird at dawn!

I knew that death is but a door;
I knew what we were fighting for –
Peace for the kids, our brothers freed,
A kinder world, a cleaner breed.

I'm but the son my mother bore,
A simple man and nothing more.
But – God of strength and gentleness –
Be pleased to make me nothing less!

Help me again when death is near,
To mock the haggard face of fear,
That when I fall, if fall I must,
My soul may triumph in the dust!"

CHAPTER 5

The Base Hospital and "T.K."

A T THE HOSPITAL, I was taken to the "eye" ward. Like most of the other wards, it was a large Nissen hut, but kept very clean and bright. The rows of beds had the usual military scarlet bed-covers and above each was suspended a mosquito-net which came down round the bed and was tucked in under the mattress at night.

At last, water was plentiful and the first thing that happened was that my dusty, sweaty clothes were removed and, as I could not bath myself, one of the sisters gave me a sponge bath. Then I was put to bed but later, after a doctor's inspection, I was allowed to become a walking patient. The bandage over my eye was replaced by an ordinary eye-shade but atropine was instilled to paralyse the ciliary muscle, so that I could not focus the eye and it was given a complete rest. I was to remain thus for ten days but I often found that, when I reached out for something, my estimate of distance was out by a couple of inches and I sometimes misjudged a step. As my optical training has since made clear to me, this was because I couldn't have proper stereoscopic vision with only one eye. Some of the other men in the ward were in a similar plight. One found that when he tapped the ash from his cigarette it landed outside the ash tray!

One young soldier, who had lost an eye, had been digging a slit-trench when he struck a land-mine and was blown yards away.

Soon, I was able to collect my kit from a store and put it in the locker beside my bed. Working with my right hand, which had some of the fingers free, I opened my valise, to discover that a pair of bathing trunks and a French dictionary were missing. Apparently someone had been busy while I lay on a stretcher.

There was a camp cinema near the hospital, which we were allowed to visit. It was one of those places built like a flimsy barn, with crude walls made of rough boarding, often with bits of bark still on it. Through the cracks in the walls, the sun would send bright shafts of light to illuminate the blue curls of smoke rising from the cigarettes of the boys in hospital blue. There was no roof, the space between the walls being simply covered with thin sack cloth, which certainly helped the ventilation. There were many such cinemas for the troops in Egypt and Palestine, most of them run by Shafto's United Film Service. Here again a particular piece of music is associated in my mind with this cinema, for they always played the *Marche Lorraine* as we waited for the show to commence.

I was soon friendly with the others in the ward, particularly a fellow-Scot from Edinburgh and a Mauritian called Émile Pastor who spoke more French than English. He was a pilot with a plane of his own, which he sometimes flew from Mauritius to the French island of Reunion. The Eighth Army was indeed a mixture of many races; it has been described as "... the most polyglot army the world has ever known". Once when I was at the cinema with Émile, he met another man he knew, a Spaniard, from a mixed Commando, also serving with the Eighth Army. This man spoke many languages, had been in Turkey, in France, in Algiers with the Foreign Legion and had taken part in the Spanish Civil War.

In the ward at night, I found it difficult to sleep at first because of the incessant noise of thousands of crickets outside! As soon as it was dark, their nightly mass concert began, a ringing noise like countless tiny files being struck together. Later, when I got used to it, it had quite a lulling effect upon me.

There were other sounds, however, that were not so cheerful. In the next ward, whose door faced ours, lay a coloured soldier of the French colonial forces, who had been severely burned by a petrol fire. In spite of a green dressing, his skin came off in sheets and we heard him moaning for several nights. He died, and the sister who told us said, he had not had the *will* to live. So, it befalls that if the spirit is not willing, no doctor can save the flesh.

During the day, there were two Egyptian orderlies to help with routine work in the ward. They were very willing and good-natured, especially one called Kemel. The fellows were always larking about with them, or playing jokes on them but they enjoyed the fun as much as anyone. Whenever somebody mentioned "Sister!" they would scuttle back to their duties, terrified lest they get a telling-off from the lady in grey. Kemel, who was only about twenty, had a wife and three of a family in faraway Luxor.

The surroundings of the hospital were dry and sandy, but we had plenty of water and a drinking supply was kept in a large chatty for each ward. The chatty was placed, not inside, but outside the door in the sun. Being porous, there was always a film of water on the outside surface and the quick evaporation of this film kept the rest of the water quite cool. One day, there was a shower of *rain* and some of the boys, who hadn't seen rain for many months, stripped to the waist and stood outside in it, just to feel it on their skins! Natives of Manchester and Greenock, please note!

There were in the ward two pet chameleons, whose job it was to keep down the number of flies, on which they feed. One thing I noticed about these queer reptiles was the fact that their eyes seem to move independently of each other, one forward and the other back, if necessary. Their bodies can change to various shades of green, grey or brown, to match the background they happen to be on. There is a tale in my native land that if you put one on a piece of tartan, it bursts! Be that as it may, our two chameleons seemed to have their likes and dislikes, for they hated red. When we put them on our scarlet bed-covers, they crawled off again as fast as they could go! Apparently they had no Communistic sympathies!

The tongue of the chameleon seems to be about nine or ten inches long and it is retracted in three folds inside the mouth, like the letter Z. If a fly settles within a foot of the reptile, nature's artillery, complete with camouflage, goes into action! First, the eyes swivel round, as if saying, "Target, enemy moving west. Zero one degree; two-o-minutes elevation." Then slowly, slowly, the head moves round, like the barrel of a gun but with infinitely more patience, lest the quarry be warned. The mouth opens, the fat, sticky end of the tongue appears, there is a flash, the body rocking under the recoil – and the fly vanishes!

When I could once more hold a pen in my hand, my diary was again kept up to date, so I will continue with extracts from it:

MONDAY – *15.6.42*
When we go to the pictures now, we are like Charlie Chan's family! Eight or nine of us line up like "disreputable offspring", while the native doorkeeper takes the bunch of tickets and counts us as we go in.

MONDAY – *22.6.42*
The Army is a League of Nations now. We have a Greek-speaking Cypriot and a Viennese Jew in our ward.

TUESDAY – *23.6.42*
Large convoy of wounded arriving. We helped to carry some of

them and their kit. They told me the K.R.R.C. are still on mobile column work. Tobruk has fallen and our forces are now back to the Egyptian border at Sollum and Halfaya.

WEDNESDAY – 24.6.42
In the cook-house there are several Palestinian A.T.S. Italian prisoners help around the wards. What a mix-up of nationalities! The Viennese is married to a Russian, and says he prefers to live in Communist Russia.

THURSDAY – 25.6.42
Since the stitches were removed, my fingers have healed quite well, except that the first finger of the left hand has not much feeling in it. Had my eye X-rayed today to make sure there were no bits of metal left. All O.K.

FRIDAY – 26.6.42
Left hospital for No. 2 Convalescent Camp, El Ballah, on the Suez Canal, north of Ismailia.

SATURDAY – 27.6.42
Swam in the canal. Water buoyant and warm. The canal is about 150 yards in breadth. Steamers passing leave a pleasant wash. We have our own "lido" with tables set out under big sunshades. Sometimes swimmers clamber on to a felucca, exchanging wisecracks with the crew as they sail along, then dive off again. I saw several starfish in the shallows.

SUNDAY – 28.6.42
Battleship went through the canal, seeming as if it was sailing across the desert, for the water is quite invisible from our tents, several hundred yards away. Swam to the other side of the canal and back again today. There is a steady current from north to south but, as in the "Med.", tides hardly cause any effect and the level never varies much more than six inches.

One day my back got badly burned by the sun when I was resting out of the water for only a few minutes. My skin had lost much of its tan during the six weeks I had been in hospital. I went back into the water and it was only later that I realised I had caught it badly. My back was painfully tender and I was so fevered I could not sleep. I dared not report sick as I might have been accused of sun-bathing, which was a military crime and could be met with a charge! The skin broke and gave way to a mass of sores. Finally I went to the cook and scrounged some ordinary flour. This I dusted over my back and in two days it was quite healed! Whether I thus discovered a phenomenal cure is a moot point but I was very much relieved.

WEDNESDAY – *1.7.42*
Enemy is now in Egypt.

THURSDAY – *2.7.42*
Camp concert. Three large bombs dropped in the vicinity. (Maybe "Jerry" didn't like our singing!)

FRIDAY – *3.7.42*
Minesweeper at work in the canal. Nine large bombs or mines dropped after dark. "Jerry" now between Mersa Matruh and Alexandria, at a place called Alamein.

A place called Alamein! Little did we guess at the historic importance that would be attached later to the name of El Alamein, a name which graced a lonely halt on the railway line.

SATURDAY – *4.7.42*
Whirlwind carried a large sunshade high in the air and dropped same in the Suez Canal! Swimmers got it out. Cinema (open-air) closed for blackout. Enemy aircraft, of course, would see the screen miles away but we are peeved all the same, for we have nothing else to do but sit in our tents in darkness. More mines dropped, the explosions signifying that most of them missed the channel and struck land.

SUNDAY – *5.7.42*
Signal station still standing. This is a bright spot, with its long red roof amongst the trees and a big white mast and yards for the signal flags.

MONDAY – *6.7.42*
News that we have held the enemy and captured guns and prisoners in counter-attack. We feel "Jerry" has now shot his bolt. Six hundred "Jerry" infantry give themselves up. We will beat him soon now, especially when the second front is opened in Europe. I believe this is the turning-point of the war!

I am still amazed at the prophetic accuracy of this sentence, which was underlined in my diary. Was it Confucius or just Ernest Bramah who said, "When the shield is bent, the sword is also blunted"? As for the Second Front, we did not know it would be so long delayed that we would take part in it! Apparently they couldn't start the damn' thing without the Desert Rats!

WEDNESDAY – *8.7.42*

The convalescent camp is now 800 over strength, mostly wounded. Some of them have been through hell. One is so badly shell-shocked (or "bomb-happy") that he wanders around in a daze and his clothing is neglected, dirty and dilapidated. About 200 of the newcomers are from the French Forces, who fought their way out of encirclement at Bir Hacheim. Some are grizzled old Foreign Legionnaires with beards and half of them seem to have arms or legs in plaster.

THURSDAY – *9.7.42*

Chaps may moan about the camp but they make a good mug of tea, and that's a lot in this dry country. Last swim in the canal – then washed my face again – in a large piece of melon!

FRIDAY – *10.7.42*

On way back to hospital. Stopped for two hours in Ismailia and went round the town with a Palestinian sapper from our party. Had coffee under shady arches by an open court with a fountain and flowers, shaded by palms and cypress. It was good to smell flowers again and look at trees and green grass, though the grass had to be watered daily. Built mostly by the Suez Canal Company, Ismailia is the most pleasant town in Egypt. A many-coloured throng at the station squatted on the platforms, or walked all over the lines! Iced lemonade was sold by a walking vendor who carried a large carafe slung under his arm. One crowded train came in with people sitting on the roofs of the carriages. Arrived back in No. 2 General Hospital and in the same ward as before.

SUNDAY – *12.7.42*

More strange nationalities! The A.T.S. orderly is a Russian Jewess called Olga. In the bed next to me is a brown-skinned Muslim in the Union Defence Force of South Africa.

There were so many different types of soldier in our cosmopolitan army that I once sketched some of the kinds of head-dress I had seen – and found I had eighteen varieties!

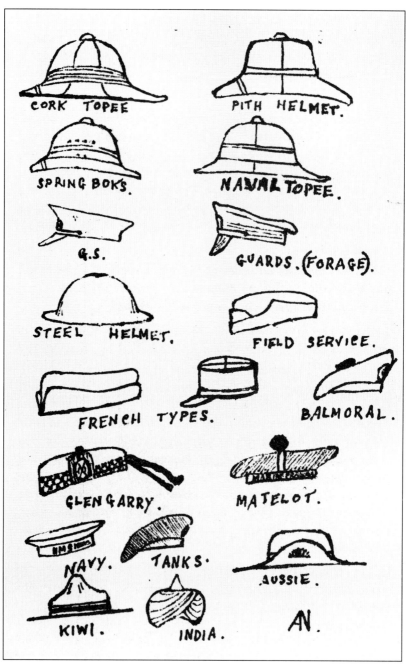

Headgear in the Middle East.

MONDAY – *13.7.42*
Moved from ward to marquee. To save us from sweeping-up, the "Aussie" sergeant in charge got some Italian prisoners to do it for us.

TUESDAY – *14.7.42*
Spoke to "Free French" soldier and found he came from near Paris. After conversing in French for ten minutes or so, he asked where I came from. When I told him he laughed and said he too was British but had been in France for fourteen years and was married to a Frenchwoman. Then, speaking with a Lancashire accent, he told how he had come out at Dunkirk to join the Free French and had fought at Bir Hacheim. His family were still in France, where he intends to return after the war. He had had no news of them for nine months, which must add strain to his service. He said he had almost lost his English once and, when he began to use it again, he could not make himself understood.

SATURDAY – *18.7.42*
Still more varied nationalities. In this one marquee there is: a Sinhalese who speaks good English; a Palestinian Arab; a coloured Mauritian taxi-driver and a black boy from Portuguese Mozambique, who speaks some English, Portuguese and a native dialect. They all crowd round eagerly when we discuss the different languages.

My final check-up was now completed and I left hospital at 6.00 a.m. on Tuesday, 21st July, to go to the base depot of Tel-el-Kebir. Almost the first thing that happened to me was that my inoculations had to be renewed. I stood in a very long queue, winding up to where the M.O. was busy at bayonet practice. He was known far and wide as "M and D" because of his habit of prescribing "Medicine and Duty"! By the time half of the queue was dealt with, the needle must have been pretty blunt and one man had blood running down his arm. Before this time, I had always been able to face these inoculations with complete equanimity but, following my injury, the sight of blood suddenly affected me and I had to put my head down between my knees to get rid of a feeling of nausea. Another man, a big six-footer, fainted outright and was carried away! Once I got the circulation back to my head, I got a grip of myself and received my "jab".

It soon became clear that I was *not* going to rejoin my old unit.

THURSDAY – *23.7.42*
Ordered to shift all my kit to another tent. Detailed for 65th Anti-
Tank Regt. (Norfolk Yeomanry). Given more kit and told to carry
it to yet another tent 200 yards away.

FRIDAY – *24.7.42*
Feeling thirsty, enjoyed a bottle of ice-cold beer from the Naafi
refrigerator. Went to see a film with the appropriate title "Dust be
my Destiny". Film cut badly. Cinema partly wrecked by "Aussies".

This was another of the "barn" cinemas of Shafto with, I think, Greek operators. Anyway, the film was Greek to us. The first reel jerked and stopped a few times, while the boys shouted for results. Then came, not the second but what appeared to be the *third* reel! There was more shouting and the panic-stricken operators speeded up the film until the figures were dashing about on the screen like the "Keystone Cops". The uproar grew and, finally, after a pause, another reel came on but whether it was the missing reel or not I could not tell, for it was upside down and, judging by the sound, running backwards! This stopped and there was no sign of any further attempt to continue the "show". The howl for "money back" arose, then suddenly a stream of beer-bottles sailed over my head towards the "screen" which was simply painted on wooden boarding. One bottle, with the neck broken off, struck into the screen and others kept bouncing off in a regular bombardment. A bunch of "Aussies" took the lead and the loudspeakers at each side of the screen were smashed. Then they picked up the vacated benches and began to use them as battering-rams on the frail walls! All this time, I believe the operators remained in their high projection-box, afraid to come down. With others of the audience, I moved outside, while the sound of crashing and splintering continued. A small crowd had gathered and some of the "Aussies" entered into the spirit of the thing. Someone said the M.P.s were coming. "Let 'em come!" growled one big "Aussie", as he tore a couple of planks from the wall.

The last thing I saw was a pile of splintered wood being built up against the wall, while the "Diggers" searched around for paper and matches! After that, I drifted away, so I can't tell what happened to the "Aussies" – or the M.P.s. However, so far as I know, the depot fire-brigade was *not* called out!

Maybe the wood was damp.

MONDAY – *27.7.42*

Air-raid warning. Tracers seen above as a dog-fight went on, then enemy plane went down in flames.

TUESDAY – *28.7.42*

Heard that the plane crashed seven miles away. Two "Jerries" bailed out, three burned.

WEDNESDAY – *29.7.42*

No show at Shafto (still wrecked) so had a shower instead. What a blessing water is! One "acker" left. Sat in tent alone, broke and browned-off.

"Acker", of course, is soldier's slang for *piastre*. A bunch of us were now slowly being brought together from various base units, hospital, etc. to form what seemed to be an entirely new L.A.D. for the Norfolk Yeomanry. As it happened, I was to remain with this unit and in the Seventh Armoured Division, until the end of the war.

One day, when our new sergeant-major arived, I was pleasantly surprised to find that it was A.S.M. Harrison, who had been with one of the recovery sections in France. He was to be in charge of us until we got an officer – which didn't happen for quite a long time.

FRIDAY – *31.7.42*

Collecting trucks from Cairo. Went to Abbasia Barracks, where a young officer named Winston Churchill once stopped on his way to fighting under Kitchener in the Sudan. On the return trip, saw: two men on one little donkey; native women carrying water from the canal while others, black-robed, "bathed" in the same place, by simply walking into the water up to their necks with all their clothes on; a distended, dead donkey left unburied at the roadside; and water being raised by the primitive shaduf, *which is just a weighted lever with a skin bag. Another way of raising water is by means of the Archimedes Screw, in the form of a wooden cylinder, about a foot in diameter, with a spiral vane running through it. It is held at a slant with the lower end in the water and the whole thing is turned by means of a handle at the top end. The water then gathers in the lower half of each spiral, until it spills over the top edge of the cylinder and into the irrigation channel. I wonder if Archimedes ever dreamed that his invention would still be in use 2,000 years after his death!*

SATURDAY – *1.8.42*
Visited Ismailia again. Swam in salt lake. Yacht of King Farouk in the bay.

FRIDAY – *14.8.42*
Evening at the Naafi with some of the boys. Almost drunk on Egyptian ("Stella") beer. On way back to camp, a group of the others stopped every few yards to debate something!

MONDAY – *17.8.42*
Little work except collecting stores. Rest of time spent reading or playing Rummy in the tent.

SATURDAY – *22.8.42*
We joined the Regiment at Almaza, Heliopolis. Spent the evening in Cairo.

We were now ready to return once more to the desert. Some of the men who came from base units had never been there, of course but, on the other hand, one of our youngest members was already a veteran for he could claim, with justifiable pride, to be one of "Wavell's 30,000". I am not sure of his first name now, but I think it was Pat but, his surname being Potter, we had to call him "Gillie". We had another "comedian" in the company, known as "Billy" Bennett.

Our kitbags, with personal effects, were left in store at the Citadel but none of us knew we would never again return to the Delta – that this was to be our last long "swan" and that it would not end until we had crossed two continents and reached the heart of Germany.

CHAPTER 6

El Alamein

WE LEFT THE FRONT on Monday, 24th August. Where previously this would have been a journey of 700 or 800 miles, it was now a comparatively short trip of about eighty miles from Alexandria but this proved arduous enough. There seemed to be hundreds of tracks and there was so much traffic of all kinds, including tanks, that the ground was churned up into powdery dust which lay a foot deep, like ochre-coloured flour.

As usual, we had breakdowns to deal with and fell behind. At one point, we fell in with some of the 4th Indian Division, who very kindly gave us tea, before directing us to the best of their ability. Later, we laagered by ourselves and found the regiment next day, after towing the stragglers through the dust for a total of sixteen hours.

TUESDAY – *25.8.42*
Join "B" Echelon, south of Alamein. Enemy expected to make a push. Bomb dropped on nearby landing ground.

WEDNESDAY – *26.8.42*
News that we have pushed "Jerry" back a bit.

FRIDAY – *28.8.42*
Hurricane of the evening patrol made a forced landing near us. His undercarriage was not working, so he skidded along on his belly and spun like a joywheel at the end. 'Plane damaged by shrapnel, but the pilot stepped out unhurt.

SATURDAY – *29.8.42*
Appointed Lance-Corporal (paid).

My one and only stripe! To me the Army was all right as a means of winning the war but as a career it did not interest me. I had no ambition to bawl at other men.

SUNDAY – *30.8.42*
Corporal Eddie Culhane, an ex-Guardsman, and now our welder,

*cut my hair – with a pair of nail-scissors! His only other weapon was
a pair of tin-snips for cutting sheet metal. Must hand it to Eddie; he
made a good job of it! If only he had had his oxy-acetylene burner,
he could have finished it off with a nice singe!*

Tuesday – *1.9.42*
The enemy's attempted forward drive has been smashed.

This was the Battle of Alan Halfa, where Rommel met his match in our
new commander, General Montgomery. The enemy was lured into a
prepared gap by our division (7th Armoured) who shot him up while
withdrawing. Once he was in the gap, artillery on higher ground on his
northern flank opened heavy fire and the 7th stopped moving back.
After several days of fierce fighting, Rommel gave up and withdrew.
This battle started only a fortnight after Monty came to the desert!

Wednesday – *2.9.42*
*Dog-fights above. Bombs dropped some distance away. We are moving
forward. Our guns have knocked out 73 enemy tanks in 3 days.*

Thursday – *3.9.42*
Third anniversary of war. More dog-fights.

Friday – *4.9.42*
*Visit to front to rob a portee. Many dog-fights. Two M.E.s chased
by ack-ack. Went out in to no-man's-land with A.S.M. Harrison
and others to remove the differential from the portee, which was
burnt-out by bombing. Returned at dusk, just missing the minefields. Bed down without finding unit.*

No-man's-land, at this part of the front, was a plain several miles wide.
From forward positions, the wrecked portee (a truck fitted for carrying
an anti-tank gun) could be seen as a toy shape about a mile away. When
we went out we were, of course, under cover of our own anti-tank guns
in the forward positions.

Saturday – *5.9.42*
*Found unit in time for breakfast. Terrific dog-fight above. Saw
captured German tank chassis with big field-gun mounted on it,
surrounded by a shield; a similar idea to our own!*

Sunday – *6.9.42*
Recovery again at front. The boys brought back many jerricans full

of petrol which smelt like paraffin; also a camera from a truck which contained a dead German.

MONDAY – *7.9.42*
Camped near sea.

TUESDAY – *8.9.42*
Maintenance of truck. Lying in soft sand which, as usual, blows into eyes, ears and inside clothing and sticks to grease-guns, etc.

THURSDAY – *9.9.42*
Stomach pains. Up all night.

FRIDAY – *10.9.42*
Bad headache. Stomach still out of order.

New long-barrelled gun mounted on a captured German tank. *(Photo W. P. Graham)*

This was known as "Gyppo-Tummy", caused by getting sand in the food.

MONDAY – *14.9.42*
Went sick with septic thumb.

TUESDAY – *15.9.42*
Old stitch removed from thumb but the main trouble seems to be a part of the old nail-root which has been turned down and is growing inwards. "Hot fomentations." Used a whole box of matches on refractory blow-lamp. Finally heated water on a petrol fire.

WEDNESDAY – *16.9.42*
Off sick-list but using ointment on thumb. Denny and Eddie develop negatives inside the truck. (Denny is a Channel Islander from St. Peter Port.)

THURSDAY – *17.9.42*
Negatives look hopeful. Shortened, hemmed and stitched a pair of shorts (!). Prints look hopeless.

FRIDAY – *18.9.42*
Wash-day. Boiled shirt, pants, underpants and socks, then scrubbed the shirt. Put on cab roof to dry.

SUNDAY – *20.9.42*
Played football versus R.H.Q. We won 2–0.

MONDAY – *21.9.42*
Fitted tyre and tube but found the tube (new) to be punctured (porous). Started all over again with three patches.

THURSDAY – *24.9.42*
Return game with R.H.Q. Drew 1–1.

FRIDAY – *25.9.42*
Tomahawk swooped low doing the "victory roll".

SATURDAY – *26.9.42*
Putrid smell around us as a group of men exhume the bodies of five troopers from the graves near us. They were taken for re-burial in a military cemetery.

SUNDAY – *27.9.42*
Up before dawn, in a damp mist, for P.T.! Moon still shining.

This physical training was one of the things that caused a lot of grousing at Monty. We were fit, for we had plenty of heavy work and, in our spare time, we played football, yet here we were roused out of bed earlier than usual to do "knees bend", etc. We were all late on parade and Lieutenant Rodway, the Regimental Q.M., who was in charge of the echelon, was waiting for us with his watch in his hand. He was ordinarily a genial and respected officer but, for once (with proper justification), he lost his temper, and as we started the preliminary run round, he roared, "Move!" And move we did for the next half-hour. But the only result was that we played less football at other times.

MONDAY – *28.9.42*
Filling empty petrol cans with sand, to build around truck radiator in case of shrapnel. Sound of strafing to the north during the night. Full moon.

TUESDAY – *29.9.42*
Cured ignition trouble on Morris water-truck.

WEDNESDAY – *30.9.42*
Airgraph censored. Told to black-out line, "Thank heavens I never joined the peace-time army." Said to be "subversive literature"! In charge of night picket.

THURSDAY – *1.10.42*

Our forces seem to consist of: 1st, 7th and 10th Armoured Divisions, 50th. Infantry Division, with recent addition of 44th Division and 51st (Highland) Division, together with the Australians, Indians, New Zealanders and South Africans. "Jerry's" Afrika Korps (the 15th and 21st Panzer Divisions) has been joined by 90th Light Division and 164th Infantry Division. Italians have six divisions, including the Ariete.

SUNDAY – *4.10.42*

General Knowledge Quiz at cook's truck, with Mr. Rodway as Chairman. Strains of an accordion in the dusk from some truck in another part of the echelon.

MONDAY – *5.10.42*

Have had no mail for over a month. Working on a portee with big end gone, when a shell from a Bofors burst near us. It was let off accidentally by the crew cleaning the gun!

TUESDAY – *6.10.42*

Change rear axle on a Jeep.

WEDNESDAY – *7.10.42*

News in Egyptian Mail: *"Assurance will be sought in Parliament that preference will be given to troops in Britain for demobilization." Encouraging news for us!*

THURSDAY – *8.10.42*

Correction in following day's paper. Should have been: "... preference will not be given." That little word "not"! Many of our bombers going over.

FRIDAY – *9.10.42*

More squadrons of bombers heading for "Jerry" with fighter escort. One of those miserable days of wind, dust and bad visibility. Sump off another portee. Big end in this one gone too.

SATURDAY – *10.10.42*

Very lights, tracers, etc. to the south at night. Sounds of heavy artillery barrage. Beer available! Did we take it?

SUNDAY – *11.10.42*

Wash-day again. Sound of artillery all day.

MONDAY – *12.10.42*
Repair gearbox on Chev. portee.

TUESDAY - *13.10.42*
*Stomach bad, head sore, pain in right armpit. Perhaps food poison-
ing. Another dog-fight overhead. After the scrap, our Bofors sent
parting shots after the M.E.s.*

THURSDAY – *15.10.42*
*Move ten miles south towards Qattara Depression and nearer front.
Heavy exchange of artillery fire and prolonged machine-gunning.*

FRIDAY – *16.10.42*
Differential packed up on our own stores truck.

(This was the 3-ton stores truck which I eventually drove from Alamein
to Tunis, a distance of about 1,700 miles.)

*Awaiting spares hopefully. Still no mail from home. Push (by us)
expected soon.*

SATURDAY – *17.10.42*
*Have collected some spares after a twenty-miles run. Many track
signs missing, so went in a circle twice. Finally had a puncture. Got
back before dark.*

SUNDAY – *18.10.42*
Spares not complete, so Eddie has brazed *the crown-wheel as a
tremporary repair! Big dog-fight above.*

MONDAY – *19.10.42*
*Completely alone in our part of the desert. 257 Battery, to whom
we are now attached, have gone. Wide-open spaces all around us!
Eddie does our cooking.*

There were so many flies about that when Eddie cut up a piece of
meat, two of us stood, one on either side of him, with fly-swatters in
an attempt to keep the insects from wiping their dirty feet on our food.
Where the blood soaked the board, one stroke of the swatter was sufficient to kill about forty flies. But still they came!

TUESDAY – *20.10.42*
*Received Airgraph from home. Good! All well. Rear axle fixed at
last.*

WEDNESDAY – *21.10.42*
Moving forward again to echelon. Three enemy fighters come low over echelon to strafe. Bofors retaliate strongly. Flashes from the ground as they fire. One tracer shell, like a ball of fire, made an arc, bounced from the ground, and burst in mid-air. Column of smoke where one plane came down. Heard later that two were brought down.

FRIDAY – *23.10.42*
Push started at 10.00 p.m. Heavy barrage at night.

And so the Battle of El Alamein began. We stood for a couple of hours watching the flashes of the guns as the incessant barrage went on. The flickering flares bobbed up and down over a wide area, making a blinding contrast to the surrounding darkness and accompanied by a continual thunder. As we finally turned in, to try to sleep through the noise, the general opinion was that Blackpool Illuminations had nothing on this! I imagine, at the receiving end, the enemy's opinion wouldn't be quite so enthusiastic.

As a matter of fact, Rommel himself wrote:

"Such drum-fire had never before been seen on the African front, and it was to continue throughout the whole of the Alamein battle … The British bombarded our known positions with extraordinary accuracy and enormous casualties resulted. R.A.F. bombers also took part in the preparatory barrage. Our communication network was soon smashed by this drum-fire, and reports from the front virtually ceased. Our outposts fought to the last round and then either surrendered or died. Under the impact of the terrible British artillery fire, which grew to World War I proportions, part of the Italian 62nd Infantry Regiment left their line and streamed back to the rear. Exposed to this tornado of fire in their partially completed defence positions, their nerve had failed."

The Rommel Papers, published by Collins.

SATURDAY – *24.10.42*
Rain in the evening. Blankets a bit damp. Continuous barrage all night. Saw two planes crash in flames.

SUNDAY – *25.10.42*
Push successful. Objectives all gained. French take and hold Hime-

imat Ridge. Radio announces R.A.F. raids on industrial plant at Turin, Milan and Genoa.

MONDAY – *26.10.42*

Sgt. Gray of the 65th (N.Y.) has captured 200 "Eye-ties" single-handed! Walking up to them, wearing an "Aussie" hat, he brandished his tommy-gun and, in broad Norfolk dialect said, "Come you on!" The "Eye-ties", viewing the "Aussie" hat, thought it might be bad if they didn't!

TUESDAY – *27.10.42*

Captain White is badly wounded. During the withdrawal from Knightsbridge, he won the M.C. for knocking out four "Jerry" tanks with some two-pounders.

THURSDAY – *29.10.42*

Move seven miles west as we advance. Now north-east of Himeimat Ridge.

FRIDAY – *30.10.42*

Barrage as continuous as rain on a tin roof.

SATURDAY – *31.10.42*

Told by Lt. Rodway to expect a tremendous barrage to be opened by Australian artillery; 320 guns in one sector, each firing 400 rounds. Move north to central sector. Laagered near wadi which contained the graves of four British and two Greek soldiers. Slept in open, to be off at dawn.

SUNDAY – *1.11.42*

Now near El Gaballa. Our freedom from bombing gives us the impression that "Jerry" has no planes left in Africa.

Newcomers to the desert sometimes wondered why the experienced men were wary of aircraft. They didn't realise it was that wariness that often kept them alive in earlier days. Before Alamein, we never waited to see if the planes bore "noughts" or "crosses" but got to a slit-trench first. After Alamein, the enemy never seemed to gain air superiority and we were hardly troubled by Stukas from one side of Africa to the other.

MONDAY – *2.11.42*

Move again by "Bombay Road" to "Star" track (near the railway lines) then "Double-Bar" track to "Springbok Road". General advance of Eighth Army.

TUESDAY – *3.11.42*

Haircut by an Indian soldier at side of track. We are now in the north sector. A captured Italian general complains of "inhuman bombing".

WEDNESDAY – *4.11.42*

Hunter's Plateau occupied by British. "Jerry" retreating fast. Rommel has taken transport away from the "Eye-ties", who are walking west and being picked up as prisoners in droves.

THURSDAY – *5.11.42*

Move by "Bottle", "Boat" and "Moon" tracks, all indicated by cut-out tin shapes fixed to posts. Pass four of the new "Churchill" tanks. Laager by Alamein Station. "Jerry" bombers over after dark, dropping flares and bombs. Ack-ack let go deafeningly with 3.7 in. guns, lighting the area with the flashes. Rifles were fired at the parachute flares in an attempt to bring them down.

FRIDAY – *6.11.42*

Chain of traffic for miles on the coast road, bringing supplies. We move thirty miles west of El Alamein. "Jerry" is moving right back towards Halfaya. Smashed tanks and unburied dead at the wayside. The dead turn black very quickly in the sun.

SATURDAY – *7.11.42*

Ground strafing at the rear. Off at dawn; petrol for 100 miles advance on board. Enemy column to south of us has captured part of our supply column. Our main forces are at Matruh. We have taken 20,000 prisoners and 350 enemy tanks have been destroyed or captured, along with 400 guns and thousands of vehicles.

SUNDAY – *8.11.42*

Rain! Whole echelon bogged in mud. Trucks tipped at all angles, engines screaming, men shoving and digging. Four "Jerry" prisoners on one truck, including a skinny, rat-faced, slovenly officer, were told to get down and shove as well. Slept on damp ground where we got out of the mud.

MONDAY – *9.11.42*

Have picked up two small Italian rifles with folding bayonets. Saw great columns of Italian prisoners, soaking wet, all along the route, waiting for transport to take them back.

This was the only way they would ever reach the Delta – as prisoners. Mussolini would never need his white charger now! One of the men of the Norfolk Yeomanry, who had been taken prisoner by the enemy but later escaped, told how the Italians took the water-bottles away from British prisoners; but when the Germans realised what had happened, they made them hand them back! Let us not deny it, the Afrika Korps, under Rommel's control, acted correctly, much more so than the S.S. divisions which we were later to meet in Europe.

TUESDAY – *10.11.42*
Working behind the regiment, we found replenishment convoy and went with them through Fuqa aerodrome to coast road and past Matruh to Siwa road. Using Italian soap, but it's not much good. Lots of Italian baggage, but sprinkled with the usual booby-traps.

On Wednesday, we turned into the desert again and over one of the roughest stretches I ever experienced. Blackened stones, all about seven or eight inches across, it seemed, were strewn for miles, reminding me once more that this used to be the bed of the ocean. Why we had to take this route, I do not know, but we crawled over it, bumping and clattering, the springs taking a tremendous hammering as the wheels jerked up and down. The whole cab rattled and the stores bins drummed until we were deafened, while the steering-wheel kicked round and back until my wrists were sore. We were more than glad when we eventually reached a smoother surface after what seemed hours.

WEDNESDAY – *11.11.42 (Contd.)*
Now making for Bir El Khamsa. News of 80,000 "Yanks" landing in Algeria! Captured material everywhere and many enemy wrecks. Terrific movement of British troops. Driving all night to find "B" Echelon.

THURSDAY – *12.11.42*
Found them at daybreak after a nightmare of breakdowns and getting lost in the dark. Have had no sleep but the convoy still moves west from daybreak. Vichy armistice with "Yanks", who are now in Tunisia.

FRIDAY – *13.11.42*
Churchill says, "Complete victory for the Eighth Army." Our 22nd Armoured Brigade are chasing main enemy column.

SATURDAY – *14.11.42*
Cross the wire into Libya for the third time at 4.15 p.m. 22nd
Brigade (to which we are attached) takes Fort Capuzzo and
Bardia. Our workshop truck, which fell behind, has not yet caught
up with us.

SUNDAY – *15.11.42*
We go north and west for fifty miles. Once we passed through a
large area of scrub, where a herd of camels stampeded and an Arab
went running after them, his galabia *flapping in the wind, like*
Nannie's "Cutty-Sark"! We have taken Tobruk and 22nd Brigade
is at Knightsbridge.

MONDAY – *16.11.42*
Move west and arrive at El Adem. We are stopping for several days.
Nobby and I have a big job on a little Jeep, dismantling clutch and
gearbox.

TUESDAY – *17.11.42*
Cold and damp. Chase is taken over by 4th Armoured Brigade
(which also is part of 7th Armoured Division) while 22nd Brigade
rest and refit transport.

WEDNESDAY – *18.11.42*
Issued with battle-blouse. In charge of guard, which is composite,
from R.H.Q., 257 and 258 Batteries.

On this occasion, one of the men facetiously suggested that the guard
ought to have a special watchword, so I obliged by scribbling the following:

> *"In watches of the weary night,*
> *Be vigilant and true;*
> *Remember that your comrade's lives,*
> *May yet depend on* YOU*!"*

Jimmy Bryant, a cheery "Brummy" with a pawky sense of humour, read
it out with much grandiloquence, to be greeted with loud guffaws and
derisive cheers!

THURSDAY – *19.11.42*
Move up into Gullies on ridge above the aerodrome of El Adem.
Saw some French troops and two girl auxiliaries with them, which
is surprising at this distance from base. Thick dust-storm; typical El

Adem weather. Fix bivvy on solid rock with piles of stones. Bitterly cold at night. We are to move to M'rassus, near the coast, tomorrow. Why couldn't we stay where we were until then?

FRIDAY – *20.11.42*

Our advance forces are now seventy miles from Benghazi. "Jerry" expected to make a stand at El Agheila, where defensive positions have been prepared.

SATURDAY – *21.11.42*

Benghazi in British hands. We are still well behind at M'rassus, about fifteen miles from Tobruk. Full moon. Heavy strafing twice during the night, machine-gun and cannon tracers from aircraft coming down on surrounding trucks. No one hit.

SUNDAY – *22.11.42*

Going back to El Adem to take track to M'rassus. Saw a Messerschmitt being flown back, with an escorting Spitfire.

MONDAY – *23.11.42*

Bombs dropped nearby at dawn. We go off along "F" Track for M'rassus. Cold and showery at night. Slept with ground-sheet on top of me. Stan has yellow jaundice.

TUESDAY – *24.11.42*

By-passing Knightsbridge and Bir Hacheim, we continue over endless, rutted tracks. Carrying eighty gallons of petrol, enough for 500 miles.

WEDNESDAY – *25.11.42*

Off again at dawn. Later, we were halted by a minefield in front of us, with no warning boundary-wire. Two graves nearby of men killed the day before. A Dodge P.U. (radio-truck), an ambulance and an armoured car lay wrecked close together in the minefield, which was sown over the track!

Either the retreating enemy forces had made the track and their rearguard laid the minefield, or an enemy column from the south had cut in and placed the mines behind our advance forces. It looked as if the Dodge hit it first, the ambulance went in for casualties and finally the armoured car was used, only to be wrecked itself.

We turned sharp left for a hundred yards or so, then right, to proceed parallel to the track but, before we did so, I noticed that the officer who was leading us at the time drew aside and waved the rest of the vehicles forward before his own!

Thursday – 26.11.42

Start at dawn. Thirty gallons of petrol left. Reach M'rassus at 4.30 p.m. Fill tanks, leaving four gallons spare. Going has been very smooth. Stan missed the Red Cross 'plane from M'rassus landing ground by five minutes!

Friday – 27.11.42

Now with 4th Light Armoured Brigade, passing Antelat, where we first contacted the enemy, almost a year ago. No more smooth mud-flats to run on. Found an old dump of petrol. Going on to Ajedabia, we pass three trucks burnt-out from strafing, all still smouldering. Two of them belong to our 260 Battery.

Saturday – 28.11.42

Dug-in for a few days. Rain following a dust-storm. Three-quarter moon at night. Little did I think, on the outbreak of war, three years ago, that I'd sleep out on the desert at the western end of Cyrenaica!

Sunday – 29.11.42

Fifteen Italian Macchis over, dropping bombs. Ack-ack pretty good, chased them off. One came low above us. They have radial engines, white cross on fuselage and fasces on the wings.

Monday – 30.11.42

News that a Russian pincer movement has encircled twenty-five (!) German divisions. Theirs must be a terrific war! We are now in the country of the Senussi. They are just as crafty at bargaining as any other type of Arab. Where is the majestic dignity we read about in romantic novels of the desert? One toothless old man wanted a pint mug filled with dry tea for two eggs. There has been some rain and he went on his hands and knees to drink from a puddle!

Tuesday – 1.12.42

I notice the large black scarabs can fly, having brown wings about four inches from tip to tip, yet they make no attempt to fly from danger on the ground. When on the wing, they whirr along as if they were the bombers of the insect world but, when they land, they are so clumsy that they often fall over, then pick themselves up and waddle away. They invariably carry five or six fleas as "attached personnel".

They also lay their eggs in a ball of dung which they hide in some cavity. I have seen a scarab with a ball of gazelle dung, two inches across, which it pushed behind itself with the two hind legs, while moving backwards on the other four legs. It proceeded in this way for about thirty feet, leaving a crooked trail in the sand. Many a "desert rat", on going to a latrine after dark, has been startled to hear a rustling noise, until acquainted with the habits of the "sacred beetle".

TUESDAY – *1.12.42 (Contd.)*
Maintenance of stores truck. Tighten cylinder-head nuts. Tighten fan-belt. Tighten hand-brake. Tighten gear-box cover. Tighten spring U-bolts. Tighten all body-bolts. Top-up battery, sump and radiator.

The emphasis on the word "tighten" shows what the effect of our rough travel was.

WEDNESDAY – *2.12.42*
Anniversary of my landing in this blasted country. Water extremely short again. Some of the large scarabs in my bed.

THURSDAY – *3.12.42*
Went along coast road ten miles south of Ajedabia, passing through the village. Tracks strewn with mines. Denny guided me through one part where torn bits of tyres showed that trucks had struck mines. Someone had dug up a few of the mines and they were an oblong type made by the French and now used by the enemy. Gathered eighty gallons of water from a well where a truck had a wheel blown off a minute or two previously (it sailed right across the road). I followed tyre-marks in to the well and carefully reversed out again, keeping the wheels exactly on the same marks, after we drew the water.

FRIDAY – *4.12.42*
Now parked near airfield eight miles south-west of Ajedabia. Disturbed by howling of desert foxes at night.

SATURDAY – *5.12.42*
The water we risked our lives for on Thursday is too salty to make a lather and leaves the skin gummy, so we try to distil it, with little success.

SUNDAY – *6.12.42*
Pancakes in truck in evening! Cooking by blow-lamp.

MONDAY – *7.12.42*
Heavy ack-ack fire at two enemy planes. A spent shell swished down near our truck. Moving again, south for thirty miles. Passed a 'drome with many planes carrying the U.S. star. Also saw an armoured car of the 2nd K.R.R.C., which was wrecked during our first visit to this area, eleven months ago.

TUESDAY – *8.12.42*
Within sound of the guns again. "Jerry" is dug-in in the "Bad Lands". Watched South Africans "mine-sweeping" a track with an electric detector.

The "Bad Lands" was an area of broken ground with salt-bogs in the hollows. The sand in some parts looked grey in colour.

WEDNESDAY – *9.12.42*
Battle for Agheila begins, with another display of artillery flashes. Many of our planes over; none of the enemy. Very cold at night.

THURSDAY – *10.12.42*
Nobby evacuated with jaundice. Fitting springs (temporarily welded) to an armoured car.

FRIDAY – *11.12.42*
Found a tail-wheel and hydraulic shock-absorber from a plane. Began to dismantle it, but found a sleeping snake coiled up inside the wheel! I didn't waken him. I expect he was there for the winter!

SATURDAY – *12.12.42*
Watched enemy fighter-bombers diving repeatedly and recklessly to bomb something in the middle distance, leaving a line of smoke-bursts. We have begun the push.

SUNDAY – *13.12.42*
Mersa Briga taken. We are advancing into the bottle-neck towards Agheila, while the New Zealanders are cutting round in the south to attack the enemy flank.

MONDAY – *14.12.42*
One hundred prisoners taken of Italian Fascist Youth, ages sixteen to eighteen. As our Lieutenant Q. humorously put it, "They are being sent to a reformatory at Almaza!"

TUESDAY – *15.12.42*
Agheila taken. We advance thirty-five miles. When we arrive at our

new position, we see on the next ridge shell-bursts from the enemy rear-guard. Prisoners taken from the 66th Trieste Regiment. German food-cans in our parking place and a carton oil-bottle, signs of recent occupation.

WEDNESDAY – *16.12.42*
Another twelve miles forward. Enemy leaving many mines and booby-traps behind him.

THURSDAY – *17.12.42*
Another twenty-four miles forward. Skirting the "Bad Lands" by an enemy military road. Ambulances go back with casualties, including some blood-stained "Jerry" prisoners. Later, come on fresh graves of men killed by mines. A soldier was still writing his mate's name on a cross near a wrecked truck.

FRIDAY – *18.12.42*
Forward another twenty-two miles. Mines everywhere. Every third telegraph pole sawn off. Three great gaps blown in the road. One truck hit a mine at the road-side and went up in flames. Our rear-axle has "burst up" again.

SATURDAY – *19.12.42*
Dozens of Douglas DC2 'planes, Mitchells and Harrows, going back and forth with supplies for a new forward 'drome. There are some high white sand-dunes here, between the road and the sea, which command a fine view of the coast in both directions.

SUNDAY – *20.12.42*
Many deep enemy dug-outs near us, where we find remnants of equipment, bayonets, steel helmets, torn uniforms, water-bottles with bakelite cups attached and a large and varied assortment of bottles, which had contained Kummel, Schnapps, Italian Chianti and some French wines.

Fitting axle taken from truck blown up in minefield. Rejoin unit near Marble Arch Aerodrome, so called because of the graceful high arch built by the Italians which straddles the road and marks the dividing line between Cyrenaica and Tripolitania.

MONDAY – *21.12.42*
Wells in neighbourhood all dry. Water situation acute. One quart per man per diem, no washing or shaving. Sample Italian canned tomato extract.

TUESDAY – *22.12.42*
Went to collect some trucks which, true to Army tradition, were not there. Passed under the white Italian arch, a really magnificent piece of work, wasting its sweetness on the desert air. There is a huge bronze plaque of bas-relief sculpture inside the arch, through which a double line of traffic can pass. Two R.A.F. men were on the dizzy top sky-watching. Sappers still mine-sweeping the road-side.

WEDNESDAY – *23.12.42*
Went again for trucks. Got four out of six. Saw General Montgomery passing up the track to inspect our brigade (now the 8th).

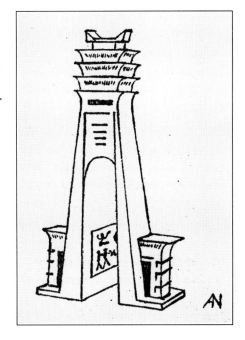

"Marble Arch" between Aghiela and Sirte.

THURSDAY – *24.12.42*
Roast pork for dinner! One bottle of beer each. News that Admiral Darlan, the French turn-coat, has been assassinated. That leaves: Laval, Hitler, Mussolini and Tojo.

FRIDAY – *25.12.42*
Christmas Day. Roast duck, more pork and some rum issued. Heard radio programme of Tommy Handley's ITMA, as we sat in the dark by the cook's shelter.

SATURDAY – *26.12.42*
We rise at dawn to go eighty miles. I roll my bed and bivvy, we pack the truck but the move is cancelled and we unpack again. I re-erect the bivvy, which is soaking from heavy night dew. "Jerry" has been pushed out of Sirte.

SUNDAY – *27.12.42*
Up at dawn again, moving to a point south of Sirte. Cover sixty-

eight miles. Surface pretty good. Bed-down with orders for early continuation next morning.

MONDAY – *28.12.42*
Further sixty miles west. Received mail from home, showing that the line of communication is up with us.

TUESDAY – *29.12.42*
We go eleven miles west, then come back twenty-five miles east, then nine miles north on a track passing a picturesque Italian fort and, finally, turn west again. Rumours that we are going into a defensive "box". Position again south of Sirte.

WEDNESDAY – *30.12.42*
About 100 tanks: Crusaders, Grants and Shermans, pass by – going south. It looks even more as if we have been placed inside a "box", while the armour is moving into the position we left yesterday. Later, another fifty tanks pass in the same direction.

THURSDAY – *31.12.42*
Hogmanay. We celebrate the turn of the year in a "hall" made by backing one truck against another and arranging the tarpaulins to cover the space between. We had "duff" and scones and a rum issue. There was story-telling and play-acting and we each sang a song, mine being "J'attendrai". Mr. Rodway was chairman. We finished by singing "Auld Lang Syne". So ends 1942.

This also ends my fifth diary. It was written in a little book purchased in Cairo. The outer cover is upside down and on the title-page is printed DAIRY!

SATURDAY – *2.1.43*
Played cards with Mr. Rodway and Mr. Drake in the stores truck in the evening. Partnered Mr. Rodway against "Gillie" Potter. Another four, including another officer, played bridge.

The Desert Army at least, was democratic! Here were three officers of the echelon, not only giving us their company, so that we could get to know and understand each other better, but also encouraging us in our efforts to provide our own entertainment.

SUNDAY – *3.1.43*
Fitting springs in howling sandstorm with "Billy" Bennett. Blankets covered inches deep in sand. Sample "Jerry" canned jellied beef.

Denny (our 'sparks') experimenting with an enemy wireless set, makes the truck sound like a Frankenstein laboratory.

WEDNESDAY – 6.1.43
Collected ten gallons rain-water from canvas hood of truck and from groundsheets laid in holes in the ground. An old Senussi comes around with two boys, one black as ink; a Sudanese. They bring four gallons of water, for which an old pair of boots is payment. They already have Italian jackets. We are now well-off for water, but our tea tastes of rubber and canvas. Orders read to the effect that we will be issued with B.M.A. (British Military Authority) currency, which can be used in conjunction with Italian lire; £1 = 480 lire. The Military Police will administer military law in the conquered territory.

SATURDAY – 9.1.43
Read in a magazine that someone is still plugging away at the official history of the First World War! We have been static for twelve days.

SUNDAY – 10.1.43
Told that General Montgomery is holding battle conference not far from us. Later warned to have forty gallons spare petrol per truck, as from daybreak on the 12th.

MONDAY – 11.1.43
Orders to prepare to move 500 miles! This will take us round past Tripoli. General push will take place, with opening moves kept secret under radio silence. Will this finish Rommel?

CHAPTER 7

Tripoli

"Here in the body pent
Absent from Him I roam,
Yet nightly pitch my moving tent
A day's march nearer home."

TUESDAY – *12.1.43*
Pack up. Move at 10.00 a.m. with the 3rd Tanks. Dust-storm blow-ing. Do thirty-three miles and stop for night near a 'drome. Ground rocky, so can't drive in bivvy pegs. Ack-ack at 'drome fires at two enemy 'planes.

WEDNESDAY – *13.1.43*
Eighteen Baltimore bombers come over and circle the 'drome, while fighter escort rises to meet them, about thirty-five fighters in all. Noise of engines like thunder. Another thirty-six fighters had prev-iously headed west. More dust-storms.

THURSDAY – *14.1.43*
Move at dawn. During halt for breakfast, eighteen bombers and escort go over. Two Messerschmitts try to interfere. Two of the escort meet them and both Messerschmitts are shot down in a whirl-ing dog-fight, one like a stone, the other like a dead leaf. The bombers sedately proceed. Three minutes later, another eighteen pass over with their escort. We continue to Wadi Bei el Kebir. Message from "Monty" says, "Tripoli by Sunday!" The 51st (High-land) Division will take over, while the town is out of bounds for forty-eight hours for clearing up. Later programme, a month to refit, and leave at a camp near Tripoli. Trouble with a salt bog in the wadi, many trucks sinking in. Have covered thirty-four miles.

FRIDAY – *15.1.43*
Go still west from Bei el Kebir. Heavy gunfire in the North. Our

planes patrol over our convoy. Cover twenty-five miles and, as we stop for the night, we see rows of big shell-bursts on a ridge as the enemy replies to our artillery. At night a great barrage starts from our guns. Flashes flicker along the ridge like an aurora borealis and the steady roll of thunder goes on for two hours.

SATURDAY – *16.1.43*
Forty-two fighters go over, followed by eighteen, then two, making sixty-two all told! We have never seen so many planes in the desert before. Forward another forty-one miles, west and north. Country becomes undulating, with valleys containing signs of vegetation, scrub and even trees up to twenty feet high.

SUNDAY – *17.1.43*
A 'plane droned around during last night and dropped one bomb. Large columns of motor transport rumble past to the north before dawn. In morning, light ack-ack opens up at enemy aircraft. We go on another forty-four miles, passing some "Eye-tie" trenches dug in the open desert, containing abandoned anti-tank guns. Later we come to broken country and a precipitous wadi with a fort on a high point above (Fort Sedada). Descending the gorge – about one in three – we come out on a flat plain, going through some sandy stretches. On our left, an M.E. is shot down by a Kittyhawk.

Heard at night that our colonel (Colonel English) has been killed and the adjutant wounded. The colonel had only taken over command a week ago. The 4th Light Armoured Brigade have advanced to west of Tripoli but the 51st Division have not yet reached the town. Our A.S.M. is missing with the breakdown somewhere behind.

MONDAY – *18.1.43*
Off at 8.30 a.m. The missing trucks turn up during the day. We do fifty miles, descending over rocky country into another steep-walled wadi with several ruined forts. Another five miles are covered on a zig-zag track along the floor of the wadi. My back axle packs up again and we are still in the wadi, being towed by the breakdown, when we halt for the night. As a consolation, we enjoy a good supper prepared by ourselves: spuds, pork-and-soya sausages, beans, tomato extract, etc. all out of tins, but good. The "Loyals" are at Homs.

TUESDAY – *19.1.43*
We replace the differential, removing half of the axle to do so, in

three hours' work. Half a mile further on, we come out of the wadi and find the echelon parked outside, where they had been all night. We arrived just as they began to move again. Fill up hurriedly with petrol and go on till we come to another great wadi with cliff-like sides and floor roughly cultivated by Senussis. Travel twenty-one miles to a position seven miles from the enemy guns. Dispersion awful, due to new mobs from Blighty, who are made to wear battle-order all the time, but don't know the first commonsense rule for safety from air attack!

WEDNESDAY – 20.1.43

Having parked in a little wadi of our own, we rise at dawn, wash in ice-cold water, which makes the skin tingle nicely, then go to the high edge of the wadi, overlooking a wonderful panorama of the scattered echelons in a wide valley. Heard that an ack-ack unit had been dive-bombed at the head of one of the wadis we had passed. They had three killed and thirteen wounded. The planes were a strange type with twin tails. Our unit moves off but we remain to repair a radiator on a battery portee. "Monty" passes by with his little convoy.

THURSDAY – 21.1.43

Still trying to repair radiator. Get it finished ready to move early tomorrow morning. Planes drone by all night, apparently taking supplies forward.

FRIDAY – 22.1.43

Radiator still leaks. More soldering. Put it back. Leaks again. Take it off for the fourth time, wondering how many more days we will be here.

Radiator "fixed", we go twenty-one miles to a wide, flat plain, partly ploughed. Find a stranded driver with portee damaged by shrapnel. Repair damage. Find radiator on the other one is now leaking in a different place! This vehicle should have been named "The Reluctant Wagon"! Stay for the night. Another broken-down truck has a radio, which we fix up. We hear the News and Tommy Handley in ITMA. Tripoli has not yet fallen.

SATURDAY – 23.1.43

Radiator fixed (we hope). We reach Tarhuna, a village of buff and white buildings interspersed with trees and situated on a hillside. It

is surrounded by groves of orange trees stretching over the slopes,
while larger hills can be seen in the distance. There are many wells
with windmill pumps but we are told the village is out of bounds.
There are some Italians remaining on the fruit farms. Many of the
square white houses are of mass-produced similarity, having two
arches in the portico, an interior courtyard, a stable, an impression
of the fasces on the front wall, a number, and a quotation from the
ramblings of Il Duce with, underneath, the single script letter, M.

I copied several of these quotations, of which I give a sample *"La vera*
fonte, la vera origine di tutta l'attivita umana e la terra." ("The true
source, the true origin of all human activity is the earth.") Another read:
"Let us worship labour, which gives beauty and harmony to life." Yet
a third began with a plaint similar to Hitler's *lebensraum* wail: "Un
popolo senza spaxio non puo vivere ..." ("A people without space cannot
live ...") and so on, *ad nauseam.*

SATURDAY – *23.1.43 (Cont.)*
There are mines and booby-traps in many places, and a few scat-
tered soldiers' graves among the fruit trees. Tripoli fell this morning,
when the 11th Hussars went in at 5.00 a.m. *The road from here is*
asphalt and takes us up among hills, gorges and defiles. It is pictur-
esque and a big change from the desert.

SUNDAY – *24.1.43*
We join echelon in position near the coast and about nine kilometres
to the west of Tripoli, which is still out of bounds. We are parked in
a cultivated field but the blades of grass are further apart than those
at home! The owner says he is pleased to have us (as if it made any
difference).

MONDAY – *25.1.43*
Went with "Cabby" and Sid to collect water for the cookhouse. It
was five kilometres towards Tripoli when we saw the sign, "Water
Point", so we did the other four kilometres into town to have a look
and got the water on the return journey.

Tripoli is quite attractive, with a palm-studded promenade, near
which stands an ancient Turkish castle. Many ships are sunk, beached,
twisted and holed in the bay and a warehouse on a mole is leaning
at a dangerous angle. The R.A.F. have certainly been busy – and
accurate! Most shops have their shutters closed but many civilians

are returning to work. The streets are busy with traffic: motor-cycles, cycles and gharries. The Highlanders have taken over a large building opposite the castle, painted their sign, on the wall and have posted clockwork sentries with scrubbed webbing, spats and even regimental kilts.

I wonder what the "Wops" think of the "Ladies from Hell"?

Received word that my kit-bag (in Egypt) has been traced!

Some time earlier, I had written a letter about this, as we were not returning to Egypt and I wanted some personal belongings which were in the kit-bag. I received no reply. The next time, Lieutenant Rodway kindly sent a covering letter and this produced results. However, it was another four months before I actually received the kit-bag or, rather, what was left of it! Most of the others never saw their kit-bags again.

TUESDAY – 26.1.43
Go to Tarhuna to collect spares from workshop unit. Trot from one truck to another in pouring rain. Pass over bridge made by R.E. to cover a crater blown out by a delayed charge since we last passed this way. Camp for night.

WEDNESDAY – 27.1.43
Set out on return journey, but find temporary track beside a destroyed bridge has been washed away by the rush of water, which now makes a river past a smashed British tank and four graves. We report back to the nearest sappers (New Zealanders) and a gang is on the job in half an hour. Men from halted vehicles are asked to help, so we grab our shovels and soon about fifty of us are digging. By 2.00 p.m., the track is clear and the tank has been dragged out, full of sand, by a Scammel. Nearer Castel Benito, we have to cross another river about two feet deep.

FRIDAY – 29.1.43
A day's leave in Tripoli. Dates seem to be the only food available, tomatoes being green and oranges bitter. Plenty of green vegetables, uncooked. We carried our ration of bully and biscuits and exchanged some of it for cups of coffee. In the Union Club cinema, (organised for the troops) we saw an American film. Came out in time to see the pipe-band marching off after changing of the guard.

One interesting edifice in Tripoli is the arch erected by the Romans

Tripoli – the historic Marcus Aurelius Marble Arch.

in honour of Marcus Aurelius, one of the wisest and noblest of Roman Emperors.

It was Marcus Aurelius who said, "If any man can convince me that I do not think aright, gladly will I change, for I search after truth, by which man never yet was harmed".

SATURDAY – *30.1.43*
Drove leave party into Tripoli. There were some loud cracks as the ack-ack opened up at a "shufty kite". Italians and Arabs scattered to the shelters.

"Shufty-kite" *is, of course, army slang for 'reconnaissance aircraft'. It is derived from the Arabic "shoofdee", meaning 'look'.*

MONDAY – *1.2.43*
Day-trip to town. Found a place where we could get a dinner, together with a half bottle of wine. This shop was later closed by the military police for some reason. Bought a copy of the Tripoli Times, *price one lira.*

This was a single sheet, printed on one side in English, and on the other in Italian, as the *Corriere di Tripoli*. I still have three copies of it, one giving an account of the visit of the Premier, then Mr. Churchill. This journal gave us news of other fronts besides our own – Russia, Tunisia and the Pacific. There had been a desert newspaper too, for the Eighth Army, called *"The Crusader"*, which was first issued on 2nd May 1942 but we did not receive it regularly. *The Crusader* should not be confused with the First Army paper, called *The Crusade*.

A small paragraph at the foot of the Italian part of the *Corriere di Tripoli* catches my eye. It says, "We have been unable to receive the Italian bulletin for lack of electricity!" Nevertheless, the Italians were very surprised that a journal under British control was still to be allowed to publish reports from Italy at all!

TUESDAY – *2.2.43*
Go to field workshops, now near Tripoli, to dismantle wanted parts from Jeeps.

WEDNESDAY – *3.2.43*
Into town to buy a radio, but all are A.C. mains, so no use. Large parade of tanks, guns and vehicles blocking the traffic. I hope our chiefs are not going to waste time "impressing" the local people, as if we had not made enough impression by getting here! There are many bigger towns to go through yet before we beat Hitler.

(This parade, however, was prepared for the visit of the Prime Minister, of which our unit knew nothing until it happened.)

Drew water at the well of a private house, the Army waterpoint being successfully hidden somewhere. Two little boys from the house spoke to us and showed that they could recognise the various types of our aircraft. We obtained some eggs from the family in exchange for bully and biscuits.

THURSDAY – *4.2.43*
Took a party to Tripoli, being "detoured" via the docks by the "Gestapo" (C.M.P.) came up a side street beside the castle just in time to see WINSTON CHURCHILL *in Air Force uniform, standing up in a tourer, waving his hat to the cheering troops at the start of a tour of inspection. He had an escort of armoured cars. The civilians were kept well back for fear of possible bomb-throwing but they, too, applauded as they craned their necks to see "The Old Man".*

*He has seen Roosevelt at Casablanca, has flown to Cairo, then to
Turkey and back to Tripoli, at sixty-nine years of age! With the P.M.
were: General Alexander, General Montgomery and General Sir
Alan Brooke.*

In a speech to the Eighth Army, Mr. Churchill pointed out that the
distance we had covered (1,400 miles) was equivalent to the distance
between London and Moscow. Then he used a quotation which I think
was most apt, when he said, "And the lines come to me of a hymn which
you must know:

> *"You nightly pitched your moving tents*
> *A day's march nearer home."*

"Yes, not only in the geographic sense, but in the sense that what you
have done undoubtedly gives good grounds for the hope that the war
itself may be shortened and home may come nearer to all than before
could have been hoped."

THURSDAY – 4.2.43 (Contd.)
*Several bombing attacks at night. Red tracer shells creep over the
sky like little red balls, marking a mass pattern framed by search-
light beams.*

FRIDAY – 5.2.43
*Received a post-card dated May of last year, which has been to
India looking for me. Bought carrots, 3 kg (6½ lb.) for 1s. 2d. and 2 kg
onions for 1s. 5d. Dates are 24 lire for 1 kg or 6d. per lb. Ack-ack busy
again at night. Over 100 shells seem to be in the air at once.*

This was the last we were to see of Tripoli for some time. The "halt
for a month" seemed to be forgotten and we were soon on the move
again.

SATURDAY – 6.2.43
*To O.F.P. to pick up spares, then twenty-three miles west to Zavia
to deliver them to our echelon. The sea is a lovely, brilliant blue.
Zavia is an Italian fruit-farming village, set among palm groves,
where the wind makes a sighing, rustling noise in the fronds.*

SUNDAY – 7.2.43
*Join echelon at palm grove, five kilometres west of Zavia. Natives
try to sell us a milky-looking wine made from date-palm sap. They
call it* legbi.

MONDAY – *8.2.43*
Move through Sabrata to Zuara. Camp between sand dunes with a few palms about. An Arab came up, mysteriously took me round a palm tree and from a spot between its roots, dug up two packets of German ammunition, which he solemnly handed to me! I just as solemnly accepted it and thanked him!

TUESDAY – *9.2.43*
Our radio (which we bought after all) has been altered from A.C. to D.C. by Denny. It works. We hear London.

WEDNESDAY – *10.2.43*
Picking up an Italian-Arabic schoolbook, I find an account of a visit of "Il Duce" in 1926 to Zuara, where we are now. This book, after teaching the native child elementary Italian, goes on to tell him about the great Italian colonies, the beautiful Italian flag, etc. "Salutiamo la bella bandiera Italiana, che e anche la nostra bandiera!*"*

Heavy rain all night.

FRIDAY – *12.2.43*
Join Rear Division echelon south of Zuara. Gale and sandstorm. The wind is cold and later there is more heavy rain.

SATURDAY – *13.2.43*
Call at O.F.P. at Sabrata. The remains of a Roman theatre can be seen from the road here, the first impression being of the red colour of the stone used in the main wall of the building but the colonnades, in three tiers, one above the other, showed white and coloured marble and grey granite.

There are many burnt-out enemy vehicles along the road, which is surrounded by marshes. There are also three wrecked British trucks and two graves, where they were caught in devastating machine-gun fire from a stone block-house, 200 yards to one side of the road.

SUNDAY – *14.2.43*
Echelon moves again, leaving us to repair three jeeps. Still blowing, with plenty of nice sand!!! We do the cooking and fix up a table with a canvas table-cloth and two benches, where the whole L.A.D. can dine.

We have an extremely disagreeable fellow with us now, the driver of one of the jeeps belonging to the regiment. He opens personal

*belongings without permission, to borrow a mirror or a comb. He
also takes a rifle belonging to someone else and some ammo and goes
out shooting at dogs belonging to the Arabs. He belongs to
Portsmouth.*

MONDAY – *15.2.43*
*For a long time we have been using leaky four-gallon petrol tins,
with soft powdery paint on them, which often fell into the petrol.
These cans caused the loss of thousands of gallons of petrol. Then
came an American imitation of the "jerrican" but it did not pour so
well. Now at last we have cans made to the same specification as the
"jerrican" but without the enamel lining. Our two-gallon water-
cans are lined with bitumen but it comes off in lumps into our food.*

TUESDAY – *16.2.43*
*We move to join echelon, leaving the coast road and taking to the
desert tracks again. Pass village of El Assa, where the Arabs all seem
to wear brown, grey or white blankets as cloaks. We see planes of
the famous "Shark" Squadron on a landing strip. Ben Gardane, in
Tunisia, has been taken, but the "Yanks" have been driven out of
the Faid Pass. At the Tunisian frontier, we cross a sapper's bridge
over a swamp, more like a gigantic duck-board, 300 yards long,
made of wooden beams and logs roped together and laid on the
reeds and scrub of the swamp. The logs dip under our tyres and
water wells up between them as we are directed over this creaking
causeway at three miles per hour. A notice-board erected by the R.E.
tells us that this is "Seven Sweeper's Bridge". Safely over on the
other side, we camp for the night.*

WEDNESDAY – *17.2.43*
*We pass through Ben Gardane and begin to see the names of streets
in French. The natives seem much the same as usual, except that they
wear bright blue cloaks.*

*The American withdrawal from Faid causes the evacuation of three
forward Allied landing grounds. Our main Division echelon lose
many vehicles through dive-bombing raids.*

THURSDAY – *18.2.43*
*Two enemy planes sweep low over the trees where we are parked.
Someone lets go with a Bren at the second one. A number of our
fighters appear later, apparently looking for them. We move eight*

miles along the Medenine road and park, while a hurricane sand-storm blows, the most miserable weather this country can produce. The radio announces that Rommel has taken another three towns, inflicting heavy casualties on the "Yanks", who have already lost 3,000 killed and 35,000 taken prisoner!

FRIDAY – *19.2.43*
Plenty of work in hand. Many tanks move up.

SUNDAY – *21.2.43*
Our position now is north-east of Medenine. When we arrived, we had to follow a track for at least fifty yards off the main road before opening out, to avoid buried mines at the verge. We have always had this danger and pass many burnt trucks and craters here and there but now "Jerry" has invented a mine which has a delayed action of anything up to three weeks! It is said to operate by the action of acid eating through a copper plate. Back at Agheila, mines were found attached to our dead, so that those who came to bury them were endangered.

The Lone Hill, Medenine.

M—— (the Portsmouth Pest) has been back again. When he had gone, we discovered that some of our rations and cigarettes had also gone!

MONDAY – 22.2.43
We move up – now five km. from Medinine. Plenty of 5.5-in. guns (60 pounders) going forward. "Jerry" has pushed the "Yanks" further back.

We were now facing a barren red hill, which lay between us and the Mareth line. Ridges of strata stuck out on it and it was split and riven with gullies, so that there were really three summits but, as it stood by itself, well away from the larger range of hills we could see to the south-west, I always thought of it as the "Lone Hill". It imposed itself on our view day after day, for we did not leave this position for some time and, finally, I sat down and sketched it. The little white house on the top soon became the target for enemy guns. As we faced the hill, we looked across the Medenine road, which ran past our echelon and a neighbouring aerodrome. From maps, I gain the impression that this hill was probably the Tadjera Feature.

CHAPTER 8

From Mareth to Tunis

TUESDAY – *23.2.43*

When I bed-down in my bivvy, Ed brings me a cup of tea and I fall asleep to the melody of Handel's "Largo" on the radio. Fine Army this!

WEDNESDAY – *24.2.43*

The R.A.F. are moving up the road beside us in force.

I hear the story of Eddie Gamble, who escaped from Benghazi once, after "Jerry" had occupied it. With another man, he joined a party of Bedouins, who disguised them to look like themselves and brought them through the enemy lines with many narrow escapes. In eleven days they walked from Benghazi to Gazala, a distance of about 200 miles. They were covered with lice when they finally reached safety. Eddie is now our Post Bombadier – that is, the man who collects all the mail for the Regiment. But he is also known as "The Benghazi Harrier"!

TUESDAY – *25.2.43*

News that the First Army has intervened to help the "Yanks" and "Jerry" has been pushed back through the gap at Kasserine. I have seen "Monty" again, going forward in his tourer, with two other cars and two Jeeps. Rumour says the 51st (Highland) Division will go in tonight to attack the Mareth Line, from our right. Sounds of intermittent gunfire all day, and many of our fighter-bombers go over. Several M.E.s also appear and are greeted by ack-ack.

FRIDAY – *26.2.43*

Greasing truck, when sky suddenly becomes filled with ack-ack bursts. Eight M.E.s fly over the nearby 'drome, where one is shot down. The other seven come past us and some of the fellows run for shelter in case of strafing. Someone has a go with a Bren and I pick up my rifle and a clip of tracers but the 'planes are already too far off for accuracy. More 'planes come over on two later occasions.

The road has a constant stream of traffic on it: tanks, transporters, 6-pounder anti-tank guns, 25-pounders, 60-pounders, armoured cars, Bren-gun carriers, Bofors and 3.7-in. A.A., 3-tonners, 8-cwt. P.Us., ambulances, jeeps, R.A.F. breakdowns, recovery vehicles and the new armoured A.E.C. portees carrying 25-pounders, to say nothing of motor-cycles, staff-cars and water trucks. They have been passing all day and for several days. Look out, "Musso"!

At dinner, 5.00 p.m., another raid came, with an even fiercer barrage, the sky being a smother of shell-puffs, while guns banged and engines droned and screamed. One A.A. shell landed near our cookhouse, leaving a small crater.

SATURDAY – 27.2.43
More aerial activity and dog-fights. Ack-ack more concentrated than ever. A shower of shrapnel whistles down around us. I have a cold and a sore throat.

SUNDAY – 28.2.43
See one of the new Spitfires with the wing-tips clipped off like the German M.E.109.

MONDAY – 1.3.43
Irish Guards go up, complete with 6-pounders.

From about 6.00 p.m. we were surprised to see many shell-bursts on the aerodrome. It was heavily bombarded for two hours, but most of the 'planes got away undamaged and flew back towards El Assa. The ground staff were also evacuated and their transport passed along the road all night. A few more shells came over in the early morning.

TUESDAY – 2.3.43
The R.A.F. return to the 'drome but not in force. More shelling on the airfield and on the other side of the road. Some come closer to us, till we hear the "whow" of shrapnel and one lands just across the road from us, quite near, but none amongst the vehicles.

WEDNESDAY – 3.3.43
"Jerry" is making a counter-attack, so the "B" Echelons will move

out to safer positions. Heavy exchange of gunfire to the west. We see many shell-bursts on the Lone Hill.

We go eighteen miles towards Zarzis on the Djerba Island road and stop in a sparse wheat-field. We are still within sound of guns as we have gone roughly north-east instead of east.

I notice a plant whose circle of leaves lies flat on the ground, until the sun rises above the horizon, then each leaf tilts up to face it and, as the sun moves round, so do the stems bend or twist and the leaves follow the light-giver like a sound-locator following an aeroplane!

Saturday – 6.3.43
Call at forward R.H.Q., near the Lone Hill where we see shells still landing, while our guns reply. Next, back to No. 1 O.F.P. to collect some trucks. Ack-ack opens up strongly on another airfield and there is a series of deafening explosions as bombs drop from a Macci which passes over our heads. We hear a whine which seems near, yet all over the sky and we duck low as a shell lands to one side of us. Our ears have hardly stopped singing when, five minutes later, there are more bombs, more ack-ack and another spent shell bursts on our other side! We return to R.H.Q. just as two more enemy planes swoop low out of a smother of flak and, as they streak over the echelon area, they leave a line of ten or twelve bomb-bursts. They are only about fifty feet up when they release the bombs but get no hits.

On the Ben Gardane road, we see the remains of a truck blown to bits and two graves dated 22nd February – the same day that we passed that way coming up! There is a crater in the road. We also have a look at one of the new 17-pounder anti-tank guns. It has a very long piece, giving great velocity and penetration.

Rain at night.

Sunday – 7.3.43
Lovely morning, still and sunny, with just a stir of a breeze. More like home, with larks singing and flowers growing among the fresh wet wheat. But the guns are still booming up the road. "Jerry" has made two strong attacks from Nareth, both broken. Our guns knock out thirty-two tanks.

Tuesday – 9.3.43
Official news that "Jerry" has been driven back into the Mareth

Line, after failing to take "high ground" near Medenine. He lost thirty-three tanks all told.* Our bombers sink three ships and leave four burning, in a convoy coming to Tunis.

WEDNESDAY – *10.3.43*

We move to R.H.Q. echelon area and park in a wadi which affords good cover and, when enemy planes come over in the first hour, we are glad of it. The ack-ack blazes away and, when it stops, some of our fighters close in and chase the enemy out of sight.

From our position, we see the 'drome at Medenine being shelled again, the shells apparently coming right over the top of the Lone Hill.

Our mail now comes via Tripoli and letters from home are expected to reach us in four days.

THURSDAY – *11.3.43*

Write some letters while shells keep bursting on the 'drome and surroundings. They have not got these guns "taped" yet. Saw eighteen of our bombers coming back from attack on the enemy.

FRIDAY – *12.3.43*

Another eighteen go over. Seventeen come back.

MONDAY – *15.3.43*

Went to Medenine for a hot shower, fitted up by the R.E. in an arabesque building. The water was pumped from a well to the showers, being heated on the geyser principle. Outside were some large shell holes and a demolished building. The long-range shelling has stopped now, so perhaps they have cleaned up "Jerry's" artillery. The native quarter of Medenine consists of hovels made of dark brown mud, set close together and completely covering a hillock, so that the general appearance is that of a big ant-heap.

TUESDAY – *16.3.43*

Flares light up the area in the early morning and bombs are dropped but they don't find the 'drome. The rear gunner of an enemy 'plane tries some "blind" strafing with a heavy machine-gun. He is swinging

---

* Later the figure was given as fifty-two.

the gun from side to side, for the green tracers "wriggle" down like a whip-lash.

More bombing in the evening. Heavy artillery barrage from our lines, causing aurora effect again.

WEDNESDAY – *17.3.43*
Working on punctured radiators.

THURSDAY – *18.3.43*
Radio officially announces that our fighters had operated for two weeks "... from an aerodrome continually under shellfire from the Mareth Line".

FRIDAY – *19.3.43*
Go to O.F.P. to dump a used engine.

SATURDAY – *20.3.43*
Our bombers still go over eighteen at a time. Enemy bombers also busy – we see the bomb-bursts forward of our position. Rumour says our push starts tonight to break the Mareth Line. Preliminary objectives have already been taken by the Guards, suported by one of the anti-tank batteries of our regiment (The Norfolk Yeomanry). The First Army and the American Fifth Army will make a push on the North Sector at the same time, while "Jerry" will be bombed from all sides, including Malta.

(LATER)
Personal message to the Eighth Army from General Montgomery:

1) On 5th March Rommel addressed his troops in the mountains overlooking our positions and said that if they did not take Medenine and force the Eighth Army to withdraw, then the days of the Axis forces in North Africa were numbered.

The next day, 6th March, he attacked the Eighth Army. He should have known that the Eighth Army NEVER WITHDRAWS; therefore his attack could only end in failure – which it did.

2) We will now show Rommel that he was right in the statement he made to his troops. The days of the Axis forces in North Africa are indeed numbered. The Eighth Army and the Western Desert Air Force, together consti-

tuting one fighting machine, are ready to advance. We all know what that means – and so does the enemy.

3) In the battle that is now to start, the Eighth Army:

    (a) will destroy the enemy now facing us in the Mareth position;

    (b) will burst through the Gabes Gap;

    (c) will then drive Northwards on Sfax, Sousse and finally Tunis.

4) We will not stop, or let up, till Tunis has been captured and the enemy has either given up the struggle or been pushed into the sea.

5) The operations now about to begin will mark the close of the campaign in North Africa. Once the battle starts, the eyes of the whole world will be on the Eighth Army and millions of people will listen to the wireless every day – hoping anxiously for good news. We must not let them be anxious. Let us see that they get good news and plenty of it, every day.

    If each one of us does his duty and pulls his full weight, nothing can stop the Eighth Army. And nothing will stop it.

6) With faith in God and in the justice of our cause, let us go forward to victory.

7) Forward to Tunis! Drive the Enemy into the Sea!

B.L. MONTGOMERY,
General,
G.O.C. in C., Eighth Army.

Sunday – 21.3.43
We are told that our troops have broken the Mareth Line in two places and our heavy forces are going through, but no news till Mr. Churchill, speaking over the radio, announces that he has just received a message from General Montgomery saying the Eighth Army is on the move and he is satisfied with its progress.

From bits of "gen" which filtered back to us, it appeared that 50th (Tyne and Tees) Division had made a bridgehead but were almost surrounded by the enemy on the other side of the treacherous Wadi Zigzaou. Sappers, working under shellfire, tried to construct a crossing for tanks and transport. Bundles of brushwood were thrown into the stream but the crossing was churned up and, by the morning of 21st March, only four tanks had reached the other side to support the infantry. In spite of this, the Durham Light Infantry attacked again and widened the bridgehead.

The enemy threw in extra forces with armour on the 22nd March and the Northumbrians were slowly pushed back, fighting hard but suffering heavy losses.

MONDAY – *22.3.43*

Move forward towards the Mareth Line. In the evening there is a full moon and enemy planes come over. The ack-ack gives a display of "fireworks". Large ground flares are dropped and make a blinding white glare among some scrub. There are some big bangs, then we see a red glow in the white area as something is hit and burns. The radio, telling of our attack on the coastal sector of the Mareth Line, says our air "umbrella" was so effective that the Luftwaffe had not shown its nose! Ed says, "Well, then, somebody is kidding us out here!" This is one of the hottest spots we have been in for some time. All night we are kept awake by strafing and ack-ack. In the lulls, one hears the click and thud of shovels digging slit-trenches in the stony ground. A Bofors near us lets go at a low-flying plane and the pilot drops a bomb towards him and flies on. I see smoke rising, just over in the next hollow. "Jerry" may not come out by day but he has an annoying nocturnal air force.

TUESDAY – *23.3.43*

It seems we passed our proper position by mistake yesterday and, by the sound of the firing, it looks as if we almost went into no-man's-land! We are being taken back.

(LATER)

As we turned back, a large explosion was seen where we had been a moment earlier. We move again at midday and, as we turn west past the Lone Hill, we see the "heavies" bursting in front; then, when we go north along a sunken track, four more burst close on our right. I expect he has 'planes spotting for him. After going along and back several wrong tracks, we finish up among scrub-covered humps beside a marshy wadi. All the desert wadis were dry but the Tunisian ones have water in them and this one is teeming with life. Frogs croak like rooks and clouds of mosquitoes hover about. We find some ants with a white "V" on their backs, so we nickname them "Victory" Ants. Another queer thing I notice is a streamlined black water-worm with a red line and a fan-tail. There are also plenty of dragonflies of all colours. Everything shimmers in the baking heat. The wadi winds along in a gorge with reeds growing in the mossy pools. We call our camp River View. If the water was germ-free we could bathe in it but there is a danger of bilharzia.

We speak to a passing Arab, who has lost his right hand. He says it was blown off by a German bomb.

While we were investigating our surroundings, however, things were desperate in the bridgehead at Mareth. Unknown to us, the gallant 50th Division troops were withdrawn during the night of 23rd March and no foothold remained in the Mareth Line.

WEDNESDAY – 24.3.43
We find a pool further down the wadi, five feet deep and running, so six of us go in for a swim. The edge is a quicksand. Jackie (a Yorkshire member of the Norfolk Yeomanry) comes pounding down the bank at full speed, does a beautiful "springboard" jump at the edge, sinks to his knees, and falls flat on the water!

Afterwards, we explore the ravine further. In one pool we see some eels about two feet long. Higher up the steep side, we watch a snake glide rapidly under a rock and, up in the heights of the "canyon", we find shelter-caves used by sheep. Lizards run upside-down on the roof of one of these caves.

These lizards are active, alert and quite harmless. Once in the desert, when we were filling our water-bottles at the water truck, a lizard came scampering across, then stopped six feet away, watching us, his tail twitching and his sides showing a tiny palpitation. He must have either scented the water or heard its trickle and his whole attitude seemed to say, "I could do with a drink!" I hurriedly folded a piece of paper into a spill and gathered a blob of water in one end of the fold. I held it out at arm's length. He looked at me for a moment and then, as I remained motionless, came right up to the spill and drank the water. I hope the chlorine didn't upset his tummy!

THURSDAY – 25.3.43
Changing engine in a Chevrolet truck.

The Mareth Line is not yet broken but has been out-flanked thirty miles inland. Fierce fighting going on.

The New Zealanders had discovered the opposition on the flank was weakened by the removal of forces to meet the 50th Division and progress was being made. I have heard it said that the heavy losses sustained by the 50th Division occasioned some bitterness against "Monty" but there seems to be little doubt that, by pinning down heavy enemy forces at the bridgehead, they saved the rest of the formations from possible attrition and made easier the final break-through. "Monty" was flexible enough to swing the main power of attack on to the flank in a strong "left hook" and soon the enemy in the Mareth Line was in danger of being cut off.

SATURDAY – *27.3.43*
Move once again to the Lone Hill. Enemy said to be out of the Mareth Line. The Navy shells Gabes, through which "Jerry" is retreating. The New Zealanders are at El Hamma. "Monty" radios to "Jerry", "Surrender or be annihilated."

A film called Desert Victory, *taken during the advance from Alamein to Tripoli, is being shown at home.*

MONDAY – *29.3.43*
The enemy has an anti-tank screen on his flank but is being harassed by bombers.

TUESDAY – *30.3.43*
Warned of indiscriminate mine-laying by "Jerry" again. We put sandbags in the floor of our truck-cab.

WEDNESDAY – *31.3.43*
Move at 10.00 a.m. Traffic congestion said to be bad at Gabes Gap. Our trucks line up in bright sunshine. There is an expectant air about everything. Where the main road goes off to Mareth, there is a constant stream of vehicles rounding the foot of the Lone Hill. We cross the road and follow the track to Matmata. Soon we come into the foothills and, as we approach the outposts to the Mareth Line, the ground is lousy with mines. Some have been lifted and are scattered along each side of the track and the sappers are scraping others up with their hands. One man has a piece of metal with which he is gently scraping the surface of the ground as if suspecting the presence of an anti-personnel mine. Another is easing up a metal

plate with the point of his bayonet, while his mate crouches on the ground to look closely underneath for hidden wires or a trigger.

As we cross an open space, the track shows a tiny, dusty ribbon, winding away up between two hills ahead of us. When we reach this ravine, we pass many anti-tank ditches and, beside trenches dug down to solid rock, there are boxes of Italian ammo. Barbed wire and trenches run around the higher parts of the ravine. The hills are really high here and machine-gun nests built on ledges and in holes in the rock cover the track below.

Out of the red hills and on to a wide green plain, we park for the night.

THURSDAY – *1.4.43*
Move north again; the whole army advancing. When we stop once more, a French-speaking Arab tells us we are twenty-four kilometres from Gabes (i.e. about fiteen miles).

I walk across an empty Arab camp site, where heaps of brushwood are lying about and some other fellows also cross the area. When we come out the other side, we find dozens of little red *fleas hopping all over us and biting like the devil! We frantically begin killing them and I take drastic action with petrol on the seams of my clothes.*

Curse the filthy Arabs! They must be immune to typhus for they live with fleas and lice.

These fleas (if they *were* fleas) had such a hard shell that squeezing them between the fingers had no effect on them. They had to be crushed between two finger-nails in order to kill them. In the cleft between the two halves of the shell, a spike protruded, which could be bent down under the insect like a spring. When the spring was released, the flea just vanished, to be next spotted about three feet away! That was how they had jumped on to us as we walked past!

FRIDAY – *2.4.43*
Some of those fleas are still around!

SATURDAY – *3.4.43*
Find more fleas on my blankets. More drastic action!

There is a native she-dog in a cavity near a heap of old timber, guarding her pups, where the evacuated Arabs have had to leave her, without food or water. We go over with some bully and goat's milk (which we obtained from another Arab in exchange for boric eye-lotion).

As we approach, we are greeted with a ferocious growl but, when I throw in some bully, she peeps out, then eats the meat quietly and drinks the milk.

In the evening, Greg "hands" us an eye-witness account of a chess game:

> "Denny moves his King, see, and then Baz brings up the Prince o' Wales and says, 'Check!' But that doesn't bother Den; he moves Nelson's Column four inches and tykes the Prince o' Wales orf the board! Oh, it's a smashin' gyme, I tell yer!"

Monday – 5.4.43

Early this morning, an enemy plane dropped flares above us. He circled while the flares came down slowly on their tiny parachutes. When they were low enough to light up our trucks, he came back in a low dive, in a straight line. I got out of my bivvy and walked away from the truck area, just before he landed two bombs a short distance away, one truck being hidden by smoke for a few seconds. After that, I kept my clothes on.

(later in the day)

We made a tin mudguard for the Colonel's car, from petrol cans! The original was blown off, along with the wheel, when he hit a mine.

See for the first time two of the twin-fuselage Lockheed "Lightning" planes overhead. An Arab arrives to collect the bitch and puppies from the wood-pile. One of the pups was given to "Floss", the cookhouse pet, to look after. Floss used to obey every little command of her master; now she won't leave the puppy.

In the evening, we have a lecture from the Colonel on the coming attack on new enemy positions at Wadi Akarit.

We have the Guards Division on the coast, the 51st (Highland) Division and 50th Northumbrian Division in the middle and the 4th Indian Division on the left flank. The 1st and 7th Armoured

Divisions are in reserve, to take armour through when a gap is forced.

We are faced by "Jerry's" 90th Light Division on the coast, Spezia, Trieste and Pistoria Divisions (Italian) in the centre and the German 164 Division inland. The 15th Panzers are behind the Italians, the 21st Panzers behind the 164 Division and 10th Panzers to the north, facing the "Yanks". The 15th and 21st Panzers have thirty to forty tanks between them and the 10th have ninety, including new "Tigers".

The "Yanks" are held by boggy ground, and can't help us much. Early in the morning of Tuesday, 6th April, the Indians will make a silent *attack on 164 Division at 4.30 a.m., barrage on wadi; 8.30 a.m. lift barrage to two hills behind wadi; 50th and 51st go through the centre. Our 7th Armoured Division will then cover the left flank of 51st Division and 1st Armoured Division will cover the flank of the Indians and New Zealanders. A tank battle may open in flat country to the North.*

The enemy is expected to make his next stand about Sousse, where the hills begin again.

The lecture was given with the aid of a blackboard and maps and I believe similar lectures were given throughout the Eighth Army, by "Monty's" orders. It is certainly revolutionary for a colonel to reveal a plan of battle, not only to his regiment, but to attached personnel!

It was the first time in history that every man of an army knew exactly what was to happen! It roused a greater interest in the proceedings and, I believe, imbued the men with a greater wave of confidence than they could be expected to have in face of wild rumours.

TUESDAY – 6.4.43
We hear the barrage and plenty of our planes go over. Told later that 2,000 prisoners have been taken. A large enemy air convoy tries to get to Tunis and American fighters shoot down 18 transports, 6 Stukas and 7 fighters.

The silent attack of the Indians was a great success. Going forward in the darkness, on foot, and without any Bren-carriers to cause a noise, the Indians, brandishing *kukris* and other weapons, infiltrated amongst the demoralized 164 Division and, according to one of our officers, "... had a happy time lopping off ears, etc!"

We also heard the story of a Scottish unit of the 51st Division, who discovered, during patrols before the battle, that there was a belt of "S" mines sown across their forward path. An "S" mine has wire prongs which stick up just under the surface of the ground and, when a foot depresses the prongs, there is a delay of about half a second (to allow the soldier to move forward!), then the mine jumps out of the ground and bursts when about chest-high, spraying shrapnel all around. Having "prodded" their way through the belt with bayonets, the patrols knew exactly the depth of the minefield. When the time came to advance, the Highlanders were lined up along the edge of the minefield and, on a given signal, they raced across it at full speed and threw themselves flat on the other side, as some of the mines began to burst behind them.

They got through with hardly any casualties.

WEDNESDAY – 7.4.43

All objectives at Akarit taken. American tropical kit, bush shirts, etc. are being issued to us. Heat and flies become troublesome again. Warned (a bit late) of the danger of bilharzia in local water. We move north again to a point near Gabes. Track and road verges mined as usual but many, including wooden ones, have been lifted by our sappers. These wood-cased mines have been made by "Jerry" to escape detection by our electric detectors, but they were not very successful because there were some nails in them and, of course, the firing pin, which still caused a reaction in the head-phones. We pass a tidy little cemetery of German dead. As soon as we get to our new position, we see our ack-ack open up at raiders. We park in a wadi.

"Jerry" over in the early morning, dropping flares and "cracker-bombs". These novelties keep exploding at intervals and jump to a different spot each time, just like Chinese crackers. Some were still banging twenty minutes after the planes had finished droning round!

THURSDAY – 8.4.43

Off again at 8.00 a.m.. As we by-pass Gabes, just near enough to see some of the buildings, the usual eighteen medium bombers go over. In one clump of palms there are twelve "Jerry" vehicles wrecked and burnt and a few graves.

We hit the main road to Gafsa, crossing a vast green plain, then go in among rugged hills where Axis equipment lies about under rock ledges. German and Italian prisoners are walking back in hundreds without guards. Many of them are limping, some with their boots tied round their necks and carrying heavy packs. One poor blighter has his feet bandaged and hobbles on with bits of blanket tied round them. They must have covered many miles without transport and are eager to crowd, a few at a time, on to a small Italian truck driven by an Indian. Some of our chaps swapped cap-badges with them!

About half-way towards Gafsa, we meet the first "Yanks", a couple of dispatch riders of the U.S. Fifth Army, coming in the opposite direction. We shake hands and exchange news. But we have come too far to the west, so we go back till we reach Star Track, then turn north on Sun Track. (The tracks still have the same names that they had at Alamein!) We finally stop in a recently used gun-pit. Later, we are found to be in the wrong place and are moved 200 yards.

Later still, we are, amazingly, found to be in the wrong place, so we move about ten miles!

We cross Wadi Akarit, where again we see dug-outs, guns and piles of enemy equipment. We stop in a small wadi, but there are regular rows of little humps where the earth has been disturbed, so Ed and I take a bayonet and prod for mines. We find none, so conclude the natives have been working, perhaps lifting plants, and we take the truck across.

FRIDAY – 9.4.43
Move early. Transport on every track as far as the eye can see. We cross the railway which goes to Maknassy and stop near the village of Graiba. The boys have been asking me what clan Maknassy belongs to!

Give a tin of bully to two hungry "Jerry" soldiers going back on their own. The railway bridge is destroyed, many Italian tanks are lying about "busted" and a British truck has been blown up on its side by a mine at the crossroads.

Rumour says that "Jerry" has used twenty captured "Sherman" tanks against us, the tanks being taken from either the First Army or the "Yanks". Both these forces are now advancing.

SATURDAY – *10.4.43*

Off again. Pass Graiba Station, which has been hit by a big shell. Halt near a large orange grove for tiffin. I pick up a letter in Italian which ends, "'Rivederci presto". ("See you again soon!") It may have been sent to one of the many prisoners we have seen.

No further move today.

SUNDAY – *11.4.43*

Move early, fast and far. I greet a French soldier, who replies, "Salut, mon vieux!" The natives also appear glad to see us. One driver faints at the wheel and runs off the road into a stationary truck, injuring himself and his mate. We go through miles of olive groves and finally stop in one, a few miles from Sfax, on a road leading to some reservoirs. Real reservoirs! We are surrounded by a blaze of red poppies and yellow marguerites under the olive trees.

MONDAY – *12.4.43*

We can see Sfax from a nearby hill. It looks a big place. Went out to recover a 3-tonner stuck in soft sand, driving for several miles through narrow, cactus-bordered lanes and found the truck near a house.

The French family here were very friendly and invited us into the house. The head of the family, an elderly man, was an agent in the olive-oil industry, whose house in Sfax was bombed by our planes.

"C'est la guerre; c'est juste," he said philosophically.

I was kept busy talking and they told me that "Jerry" took all spare clothing, footwear and even some furniture, put it on a truck and drove off with it.

Soon a younger man began to play the piano. When he played my favourite, "J'attendrai", I started to sing the words and his charming young wife joined in and made it a duet. After the musical interlude, they gave us wheaten bread, olives and almonds and apologised for having no wine as they had given away the last sixty litres already.

They seemed really pleased to see British soldiers and gave us an open invitation to visit them again.

In the afternoon, we visit Sfax, which has had a terrific smashing from our bombers, including one raid of 100 'planes. The outer, modern houses are French, with the old walled town right in the centre, a labyrinth of crooked alleys.

TUESDAY – *13.4.43*
Our echelons are going north about eighty miles but we wait to change two engines. The Holy City of Kairouan has been captured.

WEDNESDAY – *14.4.43*
Engines finished.

THURSDAY – *15.4.43*
Off early. We pass El Djem and are fortunate enough to halt for a few minutes quite near the Roman amphitheatre. The greater part of this huge eliptical edifice is still standing and it resembles the Colosseum in Rome.

When I told Greg it was in places like this that they used to throw Christians to the lions, he regarded it with renewed but rather morbid interest.

On we go to M'saken and then turn inland towards Kairouan. The country is green and fertile.

When we reach Kairouan, which is very picturesque, we find that the ancient town, like Sfax, is surrounded by a defensive wall. The brown and white domes of mosques and tombs appear at intervals. The modern French suburb is lined with trees, and tricolours hang across every street to celebrate the liberation. British, French and American soldiers intermingle on the footpaths. Many of these Frenchmen came with General Leclerc, all the way across the Sahara from Chad, to meet us in Southern Tunisia.

We stop with the echelon just west of the town. The radio announces that the total number of prisoners taken since the Mareth battle is 30,000.

FRIDAY – *16.4.43*
Move back through Kairouan to a position north of the town. There is a large German cemetery in Kairouan and also a Moslem one with two large craters in it. We see the fluted domes of the Great Mosque, in which are preserved as a sacred relic a few hairs said to be from the Beard of the Prophet. This is why Kairouan is regarded as a Holy City and a place of pilgrimage by the Moslems.

The amphitheatre at El Djem.
The "Royal Box" was above the archway opposite.

In a field outside the town, we see some huge craters, one of which is fifty feet across! We fill a sandbag with beans and another with carrots, making a good dinner supply. There is some battle wreckage lying about: tanks, guns and trucks. The big craters may be due to the enemy destroying an ammunition dump.

Mosquitoes plentiful at night. We have risked bilharzia from swimming, typhoid from drinking, typhus from fleas and now malaria from mosquitoes! What a country!

SATURDAY – *17.4.43*
See a captured "Jerry" armoured car with eight wheels – all driving and steering – independent springing and a 75 mm gun!

SUNDAY – *18.4.43*
Spent the forenoon in Kairouan. This is the most intriguing, most arabesque place I have seen of all the towns in North Africa. We wander into a maze of narrow streets, some only four feet wide and come to a line of native bazaars, where tradesmen work in full view of the passing throng. Leatherworker, tinsmith, coppersmith, saddler, rope-maker and shoemaker are all represented. In the dim interior of one large shop, carpets, tapestries and antiques are preserved from the strong light behind ample blinds. I buy an attractive tapestry, hoping to get it home with the mail.

It arrived safely and I still have this tapestry, which has a typically oriental design, depicting a sheik on horseback, with a mosque in the background.

Coming into the French quarter, I get a pleasant surprise when I meet Bill Shorter! It is almost a year since I last saw him at Bir Hacheim, 1,000 miles away, before I went to hospital. He is still with the 2nd K.R.R.C.

After a chat with Bill, I rejoin the others, we have coffee and return to camp for dinner. Afterwards, the inevitable native appears and we exchange one pair of Italian breeches for two dozen Arabic eggs!

MONDAY – *19.4.43*
Forward ten miles and park on a slope overlooking the plain where the echelons are spread out. Big mountains lie ahead of us. We find five tortoises, which must have been taken prisoner by the U.S.

forces and later released, for one has "Ike" painted on his shell and another "Joe"!

The push towards Tunis begins tonight. Fighting may be fiercer than ever. We are told a million shells will be fired in two nights.

At 6.30 p.m. we are found to be on the wrong spot on the map, so we load up the truck to go back six miles!

In our new position, we park among eight-foot prickly pear cactus, the flat oval pads of which are covered with spikes, like ivory needles, two inches long.

Radio news says we have shot down seventy-four out of 100 transport 'planes returning to Sicily.

TUESDAY – 20.4.43
Eighteen of our bombers roar back with a fighter escort, of which seven are twin-fuselage Lightnings. Two of the Lightnings go over in a victory roll; two more enemy 'planes down!

Insect life under the prickly pear is prolific. There are crickets of all colours and sizes, perfectly camouflaged stick-insects and the praying mantis, one of which is four inches long, green and yellow and almost indistinguishable in the grass. We view them through a magnifying glass and marvel. We also watch ants taking seed pods down into their nest and bringing up the "empties", the seeds apparently being stored underground. The empty pods were heaped around the "doorway".

WEDNESDAY – 21.4.43
First objectives taken. Mountain ridges cleared in face of M.G. and mortar fire. Counter attacks repulsed.

THURSDAY – 22.4.43
In the evening we find ourselves in the midst of a big electric storm, with blinding flashes and "runs" of lightning, deafening cracks and heavy rain hissing down on the cactus. Between flashes, it is pitch black and a voice from the dark asks, "Can anyone tell me where I am?" A forage cap and a black moustache appear at the tailboard of the truck and behind the moustache is "Big Sid" of H.Q. Company, whose truck is about 300 yards away. We direct him, and off he goes, feeling his way carefully through the spiky cactus.

SUNDAY – *25.4.43*
Move about eight miles north-east, crossing the River Zeroud at an irrigation dam, where a few Americans are swimmimg. Gunfire is receding. We are now near Lake Kelbia.

TUESDAY – *27.4.43*
Cross a plain of dried mud, moving parallel to the hills (that is, north-east) for ten miles. Gunfire in the nearest hills; we can see muzzle-flashes from our guns on the lower slopes.

WEDNESDAY – *28.4.43*
Thirty-six fighter-bombers go over, then eighteen medium bombers with escort.

One of the sergeants of the regiment is on a charge for taking a radio from French civilians by showing a false "chit" of "authority".

It is amusing to bargain with the natives for eggs. The Berber is just as cautious as the Senussi. Given any encouragement, he will sit cross-legged as if prepared to spend all day on the job. Indeed, he seems to derive a solemn pleasure from it and is slightly hurt if the transaction is concluded too quickly. Slowly, as the haggling goes on, eggs appear, one by one, from the recesses of his voluminous clothing, just like a conjuring trick and, each time, the egg is added to the pile, with the air of making a great sacrifice.

"Tamania, khulloss; ana mouskein!" ("Eight, finished; I am poor!")

When we jokingly suggest that we, too, are poor, he spreads his hands, raises his eyes heavenwards and says: "Ala Allah!" ("Trust in God!")

THURSDAY – *29.4.43*
Three lots of bombers with escort, followed by fifty fighter-bombers go over. Gunfire again receding.

FRIDAY – *30.4.43*
Changing a Bedford engine. Our planes fly over in larger numbers than ever. Told we are going to help the First Army! The radio announces that they have been driven back by enemy counter-attacks. We get orders to pack ready to move at dawn on a journey of 150 miles. The whole of the 7th Armoured Division and the 4th

Indian Division are believed to be going to Tebourba, the First Army country.

SATURDAY – *1.5.43*

Off at 6.00 a.m. Stop to repair the radiator of a truck which, during the night, ran on to the muzzle of a gun which was being towed. In spite of the delay, we catch up again, finding the other vehicles parked in rows by the side of the Ousseltia road. There is traffic congestion ahead. Many trucks upturned at the roadside and three on the Zeroud Bridge, belonging to forward units who moved in darkness. Lanterns had been placed at intervals on the verge but, of course, our vehicles have no headlights fitted and they were travelling at 35–40 m.p.h.

Our workshop truck has some hens aboard and every time it stops, a loud cackling and clucking issues from inside! They let them out for a bit and, when we move again, a bunch of soldiers in the next column are amused at the efforts made to "herd" them back into the coop. The cock, last out, by-passes the coop every time and finally walks in of his own accord, with a dignified air. Park for the night a few miles farther on.

The crew had pooled resources to buy these birds at a farm, so that they could have their own travelling egg supply but I think the only time the hens were happy was when the truck was off the road!

SUNDAY – *2.5.43*

Off again at 6.00 a.m. into green, hilly country almost like Scotland but drier. The road has been blown away along the side of a rocky defile and built up again by our engineers, but a bridge over a gully is gone, so we go down and up steeply in first gear. All the trucks are pulling badly as if the petrol is not too good. I clean my petrol filter at lunch stop, to make sure there is no choke there.

We pass Ousseltia, whose Church has a shell-hole in the roof, then up an "alpine" road – with gradients of one in four and many sharp bends – to a beautiful view at the top. Beautiful – except for a minefield through which we have to pass! A French tank lies at one side.

The descent is through trees and high rock spurs, where the smell of fir reminds us of home. Past some French graves, including those of colonial troops, bearing the Moslem crescent in place of the cross.

Why must every touch of beauty and peace be countered by an ugly reminder of war?

The convoy has disappeared in the distance while we have been climbing. We leave the rough metalled surface for asphalt and race on to Maktar, passing Kessera, which looks like a village of cliff-dwellers.

In Maktar, there are some Roman remains, including a large arch and also a German relic; a tank which was captured by the "Yanks" and has their star painted on it. We pass an American airfield too, and notice they have many of our Spitfires.

Past Le Ser, there is still no sign of the convoy ahead and the rest of the L.A.D. is scattered somewhere behind, so we stop at dusk.

MONDAY – *3.5.43*
The breakdown truck catches us early and we go on together but, when he brakes suddenly after attempting to overtake another vehicle, I bump into him and shear off some of his spring-bracket rivets. We limp on, find our echelon and repair the damage.

I have an old forage cap and now when I drive past any of the boys, they shout, "Taxi!"

Some French cavalry go by, in typical 1914–1918 uniforms and steel helmets, proper poilus with beards and side-whiskers, like ghosts from the past; but the horses are real and their hooves "clip-clop" on the road as they pass. They are colonials under General Giraud.

We are now between Maktar and Le Kef and amongst the First Army troops. Their trucks are not yellow but "Blighty Green" and have lights fitted. The land is almost as green as home now, though the First Army boys think it is dull. They ask why our trucks are painted yellow, not realising it is the same colour as the Libyan ground.

One of our trucks had not observed correct dispersal distance on the road and a First Army M.P. caused a laugh by saying, "I can see you haven't been in the desert long!"

The driver was almost speechless.

"Desert?" he spluttered. "DESERT? – This ain't no desert! – it's a bloody FAIRYLAND!"

(Poor First Army! No wonder we called them "The Palefaces".)

In the evening, "Hasher" (of 257 Battery) brings a large jar of "scrounged" wine to our truck and we celebrate nothing in particular.

WEDNESDAY – 5.5.43
Excellent lecture by Major Boag on the forthcoming "last push" for Tunis itself. Our 4th Indian Division and the 4th Division of the First Army will supply the infantry attack and, when they have cleared a narrow gap, the 6th Armoured Division (First Army) and our 7th Armoured Division will go through in advance along parallel routes to Tunis.

The right flank will be covered by the 1st Armoured Division, the left by the "Yanks". Between twelve and eighteen bombers will go over every ten minutes, to extend the barrage, while twenty squadrons of fighter-bombers and two squadrons of tank-busters will have a roving commission in our area alone.

General Anderson will be in command, while "Monty" will keep "Jerry" busy on the east coast with the reduced Eighth Army. French forces are now ten miles from Bizerta.

THURSDAY – 6.5.43
The echelon moves, leaving us to finish changing four engines.

FRIDAY – 7.5.43
Move up towards Medjez el Bab. Our forward troops are seventeen miles from Tunis.

When we pack, one of the hens gets on the roof of the truck and struts about, defying all attempts to shoo it off. Suddenly a well-aimed bacon tin soars up, smacks the hesitating hen in the rear and she shoots off in a fast glide, protesting loudly and leaving a few feathers behind her.

The country now looks like a colour film of Colorado; red hills with shadows that appear blue through the heat-haze. We stop near a farm strong-point on a hill surrounded by barbed wire, which is festooned with tin cans intended to act as warning "bells".

The bombers are going over, two lots going each way at one time, while fighters swarm everywhere and the air is filled with thunder. This "bus service" must make "Jerry" feel sick as he looks up!

Later, we move forward again but it rains and, as we cross the country by a track, we slip about on a skin of mud. The 3-ton stores truck is sliding broadside and sometimes backwards on hills, as I strive vainly to keep her straight. Some of our Churchill tanks have been knocked out and we stop near one which hit a heap of our own mines and was thrown bodily fifteen yards away on top of a Bren-carrier where it still lies, upside down, one man being killed. (A Churchill tank weighs forty tons.)

We hear that the 11th Hussars (first again) are in Tunis. So the 7th Armoured Division got there first! Good old Desert Rats! The "Yanks" have taken Bizerta.

SATURDAY – *8.5.43*
Radio announces the fall of Tunis and Bizerta, but says the First Army took Tunis. Cheek!

Organised resistance is ended, only pockets of troops remain in the hills of Zaghouan and in the Cap Bon Peninsula.

We move on over a track through waving wheat and come out on a major road. We pass many British graves and finally stop opposite a German cemetery containing over 200 crosses. We are ten miles from Tunis.

Many truckloads of prisoners go back, this time all Germans. Our bombers still keep up their "service".

The radio says the first troops in Tunis were the 11th Hussars – spearhead of the 7th Armoured Division – and the Derbyshire Yeomanry, who led the 6th Armoured Division.

Trucks are still streaming back, crammed with enemy soldiers and sailors. They give the Nazi salute as they pass the cemetery.

We are warned of "chocolate" booby-traps.

These were reported to have the appearance of wrapped bars of chocolate. When a bar was broken, it exploded.

CHAPTER 9

Welcome ... and Murder in Tunis

"Most honoured stranger, let me now demand
Thy name, thy lineage, thy paternal land."

HOMER

SUNDAY – *9.5.43*
Truckloads of prisoners still going back, the total number of men
captured being 50,000. Our troops get an amazing welcome, while
prisoners are booed. When some of the boys go to town to attend a
Church service, they are overwhelmed, kissed, and treated to wine.
"Jerry" had forced many of these civilians to work for him and now,
liberated, they gather in crowds along the streets and a roar of
cheering and clapping greets each group of soldiers or line of trucks.
The town is so far open only to 7th Armoured Division. The French
are keenly interested when there is mention of the Eighth Army.
The long advance seems to have caught their imagination.

In the afternoon, Les (our sergeant), Denny and myself go over to
a nearby farm to buy some wine but the farmer will not accept
payment. The wine, which they make themselves, is really good,
dark red, mature and mellow. It used to go to France but now
they have it on their hands in thousands of gallons. Denny and I
carry on a conversation in French, exchanging information with the
farmer.

Fuel for the tractors is very short, he tells us, and clothes are hard
to get. His light jacket is four years old but spotlessly clean. We
should be taking some of the wine back for the others but Les, who
has no idea what we are talking about, has nothing else to do but

238

pass round the bottle and, as soon as it is empty, another is placed before us, with the result that we get really drunk!

That was the only time I was ever completely "blotto" and I didn't like it. It simply spoiled the day's enjoyment and the appreciation of a good wine. There came a stage when, far from speaking French, we could hardly speak English! I have a dim recollection of saying good-bye to the farmer (several times) then we wove our way through a wheatfield on a hill, leaving tracks which I am sure were anything but straight, and came down to the trucks on the other side. By this time, my legs were like rubber and I sat on the steps at the back of the "stores", hardly able to hold up my eyelids.

The other two disappeared into the distance, singing, and I had just enough sense left to ask a couple of the boys to fix up my bivouac for me, which they were good enough to do. My blankets were unrolled and, with assistance, I crawled in and remembered no more!

MONDAY – *10.5.43*
Drive a leave party to H.Q., then ask for lemonade (that's right, lemonade!) in the village of Mornaghia, but the café is sold out.

Mr. Rodway tells us of a large gathering of prisoners who had their own band playing to them in the "cage".

It is now established that the "Cherry Pickers" (11th Hussars) were in Tunis just ten minutes before the First Army men! They have been first in Tobruk, Benghazi, Tripoli, Sfax and now Tunis. Altogether, the Division has travelled 1,700 miles.

In the final advance, the following units of the Eighth Army were attached to the First Army: 1st Armoured Division; 4th Indian Division; 7th Armoured Division and 201 Guards Brigade.

The first number of the *Tunis Telegraph*, a British paper, was printed on Monday, 10th May, while "mopping-up" was still going on. It announced that Sergeant Lyons of the 11th Hussars took the first armoured car into the city. A "Desert Rat" cameraman was riding on the second car when two German officers drove up in a Volkswagen and threw a hand grenade straight at him.

The guns of the armoured cars shot the two Germans to ribbons. Although wounded, the cameraman recorded the whole incident.

Tuesday – *11.5.43*

Move to position near Protville, five miles from Tunis, with the promise of seven to ten days' stop and a trip to town every second day. Eddie Culhane, Denny and I take the chance and go into Tunis at midday.

We have dinner, complete with wine, in a crowded restaurant where the manager gives us personal attention. Then we are "adopted" by a Jewish family anxious to show us around.

On the way to their home, they take us into their synagogue which, they tell us, is 700 years old. A ritual is in progress and, as usual, we remove our caps. The congregation, however, are wearing a variety of headgear and facing them sits a stout man with an ordinary tweed cap on his head. He seems to be blind and is impassively chanting in a wavering minor key.

Our hosts take us over to a wood-panelled wall and, sliding back one of the panels, show us the Scroll of the Law, a yellow parchment mounted on two wooden spindles.

Later, seated in their house, they tell us how the Germans forced them to work and how treacherous the Arabs became because of German propaganda against the Jews. Some Germans have been captured in Arab houses, they say, and two "Tommies" who got themselves drunk in the native quarter were killed.

Suddenly, in the midst of our conversation, there is a loud bang outside, followed by a lot of yelling. We go out into a lane and, a few yards away, see a few people gathering around an opening leading into a tiny back court, which has a concrete surface and whitewashed walls.

Inside the court, there is a woman slumped against the wall, bleeding from a dozen wounds, with half of one leg almost off and a kiddie lying prone in a large pool of blood, which completely surrounds the small body.

An American G.I. arrives just as we get there and he grabs the child by an ankle and turns it over. There is no face - just a mass of red pulp. Yet there is a faint snoring sound, which to my shocked mind indicates the death-rattle.

"My God!" whispers the G.I.

Both victims are beyond first aid and, as none of the people standing around seem to know where to find a doctor, we ask about the police. Felix (our host) is more alert than the others and indicates the way. Denny and I push our way through the small crowd, leaving Eddie with Felix and we hasten along the lane to a broader street, where we find a police office on a corner.

Even in our hurry, we realised it must have been a grenade of some sort that had exploded but we did not know if the child had been playing with it, or if it had been thrown maliciously. (We found out later.)

There were two policemen in that office, one short, plump and wearing a helmet; the other tall, thin, with a pointed beard. We hurriedly explained, in deteriorating French, what had happened, emphasizing the immediate need for a doctor and an ambulance.

I have seen and heard about "theatrical" Frenchmen but what followed I would never have believed if I had not witnessed it with my own bewildered eyes.

They gabbled at each other with much shrugging and gesticulating but apparently could not decide where a doctor might or might not be found.

"Shorty" seemed disinclined to do anything very much but "Lofty" finally drew a telephone towards him. This, his whole attitude proclaimed, was an emergency! Leaning forward, he began to dial a number, raising his hand after each digit, in an exaggerated gesture that would have done credit to a silent film comedy. Then he straightened himself with a jerk, the pointed beard jutting out as he waited, with the air that now something ought to happen.

However, his optimism was misplaced, for nothing happened.

I am not sure if that 'phone ever worked. Perhaps it was just a "prop" to impress chance visitors!

As neither of them seemed to have any other ideas, or showed any intention of leaving the office even to visit the scene of horror back in the lane, we left them, still spreading their hands, and went further down the street. We found a chemist in his shop and asked if he would come along with some bandages. He was very reluctantly closing the shop to do so when he saw a doctor he knew coming towards us, and carrying his little bag.

The story was repeated and, slowly, the doctor moved up towards the lane, as if he couldn't care less whether he got there that day or the next. Since there were now plenty of people to give him assistance, we left him to it and returned to our friends.

In a quieter mood, we finished our wine and were made to promise to call again.

TUESDAY – *11.5.43 (Contd.)*
As we make our way out through the town, crowds have again gathered, cheering, clapping and giving the "V" sign, "pour la victorie".

A smart, open car appears, containing General Giraud, and immediately some of our boys swarm over the running boards to shake hands with him! The General submits smilingly.

Sitting in our truck at night, feeling rather overwhelmed, we are talking about all that has happened, when someone comes along to warn us that four "Jerries" have just been captured in our area, dressed as Arabs. We are also given the news that we are leaving Tunis! Good-bye, leave; good-bye, rendezvous with Felix and the rest of our Jewish friends!

WEDNESDAY – *12.5.43*
We are going back to Tripoli! We manage to collect ten gallons of beer from Tunis before leaving.

Well, we have finished one big job! What next?

We are all rather despondent at leaving Tunis so soon, leaving civilization to return through the desert. Even Tripoli does not equal Tunis. It is a silent army which takes the road.

We go by Tebourba, Medjez el Bab and Testour. On one part of the road, near a farm, we see ten large animals: bulls, horses and mules, and one dog, all blown to bits. Several of the bulls have been completely torn in half.

These animals must have been bunched together on the road when a bomb was dropped amongst them. The road surface was gouged.

Twice we cross the Medjerda River, the first crossing being at a pretty spot where a water-mill stands beside a weir and a bridge. As usual, the centre span of the bridge has been blown out.

THURSDAY – 13.5.43
Stop at Bou Arada, which is knocked about but the war memorial still stands: "Bou Arada a ses Glorieux Morts".

There is a field of mint here but the ground has cracks a foot deep in it.

Latest figures: 150,000 prisoners; 250 German tanks; 100 Italian tanks; 500 artillery pieces; 500 anti-tank guns, etc. (Before the battle, we were told the enemy had only 120 tanks!)

The total number of prisoners taken in the North African campaign since Wavell's first action is 400,000.

We have been issued with some "Jerry" rations as extras. They are just as good as ours.

FRIDAY – 14.5.43
Prisoners now 175,000 including sixteen Generals, but not Rommel, who flew back to Europe some time ago.

Denny fetches more beer from Tunis and gets the news from Felix that the woman and child injured by the grenade both died before reaching hospital and an Italian civilian has been arrested for their murder.

SATURDAY – 15.5.43
We are, after all, allowed another day's leave in Tunis, now fifty miles away. At Pont du Fahs we see about 20,000 prisoners in a field and a procession a mile long and six abreast on the road. The "Eye-ties" are singing "Reginella Campagnola" to the tune of the "Woodpecker's Song".

A French guard (with Sten-gun) jerks his thumb towards them and says, "Souvenirs!"

I picked up the Italian version of *"Lili Marlene"* before I knew the German words, because the Italians seemed more inclined to sing than the Germans! Later, I was to hear *"Lili Marlene"* in five different languages. One English version was sung on B.B.C. programmes and a different one (which I prefer) was printed in the Eighth Army paper, the *Crusader*.

SATURDAY – *15.5.43 (Contd.)*

We pass a Roman aqueduct which runs for miles, many parts being well preserved. When we get to Tunis, we have a look at the big building where 300 Germans held out when our forces entered the city and our "Sherman" tanks fired their 75s point-blank into it from the street.

In town, no strong drinks are being sold to troops but our companions, Felix and Edouard, order two glasses of vermouth, wink, pass them to us; then they order some more.

After going round the shops for a time, we are again taken to their home, where we are given a tremendous meal of cous-cous, *all eating from one dish.*

A huge platter was placed in the middle of the table, piled high with *cous-cous*, which was made from rye, mixed with haricots, chopped cabbage and chopped meat, with spice added.

We were simply given a large spoon each and invited to help ourselves. As was their custom, the women stood back, waiting until the men were finished, before partaking of what remained.

Around the platter were several small plates containing various hors-d'oeuvres such as: artichokes, onions, asparagus, garlic and olives.

The meal is rounded off with a little Eau-de-Vie Tunisienne, a clear spirit with a kick.

Later in the day, having digested the meal, we are taken to another house, with a marble-paved court, where we find to our surprise they have arranged a dance in our honour! We are introduced to a trio; accordion, saxophone and drums and a group of pretty girls. There have been no festivities for them during the enemy occupation and this is the first dance they have held since the Germans entered Tunisia, so everyone is happy.

As we dance beneath a bright blue sky, we converse mainly in French but they all speak Arabic and Hebrew fluently as well, together with a little English, Italian and Spanish. We enjoy ourselves immensely and part with mutual good wishes, their cries of "Bonne Chance" ringing in our ears.

A few German notices are still stuck up in the quarter, saying "Betreten verboten!" ("Out of Bounds!")

Monday – *17.5.43*
Bleaching belts with chloride, polishing brasses, etc. in preparation for a parade of all the artillery of 7th Armoured Division before General Erskine. Orders say that we must get rid of all livestock except dogs, so we kill the fowls and have half a bird each for dinner.

Tuesday – *18.5.43*
Big parade. The gunners and attached personnel form a large square, beyond which are the lines of shining guns. After his tour of inspection, General Erskine makes a speech from a tank in the middle of the square, aided by a "mike" and loudspeakers but we only hear a few of the words, owing to the wind carrying the sound away.

We finish by marching past, opposite the guns; Bofors, 6-pounders, 25-pounders and 60-pounders.

Wednesday – *19.5.43*
My kit-bag finally arrives from Cairo, slashed open and with half the contents gone!

Many souvenirs, including a small alabaster sphinx, were missing. Fortunately one of my diaries, which had been in the kit-bag, was still there, intact. Without it, this story might never have been written.

We join with the whole of the regiment at Djelida Station and move off with them. Bed down in pouring rain near Kairouan.

Thursday – *20.5.43*
Continue early, by Sidi Amor, Aguareb and Mahares, a fishing village by the sea. Stop short of Gabes, beside a grounded Messerschmitt. It is an M.E.109G, with two light machine-guns, two heavy (20 mm.) guns and one big cannon of about 40 mm. which fires through the propeller boss.

Many camp-fires flicker after dark, as there is no need for a black-out now.

Friday – *21.5.43*
By-pass Gabes and Medenine, over the usual dusty, rocky, heart-breaking tracks, passing again through the Mareth Line. The natives

have now returned to their old haunts. We draw off the road at dusk, near a "Yank" laager.

Saturday – 22.5.43

Replenish petrol and water early and, moving on, find the regiment stopped this side of Ben Gardane.

Now we hear that we are going well beyond Tripoli!

This immediately starts the usual rumours. Some think we will go back to the Delta. Others lugubriously suggest we may finish up in Burma!

We are drinking German coffee with German sugar now.

One can realise the amount of our transport – guns, tanks, etc. – only when it is all gathered in one place, as it is now. It stretches for miles.

Soon we are on the move again, crossing the frontier and continuing by Pisida, Zuara, Sabratha and Zavia.

So once more we find ourselves in Libya and amongst the little white farm-houses of Mussolini's colonists.

CHAPTER 10

Leptis Magna

SUNDAY – *23.5.43*

By-pass Tripoli via Suani, then on to Homs on the coast road. Two kilometres past Homs, we pass the "Scavi di Leptis Magna". The remains of the Roman town are on the coast side of the road and opposite is a small museum, with fragments of statuary outside. Further on, we stop among palm groves.

MONDAY – *24.5.43*

Visit nearby mosque. Interior more interesting than broken outer walls suggest. Under the dome, 20 ft. high and 15 ft. wide, there is a chamber containing three large tombs, each 10 ft. long and 4 ft. broad, enclosed in carved wood and with a head-board inscribed in Arabic. Several wooden plaques lie around, with Arabic characters painted on them in black. Perhaps some sheikh lies here, or a "wise man", a "sidi" or Moslem saint. Two smaller coffins lie beside the big ones.

The edge of the burial chamber doorway is decorated with tiles. The door itself is heavy and iron-studded. Truly, the dead often have better housing than the living in this land!

Across a little whitewashed court, shaded by fig trees, is the main chamber of worship. The door is lined with slabs of Roman carved marble, and the pillars inside are made up of parts of Roman columns, with various capitals. The floor is covered with straw mats. In another chamber, there is a small well and a row of stone basins carved out of one stone ledge, where ablutions are performed. A few frogs flop about in the channel leading to the basins. There is also a private wash-room with a bowl built into the wall and a duct linking it with another bowl on the outside of the wall, where the water is supplied.

An entrance to the market of Leptis.

Irrigation well at mosque.

The mosque has no minaret but from the court a narrow stairway leads up to a small gallery at the edge of the dome.

WEDNESDAY – 26.5.43
Move a few miles to the east. The whole unit has refused leave in Tripoli, which is eighty miles away.

A native wedding is being celebrated nearby. Two Sudanese "musicians", one with primitive bagpipes, the other with a tom-tom, play outside the little flat-roofed mosque. They appear to be drunk or in a frenzy, for their eyes are rolling.

Occasionally they are tipped, and the music stops for a moment as the one who takes the money holds it to his brow and shouts something in gutteral Arabic, probably blessings. Then a crowd of women and girls in the doorway skirl on a high tremulous note like a redskin yell, and the awful music begins again.

At a well next to the mosque, an impassive old Senussi leads his ox up and down an incline, pulling a skin bag full of water to the top of the well, where a sleeve in the bottom of the bag is pulled over a roller, allowing the water to escape into a stone reservoir, where it is stored for irrigation purposes. Shallow channels divide the adjacent land into small squares. When the time comes to release the water, some of these channels will be dammed off with mud and others opened, so that the water will run to the far side of the field and every part will receive its precious share.

At midnight, the music and wassailing at the mosque is still going on.

THURSDAY – *27.5.43*
Leave is now being accepted, on the assurance that it will not be counted against our quota of leave when we get to "civilisation".

Struggling to remove a broken and jammed half-shaft from a rear axle.

FRIDAY – *28.5.43*
Still working in clouds of the usual dust. We are supposed to be here for five weeks, so plenty of jobs roll in for us. Some "rest"! Rumours

Archway, Leptis Magna.

*of discontent in the 11th Hussars, 2nd K.R.R.C., the Queen's and
3rd R.H.A.*

SATURDAY – *29.5.43*
The wedding celebrations are still going on in the mosque!

SUNDAY – *30.5.43*
*Visit Leptis Magna, one of the most amazing sights I have ever seen;
a complete Roman city, birthplace of the Emperor Septimus Severus,
who himself caused to be built the most recent parts of the city.*

*With Fred for company, I walk along paved streets with ruined
villas on either side, under great arches, past two baths which used
to be the hot and tepid plunges and come to the swimming bath. It
is 25 yards long and 15 yards wide, with a mosaic bottom, marble-
stepped sides – providing for 5 ft. of water all over – and two low
diving platforms.*

*The water once entered the pool as a small waterfall from a duct at
one side. Although now dry, the bath is in good condition and looks
perfectly capable of holding water. Marble pillars stand round the
sides, a little way back from the edge, and opposite the waterfall are
two large columns, 3 ft. thick and 40 ft. in height, each made from
one piece of green marble with a snow-white capital, elaborately
carved.*

The sketch gives an impression of these columns, on either side of
the archway leading to the plunge baths and to rooms which were heated
by hot air circulating under the floors.

The capitals of the pillars looked like sugar icing, vastly different from
our own sooty imitations of classic architecture!

*Outside the baths is the great oval court of the Gymnasium, sur-
rounded by a colonnade and statues and with two pavements crossing at right angles, one leading to the baths and the other to the
Street of Monuments, which runs towards the sea.*

*Down a little from the baths are the public lavatories, with marble
seats and a channel for running water. On the east side of the Street
of Monuments is a fountain, the Nymphaeum. Around it is a massive semicircle of masonry, rising to a height of 50 ft. and enclosing
two colonnades, one above the other, with a carved marble frieze
running between. We climb a stairway within the thickness of the*

wall, which brings us to the top and, leaning on a modern iron railing, we look at the ancient city. Now we realise the perfection of the design and layout of the courts and streets. The city must have been at least half a mile across and many parts are still half-buried under sand, away down towards the ancient harbour to the west. In other places, scaffolding stands, where the Italians carried out restoration under the Fascist regime.

We cross the Street of Monuments and enter the spacious Forum of Severus. Miniature railway lines run everywhere, part of the excavation equipment and pieces of masonry, pillars and sculpture lie around with numbers painted on them. The Forum is about 80 yards long and 50 yards wide, almost like a small football pitch. A great colonnade runs around three sides and carved faces surmount each pillar. At one end, a pyramid of steps rises to a stone dais. Square-lintelled doorways, heavily carved, give entrance to smaller rooms and some square pillars are intricately decorated with statuettes all the way up. Again, much marble has been used but some of the walls are built of three-foot blocks of stone, others of flat bricks, decorated with designs in white.

The theatre, Leptis Magna.

I lose my six-foot companion for a moment or two, until I notice a tiny-looking figure sitting up on a high dais where, perhaps, an emperor sat in bygone days.

Now we wander by the broken walls of villas, seeing an occasional rut worn in the stone paving, so fresh it seemed that the chariot wheels might have passed but a short way ahead of us. We come to the market place, again surrounded by beautiful columns, this time of polished grey granite and in the middle is a small but deep well. The marble surround is grooved by the cords of centuries but a modern can, on a length of signal cable, serves to give us a drink of cool, clear water, with only a trace of salt!

Suddenly, we hear the faint strains of music! Hush! Is this the echo of ancient minstrels? We listen a moment, then move towards some scaffolding, go through a narrow passage and find ourselves at the Roman Theatre. Someone is playing a piano. It is the "Desert Rats" concert party!

Perfect rows of stone seats rise in a half-bowl, with steps descending between them just as in any modern theatre and here sit soldiers of the Eighth Army, being entertained where the élite of an earlier legion once watched the actors of tragedy. The same sun shines down but now the pillars behind the semicircular stone stage are lying on the ground. Around the stage is a slim wall of what I take to be porphyry; purple-brown, smooth, rounded on top and carved in bas-relief.

We leave by what might be the 2s. 6d. passage and have no more time to explore. Oh, for a camera! What pictures could be taken in this city of the past, once sacked by Vandals, and so long hidden beneath the drifting sand.

It is interesting to note that Septimus Severus, the Roman Emperor, came to Britain and died in York in A.D. 211 or 212.

MONDAY – *31.5.43*
Swimming in the sea. What a comfort it is to get the dust off our skins!

TUESDAY – *1.6.43*
Making a small model of a pillar from fragments of Leptis marble.

(I still have this model, which stands about five inches in height.)

FRIDAY – 4.6.43
Move nearer to the sea and make camp on top of a red sandstone cliff. The sea has cut a tunnel through a headland near us. We find the remains of what appears to be Roman stonework and, in an enemy slit-trench, parts of two skeletons stick out of the soil, among pieces of pottery and glass.

SATURDAY – 5.6.43
In the morning, with "Doc" (of 260 Battery), dig out one of the skeletons, finding a strong skull with thirty very good teeth, the lower jaw being separate. The legs are on the other side of the trench.

(AFTERNOON)
Four guns in for repair and four trucks having engines changed.

SUNDAY – 6.6.43
Still working, but manage to have a swim.

WEDNESDAY – 9.6.43
Jackie, our Yorkshire friend, tells us how he once dived into a slit-trench when every Stuka in Africa seemed to be coming for him. His mate was already in this particular slit-trench.

"Move along," said Jackie, "I can't get my head down!"

"I can't move," replied the other, "There's a snake in here!"

There was; it was swaying about near the end of his nose, looking extremely annoyed!

FRIDAY – 11.6.43
British forces capture Pantellaria.

The 7th Armoured Division was now being held in reserve while tanks, guns and vehicles were being overhauled, following the long and hard use to which they had been put between Alamein and Tunis. We took no part in the Sicily landings and, as it happened, when we *did* go to Italy, we did not rejoin the Eighth Army.

It was about this time that, thinking over past events and considering the possibilities of the future, I sat down and indulged my poetic imagination in rhyme.

I hope the reader may be able to forgive me (in time!) for presenting the results. It's just the way I felt at the time!

Desert Victory

The Hun was at Agheila when first I came this way,
We were halted, but there wasn't any truce,
And the Stukas gave no rest, for Rommel was at bay,
And they drove us back in no time to M'sus.

Then further back to Hacheim, where the Frenchmen made
   their stand,
Retreating only when the order came,
Then the Battle of the Cauldron, with tanks in burning sand;
Again we lost, but still our lads were game.

Back across the border (even Tobruk was lost),
By Alamein at last his force was held,
Just sixty miles from "Alex" the Hun found to his cost,
That every thrust he made, the "Eighth" repelled.

After weary months of waiting, building up our strength,
With equipment of the very best design,
We sallied forth on vengeance bent, to meet the foe at length
And ... one October night ... we broke his line!

On to Fuqa aerodrome, Matruh and El Sollum,
Forward to the frontier and the "Wire",
Tobruk, and then Mekhili, and Rommel very soon
Was fleeing from Agheila's salty mire.

Onward, ever onward, till Tripoli was ours,
Further than we'd ever been before,
To Mareth, Wadi – Akarit, and Kairwan's ancient towers,
Till Tunis fell ... and then the fight was o'er.

So now the crashing gunfire stops; the echoes die away,
And silence falls; the tanks have ceased to roll.
The Afrika Korps is finished, the Allies win the day;
Revenge for Dunkirk – our accomplished goal!

I'll leave this desert soon now, and sail across the bay,
Away from blasted dust and scorching sand,
And as I feel the heaving surge, and watch the hissing spray,
I'll be thinking of a green and pleasant land.

SATURDAY – *12.6.43*

Pack everything to move 200 yards. We are in the wrong place – but we have been there for a week!

SUNDAY – *13.6.43*

Go to Leptis again, this time with "Doc". We see, laid out against a wall, parts of a marble frieze, five feet in height, carrying carvings of a chariot, horses and other figures over a length of perhaps seventy feet. We also find an original lead pipe running through a marble block at the Nymphaeum. Next, we go along the Street of Monuments towards the sea and, on our left, come upon a very early Christian Church. A stone cross stands inside, its arms broadened at the ends. An inscription on the wall of the Church refers to "Leptimagnensium".

Further on, we pass through the Old Forum (an open square with four streets entering it) and reach the harbour.

Although silted up, the oval shape of the harbour is clearly visible and the quays are in almost perfect condition. There are steps, bollards and stone rings where the galleys tied up in those far-off days, yet they look as if they were last used yesterday.

Returning to the modern coast road, we obtain permission to enter the museum, which contains mosaics, statues, pottery etc. One mosaic shows a representation of Pegasus, the winged horse. Another shows a hippopotamus and there is a lifelike statue of an elephant, indicating that the Romans had contact with tropical Africa. Some fragments of another big sculpture include a sandalled foot, about 16 in. long, and 7 in. across the toes.

There are many crates and boxes of books, notes, plans and photographic plates concerning Leptis and also other ruins at Cirene. These records are in the care of an Italian custodian but he lets us take a look at one or two of the plate negatives, which show full-face and profile pictures of carved heads, etc.

During this second excursion to Leptis, I copied two Latin inscriptions. The first was taken from a slab of stone which lay near the remains of the marble frieze I have mentioned above. There was neither spacing nor punctuation of any kind:

QVAESIINIVLTVMQVOTMEMORIAETTRADEREAGENSPRAECVNCTOSIN
HACCASTRAMILITESVOTVMCOMMVNEMPROQVEREDITVEXERCITVS
INTERPRIORESETFVTVROSREDDEREDVMQVAEROMECVMDIG

The second inscription is from a marble block at the Nymphaeum and the words are properly spaced, apparently referring to Septimus Severus.

SEPTIMIAE POLLAE L SEPTIMI SEVERI II VIRFLAM
PERP FIL P. SEPTIMIVS GETA HER SORORI
SANCTISSIMAE EXARG P CXXXXIIII S==E DECRETO
SPLENDIDISSIMI ORDINIS POSVIT EXTESTAMENTO EIVS
HVIC DONO VICESIMAM ET ARG P IIII S==E
AMPLIS QVAM LE GATVMISI ADIECIT.

I have never had a full translation of these inscriptions and, as I know practically nothing of Latin, I will leave it to Latin scholars to make of it what they can.

TUESDAY – *15.6.43*
Preparing for big parade near Tripoli. We are told we will be inspected by "General Lion", a name which is not *in Army records.*

("General Lion" was a pseudonym used for security reasons to refer to His late Majesty King George VI.)

WEDNESDAY – *16.6.43*
The radio announces that the King has arrived in North Africa by air.

Our forces now occupy several islands between Tunisia and Sicily. Sicily is being heavily bombed.

THURSDAY – *17.6.43*
Typical Libyan weather. At R.H.Q. cookhouse, we eat grit, while flies persistently stick to food, lips and eyelashes.

SUNDAY – *20.6.43*
Off at 5.30 a.m., carrying bedding and rifle for the big parade. Hang the parades! Why don't they get on with the War? We still want to get home.

We travel 120 miles, via Tarhuna, Castel Benito and Suani, arriving on the coast road at 5.30 p.m. exactly twelve hours after starting.

(The whole Division was, of course, gathered in one area for this event.)

MONDAY – *21.6.43*

Rise early, having slept without bivouacs and get busy polishing brasses and boots. Line up to match sizes of men, tall at the ends, short in the middle. March on to the road at 3.00 p.m. Line up two deep on either side of the road, dressing-off with right arm raised to the next man's shoulder and head turned right. Another unit marches through our ranks, so we keep our arms up for ten minutes, waiting for "eyes front"!

Dusters are passed along to flick the gathering dust from our boots, then we fall out and sit on the sand to wait.

An hour later we get up. Three armoured cars of 11th Hussars go by and a signaller with a field telephone says the inspection party is on the way. Next come four M.P.s on motor-cycles; a pause – then two more; then a Jeep. Each unit has a board with a regimental title painted on it. Our boots are hurriedly dusted again.

Finally, the King's car comes, we stand at attention and catch the merest glimpse of him (sitting on the folded hood) and "Monty" in the front seat, as we stare straight across the road (Colonel's orders – "no rubber-necking"!)

Another dozen cars follow, with generals, R.A.F. officers, uniformed press men, etc. We have been told the King will shake hands with every colonel but we dare not look to see; we just keep on looking at each other across the road. The occupants of the cars must realise how browned-off we are, from our faces, which they regard intently and wonderingly. The press photographers (Army Film and Photo Unit) also look fed-up. We hear the order to remove "head-dresses" and the call for cheers, which are given half-heartedly. We expect His Majesty will be fed up too, for the Indian Division were inspected yesterday and another division will come tomorrow.

When it is all over, we are rushed to change clothing and pile bedding on to the trucks. Before we can finish our dinner, we start the return journey, the idea apparently being to disperse the Division again as quickly as possible.

Stop for tea near Tarhuna and continue by moonlight, huddled on top of each other in the trucks.

TUESDAY – *22.6.43*
Arrive at our camp at 4.00 a.m.. Everybody agrees the parade was a farce and a waste of petrol.

(LATER)
Swimming is now compulsory which, of course, adds to the pleasure of it. Enjoy yourself … or else!

Naturally, we were always "grousing". Any Briton worthy of the name will persist in retaining a mind of his own!

THURSDAY – *24.6.43*
Plenty of work in. Orders published stating definitely, "We intend to invade Europe!"

FRIDAY – *25.6.43*
Saw a young black-and-white animal like a skunk, probably a striped muishond. He seemed to be only a few weeks old, with no sign of the parent animal and was obviously terrified, yet he yapped defiantly and fiercely at us, with a husky little bark. Further outlook, continuing unfriendly; so we walked away and left him.

MONDAY – *28.6.43*
Find a new place to swim, with eight feet of water and rock edges to dive from. It is like another world below, where the rocks rise from a sandy bottom and anemones grow. The water is crystal clear. Shoals of little striped fishes are swimming around too, at least until someone comes down amongst them like a dive-bomber! One of the boys is just learning how to dive. He takes off from the highest ledge of rock, his body soaring out horizontally, though his hands are pointing hopefully down towards the water. Then he comes down, Boom! and the fishes decide there are more peaceful parts of the Mediterranean.

TUESDAY – *29.6.43*
The film Desert Victory *is shown in Homs. The record of the advance at Alamein is gripping, even to those who took part in the battle, perhaps more so because they understand better the tense feeling of going into action.*

The strained expressions on the men's faces as they go forward with fixed bayonets, the lifting barrage, the sapper dropping on the ground while his mate carries on reeling out white tape to mark the gap in the minefield, are all very vivid and remind the men of the grim reality they went through themselves in the darkness of that night.

Some shots of Stukas and of Rommel were from captured German films. I wonder what pictures they took of our withdrawals.

We now sleep with rifles beside us and observe strict black-out again, owing to a parachutist scare.

WEDNESDAY – *30.6.43*
Go for dental attention at an Army Dental Centre in Homs. I notice the bungalow used by the Field Cashier has been re-named "Ye Olde Ackerage".

SATURDAY – *3.7.43*
A baking hot, dry Khamseen blowing. We work on, changing engines in the dust and grit.

Later, when we go for our swim, the hot blast rises from the rock as from a hot-plate, drying the perspiration on our skins. Then we slip into the cool sea, swimming out to a ledge of rock 100 yards away and dive down, finding the bottom at 15 ft.

Our water-bottles are immersed at the edge of the pool, so we have a cool drink as we sit, feet in the water and towels over our shoulders to protect our spines from the scorching sun.

When we return to work again, however, our shirts are soon soaked with sweat once more and any tools left lying are too hot to touch.

SUNDAY – *4.7.43*
Temperature 111 degrees in the shade; but there is no shade, except under a truck! After calling at the workshops in Homs, we buy the one and only melon in the town.

MONDAY – *5.7.43*
We now stop work at midday, owing to the intense heat. Leslie Henson comes to Leptis Magna, putting on a show at the Roman Theatre! His company includes Vivien Leigh, Beatrice Lillie, Dorothy Dickson and others. The great audience of troops must number well over 3,000. Some have brought cushions from truck seats to sit on. The sea of brown faces and khaki drill rising away above me gives a better idea of the tremendous size of the theatre

than I had when it was empty. It can only be compared to part of a football stadium!

The M.P.s had erected a notice at Leptis Theatre saying, "This building has been standing for 1,900 years. Don't knock it down now!"

SATURDAY – *10.7.43*
Allied forces invaded Sicily at 3.00 a.m. today.

WEDNESDAY – *21.7.43*
Go on four days leave to Tripoli. The harbour is once more busy with ships.

THURSDAY – *22.7.43*
We eat ripe figs, melons, grapes and even find some bananas!

SATURDAY – *24.7.43*
Several hospital ships in harbour, bringing wounded from Sicily.

SUNDAY – *25.7.43*
Return – not home – but back to nowhere. Some of the fellows in the Regiment had to take back some Blanco, to be used during a practice shoot. It makes one think that our senior officers do not take the war very seriously. To them it is just one big game. Let's get it finished!

MONDAY – *26.7.43*
We complete a model of a German Mark IV (Special) tank, which is to be the trophy for a 7th Armoured Division anti-tank shooting competition.

In Italy, Mussolini resigns *and Badoglio takes over.*

THURSDAY – *29.7.43*
All Fascist organisations in Italy disbanded. The Queen's Regiment win our tank.

SUNDAY – *1.8.43*
Visit scrap dump in a deep wadi near "Acquedotto di Homs". Saw our old water-truck, into which we had fitted a new engine, dumped here to be robbed for spares. Italian people, brightly dressed, are returning from Church in little carts and, at the village of Souk el Khemis, a native market is being held.

MONDAY – *2.8.43*
Now working from 8.00 a.m. to 8.00 p.m. (sundown)

FRIDAY – *6.8.43*
At last the L.A.D. has a new officer, for the first time since we left the Delta.

SUNDAY – *8.8.43*
Preparing for invasion exercises.

MONDAY – *9.8.43*
Proceed in F.S.M.O. (full scale marching order) to Homs harbour but the sea is considered too rough for the exercise so, after walking up and down the quay for a while, looking at the big invasion barges, we are finally taken back to camp.

TUESDAY – *10.8.43*
Clearing a big quantity of work but more is coming in, both vehicles and guns.

SATURDAY – *14.8.43*
Enjoyed a swim in the moonlight. The water is quite warm.

SUNDAY – *15.8.43*
Half-day. Eclipse of the moon. (One is about as common as the other!) We have turned out a tremendous amount of work in the last few weeks.

TUESDAY – *17.8.43*
Detailed to be driver of a machinery wagon which has been added to our strength. It carries a lathe, electric drills, charging-plant, etc.

WEDNESDAY – *18.8.43*
Sicily is now completely in Allied hands.

FRIDAY – *20.8.43*
Both hands bandaged because of "desert sores". The right arm is poisoned.

SUNDAY – *22.8.43*
Arm still swollen and septic.

SUNDAY – *29.8.43*
Still busy, fixing up the machinery lorry, painting, etc.

TUESDAY – *31.8.43*
My fourth year with the colours. Sick with sores, boils and adenitis, a lump being formed in the groin.

Many of the men have poisoned systems, and all want to get away from Libya.

SUNDAY – 5.9.43
260 Battery are on the road for the embarkation centre!

MONDAY – 6.9.43
Boiled tunny is now on the menu. It is quite good and tastes like something between rabbit and salmon. We are also getting regular doses of yellow anti-malarial tablets, in preparation for our invasion of Italy.

These tablets were mepacrin, a substitute for quinine. They turned our skins and eyeballs yellow, so that we all looked as if we were suffering from yellow jaundice!

TUESDAY – 7.9.43
New engine and gearbox fitted to the machinery truck, which weighs seven tons.

Warned to move on 10th September to rejoin Rear Divisional Echelon. Good! We'll soon be on the road to better lands.

THURSDAY – 9.9.43
Italy surrenders unconditionally. The Germans, of course, continue fighting.

SATURDAY – 11.9.43
Now parked in an area of soft dust beside Leptis Magna.

In an air-mail letter which I sent home on 12th September, I wrote:

"I hope we get to a hygienic part of Europe, with less flies, then I may gradually get rid of the habit of shrugging, blinking, waving my arms, shaking my head and generally acting like a nervous paralytic.

When I go to tiffin, I bite my slice of bread and marmalade quickly, before the flies do, while flapping the disengaged hand over my mug (of tea). I usually *let* them crawl round my ears and neck at this time, with an odd one on the end of my nose, which means less on the grub. Talk about evolving oneself to suit environment! I can almost wag my ears now!"

In another letter, I recalled the Biblical story of the Master, who fed the multitude on a few loaves and fishes and suggested that we must have someone like that acting as our quartermaster!

Our quartermaster (Mr. Rodway), who also censored our letters, passed this without comment. I expect he would just smile.

As a matter of fact, we had plenty of bread – of a sort. Where it was made I don't know but every single loaf was impregnated with small black beetles, as thickly as currants, so that it was a hopeless task to try to remove them all and we just had to eat the bread as it was. There must have been a vast supply of contaminated flour to be used, for this went on during most of the time we were in the area of Leptis.

Of course, the beetles were well cooked, so perhaps we should not have grumbled, but we did! However, as Confucius is alleged to have said, "Man with grouse always gets the bird!"

MONDAY – *13.9.43*
With several big jobs in hand, trucks dismantled, bivouacs erected and our own trucks unloaded, we are told to pack and move 50 yards. Our work (their work) is hindered for a bit of regimental meddling.

TUESDAY – *14.9.43*
George Formby at Leptis Magna. Another audience of 3,000 giving the popular George a grand reception.

There was rather a long wait for the start and, in the darkness, the shadowy figure of George appeared at the microphone to talk to the boys. Someone asked what we were waiting for and George replied, "We're waitin' for t'laadies!"

"We've been waiting for 'em for three years now, George!" said another voice. Then George answered a barrage of questions about home, frankly and, I thought, rather shyly.

I don't suppose any one man has ever been "interviewed" by so many people at one time. All round the great bowl, cigarettes glowed like fireflies, then, as the full moon began to rise over the pillars of the market place, lights flooded the stage and the show was on.

George at first appeared in baggy shorts with a little cap and a fly-swatter, clowning with his wife Beryl, then he sang and played many of his own inimitable songs.

At the end, he made a little speech, saying he had tried to get out to entertain us at Tobruk, two years ago, but could get no transport.

Now he had made it and had already given fifty-four shows in three weeks! Then he surprised us by saying he had also been over to Italy.

He had been playing at Reggio when a D.R. brought a request from "Monty" to appear at the front. He went and, when he arrived, he asked, "Where is the front?"

"You're in it," was the reply, "and patrols are operating out there and over that way!"

"Ee," said George, "it's turned out nice again!"

He added that he realised better now what we had done.

"The folks at home don't know," he said. "You can't explain it to them. Alamein to Tunis is just 'so much' on a map."

WEDNESDAY – *15.9.43*
Completely rebuilding our auxiliary gear-box. Warned to be ready to move again on Friday.

THURSDAY – *16.9.43*
Les worked till four o'clock this morning and I finished the job of fitting the gear-box by 10.00 *a.m.*

FRIDAY – *17.9.43*
Move to Tripoli, complete with shipping orders for our vehicles. The U.S. Fifth Army, who were pushed back in the Salerno beach-head, have now rallied and are attacking.

SATURDAY – *18.9.43*
Enjoyed a cold shower in a nearby villa. It is pleasantly cool in the tiled interior.

SUNDAY – *19.9.43*
Still at Tripoli. Many of the ships in the sunlit harbour are being loaded with troops, tanks and transport.

Goods now beginning to appear in the shops again; hand-made shoes, sandals and handbags with mohair decoration.

We go to a film show in the Union Club, Casa Littoria.

When we return to our camp, we are told we are moving at nine o'clock tonight! The boys are recalled from town. "Stanley", the little black-and-white dog which came all the way from Alamein with us, has been left with another unit. His mate, "Jean", has been shot but one of their pups, "Stanelli", has been smuggled on to the truck.

We go in the dark to a piece of waste ground near the docks and bed-down beside the trucks.

We were a trifle sad at losing our doggy friends but, considering the hazards of war, perhaps it was kinder in the long run.

MONDAY – *20.9.43*

Move to the docks at 3.00 p.m. We have a fine view of the town, looking over the native quarter, past the castle and the cathedral, to the Casa Littoria, but I won't be sorry to leave it. While we wait to get on to the big landing craft with wide doors in the bow, the sun goes down and all the dock and harbour lights come on.

There are many sailors of the U.S. Navy moving about.

It is 11.30 p.m. before we get aboard, the vehicles being backed on, three abreast. We have bunks along the side, one above the other, three high.

This was one of the two-decked landing ships, vehicles being raised to the top deck by a huge lift and others filling the interior. The vehicles were made fast by chains and shackles, to prevent movement when the ship rolled. Although the draught of the vessel was ten feet aft, where the engines were, it only required about three feet of water at the bows.

So now we were ready to go to Italy and, as we lay in our bunks, none of us had the slightest regret at leaving the desert behind. Electric lights shone down on our loaded trucks and I fell into a contented sleep.

Part IV

Italy

CHAPTER I

Salerno and Naples

TUESDAY – *21.9.43*

Sail at 7.00 a.m., leaving the coast of Africa at last! Smiling faces everywhere. We are told our destination is the Salerno beach-head. The sea is dead calm. There are ten invasion ships, with an escort of one corvette and two gunboats. Our landing-craft are powered by diesels.

WEDNESDAY – 22.9.43

Convoy joined by several other ships.

THURSDAY – 23.9.43

At dawn, we pass the volcanic cone of Etna and enter the narrow Straits of Messina. The mountains of Sicily and Italy rise high on either side of us and the country is green. Messina itself, we hear, was bombed two hours ago and fires are burning as we pass the town.

Later, we see another volcano, Stromboli, sticking out of the sea. Smoke rises lazily from a blow-hole at one side of the main crater and a small town nestles at the foot of the slope.

Like any other tripper, I went below to see the engines. The artificer (as usual) turned out to be a fellow Scot. He was keen to tell me all about his pets, but they were making such a thundering row that he had to put his mouth close to my ear and shout before I could hear him. There were two twelve-cylinder diesel engines with fresh water cooling and a separate salt-water system to cool the fresh water. Each engine was linked to a huge gear-box, about three feet square. There were also electricity generators and an oil-burning boiler-room which supplied steam for cooking.

As we continue northwards, one of the gunboats circles and drops some depth-charges, which jar the hull of our ship. We are warned that reveille will be at 4.00 a.m., when we will unshackle the vehicles in readiness for driving off. We have a rifle inspection.

At night, clouds obscure the stars and the coast is very dark, save for a few subdued lights glowing redly, while we creep ever northwards in an oily sea. Some phosphorescence appears around the ship. It is many months since I saw such a dark night, with all the stars hidden and so much moisture in the air.

We sleep in the bunks without undressing.

FRIDAY – 24.9.43

Up at 4.00 a.m. as per orders, but vehicles only partly unshackled as the craft – at anchor – rolls and lurches on a swell. We wait an hour for breakfast. There are gun flashes on the shore and tracer shells from some big naval vessel describe a great, slow arc, as they soar right over the hills towards some inland target.

We take our places on the vehicles at dawn, as the landing ship approaches the shore. At 7.00 a.m., the great doors before us open, the "drawbridge" is lowered and, without even wetting our tyres, we drive on to the beach, which is covered with wire-netting to prevent the tyres from sinking in.

We turn on to a dusty road leading through fields of tobacco, apple orchards and walnut trees. We ford a river and, halting, taste the apples (very sweet) and the walnuts (very tasty). High hills rise from the edge of the plain on which we stand. Allied aircraft wheel on patrol overhead.

We move on a little further and make camp in a field which is at least green, though the soil is hard and dry.

Italian soil! We are in Europe at last!

There is the continual sound of heavy gunfire. Salerno is still under fire of "Jerry" "88s" in the hills. We hear that 260 Battery, who preceded us, spent their first two days ashore burying the German dead in Battipaglia, a nearby village. The dead were thick with maggots, so there is some danger of disease. The area is also notorious for malaria.

The 46th Division and 56th (Black Cat) Division are attacking now and we see the old familiar groups of bombers going over in support. The object of the attack is to get armour through a gap in the hills and on to the plain of Naples.

We are in the province of Campagna. The American Fifth Army, to whom we are now attached, are using amphibious vehicles. They run straight into the sea, change to propeller drive and go well out to pick up supplies from ships, which they then carry miles inland!

SATURDAY – 25.9.43
Heavy roll of gunfire as the attack continues. The Navy are still shelling enemy positions and bombers go over to assist the infantry in the hills. "Jerry" dropped 200 paratroops last night, between our two attacking divisions. They dug in and made trouble. Audacious, but we do it too, and better.

This plain always seems to be misty and there are clouds of mosquitoes about. Many hundreds of swallows sweep back and forward, like a mass of black feathers in the air, devouring the insects. We use anti-mosquito cream freely.

SUNDAY – 26.9.43
Found a huge caterpillar, four inches long and as thick as my finger; green, with a red spike above the tail. Many beautiful butterflies to be seen, including swallow-tails and silver-spotted blues.

MONDAY – 27.9.43
Spoke to a couple of "Yanks", one of whom said they needed "… a guy like Montgomery".

In the dinner queue, the broad accent of a fellow Scot in front of me caught the attention of a Cockney.

"You Scotch down't arf talk funny, down't yer," he said.

There was a pause, then I said, "What do you mean – 'down't yer' – ?" A chuckle ran down the line and Les, himself from Sussex, laughed most of all.

"Good old Nick," he said, "I was waiting for that."

Rain comes, hissing down at first, then eases off and it is pleasant to hear it pattering on the leaves of the brambles. Dozens of lizards, black or dark green, run about in the bushes.

There are still many ships in the bay. The Navy are using monitors with 16-in. guns. One shell hit a large building and killed 100 Germans at once, according to prisoners.

I am feeling rather dizzy. Hope it isn't malaria!

Tuesday – 28.9.43
Feeling better; my best for three days. The Eighth Army are still advancing on the other side of Italy and have taken Foggia.

There are some fine cattle and horses in the field where our camp is. The boys have been milking some of the cows! There are also several bulls, five feet high at the shoulder and with horns spreading about four feet. They are all white.

In the evening a storm breaks, with thunder, lightning and heavy rain. The strong wind blows down some of our bivouacs and, to crown all, the cattle mill around stupidly and threaten the others. Twice during the night, I have to get up and chase them with a stick.

Wednesday – 29.9.43
Warm sun, helping us to dry out our bedding.

Thursday – 30.9.43
My hand poisoned by the last of the desert sores. Pain spreads up to the armpit. We move off at 4.00 p.m. via Salerno, our forward troops having cleared the mountains. Congestion slows us to a crawl and, past Salerno, we begin to climb into the hills in darkness. Up, up, up, between sheer cliffs where bombing would be disastrous. I drive with my hand swollen like a balloon and running a temperature. Finally I have to get "Billy" Bennett to relieve me at the wheel. We bed down beside the vehicles, still in the narrow pass. I take three asprins before lying down on the hard asphalt.

Friday – 1.10.43
Having slept fairly well, continue through several villages towards Vesuvius, which shows a steady plume of grey-white smoke. Houses are built even on the steepest slopes of hills. Many are damaged by shellfire. Some villages are as bad as those of France in the First World War (Battipaglia was a heap of rubble).

Stop at Pagani where, at last, I am able to get medical attention. The narrow streets of Pagani are laid with stone blocks in a herring-bone pattern, similar to that of parquet flooring. Took a bottle of Italian vermouth back to camp.

We are in a lane beside a field containing some American heavy artillery. The guns are 155 mm. (just over 6 in.) and every time they fire, the muzzle-blast makes the trees at the opposite side of the field bend. They have already blown out all the glass in the nearby houses. Hope they don't go off during the night. It's bad enough in the daytime!

SATURDAY – *2.10.43*
Plenty of fruit around us: grapes, passion fruit, walnuts, apples and pomodoro tomatoes growing in the open fields. These pomodoros are not like our tomatoes but are long, almost pear-shaped.

In Pagani again, my poulticed hand still in a sling, go over a rayon factory in company of Lieutenant Rodway and A.S.M. Harrison. We find the machinery used was made in Lancashire. Then we have a look inside the Basilica of San Alfonso, which has beautiful marble decoration in red, cream and white.

In the evening, we have a sing-song in a farm-house by the lane. Two Italian brothers, helped by our vermouth, burst into opera! No matter what opera we mention, or which aria, they know it and render it with great gusto and much expression, sometimes each with an arm round the other's shoulder, sometimes with arms flung wide; now quietly, now in full voice. We respond with choruses, led by Mr. Rodway, then, of all things, our hosts request that I sing the "Marseillaise" in French!

However, in the matter of music the Italians, for once, had the victory.

SUNDAY – *3.10.43*
While waiting to move again, we are pressed to partake of some spaghetti and tomatoes – and quite tasty it is too. We travel via Scafati and Pompeii to San Giuseppe, a village on the side of Vesuvius. Scafati has an impressive belfry tower, decorated with shining pillars, marble facing and bronze statues. At San Giuseppe, I peg out my bivouac on cinders.

At night, we watch great splashes of red molten material shooting high in the air from the volcano, one jet scarcely settling before another soars upwards in a different direction.

MONDAY – *4.10.43*
Move nearer to the village and park in the courtyard of a big rambling "azienda". The court is paved, with a palm tree in the middle and there is a solidly constructed well, with the date 1844 on the parapet.

We sleep upstairs in a barn-like room but it has a roof. The officers have a clean room and beds with straw mattresses – the pansies! Italian civilians still live in part of the house, which has been damaged a little by shellfire.

About six months later, San Giuseppe was reported to have been destroyed by an eruption of Vesuvius. The press recalled that the village had been destroyed before, in 1906, and eighty lives lost, but my note above the date on the well shows that it, at least, survived the 1906 eruption. I wonder if it survived that of 1944?

TUESDAY – *5.10.43*
Proceed to the area of Gruma and park in an orchard.

As we came through the narrow winding streets of the various towns en route, crowds of people stood at each corner, or lined their little balconies to wave, clap and shower fruit on us. (And the fruit wasn't bad either!)

WEDNESDAY – *6.10.43*
Our latest order is to treat the Italians as a conquered nation, not as friends! However, we can at least afford to be courteous. Now, everywhere we go, they tell us of the atrocities committed by the Germans, who are spiteful against their ex-allies. They have looted and burned, women have been carried off and men tied to trees and shot. One woman is said to have come into an A.D.S. for medical attention, with her breasts cut off!

Met some interesting personalities in a café (or caffe *as it is in Italy) in the village of Casandrio. One had been chief of the civil airport in Naples and he and two of his sons spoke French, so we were able to converse. Another had been trading in wines and clothing in France for twelve years and spoke fluent colloquial French. This fellow looked very like film star George Raft, in a loud striped shirt, soft hat and jacket over his shoulders with the sleeves hanging loose. He told us many revealing things about Fascism in Italy. France, he said, was a free country but, here in Italy, even in peace-time, you dare not speak freely. The air-chief, who must have been a Fascist to hold his position, was very quiet at this point, but he appeared to be a disillusioned man.*

The worldly-wise trader was a likeable chap and we chatted all evening, while he continued, expressively, to compare Italy with other countries. He had a commercial passport and intended to get to London, as he was fed up with his own land. Yet he stuck up for his people in some things and was, of course, proud of their music.

The burning question for both men was, had we taken Rome yet?

THURSDAY – *7.10.43*
A young student – acting as interpreter – brought a priest to me saying, in bad French, that they knew of several dangerous Fascists in the village, who would be better arrested for the peace of everyone. I told Mr. Rodway and he took them in a Jeep to Brigade H.Q., the priest looking rather ludicrous as he clambered over into the back seat with his voluminous black gown catching in the works. Finally, he was tucked in and, holding on to his flat clerical hat, away he went, minus his dignity and looking quite windswept.

FRIDAY – *8.10.43*
Nine of us, looking more like pirates than soldiers, armed to the teeth with Tommy-guns, Bren-guns, rifles, revolvers and automatics, set off for the village to round up the Fascists but – anti-climax! – the Brigade Major, after talking with the priest, decided to leave it to the Military Police.

Later in the day, paid a visit to Gruma, a bigger place than Casandrino, with more shops. In a small square an old woman and an Italian policeman were arguing and a crowd gathered. Every time the copper spoke, the crowd booed and when the old woman nagged, they cheered!

This reminded me of the old game where an audience gives the appropriate response to the comedian. Remember?...

"They've built a big new pub down the road ..." (*Hooray!*)
"But there are no pint mugs ..." (*Boo!*)
"... only quarts! ..." (*Hooray!*)

"They haven't any barmen ..."   *(Boo!)*
"... just barmaids! ..."   *(Hooray!)*

Well, here it was in real life, only there were two central figures and I can still see the policeman in his green uniform, being booed every time he opened his mouth, and the wrinkled old woman, wagging her finger under his nose and being cheered like a toreador with a bull!

FRIDAY – *8.10.43 (Contd.)*
In the evening, we provided our own entertainment as usual, by having a sing-song in the local café. One of the boys gave us music on an accordion and a Scottish tenor (from Grangemouth) obliged with solos. We drank some Cognac Bouton (egg cocktail) supplied by "George Raft", whose real name is Domenico.

During the night, big guns boom and shells howl over, directly above us, some bursting not far away. Every two minutes, we hear the distant boom of a hidden enemy gun, then a pause, then a sighing whine and, as the shell passes, it is followed up by a great roar like a train in a tunnel, echoing amongst the trees, then ... Bang!

SATURDAY – *9.10.43*
Get a leave pass to visit Naples. It is a fine city but the docks have suffered heavy damage. The bay scenery is lovely and I notice many of the trees are very similar to the Scots pine, with wide spreading heads and red bark. Had a good meal, which included macaroni soup, and pimento – a kind of capsicum – with a bottle of champagne. Music was supplied by an accordion player and his little boy, who sang "O Sole Mio" in a clear soprano.

The back streets to landward were quaint, rising steeply in irregular steps, their narrowness emphasized by the tall buildings with their many balconies. The arcade of the Umberto Gallery had most of its glass roof blown down, together with one of the four big gilded angels which graced its central dome. Perhaps it was symbolic of Italy, that Fallen Angel! The famous San Carlo Opera House nearby was closed, so I was unable to view the interior.

Returning to camp, we learn that two men were killed and seven wounded in the echelon behind us by last night's shelling. Some of the local Fascists had been playing tricks too and fixed a heavy wire across the road near our camp, so three were immediately arrested. Later, another nine were picked up from their homes. Being in Naples, of course, I missed this party.

SUNDAY – *10.10.43*
Join forward R.H.Q. All accommodation in houses is taken up and we have only a miserable little patch of weed on which to pitch our bivouacs. We do our own cooking.

MONDAY – *11.10.43*
Rise early in the rain, after a sleepless night. The 5.5-in. guns and 25-pounders crashed all night, some of them being only a few yards behind us and the rest scattered round the village. We are some-where near the town of Aversa.

The attack on the River Volturno has begun. The Royal Engineers come up with bridge sections.

TUESDAY – *12.10.43*
Zero at 9.00 p.m. Barrage goes over. The guns are now mostly in front of us; but at one end of the village, some are firing from the roadside, their muzzles in line with the trees and each great flash goes right across the road, outlining the trees vividly. Earlier, I saw some of the "Queen's" preparing to "go in" in light order: rifle, bayonet and ammo. pouches only – no haversack.

The noise is terrific now, as all the guns come in and the ground shakes as if from an earthquake. It is a cold, clear night, with a full moon. So many shells are in the sky at once that there is a continuous sighing like a great wind.

WEDNESDAY – *13.10.43*
My hand is again poisoned from the same sore, in spite of dressings. I feel fevered, weak and dizzy. When will I get rid of it?

This sore, an open yellow ulcer, was on the knuckle, almost in to the bone, and difficult to heal because of movement of the joint.

Sherman tanks go through, waterproofed for the river crossing. Attack fairly successful, except that 56th Division was repulsed. Twenty Stukas appeared at the front and some F.W. 190 fighters, a bit of Hitler's saved-up air-force.

Take some more aspirins before bed.

THURSDAY – *14.10.43*

Feeling a bit better. An enemy plane dropped its spare tank near us. Later, the official communiqué said: "Two M.E.s were seen. One jettisoned its spare petrol tank over forward troops." "Jerry" is getting reckless with his air force! Allied tanks have been taken by sea past the River Volturno and landed on the other side. Among the prisoners taken in the battle is one named Hitler – but it isn't Adolf! Another man had been caught asleep on guard, so he came over the river to surrender to us! The joke of the week, however, is that Italy has declared war on Germany.

FRIDAY – *15.10.43*

Battledress issued in place of khaki drill. I hope it will be the last time I will wear tropical K.D. "Jerry" now retreating from the Volturno. "A" echelon moves forward but we wait, as we are now rejoining "B" echelon.

SATURDAY – *16.10.43*

"B" echelon – and Mr. Rodway – join us. We have a sing-song in a house across the way, accompanied by two accordions and a bottle of Strega.

SUNDAY – *17.10.43*

After dark, "Jerry" sends over some more big shells from the elusive gun which he appears to move occasionally to a different spot. Some of the shells whine over above us but two burst quite near and short of our position.

THURSDAY – *21.10.43*

Second visit to Naples. While on the way to the city, at midday, we saw a queer thing in the sky. It was like a long, black and white streak moving broadside across the clouds. As one disappeared, another followed then, after a minute, we saw several close together like transparent waves, rippling across the sky at right-angles to the original movement. None of us had ever seen anything like it before but I suppose it was some natural phenomenon, though it caused a few wisecracks about Hitler's secret weapon!

In Naples, we saw American General Mark Clark in his car, preceded by three motor-cycles with sirens howling. The populace began a scramble, thinking it was an air-raid. The car was adorned with a pennant bearing three stars, about three times the size of the flag carried by one of our staff-cars. The D.R.s scattered the crowd and the car leaned over, tyres squealing, as it took the corner in a fast, showy manner (just as they do in films).

Collected some beer direct from the brewery (Birra Peroni) and it was surprisingly good. Outside the town again, we sat at the road-side to drink a bottle while the sun, shining out of a clear blue sky, glinted from the branches of the plane trees above us – but not like the cruel African sun!

In the evening, "Jerry" suddenly sends over quite a number of bombers and there is heavy ack-ack fire, some near us and some about Aversa, where there is a large ammunition dump.

Some shrapnel clangs on our breakdown truck.

FRIDAY – 22.10.43
Third visit to Naples. We have a fine dinner with Marsala wine, accompanied by music on guitar, violin and mandolin.

Denny requested "Catari" and, to our mild consternation, the trio left their place and assembled at our table! Then the guitar-player sang the ballad tenderly (and very beautifully) in Neapolitan.

SATURDAY – 23.10.43
In the evening, more enemy bombers and more "fireworks". We were talking to three Italian policemen when the raid started and they promptly dived into the ditch at the side of the road. We unslung our rifles and there was a click of bolts as we loaded in case any 'planes came near enough to have a shot at. None did, though one was brought down by ack-ack.

As one of the Italians said, when he breathlessly crawled back out of the ditch, "Inglese buono!"

I refrained from pointing out that the rest of the British are pretty good too!

SUNDAY – 24.10.43
In the past, we've had constantly recurring rumours that we would be going home "… after Tunis is taken" or "… after Sicily is cleared up", usually treated with derision by us. Now it is "… after Rome falls!"

This time, however, we have the added information from "high authority" that the 50th Division is on its way home, the 51st (Highland) Division is waiting for ships and we follow them!

Once again, I wonder ...?

MONDAY – *25.10.43*
Move back *from Albanova to Casandrino! Park lorries in a big yard and put bedding in a nice clean room of the casa, which has a balcony overlooking the street.*

THURSDAY – *28.10.43*
Enjoying comfortable nights in the billet, where rain does not trouble us and our blankets are always dry. The Italians do our laundry.

SATURDAY – *30.10.43*
A hawker tried to charge me 100 lire for a pair of stockings, (to send home) when I had already bought some at 30 lire! Gave him 40 lire and ran him out of the yard by the scruff of his dirty neck. He came back protesting, so Eddie ran him out again, a bit more violently and gave him a parting kick.

MONDAY – *1.11.43*
Go shopping in Frattamaggiore. It is All Saints' Day and brown-robed Jesuit monks gather round the Church.

We buy a turkey, which Domenico promises to cook for us. In the evening, we continue to provide our own amusement with a bil-liards and darts contest versus R.H.Q. The L.A.D. wins both.

TUESDAY – *2.11.43*
The rumour about going home is still strong and big bets are being made. We have a party, with a slap-up dinner, including the turkey and plenty of beer. The following sing-song started well, with "Q" Joy playing his accordion and "Gillie" on the drum, while veteran Eddie Gamble (the Benghazi Harrier) who was one of our guests, shook the company by singing "Chattanooga Choo-Choo".

Later, however, some drank themselves into a silly state and the party became rowdy and unmusical, so "Gillie" and I went to bed.

FRIDAY – *5.11.43*
Eddie (Culhane), whose wife is very ill, goes to C., R.E.M.E. (Com-mander of all R.E.M.E. in the Division) to see about the possibility of getting compassionate leave to England.

He is told, "Don't worry. Stay with your unit and you will be home for Christmas!" We are having plenty of "spit-and-polish" too, so it looks as if we may not be going forward again. Maybe our next front will be in France!

In the afternoon, Mr. Rodway gives us the official news: We ARE going home!

All the boys are excited; nobody bothers about dinner; we are half afraid to believe it. We are told we will hand over our equipment to another division and every effort will be made to get us home by Christmas. Secrecy, however, is essential for our own safe voyage and the use of "green envelopes" in our mail is forbidden.

At night, there is another raid on Naples and blast shakes our windows. Twice 'planes are caught in the search-light beams and held tenaciously, while they twist and turn and tracers stream towards them but they get away, though damaged.

Bud's dog becomes ill and is shot; "Stanelli" dies and our "Tosh" gets run over by a "Yankee" truck, so Len has to finish him off with a Tommy-gun. So all our dogs are gone!

SUNDAY – *7.11.43*
Now billeted with the regiment in a big school in Gingliana. Our room is cold, having an open doorway and two large windows without any frames. We are scrubbing all our equipment, cleaning the trucks – even underneath – checking tools and generally preparing to hand over our vehicles to a Canadian division.

MONDAY – *8.11.43*
Everybody talking about what they are going to take home and what they will do when they get there. Rumours of medal ribbons before we sail!

The favourite things to buy were real (Italian) silk stockings for the womenfolk at home. The well-paid Americans gave higher prices than we could afford, however, and soon there were no more stockings marked "setta pura" and many British soldiers had to take home rayon instead.

THURSDAY – *11.11.43*
Time seems to crawl, while we polish brasses tarnished with age and weather. There has been an air raid every other night on Naples.

Friday – *12.11.43*
We clear all personal kit from the trucks in case of a sudden move.

Sunday – *14.11.43*
In Naples again. This time I got inside the magnificent San Carlo Opera House. There are six tiers of gilded boxes, running all the way round the theatre, each fitted with mirrors, eight seats and coat-hooks. In the middle of the first row of boxes, above the main entrance, is the royal box, surmounted by a large crown. The electric lights are again in working order, enabling me to see the huge painting on the roof of the theatre. I also have a look round the dressing-rooms and back-stage, where hundreds of ropes rise high behind the great scenic curtains and narrow gang-ways are suspended near the roof amongst a myriad lights.

Tuesday – *16.11.43*
Advance party leaves for Sorrento. Only the drivers, including myself, wait behind as rear party.

Thursday – *18.11.43*
Drive our trucks to Afragola, to hand over to the Canadians. Heavy rain and mud all the way (after all the cleaning we had given the trucks!)

I remember the expressions on the Canadians' faces when they saw the vehicles they were to take over! They regarded them as wrecks and seemed to wonder how we had managed to keep them running at all, let alone depend on them during a campaign.

When I think of the desert tracks, I wonder myself!

CHAPTER 2

Sorrento

We have to leave our school billet in Giugliana clean and tidy, so we get the Italians to sweep it out!

The "Eye-ties" gathered round like a crowd of vultures when they saw we were leaving, ready to snatch up anything we left. They fought for bits of old clothing. One of our chaps had a large tin of old Army biscuits to dispose of but he was jostled so much that he finally herded them all back, then emptied the biscuits in the middle of the open space. When he signed to the crowd and said, "Come and get it!" there was a wild rush which almost bowled him over, as they scrambled for the pile of biscuits on the ground!

We were taken by R.A.S.C. transport via Castellamare and Poz-zano, into the area of Sorrento. This was the finest scenery we had yet viewed in Italy. We ran along a twisting precipitous road, high above rocky coves of the Bay of Naples, through terraced vineyards and olive groves, where the leaves were dark green. Houses peeped out of gorges, or were perched still higher above us on the cliff-tops. A lofty viaduct had one arch blown away (the work of the enemy during his retreat) and our engineers had placed a girder section over the gap but it made us dizzy to look over the side as the vehicles crawled across.

In a little village called Meta, about two miles from Sorrento, we find our billet, which is clean and has glass in all the doors, many of which lead on to balconies. The village itself is much cleaner than those further inland, perhaps because this area was a peace-time resort for visitors. Many refugees are here from Naples.

In the evening, we visit a small cinema – the "Tribuna" – in the next village, Piano, which is between Meta and Sorrento. The film is American, with Italian sub-titles.

The road through Piano is narrow and winding, sometimes bounded by high walls or dark trees, or the straw screens erected to protect orange trees and lemon trees from any possible cold spell.

SATURDAY – *20.11.43*
The electric light, which was out of commission, comes on in our billet, so we have "soft lights and sweet music", for we also have been loaned a radio by the owners of our billet – the Fascist Youth Club!

MONDAY – *22.11.43*
Parades begin – the first for ages. Scrubbing equipment; gas drill; foot drill; saluting by numbers, as if we were recruits instead of four-year soldiers.

The saluting drill must have left the Italians splitting their sides at the expense of their conquerors. We marched along a broad path under some palm trees, while an N.C.O., taking the place of an officer, stood on a grass bank which represented the saluting base. Unfortunately, heavy rain had at some time gouged a ditch across the path at an oblique angle. As the column of threes reached the "officer" with their right arms at the salute, left arms stiffly at their sides and eyes left, the right-hand man suddenly dropped down about a foot. As he clambered up out of the rut, the middle man went down (still eyes left) to be followed by the left-hand man in his turn and, when the left-hand man came up, the right-hand man in the next row started the sequence all over again. No wonder there were mutterings about being in Fred Karno's Army!

TUESDAY – *23.11.43*
Hitch-hike to Sorrento – downhill all the way – and go to the Tasso Cinema to see Tales of Manhattan.

This cinema was named after Torquatto Tasso, the sixteenth-century "Italian Shakespeare" and author of *Jerusalem Delivered*. A statue of him stands in the main piazza of Sorrento, his birthplace.

One of the local crafts is the making of beautifully inlaid tables, cabinets and music-boxes and so on, in olive and other woods and many of the shops are full of these works of art.

WEDNESDAY – *24.11.43*
Went for a morning swim in the sea below the cliffs, the way to the beach being through steep narrow streets ending in steps. The scenery is wonderful, even at this time of the year. Caves and tunnels

are cut into the base of the cliffs, often leading up to houses and hotels on the top, for this was a millionaires' playground in peace-time.

Although the sea was very rough and spouting high, the water was quite warm.

In the afternoon, we were taken to Castellamare mineral baths, where we had a fine hot bath in spa water. We also sampled some of the waters which come from subterranean springs and are led through marble spouts, each marked with the name of a different chemical content: sulphur, iron, magnesia, media, or salts. There were patches of various colours beneath the spouts, the sulphur particularly showing bright yellow, testifying to the strength of "the mixture".

SATURDAY – 27.11.43
Trip to Sorrento and back in an open victoria. *It was smaller than a Cairo* gharry, *but took "Billy" Bennett, "Gillie" Potter, "Lofty" and myself at a fair pace.*

SUNDAY – 28.11.43
To Sorrento again. The electric trams are now running between Castellamare and Sorrento. Came back from the cinema by taxi, only 10 lire each!

We have all been waiting more or less patiently for news of our sailing and trying to keep it dark (I told one family of curious Italians that we would be returning to the front after we had a rest). Now, however, they say our baggage party has gone and there are various estimates of the number of ships waiting for us in the bay!

Secrecy is important, for the Canadians who came out here were attacked in the Mediterranean by seaplane torpedo carriers and one or two ships were sunk.

MONDAY – 29.11.43
Now having lectures on our own job, which is better than "square-bashing".

THURSDAY – 2.12.43
An Army concert is held in the Tasso Cinema, a change from films.

FRIDAY – *3.12.43*
Checking kit-bags etc., ready for shipping. Our "Morale Graph" is high!

We had ironically made a large graph, which we hung on the wall and, whenever we had a "good" report, the graph line was drawn upwards. If we got a bit of "bad gen", the line fell, along with our spirits!

SUNDAY – *5.12.43*
Rumour we will be here for Christmas. Don't know what to believe. Morale down to twenty per cent on our graph.

Climb a nearby hill with "Lofty" but we have not enough time before "tiffin" to reach the summit, which is hidden in the clouds. It is a clear sunny day, however, and we have a wonderful view of the bay, all the way round from the Isle of Capri to Naples and the Isle of Ischia. The sea is very blue and contrasts with the steep, rocky hills, which have evergreen trees right to the top and the red-roofed houses, with white or yellow walls, tucked into ravines and clefts on the hillsides.

On our way down, we found an unusual cemetery with marble vaults, containing tiers of coffins. The sculpture on the private shrines was very beautiful. The largest vault had two floors and a large dome. One floor held a chapel with the marble facing of the tombs rising to the roof of the vault. We passed an iron gate, through which we saw a brown skeleton laid out on a plank, for what reason we could not guess.

THURSDAY – *9.12.43*
Saw Action in the North Atlantic, *a film full of cheerful pictures of submarines!*

SATURDAY – *11.12.43*
Detailed for advance party to port of embarkation!

SUNDAY – *12.12.43*
Hectic packing.

MONDAY – *13.12.43*
Move to a barn-like billet at Cassoria, about six miles from Naples. Visit the city, see a film show and come back hanging on the outside of a Daimler armoured car driven by Canadians. The "Yanks" won't give a lift to British soldiers, only to Americans or Italian girls.

One "Yankee" truck slowed for a moment, then drove on, as our battledress showed up in the headlights!

FRIDAY – *17.12.43*

Walk to the village of Afragola in the still winter air. The trees are now bare, except for the evergreen olive and orange trees but it is not really cold. A cartwright works on a wheel, sitting on the foot-path as he wields his adze and, farther on, a woman sells potato fritters from an open-air brazier. As a reminder of the war, six lots of six bombers go over, possibly heading for the Rome perimeter.

SATURDAY – *18.12.43*

A crowd of bootblacks start work early at the gate of our billet and do a roaring trade – 5 lire a shine!

The Indians are still doing well with the Eighth Army (the new Eighth).

SUNDAY – *19.12.43*

Last evening in Italy. We will sail on the S.S. Ormonde, an Orient ship.

MONDAY – *20.12.43*

Reveille 3.15 a.m. March six miles to a street near the docks, where we get breakfast at dawn. The Italians get out of bed to look out at the impressive sight of 12,000 troops on the march. We get a send-off by an American negro band on the quay; scrappy but cheerful and vigorous, with plenty of bass drum! They play "When The Lights Go On Again All Over The World".

Sail at 5.00 p.m., just before dark. The Colonel gives us orders to scrub equipment again, in spite of water economy on board ship.

CHAPTER 3

To Oran and the Pillars of Hercules

TUESDAY – *21.12.43*
Passing the Tunisian coast, making good time. Six troopships and six destroyers in escort, with usually three 'planes patrolling from land bases. The water at the bow and stern of each ship gleams phosphorescent in the dark, as we steam on into the night.

We now realised that we must be resigned to spending not only Christmas but probably New Year aboard ship, instead of being with the families we had not seen for so long.

The *Ormonde* (15,000 tons) was at this time completely infested with cockroaches, anything up to an inch and a half in length, which crawled up and down the white walls of our mess deck in swarms. No doubt the ship would have to be sealed and filled with gas to kill these insects but the exigencies of service had prevented any useful action being taken. The cockroaches semed to be harmless, so we just ignored them.

WEDNESDAY – *22.12.43*
Now eight destroyers on escort, plus two Spitfires and one Wellington bomber. Grey sea, mist and rain. Grub pretty good. Real butter all the time! We sleep always in our clothes, by order, but feel pretty safe with such a strong escort.

THURSDAY – *23.12.43*
Now five "troopers" and six destroyers in convoy, the others having left us for Algiers.

We call at Oran, a town built on sloping ground under a steep bluff which has a lighthouse on top. The ship ties up next to the fine modern French battleship Lorraine.

FRIDAY – *24.12.43*
An American destroyer is tied up to the side of our ship and we watch the sailors as they bring a torpedo out of one of the tubes on deck, to pump air into it at a pressure of 3,000 pounds per square inch.

In the evening, they fix up a cinema screen on the stern and, while waiting for the show to start, two of our chaps go down on to the destroyer to play their accordions, to "Gob" and "Tommy" alike, for community singing. The projector comes into action and there are two news-reels, a colour cartoon and – Desert Victory! The "Yanks" are seated on their after-deck and we watch from the rail above them, as if we were in the "front circle". (We have a cinema too, in one of the lounges, but tickets don't go round.)

During a break in Desert Victory, *when the reel was being changed, there was a stir amongst the tense sailors and one turned to his mate and said, "Jeez! T'hell wid that. I'm glad I'm in the Navy!"*

SATURDAY – *25.12.43*
Christmas day. Special dinner, with pork, salmon, duff, cake, vin rouge and a ration of rum.

The ship moves out into the bay, where a heavy ground swell is running. In the evening, the lights of Oran twinkle brightly on shore. A concert party of Desert Rats put on a show called "Homeward Bound" in the theatre lounge and it is broadcast over the loudspeakers, so we hear it on our mess-deck. The "Eastern Brothers" give a turn – "That'll be the Day, Chaps, That'll be the Day!" and they include a verse:

> *"'Monty' has an Armoured Div.,*
> *He moves it when he can;*
> *It looks like spending several months*
> *Sitting in Oran!"*

MONDAY – *27.12.43*
Leave Oran. Now twelve liners and seven warships in the convoy. No tramps, so we should travel at good speed.

TUESDAY – *28.12.43*
Pass "Gib" early in the morning. I go up on deck at dawn to see the two "Pillars of Hercules", Gibraltar itself, and Ceuta on the African

coast. Paravanes are put out in the straits in case of mines and we begin to zig-zag again with the usual signals, one to starboard, two to port.

WEDNESDAY – *29.12.43*

Radio announces the Navy has sunk three German destroyers, damaged others and sunk the blockade runner they were escorting, in the Bay of Biscay! We are almost there now.

There is a practice drill on boat stations. We'd all drown, for we wear our greatcoats, belts, braces, water bottles and steel helmets, so if the boats were smashed we could hardly keep afloat, let alone swim. Surely, in a real emergency, no one would take such a load strapped round himself.

FRIDAY – *31.12.43*

Hogmanay, still at sea, somewhere off the south of Ireland. Programme of records over the loudspeakers but no real celebration. My first wartime New Year was in France; the second at Catterick; third in the desert near the Libyan border, south of Sidi Barrani; fourth, near Sirte and now the fifth, so near home, yet so far!

SATURDAY – *1.1.44*

Enter the New Year, the morning after the night that wasn't! Another Army Concert is given in the lounge, called "Day Minus – ?" Orders say we are expected to dock on Tuesday, 4th January, so this must be D–3 in Army parlance. We had to go well off-course to avoid U-boats, which accounts for some delay. Concert verse:

> *"Old King Cole was a merry old soul,*
> *And a merry old soul was he,*
> *Till he asked for a packet of 'Kensitas',*
> *And they gave him a packet of 'V's."*

"V" cigarettes (with a large "V" for Victory on each packet) were notorious in the Middle East. Even the most hardened smokers thought they were atrocious. Although a non-smoker, I once tried one, just out of curiosity and it seemed even worse than any "ordinary" cigarette. They were issued regularly to the troops and they should have cured the Army of smoking altogether. They came from India and the general theory was that they were made from jute!

SUNDAY – *2.1.44*
Man found dead in the lavatory next our mess-deck, with a revolver beside him, in the early morning. He is consigned to the deep at 4.00 p.m. in a rough, grey sea. Spray is being carried from one wave-crest to another by a strong following wind and even on to the deck.

We are now heading north-east, with a Short Sunderland flying-boat in escort and must be rounding the north of Ireland.

MONDAY – *3.1.44*
Land to starboard. A destroyer drops some depth charges and the blast bangs the sides of our vessel. It must be just preventive action, for no alarm is given.

Later, each ship shows its navigation lights, so we are now in safe waters.

TUESDAY – *4.1.44*
Pass Gourock in the early morning and wake to find ourselves in the estuary of the Clyde, near Greenock. As dawn breaks over the fresh, green, snow-topped hills – a wonderful sight – tugs, Red Cross launches, Customs pinnaces, etc. fuss out to our ship.

The first question asked by a Scot amongst us is, "What was the result of the big game?"

The answer comes from a tug – "Celtic 1, Rangers 3!"

A launch passes with four "Wrens" in it, accompanied by much whistling and many remarks from the troops. They smile, wave and pass on. I can see the familiar maroon double-decked 'buses running on the shore. We won't be off for some time yet. The yellow quarantine flag flies at the mast and there are many formalities to go through and arrangements to be made.

Later, we are told we will be taken off by a lighter to Prince's Pier, then by train all the way to Wymondham, in Norfolk! Then presumably I – with other Scots – travel with my kit all the way back for leave. And I could be home from here in a couple of hours!

We will not leave the ship till Thursday morning, two days hence. Meanwhile, the estuary looks lovely. There is every type of craft on the water, from motor-boats to aircraft carriers and, above, Catalina flying-boats are circling.

WEDNESDAY – *5.1.44*
Bored stiff waiting. Money changed to real British notes and solid coin.

THURSDAY – *6.1.44*
Get on to lighter with kit. Fred's kit-bag, containing a bottle of cognac, was accidentally dropped thirty feet on to the deck of the smaller vessel but miraculously the bottle was unbroken!

Harry Garfield – the Regiment's champion chump – somehow contrived to turn the wrong way as we were leaving the lighter. Instead of going on to the pier, he got on another lighter, which immediately steamed away. He is still missing.

This was written in the afternoon, when the special train had commenced the long, weary journey which was to stretch through the night and into the dawn of the next day, before we reached Wymondham. But we were "home"! When we landed at the pier, one of the men knelt and patted the ground, as if to say, "Good old Blighty!"

Could our feelings be described more aptly than in the words of Scott?

> *Breathes there the man with soul so dead,*
> *Who never to himself hath said,*
> *This is my own, my native land!*
> *Whose heart hath ne'er within him burned,*
> *As home his footsteps he hath turned,*
> *From wandering on a foreign strand!*

Second Interlude in Blighty

WHEN WE ARRIVED at Wymondham (pronounced *Windam*), ten miles from Norwich, we were taken a further three miles by lorry to Kimberley Hall, on the estate of the late Earl of Kimberley, where the Regiment was to be stationed. The L.A.D. were billeted in one of the wooden huts beside the Hall.

SATURDAY – *8.1.44*
Still waiting for leave. Visit Norwich but leave early as the last bus is at 8.20 p.m. "Yanks" everywhere. The cleanliness of British towns is appreciated after seeing some of the foreign places. Had a "beer" at Wymondham on the way back. Very watery. In a fish-and-chip shop, a bombardier of the Regiment began yelling Arabic at the proprietor and he replied in the same tongue, having apparently been in Egypt in the 1914–1918 war. The ensuing back-chat in Arabic caused some amusement amongst the customers.

Walked the three miles back to the Hall in the cold, fresh air, by moonlight.

As there was little of interest, I made no further entry in my diary until March. Meanwhile, I had enjoyed two periods of leave.

SATURDAY – *4.3.44*
Snow on the ground. Feel very browned-off now. Local dances do not amuse me. They just shuffle round and round the floor, like the bears in the zoo! All Norfolk beer is poor and whisky is unobtainable, which is perhaps just as well, for the boys have nothing else to do but go out drinking. Norwich is crammed with "Yanks", mostly on what they call "Skirt Patrol".

We have now been definitely warned for overseas (again!). Expect it will be France once more. Well, the quicker it's finished the better, then we may get settled into decent jobs in Civvy Street, away from Army restrictions. But I hope the troops who have spent three years or so in Britain will have a go as well. It's all very well saying we are experienced troops – the others won't get their experience unless they get into action.

If these strange people, the British, were more hospitable we might find some interest here but it is a lonely, meaningless existence for the most part.

Monday – 6.3.44
A grand little show by a civilian concert party called "The Hurricanes", in one of our huts, helps to brighten us up.

Sunday – 12.3.44
Visit the Norman Abbey of Wymondham and sign the visitors' book. Fine oak roof (fifteenth-century), ancient stonework and a beautiful reredos of gilded figures in niches.

Tuesday – 21.3.44
Leave for Ripon to take a course on mine-lifting under the Royal Engineers.

This instruction came a bit late as far as I was concerned but still, I learned a lot more about mines and, when I returned to my unit, I had to pass on the information in lectures to members of the L.A.D., including newcomers.

Thursday – 23.3.44
Lay, and then lift, a complete minefield at night, "freezing" like statues every time an "enemy" flare goes up. Removing the fuses from the mines later, in the dark, a heart-breaking time was had by all.

Friday – 24.3.44
The Royal Engineers put on a very realistic demonstration of what happens when infantry advance into a minefield when they are untrained in mines. The platoons advance, are blown up with flash, smoke and bang and are followed by two Bren-carriers which also hit mines and are set on fire. "Dead" bodies everywhere. Another scheme showed what I have already seen in actuality, a convoy of vehicles striking mines on a road and on the grass verges.

We set and clear booby-traps quite successfully, in two squads, each squad undoing the other's work.

SATURDAY – 25.3.44
Learning to use mine detectors which can discover a small piece of metal two feet under the surface of the ground.

SUNDAY – 26.3.44
To finish off the course, I lecture the rest of the class on an igniter used with the German "Tellermine".

TUESDAY – 28.3.44
Return from Ripon to Wymondham.

SATURDAY – 8.4.44
Now wearing our first issue of berets (khaki). We are part of the Second Army now.

MONDAY – 10.4.44
All leave cancelled and mail being censored, which is unusual in Blighty. I don't think the invasion will be long now. Bombing is being intensified and each morning there is a constant drone in the skies.

TUESDAY – 11.4.44
Bombers have come back this evening, several with an engine out of action. The weather is grand and birds are singing all over the estate, while waterfowl sport on the lake. Meanwhile, the Flying Fortresses circle down, many, no doubt, carrying wounded men.

FRIDAY – 14.4.44
"Titch" has a beautiful black eye. It happened during the Regimental Dance. His pal, Mike, was telling a "Yank" how he had got "busted" from corporal to private for striking his sergeant. He was making a demonstration of the swipe that had caused the trouble when "Titch" walked in the way. He sat down suddenly. For the rest of the evening he ducked every time Mike moved his arm!

SATURDAY – 22.4.44
Air-raids as "Gillie" and I leave a cinema in Norwich. Two aircraft down in flames. We see our own planes returning from raids with navigation lights showing, then they switch on great headlight beams as they come in to land on the 'dromes. The flat Norfolk land is ideal for airfields.

At the end of almost exactly four months at Kimberley Hall, we were warned for moving again, this time to Essex, where it became obvious we were to prepare for a landing in France and on no small scale. This was to be the invasion which we all hoped would end the war, and which led us on the last long "swan" to the heart of Germany itself.

Part V

The Invasion
and the Final Advance

CHAPTER I

Normandy

MONDAY – *8.5.44*
Hectic preparations for moving. For several days we have been
working long hours and four electric welders have been kept busy
on waterproofing the tanks.

(We sometimes referred to the S.P.s – self-propelled artillery – as "tanks",
though the turrets were open-topped. They were, in fact, built on the
same "chassis" as the General Sherman tanks. The regiment now had
two batteries equipped with S.P.s and two batteries with 17-pounders
towed by half-tracked armoured cars.)

TUESDAY – *9.5.44*
Move to camp near Brentwood, Essex, where we go under canvas.
Still working on waterproofing till 7.00 p.m. and confined to camp.
Many other units are on the move and there are thousands of troops
in this assembly area.

Our bombers go over continuously, mainly Marauders.

THURSDAY – *11.5.44*
Allowed out of camp and find Brentwood a bright little town. The
beer is much better than that of Norfolk.

SATURDAY – *13.5.44*
Our turn for a day off, so "Gillie" and I went to London by the
first train after breakfast.

During the day, we visited a waxworks in Oxford Street – "The
War in Wax" – and were much surprised and amused to see two
"desert soldiers" with 1908 equipment and white knees!

Later, we took a quiet stroll from Westminster Clock Tower along
the Embankment to Lambeth Bridge. A simple occupation but a
pleasant one, for this was the capital city of our land; this was The

Embankment; and many a time in Africa we had wondered if we would ever see it again.

In the evening, we saw Revudeville *at the Windmill but I found it dull compared with the* Folies Bergère.

Returned by the last train at 11.00 p.m., which was packed to the doors and did not arrive until 12.30. Our passes ended at midnight, so we had to "infiltrate" into camp through a wet wheat-field!

SUNDAY – *14.5.44*
Working late again.

WEDNESDAY – *17.5.44*
Now we are working day and night shifts on the S.P.s, which carry 17-pounders.

SUNDAY – *21.5.44*
I will be in the "second wave" part of the L.A.D.. The "third wave" part has gone to Brandon, Suffolk. We stand by on three hours' notice to move. All the work is finished and the tanks ready for action.

We pass the time in one of the camp "cinemas", in a big marquee. There are two, the "Odeon" and the "Ritz"!

MONDAY – *22.5.44*
Invasion instructions. We will be given forty-eight-hour concentrated rations and the equivalent of one pound sterling in the currency of whatever country we invade, irrespective of rank, debit or credit. Each truck will be numbered according to its place in the assembly for embarking. "B" stage of the waterproofing will be done at the assembly area. We hope it will not be put to the test and the landing will be "dry" as at Salerno.

FRIDAY – *26.5.44*
All personnel confined to camp for security reasons. The time must be getting near, for we are told we will be getting new currency very soon, probably within two days, and before leaving the camp.

SUNDAY – *28.5.44*
New breakdown comes at the last minute, an American Ward la France and we feverishly begin waterproofing again with pressure-plastic and asbestos compound.

Orders are coming steadily over the loudspeakers for vehicles to marshall and long lines of tanks, trucks, jeeps, half-tracked armoured cars and Bren-carriers form up, all fitted to run, if necessary, through 4½ ft. of water.

These vehicles were now on their way to the docks to be loaded on to ships. As I was not numbered amongst the drivers this time, I remained with the others in camp. The strength of the L.A.D. had been much increased.

We now have our forty-eight-hour rations – in concentrated, small cubes: tea, sugar and milk in one powder-block, biscuits, sweets and a folding chemical heater.

The rations were actually in two twenty-four-hour boxes. I have before me one of the instruction leaflets which were enclosed in the boxes, and the contents were listed as follows:-

10 biscuits	*Boiled sweets*
2 sweetened oatmeal blocks	*2 packets of chewing gum*
Tea/sugar/milk blocks	*1 packet of salt*
1 meat block	*Meat extract tablet(s)*
2 slabs of raisin chocolate	*4 tablets of sugar*
1 slab of plain chocolate	*4 pieces of latrine paper*

There was a "suggested menu" for breakfast and supper, the rest of the ration to be carried in convenient pockets for use during action. On the other side of the leaflet was a further hint: "If circumstances make heating with water impossible, the oatmeal and meat blocks can be eaten dry – in which case, (1) eat them slowly, (2) chew them well, (3) drink some water at the same time or soon after.

So everything was planned to the smallest detail.

TUESDAY – *30.5.44*
Talk given by C., R.A. (Brigadier), relaying "Monty's" message to the troops. He ("Monty") reveals he has two million men under his command alone! Britain has 6,000 bombers and 4,500 light bombers and fighters. The forty most important production centres in German Europe are half-destroyed and will be completely flattened before we go in.

The weather is very warm now, so we go en masse to a boating lake near the mansion for a swim. The residence is the property of Lord Lonsdale and a golf course runs past the lake.

While a few hundred soldiers swam or ran about, mostly nude, a young lady and her golfing instructor came along. She hurriedly missed the green by the lake and went round another way!

WEDNESDAY – *31.5.44*
Drivers return from Tilbury Docks, where the vehicles were loaded by crane on to "Liberty" ships, not on L.S.T.s. It seems we have to change over to landing craft when we are offshore, which might be slow and risky.

Saw a film called Commandos Strike at Dawn. *Each hand-grenade made a burst like a 6-in. shell and, immediately after the scrap, the commandos lined up and took their dressing with arms outstretched as if on the barrack square! They must think we are daft!*

THURSDAY – *1.6.44*
We march to the Palace Cinema, Brentwood, for a free show. Opposite the cinema, our officer (260 Battery) yelled, "Battery – Halt!" and, as we came down smartly, our boots crashing on the road as one, a company of the "Queen's" raised a derisive cheer, which made the passers-by laugh.

Still, we can take it!

SATURDAY – *3.6.44*
March to Warley Barracks.

SUNDAY – *4.6.44*
Short before-battle service in the Chapel of the Essex Regiment.

Hitler's biggest mistake was that he never asked God for His help. We did; so how could we lose?

Leave Warley by truck and, at Tilbury, a lighter takes us out to a "Liberty" ship. Quarters crowded and stuffy. We have oxtail soup from self-heating tins for supper.

MONDAY – *5.6.44*
We hear that Rome has been taken by the Allies. Move down river and anchor near Southend Pier. There are hundreds of "Liberty" ships and liners in the estuary and away out through the gap in the

boom. It's a big target but "Jerry" could not take advantage of the Armada at Sicily, so why should we worry?

TUESDAY – 6.6.44   *"D" DAY*
It has started! *Allied paratroops land. Big bombing raids on bridges and communications. Rumour that the "Jerry" fleet has come out at last! German reports say action is in northern France. No coastal landing yet. No Allied communiqué. Naval battle said to be raging off the mouth of the Seine.*

12 NOON
Radio announces coastal landings from Le Havre to Cherbourg, including Caen. Marines take part and battleships shell the coastal batteries.

LATER
Churchill says initial casualties comparatively light. Invasion going better than hoped for.

Procession of oil tankers going down the estuary with supplies for the forces. Many other ships leaving too. We go tomorrow.

WEDNESDAY – 7.6.44   D + 1
We are now sailing round Kent, heading for our corps beach-head, which is north of Bayeux. The "Yanks" are on our right in the Cherbourg Peninsula and the Canadians on our left at Caen. The 50th Division (our old companions) are in action today, followed by our 22nd Armoured Brigade. The rest of us are due to land tomorrow.

Now we are passing the white cliffs of Dover and the French coast is in sight, so corvettes are laying a smoke-screen in case "Jerry" tries to shell us with his 16-in. coastal guns. We are all wearing our "water-wings" – a new type of life-jacket which you blow up. Our destroyer has both funnels belching black smoke and also chemical burners at the stern. Other chemical burners are left floating on the water, still pouring out smoke. Two of our own coastal guns let off a round each with a great bang and a puff of brown smoke, away up on the cliffs above us. Slow biplanes circle round on anti-submarine patrol.

Our vehicle (the wrecker) is on deck and will be one of the first off. It is already cradled and hooked to the derrick in readiness. Six of us, including our Captain and the Padre, are going ashore with it.

A message from "Monty" includes the quotation:

> *He either fears his fate too much,*
> *or his deserts are small,*
> *Who dare not put it to the touch,*
> *to win or lose it all.*

As we proceed down-channel, all lights are switched off and the nightmare feeling in the dark hold, with the rumble and swish of the engines, reminds me of the time when I left France in 1940. Now I am returning, again in a ship's hold, and almost exactly four years later, in the same month of June.

Thursday – 8.6.44   D + 2

At 8.45 this morning, still no sight of land. Many lines of vapour in the sky, as our air armadas return from the attack. I can hear distant booming of gunfire.

Land in sight at 9.30 a.m., also scores of ships, as far as the eye can see, with a balloon barrage as big as that of a city. "Jerry" radio reports he shelled one of our convoys in the channel but the escort put up a smoke-screen. I didn't hear any of his shells.

Now we are told we cannot go off today, as petrol tankers are being unloaded first. Some large warships (I think three battleships and one cruiser) are lying close inshore, sending over some heavy stuff (probably 15-in.) at an invisble target. The gun flashes are tremendous and brown smoke covers the control towers, while each bang rolls across the water to us, seconds later. They may have an observation post some miles inland, or perhaps aircraft are spotting for them, for the steep coast hides the country from view, though we can see trucks running over the rise on dusty roads.

Friday – 9.6.44   D + 3

From dusk last night, as soon as our fighters had to return to Blighty, there were almost continuous air raids by "Jerry" throughout the night. Our ship shook and rattled as the Oerlikons (20 mm) opened up and the streams of tracers left a flickering green reflected light on the hatch openings. There was a flare as one of our own barrage balloons came down in flames but "Jerry" was scared off again and again and eventually the banging, rattling inferno ceased.

Now, in the calm morning air, we wait to go ashore. At last a small

L.C.T. (Landing craft, tank) comes alongside, our wrecker is first over and is lowered towards the deck of the smaller craft, which is rising and falling on the swell. As the deck rises to touch our tyres, the derrick is released just a fraction late and the heavy wrecker drops about a foot but without damage.

We are taken through a maze of cruisers, destroyers, "Liberty" ships, hospital ships, landing craft and tankers marked "Petrol", "Diesel", "Water", "Food", etc. in letters more than a foot high and finally, just after noon on D + 3, we drive on to French soil. Our tyres just touch the edge of the water as we leave the L.C.T. but around us are many more abandoned vehicles than we saw at the Salerno beach-head. Some are well out from the beach, where they have run into pot-holes or gullies in the sea bed and have dropped into deeper water.

But we have no time to look around as we drive up on to a narrow road and head inland. There are plenty of signs of the scrap and houses in the villages we pass through have been badly shelled. We go through Ryes in the direction of Bayeux and, two kilometres past Ryes, near the village of Sommervieu, we stop at a farm, where our forward R.H.Q. has been established.

Civilians, who had to leave their homes, are returning already and they seem pleased to see us but a little reserved. We are parked under some trees near the farm when, at 9.00 p.m., several M.E.109s come over through a smother of light ack-ack fire and let go a few bombs. There is a bit of strafing too and a vicious noise which I take to be the rocket guns on "Jerry's" fighters.

SUNDAY – *11.6.44*
The echelons move up into position, leaving us with a tank which has got water in the engine. Efforts are being made to gain and consolidate high ground south of Bayeux but it seems the necessary forces are not getting ashore quickly enough. Everything depends on getting there before "Jerry" concentrates and taking the high ground which will form a strong point covering the surrounding country with the guns. If "Jerry" gets there first, it may take a lot of hard fighting to remove him, as it did at Salerno.

Later, looking for 131 "B" Echelon, we pass through Bayeux but have to come back when we find they have not yet moved up. As we leave Sommervieu, two M.E.109 Gs sweep over low, machine-gunning. We find "B" Echelon at a hamlet called Magny. The French people seem to be coming out of their shells and are waving and throwing flowers into our trucks.

Monday – 12.6.44

We explore a bit and come upon a house which "Jerry" used as a strong-point. The house is burnt out and enemy "ammo." and steel helmets are lying about. The ammo., we find, fits a Hotchkiss machine-gun which "Jerry" has been using but which is now part of Eddie Gamble's armoury!

There is a neat swimming-pool by the house, ranging in depth from three to eight feet and fitted with ladders and a springboard. A fire-extinguisher has been blown into the pool and is spreading its chemical contents on the bottom but that does not stop us from enjoying a swim! At least, we feel, there won't be any bilharzia in the water!

In the next field there is a German radio-location post, with sixteen of our bomb-craters around it and one slap by it, which has blown the wall in.

In the afternoon, went forward to pick up a smashed motor-cycle. At one crossroads, all buildings were wrecked and there were two of our armoured cars knocked out. Farther on, I saw three German Mark IV Special tanks smashed and several burnt enemy trucks. In one field, a battery of self-propelled 25-pounders were banging away, watched by a French man and a boy. On the other side of the road, some flying O.P.s were drawn under some trees. They apparently took off and landed in a lane cut through the corn. These are very slow monoplanes which spot for the artillery.

Everything is green and beautiful, except the dusty roads, along which a stream of tanks, guns and men move to the forward positions.

In Bayeux we went into a café and I was surprised to find they had most of the old drinks, including beer, but Mam'selle said the beer would soon be finished, as it is made not here but in Le Havre, which is still in enemy hands.

"B" Echelon have moved forward a little and we join them again

*and sit beneath the trees, eating canned sausages and fruit. They say
our 258 Battery have lost two tanks, with several casualties. The
whole Division will soon be in action in the attempt to get the rising
ground which will cover the area where we hope to amass the great
force which will later reach Germany. Many of the guns which were
firing over our heads at "Jerry" have moved up too.*

*At night, artillery fires from the field next to us, enemy bombers
come over and we hear some spent ack-ack shells come howling
down.*

TUESDAY – *13.6.44*
*Out on recovery work south-west of Bayeux, near the "Yankee"
sector. On the way back, at a café in Subles, we had a black coffee
with Calvados.*

WEDNESDAY – *14.6.44*
*Went to 30th Corps Workshops on the beach and I noticed they now
have floating jetties pushed over the shallows and are getting the
reinforcements and supplies ashore much more quickly.*

This, though I did not know it, was the beginning of "Mulberry
Harbour".

*In the evening, more recovery in the same direction as on Tuesday,
a White half-tracked armoured car turned on its side. After working
in the twilight, got back at 12.30 and in bed at 1.00 a.m.*

A duplicated news-sheet was now being issued, called *The Jerboa
Journal* and, in No. 5, the following report is given:

> "On the central sector our armoured forces on Wednesday
> night withdrew from Villers Bocage to link up with the
> American positions at Caumont. In carrying out this move-
> ment, they fought a most successful action with troops of the
> 2 Pz. Division. After the orders for withdrawal had been
> received, strong German infantry attacks, supported by tanks,
> developed. The German infantry suffered very heavy casual-
> ties but they moved forward until our gunners were firing air
> bursts over open sights at 500 yards range. Only after a num-
> ber of Tigers had been knocked out at 200 yards, and their
> infantry heavily engaged by the whole of the artillery at the
> disposal of the C.R.A., did the enemy decide to withdraw.

Practically the whole of our Brigade, including all available vehicles of Tac. H.Q., was committed. Throughout the battle the situation was made extremely difficult by snipers actually sitting within a few yards of our vehicles.* We destroyed up to 12 tanks, and it is estimated that German infantry losses were between 700 and 800. The Corps Commander has sent the following message to the Divisional Commander:

> "'Hearty congratulations on successful actions yesterday. You have dealt 2 Pz. a hell of a smack. A major contribution to general plan. Well done all ranks'."

So the Division were still proving their capabilities, although this was a vastly different sort of war to that of the desert.

THURSDAY – *15.6.44*
Visit the beach again. It seems they are going to sink the large concrete structures which were floated across the Channel, to form a harbour. Later, I take a walk round the busy streets of Bayeux and have a couple of cognacs in the "Lion d'Or"; which reminds me that there is a hotel of the same name (Golden Lion) in my own town of Stirling, where Robert Burns once scratched a verse on a window-pane, still preserved.

FRIDAY – *16.6.44*
"Jerry" bombers over very low in the early morning. Bedlam let loose as the ack-ack fires almost horizontally, the shells bursting above the trees beside us. We hear the shrapnel cracking through the branches.

SATURDAY – *17.6.44*
"Jerry" over again early this morning. Managed to sleep through the ack-ack for a while but two heavy bombs at the foot of our field awakened us.

Later, on visiting the beach dump for spares, I found an abandoned

---

* These snipers were possibly using special infra-red ray equipment. A small searchlight sends out a beam of light invisible to the naked eye, but which can be seen through a special telescope. The press later announced the capture of such equipment.

Jeep with a very apt inscription painted under the windscreen. It was the ITMA *line, "I go ... I come back!" (Dunkirk ... Normandy?)*

SUNDAY – *18.6.44*

Move to a position by Noron la Poterie, five miles south-west of Bayeux on the St. Lo road. Quiet night, for a change. We brought in a Jeep riddled with shrapnel. The name painted on it was – "Hellzappopin".

MONDAY – *19.6.44*

Forward again to 257, taking reinforcements on the way. This battery lost several guns and their crews in a night action against tanks. We take back three Morris gun-tractors on one trip, behind the big wrecker, then go out again for a Daimler armoured car. It rains all day and we are soaked, so we are glad of a rum ration before bed. Some bombs dropped in the vicinity at night.

I have just remembered that Bayeux is connected with the famous tapestry!

TUESDAY – *20.6.44*

"Titch" Houghton, the cheery blond lad from Durham, has been evacuated with both hands blown off by an "88" shell-burst. While we worked on the wrecks we brought in yesterday, eight enemy fighters of a new type suddenly swept over our field, strafing. We scattered and a French farm-worker, who had been cutting hay, was down in the ditch with us. The 'planes were so low and passed the high hedges so quickly, that the ack-ack had no chance to hit them.

Up forward, F... D..., one of our L.A.D., who is pretty good with a rifle, was called on to have a go at a troublesome sniper hidden in a tree. He got him.

Some of the boys have been fitting tracks to damaged tanks in no-man's-land, under cover of a barrage laid down specially for that purpose. Fighting is vicious to the south and we hear the guns all day.

At night, enemy 'planes come over again and two bombs are dropped quite close, perhaps intended for Div. H.Q. and, down by the beach, a great red glow appears.

WEDNESDAY – *21.6.44*

They say the fire-glow of last night was a petrol dump that "Jerry" hit. We move further inland to Castillion, a small commune near

*Balleroy and park the wrecker beside a small disused quarry. In the
evening, just as Greg had gone to bed in our lean-to tent, the
ack-ack opened up with a crackle, bang, thud; an enemy fighter
dived and zoomed over the road and bullets ripped through the
trees above us. Greg, in his shirt-tails, was down in the old quarry
in a flash – and we were not far behind!*

Wish I had a Bren-gun and some tracers.

THURSDAY – 22.6.44
*"Jerry" strafing at 6.00 a.m. got us up nice and early. Spend the day
dismantling a Jeep. A few groups of our bombers pass over in the
evening and we see a great smother of "Jerry" "flak" greet them
towards Villers Bocage. The "Yanks" are said to be within four
miles of Cherbourg, which is cut off. I have now acquired several
clips of tracers.*

FRIDAY – 23.6.44
*We are getting newspapers now – but usually four or five days old.
Two French children have been killed by a shell which landed at
our Tac. H.Q.*

*Just before dusk, we heard "Jerry's" ack-ack going off, then we saw
one of our Typhoons – the new tank-bursting type with eight rockets
and four heavy machine-guns – passing over with his engine pop-
ping and smoke coming from it.*

*Suddenly, it burst into flames, the pilot baled out – after an age –
and the 'plane crashed not far away, leaving a great column of
smoke above the trees. Other fighters, including Mustangs, circled
to see if the pilot had got out and down safely, then carried on.*

SUNDAY – 25.6.44
*Go forward to do welding repairs on tanks for 260 Battery. Our
guns were behind us, firing over our heads, and several return shots
landed in the fields around us. "Jerry" also sent over air-bursts,
some of which were quite close. Saw his ack-ack have a go at several
of our planes, including a lone Marauder which had to twist and
turn to get out of it.*

MONDAY – 26.6.44
*Long and heavy barrage going over in the morning. Small push by
us in the Tilly sector. Advance only 1,000 yards. Heavy rain.*

TUESDAY – *27.6.44*
After rain all night, woke to a brighter morning to hear that Cherbourg had been taken.

WEDNESDAY – *28.6.44*
Went to a position just 2,000 yards from "Jerry" to pick up a Crusader A.A. tank fitted with just two Oerlikon guns. A few shells whined over but burst no nearer than 100 yards away.

I am now reading Over the Hills *by Jeffery Farnol; an enthralling tale of the '15 Rebellion.*

THURSDAY – *29.6.44*
Forward past Livry village to get a Morris Quad (gun-tractor). Just before we went through the village, "Jerry" sent over about a dozen shells which burst in the street, on roofs and on the front of a little shop, killing two of the "Queen's" and wounding several others. When we got to 259 Battery H.Q., there was barbed wire across the road, on the brow of a hill and a notice said, "You are under enemy observation". A blind old woman was caught in the wire and the Battery Major helped to disentangle her skirt. Then on she went, down the slope towards the enemy, tapping her way to her home, somewhere along the road, ignoring the noise of the guns. We picked up our wreck from a narrow track and returned through Livry before the next shelling, which was due in a few minutes.

FRIDAY – *30.6.44*
At 8.15 p.m., a dull thunder announced the arrival of a great procession of our heavy Halifax bombers. This was the first time I had seen them dispersed to offer less of a target to enemy guns and they seemed to cover the sky as they passed, apparently serenely, through a smother of "flak" to their target in the direction of Villers Bocage. We saw them wheel steadily over the target and stream back, while more and more bombers were still arriving. Then, under the point where the bombers were turning, ten miles away, we saw the dust beginning to rise from the earth. Higher and higher, thicker and thicker it rose, until that disc on the map was obliterated beneath an impenetrable pall.

This was the first time we had seen our heavy bombers used in daylight in large numbers to help the ground forces. It was an awful spectacle; a small town (Villers Bocage itself) being wiped out as we watched. Yet we could not help being thrilled, for we felt that now the power was on our side and that retribution was surely coming to the supporters of the inhuman Nazi regime.

SATURDAY – *1.7.44*

Move back to Subles. They say the division is now being held in reserve. We are not in billets, but still sleep in our lean-to tent, made with a tarpaulin.

Yesterday's big raid was for the "benefit" of a Panzer concentration at Villers Bocage. "Monty" thanks the R.A.F. for an "inspiring sight".

SUNDAY – *2.7.44*

Visit the beaches again. The quaint little town of Arromanches, with its narrow streets, is nearly all occupied by naval, military and air force H.Qs. now. Great camps, dumps and stores have sprung up everywhere, roads have been widened and improved and a large harbour has been made, with a line of small ships deliberately sunk to protect the floating quays and concrete breakwaters at either end.

There are plenty of French people about in Bayeux, all in their Sunday best.

TUESDAY – *4.7.44*

"Jerry" over, strafing but the Bofors chased him. One gun in the field across the road kept blasting away, while we felt each concussion like a blow. Rain and sunshine, turn about, all day. Plenty of mud but we keep dry in our tent, augmented by odd bits of canvas.

WEDNESDAY – *5.7.44*

Go to Colombiers, near Creully, to pick up a Ford rear axle. See many troops from Blighty who have never been in action, after nearly five years of war. They sit in neat rows in their transport, wearing green-blancoed haversacks and camouflaged helmets as if they were on manoeuvres.

THURSDAY – *6.7.44*

We are taken to a film show in the "Cinema Grenier", or Barn Cinema. It was a barn, in a big farmyard near Damigny, south of Bayeux. We sat on rows of "Compo" boxes, that is, the boxes in which our "composite" rations are delivered.

FRIDAY – *7.7.44*
In the newspapers it is said that "Tommy" in France is being paid every fortnight. We've been here a month and have had no pay. If I had not changed all my money before the invasion, I would not have anything left. I have been buying some Camembert cheese, of which there is a surplus now, since the Paris market is cut off.

Working on greasing our wrecker, when some Messerschmitts came over. The ack-ack opened fire and I shot off three rounds with the rifle, using tracer to see where they went. My third skimmed a wing-tip as I aimed about six lengths in front. I was nearer than any of the Bofors!

SATURDAY – *8.7.44*
At midnight, our "residue" arrives; all the fellows of R.H.Q. and the L.A.D. who remained behind in Blighty. Much shouting and crashing of branches as each truck comes in.

SUNDAY – *9.7.44*
Seems the boys have had a good time in Wisbech since the invasion began. Our field is now crowded, though some are going forward to join the S.P. batteries. In the café at Subles, I enjoyed a drink with Denny, while Mam'selle put on a record of Tino Rossi singing, in French, "Sérènade près de Mexico" – "South of the Border".

During the night, two shells came screaming over, one landing in the hollow short of us and the other near the village behind us. Surprising, for we are ten miles from "Jerry" now. Why pick on us?

MONDAY – *10.7.44*
The "residue" are amazed to find us eating hard biscuits. They read in the papers that we were getting bread. The usual propaganda!

TUESDAY – *11.7.44*
Walked to Bayeux with Denny and visited the beautiful cathedral, where, in a side-chamber, we saw a copy of the long Bayeux Tapestry, depicting William the Conqueror's preparations for his invasion, the landing at Pevensey and the Battle of Hastings. The original, put in a place of safety for the duration of the war, is believed to have been made by William's consort, Queen Matilda.

The town was crammed with troops and the cafés were practically all sold out. Saw two British nurses in smart uniforms, the first of the invasion. On the outskirts of the town, a smashed house had only six feet of the gable standing, with a pump attached and a soldier was drawing water from this, the only useful thing to survive.

SATURDAY – *15.7.44*

In the area of Ranchy, two kilometres away, there are half a dozen field hospitals, with a large number of nurses, already established. During the night, the ack-ack fires at something roaring above. Two pass over but the third goes "pop-pop" as if the engine was failing, then the sound stops, to be followed, a few seconds later, by a big explosion in the hollow below our field.

SUNDAY – *16.7.44*

Some of the "residue" tell us that last night's "foreign object" was a flying bomb, "Jerry's" new toy.

MONDAY – *17.7.44*

Our canteen actually produces some beer; one bottle per week. Griff-talk: We are joining 8th Corps, composed of 7th, 11th, and Guards Armoured Divisions (three armoured divisions instead of the usual one with two infantry divisions). The attack will go in by a small bridgehead north of Caen and not by the large one south of the town, which will only foster a minor attack to occupy the enemy Panzers, which are concentrated there in expectation of a break-through; 11th Armoured Division will join the rear of the southern bridgehead, cutting off the enemy opposite Caen. We, (7th Armoured Division) will go due south as far and as fast as possible and the Guards will turn east along the main road past Lisieux. "Monty" wants an advance of twenty miles a day for the first fortnight, increasing to forty miles a day when the breakthough is complete and the advance gains momentum! Zero may be tomorrow, Tuesday, but depends on good weather for intense air support.

TUESDAY – *18.7.44*

Weather good, sky clear; bombers and fighters are out and the attack begins. We move to Cully, half-way between Bayeux and Caen. In the evening, as we make camp between a farm and a church, we are told that "Jerry" is retreating at three miles an hour!

WEDNESDAY – *19.7.44*

2,000 aircraft went into the attack. We lost nine. Advance going well. We are warned to move again and later arrive at a spot near

Douvres la Delivrande. We are now in more open country and vehicles are dotted over the rolling wheat-fields and stubble for miles.

THURSDAY – 20.7.44
Standing-by for a further move. Hot sunshine changes to heavy rain and we quickly put up our tent again and get inside. Heavy barrage going over, the rumble of the more distant guns being broken by the thuds, cracks, bumps and bangs of those nearer. The French people cycling along the road now and then seem to have no shortage of rubber tyres or bright dresses.

We do not move. More rain.

FRIDAY – 21.7.44
Steady downpour.

SATURDAY – 22.7.44
A flying bomb – or "doodle-bug" – passes over, with a dull, spluttering roar from its jet propulsion.

An attempt to kill Hitler fails, but shows dissatisfaction in Germany. Several German generals shot.

SUNDAY – 23.7.44
Out at 5.00 a.m. to get an ammo. truck out of the ditch at Basly. This was not a Regimental job, but done at the request of the Military Police, in order to get the shells forward and clear the road.

MONDAY – 24.7.44
Move to Thaon. We pitch camp at the edge of a big hollow, which contains a farm set amongst giant trees.

"Jerry" over at dusk, dropping strings of "chandeliers". Then we have ack-ack; bangs; red tracers; strafing; droning; the glow of bombs; thumps; the swish of shrapnel; and so we are "lulled" to sleep.

TUESDAY – 25.7.44
My wash-day!

WEDNESDAY – 26.7.44
Out on recovery, we pass through Caen. Gone is the city I saw when I passed through by rail in 1940. Now it is the scene of the most terrible destruction. Huge bomb craters overlap for acres; great heaps of masonry spill on to the streets; ruins are smouldering; shops

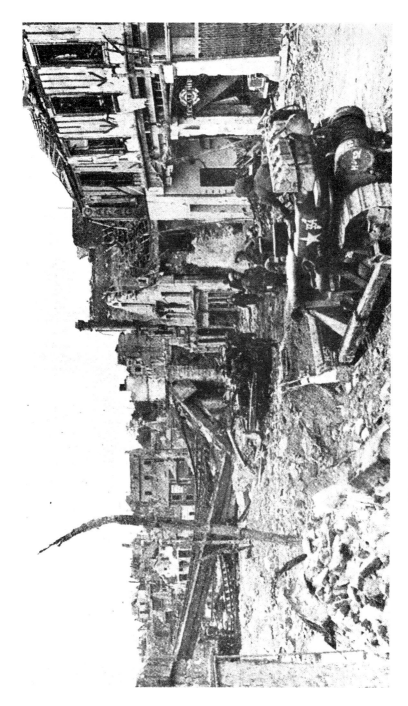

The actual bridge under which we took our Wrecker.

are smashed; churches are empty shells; roads are blocked and we zig-zag along where bulldozers are pushing the rubble aside. The whole place stinks of the dead. Water, light and sewage are non-existent. The town is out of bounds to all not with special duty. Our wrecker barely gets under a railway bridge which has collapsed. Smashed cars are lying in craters. A few citizens, bewildered, wander amongst the desolation, some living in broken basements under the wreckage, some shaking out salvaged linen and other belongings. Here and there a gaunt wall rises above the debris and I see a settee perched high on a ledge; pictures still hanging; bottles on shelves; smashed furniture and torn bed-clothes. And what lies under the mountains of stone and brick, God alone knows. Some streets have completely vanished under rubble. In one small area, there are still asphalt and kerbstones and houses and cafés with billiard tables; but even here the buildings are pierced by shells and pitted by shrapnel. The destruction is not in patches as in London, but is continuous from one side of the city to the other. Only the Cathedral of St. Étienne has, by a miracle, escaped damage. Even the surrounding villages are in ruins and trees stand as naked stumps. We cross the River Orne by a Bailey bridge named "Winston Bridge" and go further east to the front, where we pick up the wreck, a water-truck riddled with shrapnel, with three flat tyres. The flat ground here has our tanks dotted all over it and in front is a low rise, behind which is "Jerry". Some 25-pounder S.P.s are firing near us and we watch our Typhoons diving down and ripping off a salvo of rockets on "Jerry", ignoring his flak. Then we see a line of smoke puffs rising behind the ridge and hear the reports as the "Hun" gets his share of the fireworks.

We return via Colombelles, a factory town, which is battered too. A few enemy shells whine across but none close. Back through desolate Caen, with the wreck on tow. It is terrible that we had to smash Caen so completely to get the enemy out of it. An old French ex-soldier of 1914, to whom I spoke, said as usual, "C'est la guerre!" and with the usual shrug; but what a tragedy, hardship and loss the French people have suffered! Caen is the worst thing I have seen in this war, but then the enemy held it stubbornly. The Germans have always been clever enough to fight on other people's territory – but their time is coming.

A notice in the outskirts of Caen says, "You will be placed under arrest if you enter this town when not on duty."

THURSDAY – *27.7.44*

Went to Colleville for two 3-ton wrecks. Colleville is near the mouth of the River Orne and, as soon as we showed on the skyline, shells began to whistle over from the other side of the river, where "Jerry" is in possession of the coastal town of Cabourg. We could clearly see the high ground beyond Cabourg and some of our cruisers offshore opposite Hermanville.

While hitching one of the trucks on tow, we had trouble with a jammed shackle-pin and the shells burst closer and closer, as the enemy got the range. The truck had to be suspended with front wheels clear of the ground and, while I struggled with the shackle-pin, with Sergeant "Les" Harman beside me, two of our newer men, who joined us shortly before the invasion, crouched shivering in a slit-trench with their steel helmets on, instead of lending a hand. Obviously, the vehicles showing above the skyline were the target for the enemy fire, so the quicker we got them hitched up and moved out of sight, the better. Eventually we managed it and signalled the driver to move off, just as another shell landed very close on the brow of the hill.

THURSDAY – *27.7.44 (Contd.)*

We go to the same place in the afternoon but find the Battery (260) gone. They had been shelled out with heavy air-bursts! We return to Thaon via Douvres.

FRIDAY – *28.7.44*

We have no more official news of the big push around Caen but rumours are going around that the Blanco divisions from Blighty let us down. The Guards took their objective but stopped for further orders, when they might have taken more ground and prevented "Jerry" from settling. The 11th Armoured Division could not reach their objective and we had to come back, to keep the line straight. This may be all wrong; but "Jerry" has apparently held our 900 tanks, or we should be much farther ahead. The radio says it was a blind to draw the enemy armour and allow the American infantry to advance in their sector! But if so, why tell "Jerry"?

SATURDAY – *29.7.44*

Up at 4.30 a.m. for a quick move back to the area south of Bayeux. At 10.00 a.m. we have only covered one mile and are queued up waiting. We have two 3-tonners on tow but drop them to recover an R.A.S.C. truck lying on its side at the foot of the bank. We unload the breakdown to use the crane, finish the recovery, reload, go back to the 3-tonners and find we (and all the echelon) have to return to our last position! We do so and pitch our tent once more. Love's Labour Lost!

At 9.00 p.m., we again pack to move and, after crawling along dark side-roads, we reach a position near Trungy, in the middle of the night.

SUNDAY – *30.7.44*
Wakened at 6.00 a.m. by our bombers going over. They were still going over at 7.00 a.m.. Broke the jib cable on a stubborn recovery job and spent the afternoon repairing same.

MONDAY – *31.7.44*
As we drove along the Tilly–Bayeux road, a truck-load of 2-pounder ammo. suddenly went up in front of us, nearly bursting our ear-drums. A great mushroom of smoke arose, with tracer shells shooting out of it, to the accompaniment of more bangs. Something clattered down beside me. It was a rifle barrel, twisted and smoking hot. The M.P.s led two ambulances towards the scene but, before they got there, a roadside petrol dump next to the ammo. truck went up. Black smoke now rose in billowing clouds and flames swirled high above the trees, which began to crackle. Several of our own aircraft circled round the smoke column in curiosity. Petrol ran along the road and even the tar burned and the hedges shrivelled in the blaze. We were sent on our way by a different route.

TUESDAY – *1.8.44*
Four dead in yesterday's inferno. Work all day on a Quad. Valve-timing, necessitating removal of radiator to reach turning gear; grind valves, adjust tappets, cut two holes in a bracket with oxy-acetylene and "manufacture" a valve-cotter. Just a small job! I have lately become a little more expert at cutting and welding as when I welded a thin plate to a thick rod to make an L.A.D. sign.

WEDNESDAY – *2.8.44*
Move south towards Caumont. The 25-pounders are now all round us and make a deafening noise. The gunners sit casually around their guns, pass the shells as if they were passing the salt and press the trigger-push at regular intervals. Each time, the muzzles recoil about

eighteen inches and, as the blue smoke rises, we smell the cordite. There is also the smell of some dead cattle, about a quarter of a mile away.

THURSDAY – *3.8.44*

The guns have moved forward again. "Bud", who was our ration bombadier for many moons, before being posted to one of the batteries, has now been seriously wounded.

FRIDAY – *4.8.44*

Pass through Livry to another village, smashed and deserted. In the wrecked houses, everything has been looted and strewn about. We intended to bring back a Jeep wreck for spares, but all we found was the chassis.

SATURDAY – *5.8.44*

The "Yanks" are now past St. Malo and moving on towards Rennes. We also advance and re-take Villers Bocage. The guns are now almost out of hearing. At last we seem to have "Jerry" on the move. Guinness from our canteen – and two bottles this week!

We stand by to move at any hour to follow the advance. Tents are packed, stores, equipment, everything except blankets. I lie down across the seats of the wrecker for a few hours' sleep.

SUNDAY – *6.8.44*

At 3.00 a.m. we move. Again we pass through Livry, scarred and dusty but its damage now softened by moonlight, till it looks like a scene from a Christmas card. A mist is rising under the full moon, giving everything a ghostly look, as we go along quiet roads and through deserted villages, their torn rafters spread to the sky. Now and then we glimpse a smashed tank or armoured car. One place we pass through stinks horribly of death. At 5.00 a.m. we stop in a field for another two hours' sleep, then with daylight we move to another field by a farm-house. We are at Coulvain, five miles south-west of Villers Bocage. The farm has been looted by "Jerry". I found a row of his little dugouts in a narrow lane. Enemy equipment lay around and the farmer's best sheets and blankets were lining the earth walls. Chairs, stools, jugs and bottles of crude wine were scattered about. The dugouts were stinking and lousy. A large box contained cups, saucers and tumblers, all from the farm. Wings of chickens were strewn in the house itself, where they had been killed for food.

Our colonel (Colonel Stewart, D.S.O., M.C.) has been killed by a mine. He has been with us a bit longer than most of the last six C.O.s His Jeep was blown on to the bank at the side of the road, the colonel himself being thrown several yards away. His driver, wounded, staggered several miles for help.

The enemy is believed to be withdrawing to the Seine!

Had a walk to some other deserted enemy positions and stopped when a horrible stench struck our nostrils. There was a rough cross marked just "German Soldier". He had been shovelled into a slit trench and covered recently but there were maggots on the ground where he had lain for some time.

We found a bewildered dog in a grain store at a farm. He was lying behind a barrel, looking at us with pitiful eyes, but would not come out, apparently intending to remain until his master returned to the farm. We had no food with us and he only growled when I spoke to him, so we had to leave him. Later, we returned with food.

MONDAY – 7.8.44

I am taken off the wrecker to drive a Jeep. All the other fellows are changed round too, by our officer, in a needless effort to shake the boys up and make them work harder. Yet we have turned out every job given to us! The fellows have no interest in a static war. They want to get it over and an advance is all the encouragement needed for them to turn out a superhuman effort when necessary. The officer is said to be annoyed because some of the boys were throwing crab-apples at each other. Why should they not be light-hearted some time? Must they always be miserable? If he had tried to provide some means of recreation, it would have been more like the thing. We are all disgusted.

Meanwhile, the forward section of the L.A.D., under Sgt. Ed. Culhane, has been taken in front of the infantry, where patrols were operating, by order of one of the Battery Majors. They had no cover to allow any useful work, but just had to keep dodging enemy fire.

One shell landed between Ed's Jeep and another vehicle, blew the Jeep upside down, blew Ed on his face and left a crater. They turned the Jeep upright, pressed the starter and, miraculously, the engine worked! The starting handle could no longer be used because, as Ed reported, it couldn't "go round the corners"!

But what chance of doing a job of repair?

Taking a truck out on test after repair, I had my first look at Villers Bocage, which is completely smashed. (This was also the scene of bitter fighting.) Rennes has been taken by the "Yanks"

TUESDAY – *8.8.44*

Fighting in Brest, Lorient and Laval. The "Yanks" are passing through miles of country without any Germans in it. The enemy is concentrated against the British-Canadian sector in the Caen-Vire area, hence our slow advance.

WEDNESDAY – *9.8.44*

Move to a spot north of Aunay. The rising ground gives a good view of the rolling country. We have advanced only a little and the guns are not far off. My "transfer" is in abeyance, so I travel on the wrecker as usual. Beautiful weather; grasshoppers all chirping.

FRIDAY – *11.8.44*

Rumour I may go to the section attached to 260 Battery. We move to the Regimental area south of Aunay for a general's inspection. Aunay itself is just a heap of stinking rubble. The church spire is the only thing left standing. We never see civilians now. The Army are using water-carts in Aunay to lay the thick dust.

In the field next to our camp, dead cows are being burned.

These animals were distended and stinking and, being too big to bury easily, petrol was poured over them and they were cremated. The shells which killed them had been so delicately adjusted that they burst without digging into the ground so, instead of a crater, each shell left only a burnt patch on the ground, while shrapnel often cut horizontal grooves through the grass for many yards. Many cows, too, must have died through not being milked.

SATURDAY – *12.8.44*

We have been working till dark on Quads, which give a lot of trouble, particularly with steering and valve-springs. Today, however, I am told to finish at 6p.m. so I have a wash and enjoy a drink of cider (from deserted vats) after a broiling hot day.

... And the many that died.
The slaughter that no soldier who fought in Normandy will ever forget.

SUNDAY – *13.8.44*
Sunday, but no Church bells. One thousand bombers go over to blast the German divisions now almost encircled between Vire and Falaise. "Jerry" is supposed to have got his S.S. divisions out through the gap, which is only twenty miles wide. We lose forty-nine 'planes.

MONDAY – *14.8.44*
Treated to a film show (in colour) at the Jerboa Club, in a portable workshop structure like an aircraft hangar.

In the afternoon, I was at "B" Echelon and picked up two Canadian Air Force men, who asked for lift in the Jeep I was driving. I brought them forward via Aunay. They were heading for the front to "have a look around".

Tuesday – *15.8.44*

The newspapers seem to think it's about all over bar shouting but there's a long way to go yet to the Rhine and the Siegfried Line! Meanwhile, crops are wasting here, because "Jerry" has driven the people away and there is no one to bring in the harvest. This will mean a big loss of food for France. Cattle are wandering about un-milked too.

We have a "griff" talk from the Padre: *the gap at Falaise is now only six miles wide, containing one small road which is being shelled from both sides, and bombed. Seven German divisions are trapped and have made no attempt to run the gauntlet. These divisions include four armoured (Panzer) divisions but the 1st, 3rd and Lehr Divisions (S.S.) were pulled out before the gap closed. We are being "rested" for a later drive towards the Seine. At Falaise, we have the American Third Army, which was landed secretly and came up through Argentan. A French Armoured Division is also there and has made a mess of a German Grenadier Regiment.*

A fresh invasion took place this morning in the south of France. British, Canadian, American and French troops took part and reached their objectives in one hour.

We now have – under my care – a Mark IV mine detector, the latest, very sensitive, light and compact.

Major B., second-in-command of the Regiment, is now taking charge. As he has only one eye, he has always been known to the men – rather irreverently – as "Wahed Shufty", which may be taken very roughly as Arabic for "One Look"!

CHAPTER 2

The Breakthrough

WEDNESDAY – *16.8.44*

The regiment moves early on sudden orders to join the Canadians in their sector at Eterville, near Caen. The L.A.D. will only move later, when several trucks are put back on the road. One we brought in at 6.00 a.m. was full of ammo. and the steering was gone. We suspended it on the crane but, when we tried to turn round in Aunay, the weight of the shells raised our front wheels and pushed them broadside over the road. There was a traffic jam, until we went on to the big roundabout which used to be the centre of Aunay and managed to turn there.

THURSDAY – *17.8.44*

Move towards Eterville. Civilians are just coming back to their wrecked homes. Many are weeping. A few can still give us the "V" sign. By the roadside and in the fields are heaps of charred bones and horseshoes where dead animals have been burned. Crossing the river by a Bailey bridge near Eterville, we turn south and east on dusty tracks.

The Canadians have had some desperate fighting for a wheat-covered ridge here. German and Canadian dead are all mixed up, little white crosses being scattered amongst the wheat and the shell-holes. A few Bren-carriers have been knocked out and some German tanks. In one spot we saw another of our vaunted "Churchill" tanks knocked out. In another place I saw a cross marked "Anglais Inconnu". The civilians must have buried him.

We stop at St. Aignan, still deserted and wait for news of the whereabouts of the regiment. Later, we join them at Conteville.

Falaise is now in our hands. The "Yanks" are at Chartres; and the Marseilles beach-head is now fifty miles in length.

FRIDAY – *18.8.44*

Move south to Maizieres. As we came on to high ground, two shells landed beside the road but we went on down a slope and parked behind an orchard.

We went to bury a dead German pilot and found three more German soldiers in their slit-trenches, partly hidden by sheaves of wheat. All had been there some time and their faces were black, swollen and negroid, with hordes of tiny maggots on them. Each had his photograph in his service book but could not have been identified with it. The airman had been thin-featured, good-looking; but now his face was like that of a fat negro. His name was put on the cross; Josef Schoferle.

Two French farm-workers cut the equipment away from the others and buried them. One of the Frenchmen carried a small cask of cider and, while they worked, they kept taking copious draughts of the stuff until they were half drunk. A Polish division sent tanks and infantry here and they had no mercy on the hated Nazis. A Polish A.A. gun was burned out in one corner of the field, with a grave beside it, only half the length of a man.

It seemed as if the pilot, Schoferle, had come low, hit the gun but was himself hit either by that gun or some other. He then tried to bale out but was too low for his parachute to open. We could not remove the parachute, so buried it with him. One of the German soldiers had a red Cross on his arm and the tracks of a tank passed near his body. The sheaves of wheat which had been used to camouflage the slit-trenches had been set on fire by flame throwers and, when the Germans jumped out, they were shot down. The carcase of a dog also lay beside one of the trenches.

We had just got into our blankets when flares lit up right above us and bombing and strafing began. We got our clothes back on again and dispersed to trenches. One flare came down very close and we saw the little parachute distinctly. The ground showed as clearly as in daylight but "Jerry" hit nothing near us. Away towards the new front, however, were more flares and there an ammo. dump went up. Three splashes of orange flame appeared, then kept erupting like volcanoes and the church spire below us was silhouetted against the glow. Mosquitoes are plentiful and troublesome when we try to sleep.

Saturday – *19.8.44*

Went forward with the wrecker towards St. Pierre sur Dives to pick up a 3-tonner riddled with bomb-splinters. Dead Germans stilll lie by the roadside in grotesque attitudes.

In the evening, more strafing. One plane came so low over us that the tracer shells of a Bofors travelled horizontally a few feet from the ground, chasing him.

Sunday – *20.8.44*

More evening activity; strafing and bombing. We watched a truck blazing some way off, then we heard a swish and threw ourselves flat as a cracker-bomb landed. Still no casualties in our area.

Monday – *21.8.44*

In heavy rain, we pack ready to move. We go through St. Pierre and stop in picturesque country three miles east of the town. About ten miles advance.

Tuesday – *22.8.44*

The gap east of Falaise has been closed by the Poles. "Jerry" is being mopped up inside the pocket. The "Yanks" are now over the Seine north of Paris. According to a "griff" talk given by an Army Educational Corps officer, our front from north to south consists of 6 Airborne Division, 49 (Polar Bear) Division, 51 Highland Division, 7 Armoured Division, Canadians, Poles and so connects with the Americans. 12th Corps and 30th Corps are attending to the trapped Germans in the pocket. The names of the enemy divisions are too many, new and strange, to remember.

The southern invasion has produced a thrust near Avignon (Sur le Pont?). The furthest advance on our sector is to Lisieux.

Wednesday – *23.8.44*

Paris is free! "Jerry" evacuates and the French people take over control. Vichy, Lyons and Toulouse are also in the hands of the Maquis. Traitors have been shot or imprisoned and French Courts set up.

The enemy is said to have lost 60,000 killed in the Falaise pocket and 50,000 taken prisoner. The Regiment (65th Anti-Tank) moves again but we are changing several engines.

Thursday – 24.8.44

Move north-east towards Lisieux and halt at Lessard. Went out to recover Jack A's truck, upside down in a stream below a bridge. As a recompense, he gave us a taste of some real "Johnnie Walker" which he had aboard!

Rumania is out of the war and Bulgaria also asks for peace terms. So rats desert a sinking ship. "Jerry" is retreating all along this front, as he realises he is trapped with the Seine at his back.

Friday – 25.8.44

All move again except two vehicles of the L.A.D., one being our wrecker. We finish off changing two engines, using the crane to lift them.

Saturday – 26.8.44

On our own, we cook breakfast for ourselves feeling almost as if we were on a camping holiday. Join echelon at midday near Marolles, 8 km past Lisieux. The cathedral of Lisieux, standing on a hill, is a beautiful piece of architecture in white stone, with a large dome. The echelon is ready to move again, so it looks as if "Jerry" is really on the run now.

We travel along a first-class road, passing the boundary stone as we leave the département of Calvados and enter Eure. Finally, we take a side road and halt near Giverville. The people are now much more friendly. This area abounds with red brick half-timbered houses, reminiscent of Old England.

When we go through a gateway into a field, I find a large bomb half-buried, with just the fin sticking up. We move to another field, just in case ...!

Sunday – 27.8.44

Church bells again. All the civilians have remained here, as "Jerry" had to get out too fast to take them with him. The crops are safely cut and stacked. I have now to go forward to be attached to 260 Battery.

The R.A.F. find an enemy column fifteen miles long, smash the leading vehicles, blocking the convoy, then bomb and strafe it for an hour or two. Poor "Jerry"!

I join the "A" Echelon of 260 Battery near St. Georges.

We went up to a farm to obtain milk (one gallon) and cider (three gallons) and I had quite a chatter with the whole family. The old boy was full of cider and reminiscences of the last war. Another man was quite surprised that I, a Scotsman, had no "short skirts"!

TUESDAY – 29.8.44
I sleep now on a bench in a covered trailer, fairly happy. We do all our own cooking.

WEDNESDAY – 30.8.44
Move to the Lisieux - Evreux road and travel along it for some considerable distance. Turn left near Neubourg and park at the village of Tremblay. Got potatoes from a woman whose husband had been a prisoner for four years and eggs from another couple who gave us a great welcome, invited us into their spotless house, and told us about their life under German occupation. During the enemy retreat, one young Nazi had threatened the woman with a knife to get some food.

Later, other friendly people brought us butter, cream and even some Calvados, a liqueur made from apples.

In the evening, I was in conversation with a man who was born in Egypt, his father being employed by the Suez Canal Company. He spoke (besides French): English, Arabic and a little Italian and lived now in a fairly large house. He showed me some "soap" he had made himself from potassium and distemper, a pasty substitute for the real thing, which was apparently unobtainable. Cigarettes, he said, were rationed to forty a month and extras cost 200 francs (one pound sterling) per packet on the Black Market. He warned us about Frenchmen who put on the arm-band of General de Gaulle two hours after our troops arrive, instead of showing their sentiments earlier by sniping the German ambushes left as rear-guard. These ambushes had cost us lives and time.

"Surely," he said, "that was the time to do something!"

He added bitterly that France was decadent and would be no help to Britain after the war, as every man had different ideas and their politicians would be at loggerheads again.

I was silently thinking that perhaps things would be much the same in Britain!

THURSDAY – *31.8.44*
The fifth anniversary of my entry into the Army. Move at 7.00 a.m. through Neubourg towards the Seine. Coming down towards Louviers, we have a wonderful view of a wide valley of rolling fields under bright sunshine, the farms and trees looking like tiny models and the town nestling in at the left of the hollow. In Louviers itself, we get a great welcome, taking its practical form in gifts of pears and tomatoes.

We cross the Seine at St. Pierre de Vauvray, near Les Andelys, where there are remains of enemy pontoon bridges. The broad river is split at this point by tree-covered islands. We cross one of our own pontoon bridges to an island, then off the other side by the original stone bridge. We drive on into the night and finally bed down in the market square of Lyons la Forêt after sixteen hours of travel. The town is asleep, shutters closed, the people perhaps tired from the excitement of welcoming the troops who are chasing the Germans out of their country. All night convoys of trucks, tanks and guns rumble through.

FRIDAY – *1.9.44*
We rise again at 4.30 a.m., brew up and away before the people awake. At last we catch up with the battery at Gournay, now in Seine Inférieure. There was evidence of the great damage wrought by the R.A.F. on enemy convoys, for every fifty yards along miles of the main road, were burnt-out wrecks of vehicles.

From Gournay we turn on to the Dieppe road, halt for breakfast and a wash, and off once more at 9.00 a.m.. Prisoners are now going back. We leave the Dieppe road again, turning right to Gaillefontaine. The people are very friendly and talkative. We get plenty of fresh butter now, which makes even Army biscuits a delicacy. We also have a large, dilapidated dog, with brown eyes and sleepy habits. He has adopted us wholeheartedly. We still have no name for him.

A burnt Daimler armoured car by the roadside is still hot, with smouldering tyres. Inside are two burnt bodies, British. The floor is blown in; a Frenchman tells us it was hit by a shell from a German gun hidden on a ridge but another armoured car crew shot up the enemy gunners with machine-gun fire. Now some men of the Rifle Brigade are lifting out the charred remains to bury them by the roadside.

We go on into the Oise département and, at Romescamps, we are welcomed with gifts of fruit and much hand-shaking. One café owner produced two bottles of beer and refused payment, pushing my money back into my pocket. There were six Germans in the local jail!

The echelons park at Fuilloy. After sending a message saying we are settling down for the night, Divisional H.Q. changed its mind in the middle of the night and, at 3.00 a.m. (Saturday, 2nd September), we got up and moved again, going into the Somme département and crossing a bridge at Chaussée, probably over the River Somme itself.

SATURDAY – 2.9.44
Park in chalky fields at 8.00 a.m. near a flying-bomb launching site. We go on again at 4.00 p.m. and halt for the night (we hope) at Bouques Maison, where some of the boys sleep in the local sports pavilion, as it is raining. Some Americans are on the other side of the Maginot Line already and British troops are at the Meuse on the Belgian border.

SUNDAY – 3.9.44
Allied troops are now thirty miles from Brussels. We move at 8.30 a.m., having had a good night's sleep. Arriving at Frévent, we have breakfast. I do a bit of oxy-acetylene brazing on the captain's kettle! We are now in the Pas de Calais and have seen another launching site with four huge concrete shutes, used to dispatch pilotless missiles to England.

Later, we proceed in the direction of Arras. St. Pol, on this road, is in the hands of the enemy, in a pocket encircled by our guns. We by-pass it through side roads, where we see the 5.5-in. guns pointing towards the pocket, and return to the main road beyond St. Pol. Again we turn off, towards Béthune, and bed down somewhere between Béthune and Arras.

CHAPTER 3

Belgium and the Dutch Corridor

MONDAY – 4.9.44

Still moving. After waiting for miles of military traffic to pass, we start at 4.00 p.m.. We hear that Brussels has been cleared of the enemy. We are now in the area in which much of the First World War was fought and pass the cemeteries of Quartre Vents and Dud Corner. In them are the remains of men who, a quarter of a century ago, laid down their lives to end war and now we follow in their footsteps because war was not ended; because the Germans cast their greedy eyes beyond their own borders.

We go on by Loos and Lens. As we come over the brow of a hill, a vast plain bursts on our view below us, an industrial panorama of coal slag-heaps, red brick houses and fields of sugar-beet. Along the miles of roads our fathers trod and in the streets, crowds of French people wave, cheer, throw kisses and flowers and give the "V" sign. This is the Nord département and, in one place, we see our 25-pounders sending their flashes almost horizontal as they fire into another patch of resistance near Lille.

Unfortunately, we had to by-pass Lille, which held a special interest for me, as my father has told me of its liberation in the First World War, when he and his comrades received a welcome similar to that accorded to us in various other towns in 1944.

At dusk, we suddenly find ourselves in Belgium, having crossed the frontier between Toufflers and Nechin, so far as I could judge when I asked the people the names of the villages. Here, the folk went crazy, crowding the road so that we had to slow down, grabbing our hands, kissing them and both cheeks, passing us bottles of beer and other refreshments and, when a fork appeared in the road and we were doubtful of the way our convoy had gone, they blocked one road and pointed to the other, and we were racing on again. As we passed a burning Bren-carrier, we ducked behind the armoured sides of our White Scout Car as ammunition cracked off over the road. We park in a field about 15 km inside the frontier, between Espierres and Helchin.

TUESDAY – 5.9.44

The Belgians tell us we are on the Oudenaarde road. So far we have no large-scale maps. The name of each town has two spellings, in French and Flemish. We move on and stop for dinner at Petegem. Then on again through Oudenaarde to the village of Leeuwergem, where we stop for the night. In a small café, we make friends with the local people over a glass of beer. We were also treated to cherry brandy, on the house, and I spent the rest of the time learning Flemish phrases, translated with the help of French.

WEDNESDAY – 6.9.44

Two British soldiers are buried near us. They were sniped last night near the pocket of resistance at Ghent, which our division is mopping up. We are suddenly called out of the village to move again. Girls crowd round our vehicles and kiss us all goodbye. Some give us addresses and ask us to write to them. Proceed to Oosterzele, where we park close together in a small field.

FRIDAY – 8.9.44

Rise at 5.30 a.m. to go all the way back into France with a Regimental party to pick up new trucks. We go first to main Echelon, hang around, go back to Tac., near our own echelon and eventually leave at 10.00 a.m., having to pass "Main" again; a double journey of six miles for nothing. This is what is called "organisation"! We find the new vehicles at Estrée Cauchy, a small village 15 km from Arras. Spend the evening in a café.

SATURDAY – 9.9.44

Off again to Belgium. Our route lay by Mazingarbe, Vermelles, Hulluch, Wingles, Carvin, Seclin, Lesquin, Toufflers, Nechin, Pecq., Avelgem and Oudenaarde. From one part of the road, looking south, we could see on the skyline the Vimy Ridge Memorial. Again we by-passed Lille, all I saw of the town being the tower of the Town Hall in the distance.

At the frontier, in daylight this time, I saw the broken barrier and the Douanes or Customs buildings on either side. The first Belgian province we enter is Hainaut and the next Oostvlaadern (East Flanders).

We find the Battery has moved and meet them in Lede, a town near Aalst. In the evening we visit a café where there is music and dancing, mostly circle waltzes danced in fast tempo in the old style. When they dance a fox-trot, they "jig" with their elbows jerking up and down, reminding me of the old silent films.

Sunday – 10.9.44
Join the Battery at Quatrecht to do a tank job. I also manage to do my first washing since leaving Normandy.

Later, we re-visit Lede, where we find community dancing led by a band in the town square. Several people have given me cards and asked me to call on them if possible.

Monday – 11.9.44
In a covered area beside the café in Quatrecht, we watch four men playing a queer form of bowls in a special court, with a "jack" peg at each end. The bowls are wooden discs about 8 in. wide by 2 in. thick and are biased to roll in a curve. If one player gets his wood leaning against the peg, his opponent skims his one flat along the floor with great force to smash the first one off the target.

Tuesday – 12.9.44
Return to Lede.

Wednesday – 13.9.44
Move via Boom and Mechelen to a summer resort called Rijmenham, where there are hotels and cafés scattered among pine trees in an area of sandy ground called "The Campine". We park beside a hotel called "Solarium des Pins", which has a swimming pool. However, they seem to cater for snobs, for they ask 40 francs for a brandy, which should cost 10 francs.

Thursday – 14.9.44
Swim in the pool to the accompaniment of music through a loud-speaker. The old songs about the Siegfried Line are back in popularity again. We are going to have a week's rest here! Later, we are taken into Mechelen, the famous lace centre. The first thing to be

seen at the end of the road leading into the town is the massive unfinished tower on the ancient cathedral which reminds me of the Boston Stump. The town hall is also interesting. This is the province of Antwerpen.

FRIDAY – *15.9.44*
In the Café Campinoise, had a long talk in French with the owner and his daughter. He had been a ship's cook on a Belgian vessel and had seen a lot of the world, including many of the places we have seen, so we had plenty to talk about, while enjoying a French vermouth. Left the café at ten minutes to twelve!

SUNDAY – *17.9.44*
Short day in Brussels. The capital was crowded with people in their Sunday best, so that we could hardly move through the colourful throng. The city is beautifully laid out but we hardly had time to see all the sights, as we had to return to our truck by the Gare du Nord in the afternoon when other units were just arriving. The Grand Place is surrounded by architectural gems: the King's House; the house of the Dukes of Brabant and the great Town Hall, which has a wonderful row of statuettes over the whole stretch of its long facade. Down a narrow street beside the Town Hall stands the Manneken Fountain, depicting a little boy, urinating. It was erected by a rich man in 1648 to commemorate the finding of his son, who had been lost for five days.

At different times in his history, the Manneken has been dressed in various costumes and miniature uniforms, some of which are still preserved. He is known as "The oldest citizen of Brussels" and Louis XV even invested him with the Cross of St. Michael.

When we had lunch, a lady at another table insisted on paying our bill, a kindness which we acknowledged as best we could. Great advertising signs and neon lights were beginning to blaze when we had to leave.

MONDAY – *18.9.44*
At the Café Campinoise again, we were given a conjuring show by a fellow who did something on Brussels stock exchange, and was "rolling" in money.

TUESDAY – *19.9.44*
A fleet of Douglas Dakotas go over, towing gliders behind them, en
route *for Holland.*

*We hear from a soldier in the Signals about a concentration camp
that he has seen at Breendonk, near Mechelen. He had been reluctant to believe the propaganda about enemy atrocities until he visited this camp. He saw where people had been shackled to a wall
and the Germans had fired wooden bullets at them. Channels were
cut in the floor where the blood ran to a loose tile. There were
appliances to jerk arms from their sockets and other forms of torture.
This camp is now in the hands of the Belgian "White Army" and is
filled with Gestapo and collaborators!*

WEDNESDAY – *20.9.44*
*We prepare roast pork, roast spuds, chocolate cream and stewed
apples; and Georgette from the café brings a contribution of celery
and helps us to prepare same.*

THURSDAY – *21.9.4*
Farewell party in Café Campinoise.

FRIDAY – *22.9.44*
*Our week's rest finished, we go forward again via Heyst op den
Berg, cross the Albert Canal by a Bailey bridge, through Westerloo
to a small village called Hulsen.*

SATURDAY – *23.9.44*
*A man from a nearby house invited us to pull our trucks near his
dwelling, where we could cook under shelter, as it was raining. He
gave us potatoes and showed real consideration for our comfort,
without grumbling about how he had suffered under the "Boche",
as others have done. We exchanged a white loaf for one of his brown
ones and he in turn treated us to some very good porridge with fresh
milk (ours is, of course, canned). His elderly mother did all our
washing. Altogether, they are the kindest people we have yet come
across. He even helped when we packed the trailer in expectation of
a quick move in the early morning and we ended the evening sitting
beside him in the house, listening to his radio. His name, I discovered, is Jan Hykmans.*

SUNDAY – *24.9.44*
Start at 6.30 a.m., going via Mol and Lommel, crossing several

Bailey bridges and so into Holland by Luyksgestel, stopping at Riethuven in Braband. The people are still very surprised that we do not billet ourselves more than is necessary in their homes, when the Germans always demanded room, even if it meant turning out the people.

MONDAY – *25.9.44*
Off early via Veldhoven and Eindhoven, scene of strong resistance. North of Eindhoven, in the corridor through which our troops are trying to reach Arnhem, the enemy has again cut across the road and we sit in column, watching German shells bursting around a tower some way off. He sprays the area with shrapnel from air-bursts, while it rains steadily. Nearby lie the tilted gliders of the 6th Airborne Division. When the road is again clear, we will go through towards Arnhem, the idea being to take a chance and run every bit

Dutch Corridor.

of support possible to the Airborne pocket across the Rhine, which has been contacted by 2nd Army troops. Arnhem is in Holland but, if we can hold the bridge-head over the Rhine, the way is clear to Germany.

The rain stops, we pull into a field and cook a meal, while machine-guns rattle, guns rumble and bang and observation planes drone above the battle. Stan and I inspect some of the abandoned gliders and Dakotas which crash-landed.

Later in the afternoon, a fleet of Douglas transports fly over and drop bundles of supplies by parachute around us, including 17-poun-der shells! We watch the clusters of orange-coloured parachutes come down in hopeless chagrin. Surely these supplies should have been dropped on the other side of the breach where the enemy has cut across the corridor, to give the advance troops what we cannot get through to them by road. We don't need supplies but our cut-off forward troops do.

Some bombers go over too but, luckily, they do not drop their cargo on us!

TUESDAY – 26.9.44

Many more transport 'planes go over with fighter escort. Our Ty-phoons give "Jerry" a plastering with rockets, which make a terri-fying noise, The road must be clear again, as vehicles have been streaming along all day, though we still wait. Our "five-fives" are still thundering out but the target area seems to be off to the west of the road now and we do not hear so much machine-gunning. A barrage opens up at dusk and the noise is deafening. At intervals in the night they break out again and the nearest guns shake our trailer with their muzzle-blast.

WEDNESDAY – 27.9.44

We are being issued mainly with captured German rations now, as our lines of communication are long and it takes a week for road supplies to come from the Normandy beach-head. The artificial harbour at Arromanches is still used, as the Channel ports are cut off or destroyed. The German rations consist of tinned cheese, ersatz coffee, quite good margarine and cartons of frozen greenstuffs, peas, runner beans, spinach, etc.

We move on five minutes' notice, going eight miles further north in the corridor. Now the flanking battle is closer and we hear not only machine-guns, but rifles. We have a double guard and sleep with loaded rifles beside us, in case "Jerry" manages to cut across the vital road again.

THURSDAY – *28.9.44*

Shells whine over and burst near the road as we finish our morning wash. "Jerry" is still fighting on the west side in an attempt to stop the supply traffic. Where the road was cut off before, we passed several dozens of our trucks burnt out but, when the enemy was pushed back again, we got 4,000 vehicles up to Nijmegen! The airborne tropops are having a desperate time, with heavy losses, while the forward elements of the Second Army try to relieve them.

Our own report, later, from H.Q. says that the airborne troops were withdrawn, 2,000 coming back out of 8,000.

We have consolidated only as far as Nijmegen, so we have lost the bridgehead over the Lek, the northern arm of the Rhine. The B.B.C., so far, makes no mention of this, in spite of the heroic fight of the airborne lads against overwhelming odds; but perhaps they are only interested in victories. They do say, however, that this corridor has been widened to the west, thus narrowing "Jerry's" escape route to the north, yet his shells come nearer and nearer to us, until his air-bursts are almost directly overhead! Why don't they give straight news?

FRIDAY – *29.9.44*

We again move a few miles further up the corridor, seeing more signs of scrapping. Park at a farm, where I collect a few Dutch coins, apparently made of zinc, including a square one of five cents. The people are very friendly.

SUNDAY – *1.10.44*

Go to Uden for a bath, then return to Veghel, which is the village nearest to our position. A new engine has been fitted in our White scout-car. Stand-by on one hour's notice to move.

TUESDAY – *3.10.44*

Still here. We are collecting spares from derelict trucks. Saw an enemy "S.P." made from a French tank and carrying a Russian 47 mm gun.

The British Army is smoking cigars! Made in Eindhoven from Dutch home-grown tobacco, the cigars are being issued in place of cigarettes.

SATURDAY – 7.10.44
We have taken the 0.5 in. machine-gun from the back of each tank – where they were fitted as anti-aircraft weapons – and are welding the mountings in front, so that they can also be used against the enemy on the ground. Woe betide "Jerry's" infantry!

WEDNESDAY – 11.10.44
Still at Veghel. Orders issued for future entry into Germany: no fraternisation; strict segregation; treat them with silent contempt.

FRIDAY – 13.10.44
Captain H. is dead. He threw a loaded Sten-gun into the back seat of his Jeep, it went off and he received the full charge.

The original Sten (we called it the gas-pipe gun) was dangerous, as there was no safety-catch. If dropped butt first, the heavy bolt jerked back, cocked the gun and, unless the trigger sear checked the bolt, the gun fired itself. Later, it was modified to take a safety pin.

FRIDAY – 20.10.44
At last, we are packing! We don't know where we are going, but we are hoping it will be the last big push.

SATURDAY – 21.10.44
Still here; but an attack has gone in north of Antwerp, probably only a secondary attack to clear the estuary leading to the port.

EVENING:
Big "griff"! We must prepare to spend the winter over here, as the armies cannot undertake the last push owing to lack of supplies! The port of Antwerp must be cleared first, in order to build up for the spring offensive. The infantry will remain in the line throughout the winter but armour will not be required, so we are going back – after a couple of local jobs are finished – to train for the spring push.

CHAPTER 4

The Last Build-Up

SUNDAY – *22.10.44*
Warned we are all going to "B" Echelon again to carry on as a complete L.A.D.

MONDAY – *23.10.44*
"B" Echelon assembles – at Veghel!

TUESDAY – *24.10.44*
Prepare to take Eddie Culhane back to Belgium en route *for England, as his wife is again very ill. We are going in a Jeep.*

WEDNESDAY – *25.10.44*
Travel half round Holland looking for Second Army H.Q. to get Eddie's visa to fly to England. Eventually we find where they used to be, at Helmond, and are then directed to their present situation at Hasselt in Belgium. Next we go via Louvain to Brussels where, in the big "Shell-Mex" building – taken over by the Army – we receive instructions to proceed to Antwerp. Passing through Mechelen, we visit the folks in the Café Campinoise and some people known to Eddie in Keerbergen. A flying bomb had fallen in Keerbergen, killing one person and wounding several. "Jerry" is aiming these bombs at Antwerp but they are quite inaccurate. While we are still at Keerbergen, another one comes over at no great height and we see the flicker of flame at the tail as it goes on its way. We arrive at Antwerp Airport at 11.30 p.m. then wander up and down miles of concrete roads and runways in the dark. Finally, we bed down in a hangar and sleep fairly well, in spite of the fact that several more flying bombs come over. One cuts out its roar directly overhead. I lie waiting for the bang, counting the seconds. Will it come straight down, or will it glide? Three, four, five, six – after twelve seconds, the bang comes, from the opposite end of the aerodrome. Ah, well! We turn over and doze off.

341

THURSDAY – *26.10.44*
This morning, as we washed, an R.A.F. chap in the hangar looked at his watch.

"Next flying bomb is due at 8.15," he said, sounding just like a station-master. Nothing happened until we were having our breakfast in an old fort used as a dining-hall, then the bomb roared over. We checked up – 8.35 – twenty minutes late. Eddie laughed as I said, "We'll have to put in a complaint to "Jerry" about this!"

Bad weather holding up the 'planes from Blighty, we went to town till midday. There, the flying bombs did not seem so funny. Police kept back a crowd of people from a corner where heaps of rubble were being cleared. White-robed doctors and nurses waited beside ambulances. One three-storied building was sliced away and glass littered the neighbouring streets.

Later, several Dakotas arrived at the airport and, as soon as Eddie was sure of his passage, I set off on the return journey to Holland, alone in the Jeep. When I got to Eindhoven, I fortunately met two of the boys of the Norfolk Yeomanry, who told me the Regiment had moved, otherwise I would not have known where to find them.

Eventually, I found the L.A.D. at Oisterwijk, near Tilburg.

MONDAY – *30.10.44*
Enjoyed a cheerful evening at a dance in a little hall in the village. Each slow waltz was announced as the "English Wals" and, when some of our bright lads introduced that piece of nonsense called the "Hokey-Pokey", it made a great hit with the local people.

There is quite a bit of shell damage here from the recent battle. Many collaborators have had their hair cut off in the public square.

FRIDAY – *3.11.44*
Move to Berkel-Enschott, where we are billeted in a big loft where strings of tobacco leaves are hung up to dry.

SATURDAY – *4.11.44*
Clean out the large stable which we are using as a workshop. Flying bombs are occasionally dropping on Tilburg.

WEDNESDAY – *8.11.44*
Visit Tilburg, where there is now a "Jerboa Cinema". Heavy traffic

*holds us up, as scores of tanks come through. It looks like a whole
division on the move. To make up for a shortage of policemen,
Dutch Boy Scouts are on points duty at every crossing – and making
a good job of it, too!*

THURSDAY – *9.11.44*
*Tanks are still going up. Rumours that we will soon be going back
into Belgium.*

SATURDAY – *11.11.44*
*Pack up and rejoin "B" Echelon at Oisterwijk, where they are lined
up ready to move. Many of the Dutch people come out with cameras,
taking snaps of the column and various groups of soldiers. Off we
go and find our new position at Meeuwen, near Hasselt.*

SUNDAY – *12.11.44*
*Some of the boys go on forty-eight hours leave to Brussels. I go out
with the wrecker, on loan to 5th R.H.A. and we go into Holland
again, a short way, to stand by near Stamproy.*

MONDAY – *13.11.44*
*We are sleeping on the floor of the farmhouse at Meeuwen, which
is warmer than in a vehicle.*

SUNDAY – *19.11.44*
*Weather cold and wet and we have had our first frost and a little
snow. General advance on the Franco-German frontier, but may be
only intended to reach the Rhine.*

WEDNESDAY – *22.11.44*
*Transferred to stores truck as driver and assistant storeman.
Weather atrocious.*

TUESDAY – *28.11.44*
*Go to Brussels for forty-eight hours leave but spent most of one day
getting there, as we have the usual Army muddle. We tour all the
batteries before we get away and only arrive in the city at 4.00 p.m..
The leave hostel is in the Royal Institute. Prices in the shops are
ridiculous. Wages have to be high to buy food on the black market,
so prices also run high. Half a dozen gift handkerchiefs cost me 210
francs or roughly 24s.!*

WEDNESDAY – *29.11.44*
*Out sightseeing and shopping carefully – i.e. as little as possible.
Later visit a magnificent cinema in the Place Brouckere, now being*

*run by N.A.A.F.I. for services only and free. The only other thing
that was free was transport on the trams but this was restricted
owing to strikes. Passengers hung on to the outside of the platforms,
stood on buffers and even climbed on to the roof to get home!*

THURSDAY – 30.11.44
*Return to Meeuwen. En route, a flying bomb crossed our path and
the A.A. guns had a pot at it, without success.*

*On arrival at the billet, heard the shocking news that our D.R., Bob
White, was killed when his motor-cycle was in collision with a
water-truck. He has already been buried.*

We also learn that our cook-house (a barn) has been burnt down.

SATURDAY – 2.12.44
*Painted name and particulars of Bob White on the cross made by
Joe Brown. "Chalky" has been buried at Hamond, near Bree. The
R.E.M.E. badge and colours are also on the cross.*

THURSDAY – 7.12.44
*After almost a month in Meeuwen, we get orders to pack and move.
I shift my kit on to the stores truck, say good-bye to the good folks
at the farm and drive the heavy stores to Dilsen, close to the narrow
"appendix" of Holland which comes down between Belgium and
Germany. We are now in the Province of Limburg. Our billet is in
a comfortable house and the people seem quite pleased to have us.*

SUNDAY – 10.12.44
*The people are treating us extremely well, doing one big washing
for the five of us in this house, cleaning our boots, washing our dixies
and generally spoiling us. It is good to sit at a table to eat. Our hosts
are Henri van Daemen and his wife Marie and they have a little
boy called Piet.*

*In a small cinema in the nearby village of Stokkem, we saw a very
interesting newsreel taken by someone in Antwerp, showing the
Germans retreating through the city at speed, except where some
had to push their car in an attempt to start it. The camera was in a
concealed position. Next, the civilians wrecked the houses of collaborators and then the first British tanks came along the streets and
were surrounded by cheering, laughing people.*

As we walked back from the cinema, it rained and the muddy road got worse, great puddles gathering, while the wind whined and the reflected light of the moon and of searchlights gleamed on the great sheets of water in the fields at either side. There is little drainage in this flat country.

SUNDAY – *17.12.44*

Over at Stokkem again. Some air activity as "Jerry" brings out some of his hoarded air force. I saw one 'plane clearly against a cloud which was floodlit by searchlights. Tracer shells streamed upwards but the plane escaped into the cloud. While we were watching a newsreel of the V-I flying bombs landing on London, our own A.A. rumbled outside.

Later, when we returned to Dilsen, more enemy planes came over, apparently trying to get our bridge over the Maas. We hear that "Jerry" has begun a counter-attack with three Panzer divisions. We have already shot down 140 of his 'planes. Some of our night-fighters are up too, for they drop Very signals when caught in the searchlights.

Maybe "Jerry" thinks he is going to push us back!

MONDAY – *18.12.44*

Captain B... was wounded in last night's bombing. Three enemy 'planes actually come over in daylight, taking advantage of low cloud to hide from our Thunderbolt patrols. They whine over very low and again the ack-ack rolls out like an irregular drum-beat. Later, a single enemy 'plane scoots back to Germany and I get a good look at it. It is a new type of 'plane with a slim fuselage and two engines, probably jet-propelled, *as there is only a shrill, whistling whine, no roar and apparently no propellers.*

Although claims have been made that Britain was first with jets, these German 'planes were the first jets any of us saw in action, apart from the V-I bomb, which must surely count as the primitive prototype. At the time of which I am writing – December 1944 – the Germans had both single-jet and twin-jet aircraft in operational use. Owing to their superior speed, our A.A. shells always seemed to burst *behind* the 'planes, as if the radar allowances required readjustment! For some reason, the twin-jet type of plane became known to the troops as "The Black Widow".

In the evening, things seemed a bit quieter and Jim and I were having a game of chess when, without warning, there was a series of explosions, shaking the house and the electric light went out. Marie had run half-way down the stairs to the cellar for shelter but she came back up. We lit a paraffin lamp and then went to see where the bombs had dropped.

Some had straddled the main road and one house had been hit. The people in this house were playing cards with the soldiers in one room, which was untouched but the rest of the house was destroyed! In our billet, all the glass is out of the front windows and lying on the pavement. The power cables are down on the main road but we get the radio news on a battery set.

It seems "Jerry" made considerable gains on the American First Army front during last night. They say nothing about our sector.

TUESDAY – *19.12.44*
Our air forces have knocked out ninety-five enemy tanks.

WEDNESDAY – *20.12.44*
"Jerry" advances twenty miles on a 100-mile front against the "Yanks" at Malmedy. No change on our front but enemy attack expected, as our patrols find that armour has been brought up. Our own forces are moving to meet the threat. We in Dilsen are also warned to prepare to move.

THURSDAY – *21.12.44*
Move postponed until after Christmas!

FRIDAY – *22.12.44*
Sleeping with rifles beside us, being warned of the possible use of paratroops by the enemy. He has already used large numbers of them in his attack further south. General Eisenhower says this is our chance to inflict on the enemy a "colossal defeat". "Jerry" is now thirty-five miles into Belgium and claims 20,000 American prisoners.

Perhaps it should be remembered that, at this critical time in the struggle against the Nazis, the miners at home were on strike!

The radio announces that another quarter of a million men are going to be drafted into the British Army.

"Gillie" is the first of our L.A.D. into Germany as he crossed the

*frontier from the narrow strip of Holland near Sittard to visit one
of our forward positions.*

SUNDAY – *24.12.44*

*Frost hardens all the mud but it is a beautiful day, with the winter
sun shining from a clear sky. There are wisps of vapour high in the
blue as our aircraft sweep over.*

MONDAY – *25.12.44*

*Christmas Day, the sixth of the war. Came downstairs to find that
Marie had prepared a special breakfast for us. We presented her with
some small gifts we had bought between the five of us – "Gillie",
Jim Bryant, Joe Brown, Len Lambert and myself. It was just a small
appreciation of the way they have looked after us. The Christmas
dinner of canned turkey was supplied by the Army in the village
hall. Then we heard the programme of radio messages from all over
the Empire and liberated Europe, the most moving being from a
British corporal in Germany. The programme was called "Journey
Home". Then came the King's speech, heard in a hushed room.*

*Later, "Gillie" and I went skating on a long stretch of ice over a
flooded field, with old-fashioned wooden skates which we borrowed
from Henri – or "Harry" as he is called. Tea was provided in the
house, as all the cooks were "blotto"! It was a fine tea, too, with
plenty of custard pie! Dank u, Marie!*

*In the evening, we visited the house of Theodoor Daemen (a relative
of Harry's) where some more of our lads are billeted and we had a
party, with songs and the usual party games (they play "Forfeits"
exactly as we do!). The family sang Flemish carols and we organised
a little choir, reaching great heights of harmony. Our hosts were so
captivated they would not let us go until three o'clock in the morning. They said it was the merriest Christmas they had had since the
war began.*

*I think it is also the most enjoyable war-time Christmas I have had,
especially since the official situation report says that things are now
going well and "Monty" believes we may be able to crush "Jerry"
now that he has left his prepared positions.*

TUESDAY – *26.12.44*

Volunteers required to go looking for 200 German prisoners who escaped from a smashed P.O.W. train. Those not wanting to go were told to fall out but no-one moved from the ranks. We were driven to a village called Neroeteren, where we were rather disappointed to find we were being held in reserve. We had taken our recovery tank with us (the old S.P. minus its turret) and two armoured cars, which bristled with rifles and we had a following of the Durham Light Infantry, Queen's Regiment, R.H.A. and others in Bren-carriers and trucks. The troops of 12th Corps were already combing the woods where the Germans had been spotted, so we were ordered to stand by, which we did – in a café – until 4.15 p.m. when we were told to return to Dilsen, with no news of what had happened.

WEDNESDAY – *27.12.44*

Two large bottles of ink, one red, one blue, both frozen solid in our stores truck.

SUNDAY – *31.12.44*

Last day of 1944. As the old year died, we drank in the New Year with cognac but it was not too cheerful and we went to bed at 1.30 a.m.. This is the sixth New Year I have not spent at home. However, the situation has improved around Malmedy and we have the initiative again. In any case, things are much better than they were at this time last year, so here's hoping 1945 will be the last year of this war.

MONDAY – *1.1.45*

A cloudy day, so quite a number of enemy 'planes come over and start strafing. The echelon slings everything at them. "Gillie" mans the Browning 0.5-in. machine-gun on our recovery tank and I get in beside him, my rifle loaded with tracer. There are all types of "Jerry" 'craft, M.E.262 (twin-jet), M.E.109F, and even a Junkers 88. We bang away but "Gillie" gets a jam on the Browning, so I carry on with the rifle. They dive over the main road and I see one skimming the village with flashes flickering from his wings as he opens up with his guns. I get some shots very close while "Gillie", cursing, discovers a split cartridge in his gun and changes the barrel. Then another 'plane comes over very low and I graze him with tracers. He banks frantically from side to side and we suddenly realise it is one of our own Mustangs which has arrived on the scene! The black and white bars on the wing are very misleading, as they look like the Iron Cross at first glance.

In the midst of all the din and excitement, Harry and Marie, dressed in black, go quietly along the middle of the street to attend the funeral of Marie's brother, who died from complications following appendicitis.

Smoke is rising from the village where an enemy 'plane has crashed on a house. The ack-ack hits another and he comes down in a spiral of smoke. One of our Thunderbolts comes along looking for trouble but things quieten down.

After a bit, "Gillie" unloads and I am half-way out of the tank, when a lone straggler skims the treetops towards us, no more than sixty feet up and, before we can get into action again, he is past. We cuss, for we could have riddled him, if the Browning had been loaded!

Total bag for the echelon: 3 'planes, against 1 truck shot up. Later, the radio gives the total brought down over the whole sector as 125, out of 300 sent up by the enemy in an all-out attempt to break the supremacy of the R.A.F.; 84 of these were shot down by the R.A.F., 31 by A.A. and 10 "elsewhere".

TUESDAY – *2.1.45*
The latest figure is 193 enemy 'planes brought down but we have had many of ours shot up on aerodromes, though we only lost four pilots in the air.

Later, we heard that practically all the aircraft shot up on the ground were replaced within twenty-four hours by 'planes flown from Britain, so the enemy gained no advantage. Our air forces were still supreme.

A propaganda leaflet I have before me was dropped by the Americans during the war. It shows Flying Fortresses in daylight and British Halifaxes flying on into the darkness, with the caption: *"Tag und Nacht, mit Vereinten Kraften"* – "Day and night, with united strength!"

I have several such leaflets, in various languages, which I picked up at different times: some in Italian; Allied ones in German and French; and German ones printed in English! Another Allied sheet had a safe conduct on one side for any German soldier who felt like giving himself up!

A German leaflet says:

"STALIN – OR YOUR WIFE? Who has the greater claim on you?
If you were defending your own country, it would be a

different matter. But as it is, you are fighting only to help the Red Army! ... At present, the German Army on the East Front is standing as a defensive barrier against the enemies of civilisation."

And so the war of words went on, ad nauseam.

WEDNESDAY – *3.1.45*
Ballot held for home leave. I come out fifth, which means I will go in the first half of February.

THURSDAY – *4.1.45*
Marie adds variety to our dinner with a chocolate pudding!

Our rations were still supplied at the unit cookhouse but we always had them prepared at the house. The chocolate was either issued or bought from our canteen, for it had not been seen in Belgium during the years of enemy occupation. It became the favourite gift from a soldier to a Belgian friend. Indeed, one of the Belgian newspapers contained a little verse about it:

> *Zwart gelaat,*
> *Meisj 'op straat,*
> *Aangepraat,*
> *Eerst heel kwaad,*
> *Chocolaad,*
> *Goede maat!"*

As it would be difficult to translate this and retain the rhyme, I have prepared my own version which, if not a translation, at least indicates the general trend!

> *Dark and late,*
> *Girl at gate,*
> *Shy and sweet,*
> *Soldier greets;*
> *A chocolate bar!!*
> *Her eyes are stars!*
> *Tomorrow's fate?*
> *They've got a date!*

So chocolate, it would seem, paved the way to a Flemish girl's heart!

SATURDAY – *6.1.45*
There is enough work for every fitter in the L.A.D., but all work is stopped to allow us to scrub our web equipment and polish brasses, because the C., R.A. (Brigadier Smith) is coming to inspect us. Meanwhile, the vehicles lie untouched.

This, of course, produced the usual outbreak of "grousing" amongst us! We felt it would be a fine state of affairs if the regiment should suddenly need these vehicles to go into action with!

SUNDAY – *7.1.45*
Following the Brigadier's inspection, went to Stokkem to see the film, Sun Valley Serenade, *featuring Glenn Miller, the band leader, who is now missing on a flight to Paris.*

We quite enjoyed the walk back through the powdery snow, which is quite deep.

TUESDAY – *9.1.45*
My twenty-eighth Birthday. Big icicles now hang from the eaves of houses and all round our vehicles, which are covered with deep snow. Marie brings in clothes from the drying line which are frozen stiff as boards.

WEDNESDAY – *10.1.45*
Part of the L.A.D. have already gone to a new position. We go tomorrow.

THURSDAY – *11.1.45*
Left Dilsen. Marie was crying, quite upset because we were going and in other houses people were weeping too. They have really taken us to their hearts.

We travel over ice-bound roads via Eisden and Maastricht, where we cross the River Maas by a pontoon bridge and arrive at Geleens, near Sittard, in Holland. Now Germany is only about three miles in front and Belgium three miles behind, for we are in the narrowest part of Holland. We are stationed at the pithead of one of the largest and most modern coal mines in the world. They extract both gas and benzene from the coal. We may use the baths, we dine in the canteen, there is boiling drinking water on tap for tea-making and our sleeping quarters are in a large, clean air-raid shelter, heated by steam pipes. We hope later to find civil billets again when the dense concentration of troops moves on. At the moment, every house is full.

The big gasometer is empty. Apparently some of our Mosquitoes "bit" it and the top blew off!

FRIDAY – *12.1.45*
Woke up feeling heavy after spending the night in the stuffy shelter. Later enjoyed the luxury of a hot bath.

In the evening, when I was having some practice on the piano in the little theatre hall at the pit-head, some of the boys switched on the lights, including the footlights, pulled open the curtain and "announced" me to the hall which, thank goodness, was empty!

SUNDAY – *14.1.45*
Go into civil billets again. The house I am in is attractively furnished and our "landlady" speaks good French.

MONDAY – *22.1.45*
"Gillie", Joe and I played "Rummy" with Piet, our present host, after much explaining in a mixture of French and Dutch. Then he caught on and licked us!

MONDAY – *29.1.45*
Still quiet, though another flying bomb went over today. Cold, but sunny.

TUESDAY – *30.1.45*
Blowing a blizzard! Snow drifting just as the sand used to in the desert, skimming the ground with a rustling noise; but what a difference in temperature! Still, this is cleaner and healthier than the desert.

SATURDAY – *3.2.45*
Snow now thawed.

SUNDAY – *4.2.45*
Return visit to Dilsen with "Gillie". We again cross the Maas, which is swollen with the thaw, so that the broad waters race past the pontoons of the bridge. The ground is very muddy. Half the village turned out when we appeared and Janne and Elizabeth, two young nieces of Marie's, clambered on to the Jeep for a ride. Marie and Harry were very pleased to see us and instantly prepared coffee for us, while plying us with questions about the rest of the boys. Harry

has now added to his collection of "brass-ware" a 17-pounder shell-case, which stands over two feet high on his mantelpiece!

On returning to Geleens, I find my leave has been postponed for a day, owing to bad seas in the Channel.

MONDAY – 5.2.45
Leave postponed for another twenty-four hours.

WEDNESDAY – 7.2.45
"Gillie" and I have to collect our leave passes at Main H.Q. in Echt, which we reach via Zusteren. Both places have been under a rain of shells, all roofs are smashed and the people are just beginning to trickle back to their ruined homes, which are mostly occupied by troops. Later we go to "B" Echelon at Cutterhoven, where we spend the night.

THURSDAY – 8.2.45
Proceed through Sittard to a transit camp at Burg Leopold in Belgium. At 3.00 p.m., a message from "Monty" is read out over the loudspeakers, saying that the final round is about to commence.

"There was a time," (says "Monty"), "When it seemed we could not win this war. Now, the position is that we cannot lose it. On this last move, there will be no easing up until we have forced a final decision."

And we are going on leave! Hope we don't miss the finish! the Russians will also continue their attack from the East, where they have been held on the Oder, only forty-five miles from Berlin.

We leave Burg Leopold by train, reach Lille at 1.30 a.m. (Friday) and get tea and buns on the station platform.

FRIDAY – 9.2.45
Arrive at Calais, 6.00 a.m. Here it is fresh and breezy. Did not get much sleep on the train, though the coaches were "civilised", having padded seats, unlike the ones which took me to Cherbourg in 1940. Five years ago to the month, that last leave from France! Many French civilians – men, women and girls – are now working in the army leave camps.

Sail from Calais (which is sadly battered) by the Princess Astrid *at midday. The cliffs of Dover are sighted within an hour but we continue up the coast towards Harwich. Weather clear, sea choppy, spray coming aboard. We reach Harwich at 5.30 p.m.*

Later, on the train for Edinburgh, tea is again supplied, and a daily paper for each man! I must say everything has been really well organised, the country being split into zones, so that all the men on this train are either Scots or North Countrymen. "Gillie", of course, has gone to Leicester.

Leave over once more, I eventually found myself back in a Transit Camp at Dovercourt, near Harwich, amongst a silent, miserable crowd of men, all "going back".

Monday – *19.2.45*
Weather clear and warm and the R.A.F. keeps roaring over in great force. Wonder what the "Jerry" prisoners in this camp think about it?

Tuesday – *20.2.45*
At Harwich docks, our faces must have looked pretty glum, for a voice over the loudspeakers said, "Come on, smile, you've had it!" Sail at 5.00 p.m. but drop anchor off the South coast at 9.30 p.m. and are told we will continue the voyage in the morning. The vessel is the Lady of Mann.

Wednesday – *21.2.45*
Land at Calais at 10.00 a.m. The train does not leave until evening, so I spend the day in town with another chap (you team up with anyone in these circumstances). A French variety company put on a bright little show for the troops in the Town Theatre. Each act was announced in English, with and without accent.

Thursday – *22.2.45*
Arrived Burg Leopold 8.00 a.m., after a miserable journey. The seats were wooden, there was no heating and so we shivered all night. Why the difference between the homeward journey and the return journey? Were they afraid we might carry home complaints to the United Kingdom?

Reached Divisional Report Centre at 2.00 p.m.. Here, we had to wait several hours for regimental transport. Ours was the last party to go and eventually I found the L.A.D. in a little village called Hunsel, near Roermond. I am billeted along with five others in a house which already has sixteen of a family in it!

SUNDAY – *25.2.45*
The folks in our billet have prepared the bedrooms upstairs for the six of us, so that we won't have to sleep on the floor. Yet some people at home grumble if they have only a few children and are asked to billet a couple of soldiers or evacuees!

MONDAY – *26.2.45*
Warned to scrub valise, haversack and web equipment till white, for the C.O.'s inspection on Friday morning. All this equipment was, of course, dyed khaki at the factory where it was made. Perhaps if we carry on parading, somebody else will win the war for us! This morning too, some of our boys had to go round the village, picking up papers, while the Dutch people looked on in wondering amusement! Censorship, of course, prevents any of this being mentioned in our letters home.

TUESDAY – *27.2.45*
Spend all day scrubbing and bleaching equipment. No other work done. As the men are saying, if there is nothing useful to do, why not send more men on leave? Only three men are going home in March.

This evening, one of the older sons of the house, Chris, showed us an interesting collection of Stone Age axe-heads, flint arrow-tips and Roman pottery, all dug up around this village! He also has a collection of antique guns.

THURSDAY – *1.3.45*
Off for forty-eight hours to Brussels again. Prices still high. Stayed in a hotel, as the leave camp is now six miles outside the city. Viewed: the Royal Palace; the beautiful Palace of Justice, which is now a burnt-out shell; the Congressional Column and the tomb of Belgium's Unknown Soldier.

SATURDAY – *3.3.45*
Take tramcar to Meise, pick up our truck at the leave camp and return to unit, to find that the inspection has been postponed until tomorrow, so we won't miss it after all!

TUESDAY – *6.3.45*
Sudden move early in the morning, to Kessel, near Venlo. Every house in Kessel is damaged, but we are lucky enough to find billets. There is no electric light, however, as the grid is destroyed. Along the roadside are little notices, painted roughly on bits of board, such

as: "*Spandau Alley, run next thirty yards!*"; "*Visiting 8 Platoon? Use ditch!*"; "*Under observation – duck next 100 yards!*"

WEDNESDAY – *7.3.45*
Visited a nearby windmill, which is surprisingly high when you climb the stairs to the windy wooden gallery. There are a few shell-holes in the upper structure and, looking down through them, the ground seems to be a long way off. The sails must measure about sixty feet across.

Cologne is now in the hands of the Allies.

SATURDAY – *10.3.45*
Funeral of a young Dutch boy who was killed by a German mine. He will be buried in the cemetery beside the smashed Church which stands by the River Maas.

SUNDAY – *11.3.45*
Today, I saw many of the dangerous wooden Schumines, which had been emptied at the edge of an enemy minefield. These mines can be set off by the pressure of a foot and are difficult to detect, except by prodding, as the only metal in them is the release pin.

Plenty of tanks, trucks and guns moving up. Looks like we are preparing for an advance over the Rhine.

Tonight there was a dance in the village hall but it was over-crowded. We had to bring a piano from a house seventy yards away, for the band.

MONDAY – *12.3.45*
Many more "Churchill" tanks and amphibious "Buffaloes" moving forward. It won't be long now!

TUESDAY – *13.3.45*
Concert in the village hall, arranged by the Burgomaster in con-junction with R.H.Q. The stage was well decorated and lighting effects, including spotlights, were fitted up by our electricians. The village silver band played marches and Dutch folk-songs and our dance band also gave a few numbers. There were comic turns in both languages, including one by our Padre. *There were speeches by the Burgomaster and our Colonel – and the compère of the show was the local police corporal, complete with huge white lanyard! We invited the folk from our billet: Jo (Johanna); her brother, Jaques*

and another friend and we all enjoyed the show very much, helping each other to translate. (It's amazing how many things you can explain with only slight knowledge of a language!)

WEDNESDAY – *14.3.43*
Jo tells me that, when the battle came to this area, the people had to go into some big cellars in the village. Luckily, "Jerry" had no chance to use this house as a strongpoint and there was little fighting actually in the village. As it was, Jo's father visited the house during a quiet spell and was just in time to see a German soldier disappearing out of an open window. When the battle was over, their belongings were still untouched, though the house was hit by one shell. In spite of their troubles, they were cheerful and have made us at home. We are the third lot of soldiers they have had.

SUNDAY – *18.3.45*
The continual stream of matériel *is still going forward, even after dark.*

TUESDAY – *20.3.45*
Went to Weert to see the replay of the final football match for the Championship of the Division, between the Norfolk Yeomanry and 131 Brigade Field Hospital. As we drove along the road, amphibious "Buffalo" tanks were still being taken forward. The game was a hard-played one, influenced by a fairly strong wind, which helped the Medical Corps in the first half. In the second half, with the wind behind them, the Regiment overran the Hospital and got the extra goal for a well-deserved win, 3–2.

The game took place on a factory ground, and outside was a column of parked trucks, both teams having good support and many neutrals from the Division were there too.

TUESDAY – *22.3.45*
Today has been perfect, warm and sunny, with a clear blue sky and a slight breeze. During last night, I heard our bombers thundering over, and the sound of Bren-carriers moving up on the main road. Today, the never-ending procession of tanks and trucks continues. I have even seen small invasion craft with naval personnel being carried through on transporters! All day our planes have taken advantage of the brilliant weather and rumour says the big attack on the Rhine begins tomorrow. The Second Army will thus make its own bridge-head, in addition to the American one at Remagen.

CHAPTER 5

"Over the Rhine, then, Let Us Go!"

FRIDAY – *23.3.45*

Good weather and air activity continue. Our medium bombers are doing a shuttle service.

SATURDAY – *24.3.45*

Some old, doubtful ammunition had to be got rid of, so half the L.A.D. were taken for a bit of practice with rifle and Bren-gun. I fired about 200 rounds myself. Our target was a derelict house on the opposite bank of the Maas and we were quite childlishly amused when our shots sent chips of brick or woodwork into the air. The most popular targets were the number plate by the door and the tiles on the shell-smashed roof. Sometimes a tracer would stick in the wall and continue to glow bright red for a few moments.

There is a strong rumour that British airborne troops have landed over the Rhine. Runstedt, Commander of the German Army in the West, has been replaced by Kesselring.

SUNDAY – *25.3.45*

"Griff" talk by the Colonel. He tells us the big attack went in on Friday night at 10.00 p.m. and airborne troops landed at ten o'clock next morning. The bridge-head is now fifteen miles long and three miles deep and our division will soon go in. Two Scottish divisions, 51st Highland and 15th Lowland, made the actual crossing. The barrage was laid down by twenty-three regiments of artillery! One troop of our 260 Battery stood by to shoot out any searchlights the enemy might switch over the river, but none appeared.

The Colonel said, "They then watched 'Mr.Harris's boys' bombing

358

'the Hun'. They could see the bombs coming down and the houses going up; and they went up to no mean height!"

An interesting point is the extreme secrecy which surrounded this attack. This is the first official news we have had. "Security" is said to have been perfect.

As I write, a long column of tanks and armoured cars of 7th Armoured Division are going up towards the bridge-head, so it won't be long before we follow. When we get into the Reich, we expect to have to carry arms at all times. I don't suppose life will be very bright for us in Germany but the quicker we get there, the quicker we will get out again.

(EVENING)
All day long, matériel has been churning and rolling its way forward. We hear nothing but roaring engines, squeaking tracks, whining gears and clanking transporters. What a build-up! Yes, "Jerry", you've had it.

MONDAY – 26.3.45
Feverish packing, as we have to be ready to move as from 7.30 tomorrow morning. This, as "Monty" said, is the last round.

TUESDAY – 27.3.45
Rise at 5.30 a.m. Our Dutch friends get up early too and prepare breakfast for us. We say good-bye and line our vehicles in the roadway. It is a misty morning. We wait patiently as long columns of trucks move slowly away up the main road to Venlo. At last we go, about nine o'clock and cross the Maas by a magnificent wooden bridge built by the Sappers at Venlo. Just after ten o'clock, we cross the frontier into Germany, the ninth country I have been in during my overseas service.

By midday we have covered only nineteen miles and then we find the concentration area is congested, so we pull off up a side track, forming three sides of a square, half a mile across. Here we wait, hungry and "browned-off", till we are finally provided with a meal at 5.30 p.m. – the first since our breakfast.

Later, we are told to bed down where we are, so we level off the loose material in the stores truck – axles, springs, oil-drums, etc. –

*lay two folding tables on top and the three of us – Joe, Jim and I,
sleep thus.*

WEDNESDAY – *28.3.45*

*Having slept well, we rise at six o'clock, wash and have breakfast,
literally "in the field". The morning is clear and sunny, with a cold
breeze. Larks are singing cheerily above. The land is still flat and
fertile, and German farmers are working in it with no lack of fine
horses, though the Dutch, Belgians and French were left short of
animals.*

*At 5.00 p.m. we move again, passing through Sonsbreck, which is
not smashed quite so badly as, say, Villers Bocage was, but it will
give the Germans a taste of their own medicine and will be a
reminder for some time to come, that war does not pay.*

*Before dark we come to barrage balloons and then we see the Rhine.
We cross the wide river by a pontoon bridge at Xanten and so enter
the British bridge-head. Gunfire is near, especially some of the
heavies and, when we reach echelon area, there are machine-gun
tracers streaking about and a searchlight shows its glare in the dusk.
An electric railway goes past our area, but all the wires are down
and the fields are pitted by the creeping barrage of our guns laid
down before the crossing.*

*Now we must wait till the Division takes over and leads the usual
break-out, on to the plains of northern Germany.*

We have tea and bed-down as before.

THURSDAY – *29.3.45*

*Joe and I went exploring, taking our rifles, and came upon half a
dozen individuals dressed in mixed grey, green and khaki uniforms,
very tattered. I said to one, "Deutsche Soldat?" and he replied,
"No, Italiano!" So I said, "Come si chiama?" to which he answered
by giving an Italian name, so he seemed genuine. Then an officer
of the Tanks came along to investigate and we went into the doorway of a farmhouse, where some more of these men were. They were
obviously starving, and nibbled away at slabs of honeycomb which
had been taken out of some hive, but had little honey in it. They
showed their identity cards, one being marked "Allied Expeditionary Forces". Its owner was a shifty-looking Rumanian. Then the*

woman of the house came forward, weeping and saying something in German. Seeing that we did not understand, her husband tried French and told us these "refugees" kept coming to them for food and what was he to do? The officer asked us to take all the stragglers to a camp which lay down the track a bit, and this we did, but found no one in charge of the camp, only a row of tents with straw and filthy Italians in them. They had all been released from German labour camps and told us the next camp contained Frenchmen and Poles.

Several shell-holes nearby were full of feathers, where the "League of Nations" had plucked the German farmer's chickens! Good luck to them! They have suffered enough at the hands of the "herrenvolk".

In the afternoon, we suddenly move again, minus our sergeants, who have gone back to look for our wrecker, which was on a recovery job in the mud. As our captain is on leave and the "Q" returned to Blighty permanently some time ago, there are only four lance-corporals in charge.

We go via Hamminkeln. Between here and Brunen was an area littered with gliders, which had landed in ploughed fields, over ditches, through fences and crashed into houses and trees. There were many signs of battle: burnt-out German armoured cars, broken rifles and small kit of the Wehrmacht. Some civilians had stayed in their houses, which had white flags flying, and others were returning on cycles and on foot. Now they are getting a little of what other countries have had to suffer because of Hitler.

We halt at dusk, on the road to Borken, and pull off into the fields. Again we hear the artillery, which had vanished earlier in pursuit of the enemy.

FRIDAY – 30.3.45
After breakfast, I hear music from the radio on the next truck. Paul Robeson sings "Dream River". "Monty's" ideas on rivers are differently expressed. In his order of the day before the crossing, he said, "Over the Rhine then, let us go …"

Two more wanderers come along, wearing grey uniform. I stop them and they say "Polish". I ask if they have cards and they produce passports with photos, stamped by German authority and giving their home as Lublin, the place where some of the German atrocities were committed. I pass them to an officer and later see them going their way behind our lines. We stay here tonight.

SATURDAY – *31.3.45*
The echelon moves on but we remain to repair two half-tracked vehicles. Sergeant Ed. Culhane is now in charge.

At 2.00 p.m. we follow the echelon through Borken, which is knocked about and still burning. A dead calf lies beside a shell-hole and a live one stands wonderingly over it. Fighting has been recent and infantry are standing by (against infiltration) with Bren-guns in trenches. I pick up a German officer's sword with the monogram of Kaiser Wilhelm II on the hilt. We find the echelon at Weseke and settle for the night.

CHAPTER 6

Germany

"If you remain as simple there as here
And still think love the sovereign power through space,
You will indeed find men, just as you fear,
A cruel and crafty race,
Who most exalt the heartless and the strong,
And force the gentlest to endure most wrong."

CLIFFORD BAX

SUNDAY – *1.4.45*
Our troops are now seventy miles east of the Rhine, near Minden.
We depart from Weseke at 9.00 a.m. and pass through Sudlohn. Stop
at midday, in a farmyard. We are apparently the first British soldiers
the people here have seen and they are quite curious until we herd
them all back into the house.

Civilians walking about here carry little white flags, so the "master
race" are scared now.

MONDAY – *2.4.45*
Told to move at 8.00 a.m., so the Division is still advancing. Pass
through Wesendorf. This place is very pretty, full of large craters,
but still not as bad as Aunay in Normandy. Civilians here are
looting their own countrymen's houses. On the pavement outside
wrecked buildings, I saw a dead sow, its throat gaping red, and a
German steel helmet on its head.

Some of our boys must have left this as a macabre sign to the German
people.

Later we go through Ahaus, which is almost as bad as Caen, but
not so big. The route then is by Heek and Metelen, both untouched

363

and full of white flags. We are on the main road to Rheine and may be going north to cut off the enemy in northern Holland.

In the evening, we are told there is a pocket of about 600 "Jerries" nearby, making a counter-attack in an attempt to break out. We stand-to with rifles, ammo. and steel helmets and take up positions along a winding bank linking up with R.H.Q. The infantry are back in front of us and there is an odd spot of machine-gunning and scattered rifle fire. There are also several "bangs" which might be from mortars or tank guns. The situation must be in hand, however, for we stand-down after an hour and retire. So ends our turn as second-line troops!

TUESDAY – 3.4.45
Eggs for breakfast and chicken for dinner! Some of the boys even have a young pig, for which they gave fifty cigarettes. We are beside another farm-house and, every hour or so, soldiers go into the hen-house (causing the squawking inhabitants to evacuate in a flurry of feathers) and, hopefully, look for eggs. The protesting hens, how-ever, refuse to work overtime! As for the fraulein *from the house, she hardly gets any eggs, as some soldier is always there before her!*

WEDNESDAY – 4.4.45
Still "static", but hoping to move soon, as the Division is still ad-vancing. Pork for dinner. The radio actually mentions the names of divisions, saying that the Guards are at Emden and the 11th Ar-moured are across the Ems lower down, so the enemy in northern Holland has been cut off.

Meanwhile, the 7th are wearing down strong opposition between Rheine and Osnabruck. We shall probably move more to the east now. Rain most of the day.

THURSDAY – 5.4.45
Although the press says the security black-out is lifted and they believe they are getting the latest news, we seem to be at least twenty-four hours ahead of them, for we are under orders to travel fifty miles, which will take us far beyond any point named by the papers as being in our hands. (We have yesterday's journals, which must be flown over.)

Move at 12.30 p.m. Route: Burgsteinfurt, Emsdetten, Riesenbeck, Brochterbeck, Tecklenburg, Westercappels, Wallenhorst.

Refugees from forced labour camps are going back, some on bicycles. Some are Poles, some are Dutch. The latter have no great distance to cover to reach Holland. The Ems-Weser Canal runs along past Riesenbeck and here a bridge is blown down and sags over the water. There are some barges in the canal, with the Belgian flag flying. Our guns are firing from the right, over our heads, at a wooded ridge. While we are stopped for some obstruction ahead, we watch our "Tempests" go over and can see them dropping bombs on the enemy. An old bearded man comes past, leading three others, all carrying bundles or old suitcases and wearing green greatcoats. They are Russians.

We cross the canal by a Bailey bridge, the delay being because of one-way traffic at this point. Then we pound on, trying to keep in the centre of the narrow road, which is badly broken, rutted, and falls away on either side. In Brochterbeck, some houses are still smouldering. Suddenly, we turn into some hills, climb sharply and find ourselves in Tecklenburg, a very picturesque village, almost Bavarian in appearance, where the streets wind in and out, up and down, and spotless châlets overhang the sidewalk.

From here on, it is dark and the journey becomes a nightmare, recalling the drive to St. Nazaire in 1940. The trucks in front speed ahead, then stop suddenly, then go on again. All I see is two bobbing red pin-points ahead, then they seem to rush back at me, and on go the brakes. Skidding, lurching, skimming trees on sharp bends, on we go. Clutch, gear lever, red lights, brake; clutch, gear, accelerator, on into the blackness. The sign of Westercappels looms up and fades behind. Houses, trucks, men, trees, come and go. Joe has fixed a torch on the bumper, which helps a bit. We have no headlamp and, anyway, it would blind other drivers. Now we pass trucks tilted over in the ditch and we almost go over the other way ourselves, in scraping by. A jeep comes along with a blazing headlight and we can see nothing else. Our 3-ton truck goes crabwise as one back wheel goes in the ditch, then I line up on a tree and hold my ground. Joe looks back and says, "He's in the ditch, and serve him bloody well right!"

By another village, we stop for half an hour and I fall asleep over the wheel. Then we hear "Start up!" and off we go again, but not far. We draw in to the verge and are told to bed-down. We flop down gratefully at 2.30 a.m.. Fourteen hours at the wheel, six of them in darkness, just to cover fifty miles!

Friday – 6.4.45
Awaken to a clear, sunny morning and find we are at Wallenhorst. Wash and shave (wonderful luxuries) and have breakfast. A number of Bren-carriers are standing in the field across the road. They are of a type I have not seen before, called the Windsor.

Move again at 12.30, by way of Engter, and climb a long steep hill track amongst beech trees and fern. During a pause, we see a tight formation of "Fortresses" going lazily over in a brilliant blue sky, looking like silver fish.

I must say that all the German farm-houses are very well kept – tidy and spotlessly clean. We continue via Venne, Hunterburg and Stemshorn, coming on to the Bremen road, and halt for the night in Lemforde. We see more and more escaped prisoners and I speak to two French soldiers, who tell me they have been prisoners for five years, here in this village. Lemforde is very pretty, with half-timbered houses, but its peace is disturbed at 8.00 p.m. by a visit from three Messerschmitt 109 'planes which do a bit of strafing.

For an hour, until dark, we bang away at them with rifles and Brens, while they persistently circle and dive. The German civilians run for shelter but a group of French ex-prisoners stand watching and act as spotters, pointing out to us where "Jerry" is coming from each time. One dives straight towards where I am standing. I fire once. Then, as I see the flicker of his guns, I dodge behind the corner of a house, waiting for him to appear beyond the line of the wall before having another shot. His bullets ricochet and whine from the road, probably aimed at some of our vehicles, though he may have spotted the flash of my rifle. At dusk, they vanish and peace reigns once more.

The news at this time told of the tanks of the Desert Rats racing on with open throttles, meeting very little opposition.

SUNDAY – *8.4.45*

Move at midday, by Lembruch, Strohen, Varrel and Sulingen, all untouched. Many Russian soldiers on the road. They come to attention and salute us, smiling all over their faces. Their uniform is green and some have red-banded hats, others fur caps. We stop at Schwaforden.

TUESDAY – *10.4.45*

Still in the same place. The whole L.A.D. are working hard and long hours to put M.10s and trucks back on the road. The forward part of the Division is near Bremen.

The Germans are impressed by the quality of our soap and point out to each other the white bread we eat. Their own soap makes no lather, only a paste; and their bread is dark grey-brown. I spoke to a liberated prisoner who reached us tonight. He is a Dundonian, was in the Black Watch, in the 51st Highland Division, and was captured at St. Valery in 1940. Now he will go home, after five years in various prison camps from Poland to West Germany.

WEDNESDAY – *11.4.45*

Hanover is now in our hands and, to the north, the 7th are swinging round Bremen and heading straight for Hamburg. The Americans are near Schweinfurt and the Russians are in Vienna, so we are all doing well!!

THURSDAY – *12.4.45*

Walked through Schwaforden and photographed a German Mark IV tank with its turret blown off and a small group of freed Yugoslavian prisoners, still occupying their prison quarters until they can get home.

(I brought a small camera back with me from leave in February.)

Move at 2.30 p.m. via Borstel, Lemke and Oyle. At Oyle, we saw some of "Jerry's" huge V-2 rockets lying on railway wagons, where they had been bombed and shot up by our aircraft. Unfortunately, the convoy was moving too fast for me to get a photograph. We stop a few miles past this spot and camp in a clearing in an extensive forest.

FRIDAY – *13.4.45*

President Roosevelt is dead. So this great man will not see the victory he has done so much to secure.

I managed to get a lift back to the giant rockets, with Jim and Joe, and took some photographs. Only one of the rockets was intact and I estimated it to be about 45 ft. in length and over 5 ft. in diameter. The others were wrecked by bomb-blast. They were lined with glass-wool to prevent freezing in the stratosphere. The warhead itself was only 6 ft. long, all the rest of the space being taken up by huge tanks for alcohol and liquid oxygen. The total weight to be raised into the air must be colossal, yet these massive things are believed to have covered the 150 miles to Britain in five minutes, an average speed of 1,800 miles per hour!

Between the rear fins was an aperture large enough for me to crawl into, and here the expansion tubes, each 6 in. in diameter, protruded from the interior. From these would come the propelling jets; but this is one monster that did not go on its way, carrying death and destruction for the people at home.

SATURDAY – *14.4.45*

Move 9.00 a.m. via Nienburg, a town on the Weser. The bridge lies broken in the water and we cross by a pontoon bridge. We pass through more wooded country and I stop to photograph a 105 mm German gun, a larger edition of the famous "88". From here we go through Steimbke, Wendenborstel and Rodewald, near which we halt. There is a German camp here, which has been hurriedly evacuated.

In the evening, we see our "Typhoons" wheel and dive recklessly on the "Jerry" lines, letting go their rockets after a long slanting dive and ignoring the enemy flak. Then smoke rises from the target area, showing they have hit the mark.

At the farm near us, there are several Polish workers and one Italian. Most German farms have their quota of foreign workers drawn from the slave army of the Reich. They must remain here until transport is arranged for the great migration back to their own lands. Even Polish and Russian women are slaves but fairly well treated and at least fed, so they are better off than those in the prison camps.

This slave labour under the Germans was one thing that the people of Britain – thanks to "The Few" – never had to face.

We have had two eggs to each meal for four days now! One of 260 Battery S.P.s has knocked out a Tiger, damaged another and repulsed 200 enemy infantry, machine-gunning them and directing artillery on them, causing heavy casualties. The S.P. – the only one which could see the action – was parked beside a house and the sergeant in charge kept in touch with the artillery over the radio, though enemy shells were landing all round (one hit the house, three feet above his head). When our artillery fire came down, his comment over the air was, "That's sorted out the bastards!"

However, at 258 Battery, there was a different kind of action. A German tank came into a village in their area, shot up two S.P.s, putting them on fire and knocked out an armoured car, a Jeep and several 3-tonners. All the time, the tank commander stood in the open turret, frantically yelling, "Heil Hitler! Heil Hitler!" They were stopped by another of our tanks, all the German crew being killed. Our losses were two dead.

SUNDAY – *15.4.45*
I had the welding torch in my hand when an old man, seeing welding and soldering being done, came over with an enamel jug with a hole in it, for us to mend! The wheedling old hypocrite started to say, "Kamerad" too, just as if he had nothing to do with Hitler's Germany! I promptly told him to scram. He seemed quite surprised that the "soft" British could be at all firm. What sort of mentality have these Germans? They have a sentimental, hero-worshipping streak which makes them admire a loud-mouthed dictator like Hitler, while they accept Nazi doctrines as being wonderful – so long as they show results! When they fail, they claim to have had no sympathy for the Nazis all the time. Yet the children around here, boys from six to twelve years of age, wear uniforms of field grey and caps of "field service" type with long peaks. No doubt they were all in the Nazi Youth Movement and have almost forgotten what it is like to wear ordinary clothes. So, instead of thinking for themselves, Germans of all ages have a cruel creed instilled into them.

Monday – *16.4.45*

I have seen photographs of British soldiers released from German prison camps – emaciated, legs and arms as thin as a child's and the bones showing, due to starvation. Now we hear that our division has overrun two more Stalags and, here again, about half the prisoners were in hospital and others were so weak they would have been in hospital in any civilised country. I think of the line from the Koran: "Your prisoner is your brother." But the Aryan Master Race have no such philosophy.

This evening, at eleven o'clock, the L.A.D. captured two German officers. They came along the track on cycles and our two sentries, Tommy Bedford and Titch (The "Killer") yelled, "Halt!" One said, "Pole!" but the other lost his nerve and made a dive for the ditch. Titch said, "I'll give you 'Pole'!" and there was a bang as he fired into the ditch. The German came up out of the ditch quicker than he went in. We heard the shot and turned out. In the middle of a group with torches and rifles, stood the two lieutenants, with their hands up.

The younger man, who had been in the ditch, was unhurt and looked resigned, though ruffled and scared. The other, a round-faced man, compressed his already thin lips in bitter hate. They were searched, two automatics were removed and they were taken to R.H.Q. in a Jeep.

Each of the prisoners carried several studio potraits of himself in dress uniform. The younger officer, who was quite a handsome type, wore the ribbon of the Iron Cross with crossed swords. The older man was called Wellnitz and his home town seemed to be Schneidemuhl, close to the Polish frontier, which meant that his family were already under Russian jurisdiction. He had in his possession two photographs of Hitler's châlet at Berchtesgaden and a postcard showing various sections of the Wehrmacht manoeuvres, with Hitler in the centre, striding along with his right arm raised in his usual pompous manner. Underneath were the lines, *"Mit Herz und Hand, fur Fuhrer und Vaterland"* – "With heart and hand, for Fuhrer and Fatherland!

Tuesday – *17.4.45*

Move early by Lichtenhorst and Retham, where we crossed the Aller by a pontoon bridge which "Jerry" bombed once and we rebuilt. The enemy fought here and, judging by the damage, paid for it. The road was atrocious. The cab rattled so much I could not hear the engine. It might have been described as a patchy surface but the patches were worse than the holes!

Stop in a wood near the village of Schneeheide. Here I spent an hour talking to several French soldiers – prisoners for five years – and French girls who have had to work in munitions. They have had a tough time, but they say it is worse still for the Russians, who have died from starvation in thousands. The Germans just dug a great hole, threw in the bodies, covered them with lime and left the hole open to receive the next day's dead. They also told me of seventeen British soldiers taken prisoner by the "Boche", who were lined against a wall and shot. Well, we can be just as ruthless, if that's what they want!

These Frenchmen warned us never to be "soft" with "Jerry". One of them had gone through Dunkirk to join the Free French in England. He still had a souvenir, in the shape of an A.T.S. badge in his cap! When he discovered I had once been in Nantes, he brought two of his friends who belonged to the city and they nostalgically remembered every street I mentioned and even the old Château de Breil!

WEDNESDAY – *18.4.45*
Move again via Valsrode and Honerdingen to Fallingbostel. We pass the village and park by a large farm. There is no dispersal these days; we all just huddle round the farm buildings, with our trucks and tents.

Fallingbostel is the village near which lie Stalags 357 and 11B, containing 7,000 British and 12,000 Allied prisoners. These prisoners must remain in the prison camps at present, as there is much typhus. Tough luck after their long suffering, but medical help is being rushed through.

We are supposed to be on the main road to Hamburg but it is only a second-class road. Hitler might have spent some time and trouble on these "highways". When a government does everything possible to improve services within its own frontiers, it has no time to cast envious eyes on other territories.

Warned to prepare for a long "swan" in the morning.

THURSDAY – *19.4.45*
The "long swan" turns out to be only nineteen miles, via Wierde, Dorfmark and Jettebruch. At the last-named place, we see a train of fuel tanks which has been shot up. Next we go through Soltau, a bigger town. The first half of it is smashed and wooden beams are still blazing among the ruins as we pass. The farther half is undam-aged and here we come upon a large crowd of German prisoners, mostly old men and young boys. Past Soltau there has been fighting in the woods and great stretches of ground under the trees form a black carpet of burnt pine needles, where our flame-throwers have cleared the enemy from cover. We park in a field near Heber. The weather is clear and sunny but with a cold wind. Later, the wind becomes a gale and the smouldering parts of the woods are fanned into flame, until several fierce forest fires are blazing in our vicinity and billowing clouds of smoke blow across the field in which we lie. Fortunately, the woods are separated by wide fields, so each fire eventually burns itself out but, for some distance on either side of the main road to Hamburg, the trees make an inferno through which trucks have to race at full speed, with the constant danger that their petrol tanks may be set alight.

FRIDAY – *20.4.45*
Taking advantage of low cloud, several Messerschmitts came over. One drops a bomb rather hurriedly on a nearby echelon. We see it leave the plane and, as he pulls out over our position, we sling all our small arms at him but he vanishes in the cloud.

SUNDAY – *22.4.45*
Move by Welle, Hockel, Langeloh and Todtglusingen and stop by the railway station at Tostedt. There are many French *railway trucks in and around the station.*

We have heard a report that troops of one of our regiments, captur-ing some of the infamous black-uniformed S.S., tried to find out who gave them orders to shoot their British prisoners but failed. They made the S.S. men dig their own graves, then shot them, while the ordinary Wehrmacht soldiers looked on.

Two wrongs will never make a right, of course, but those are pre-cisely the methods used by the Germans and, if the report is true, then the Wehrmacht prisoners who live to return to Germany will remember that the British are not so soft as they imagined.

MONDAY – *23.4.45*

R.H.Q. took fifty-one prisoners this morning. I have an automatic rifle taken from one of them. It has a curved magazine like that of the Bren, but longer.

TUESDAY – *24.4.45*

A Dutchman, forty-eight, who has been an "arbeiter" (slave), has been given a little food by us and is working eagerly with the boys at the cookhouse, to show his appreciation. Under the Germans he, with others, had to work on railroad repairs, carrying heavy sleepers at the double through mud and rain for twelve hours a day, with only ten minutes break for a "dinner" of water and turnips, such as cattle eat. He has given me a small photograph of himself. He says we will remember him as the "Man met de Rood Haar" ("The Man with the Red Hair"), which seems to recall to me the title of a well-known painting.

WEDNESDAY – *25.4.45*

Many more refugees arriving from the direction of Hamburg. I spoke to two French girls who were accompanied by a Neapolitan. One of the girls came from Caumont, in Normandy, and was anxious to hear about conditions there.

Nieuwerhuizen – the Man with the Red Hair – told us he was going to try to reach Holland on a bicycle, leaving at 6.00 a.m.. He clasped our hands in both of his as he said goodbye. We wished him good luck and he called us "Schoon kameraaden!" and broke into tears. I have given him a note asking anyone who can, to give him a lift. He is a good-hearted soul and I hope he manages to find enough to eat on his long journey home. His cheeks are much more shrunken, in reality, than shows on the photo he gave me, which was taken some time ago. He had also sent a copy of the photo to his wife and children, who have not seen him for three years.

THURSDAY – *26.4.45*

Some 600 liberated slaves are living in railway vans in the sidings. There are: Russians, both men and women; French girls, some very young; Italians; Poles and Dutch, a very Babel of tongues. They have set up tables and chairs in the vans and sleep on straw.

This evening, some of the boys were careering up and down the railway lines on a little petrol-driven trolley, when someone put a fog signal on the line. There was, of course, a loud bang, a puff of smoke and one wheel of the trolley leapt in the air, then came down on the line again. The expressions of the passengers, both facial and verbal, were quite amusing. For a moment, I believe, they thought they had struck a mine!

I was just going over to take a snapshot of them, when three young, unwashed German soldiers came up the line, wearing camouflage capes, with the rifles of Bill Thomas and Allan Thornewell behind them! So I took a photo of them too. They had been picked up in some wood nearby. Later still, three more "Jerries" gave themselves up, after two of our boys fired a few shots at them.

Friday – 27.4.45
The Man with the Red Hair comes back. He has been turned off the main roads by our M.P.s and told he must stay in Tostedt, which is the concentration area for freed slaves. He gets one dish of potatoes per day and it will be three weeks before he is taken to Holland. He is philosophical about it and says three weeks is not long, after three years in Germany, so long as he has something to eat, so he will come round tomorrow to work for us!

One more prisoner for the L.A.D. tonight. "Gillie" spotted him beneath a bed in a wooden bungalow and yelled "Come out!" He apparently didn't understand good English, for nothing happened, so "Gillie" sent a round through the bed and out he came, howling but unhurt. He thought he would be shot but was quite pleased when he learned he would go to England as a prisoner. The L.A.D. bag is now nine!

Goering "resigns" from the Luftwaffe!

CHAPTER 7

The Final Surrender

"Oh these were hours, when thrilling joy repaid
A long, long course of darkness, doubts and fears!
The heart-sick faintness of the hope delayed,
The waste, the woe, the bloodshed, and the tears ..."
SCOTT (*Lord of the Isles*)

SATURDAY – *28.4.45*
Himmler, chief of the Gestapo and one of the worst of all the Nazis,
is believed to have offered surrender to Britain and the U.S.A. only.
Which just shows how the Germans hate Russia. Britain states there
will be no peace without our Russian Allies. The Russians have now
completely encircled Berlin and are fighting in the city and in the
underground railway tunnels.

Mussolini shot by Italian patriots.

Weather here now cold and wet.

SUNDAY – *29.4.45*
Very cold.

MONDAY – *30.4.45*
Bitter.

TUESDAY – *1.5.45*
Hailstones.

Bernadotte, the Swedish diplomat who brought Himmler's message
to the Allies, has again contacted Himmler in Copenhagen. Chur-
chill seems to expect something big within a few days. Detailed
information has been given as to when and how work will cease in
factories, etc., for celebration if the war in Europe ends, but there

seems to be some doubt, even in Parliament, as to whether anyone will wait for instructions!

Borneo, where Uncle A... is held prisoner, has been invaded by the Allies, including Australians.

News flash at 10.00 p.m. German radio announces Hitler is Dead! He is said to have died of haemorrhage in Berlin. I wonder if the Russians will make sure by finding his body?

WEDNESDAY – 2.5.45
Admiral Doenitz is the new Fuhrer and says Germany will fight on against Bolshevism. Is he, too, so stupid as to imagine we will break faith with an ally? And where are Goering, Goebbels and Himmler?

More than half the liberated slaves here have gone from the railway vans, leaving only the Russians and others who cannot yet make their way home.

Today we had an inspection and talk by the C., R.A., Brigadier Smith. He told us of the horrors of Belsen, which he had seen. Hundreds of men, women and children had lost all power of thinking and could not remember why they had been brought there, or where they had their homes. There were no latrines and no washing facilities for 30,000 people.

The Brigadier also told us we will be going over the Elbe shortly, to encircle Hamburg and we may even continue into Denmark if the enemy doesn't pack in first!

The German armies in Italy surrender. A well-deserved victory for the boys out there, who carried on where we left off.

Runstedt, captured on the American front, said the German Forces were not fully aware of what was happening in the torture camps and Himmler had told him that he himself had been ordered to do these things, hinting that Hitler was responsible! Passing the buck?

Events were now moving with bewildering rapidity. Every hour brings something new. At 10.00 p.m. another news flash comes over the radio – Stalin announces the complete fall of Berlin, with 200,000 prisoners in and around the city. Meanwhile, the estimated number of prisoners surrendered to Field Marshall Alexander is one million!

Fritsche, German propangandist, taken in Berlin, says both Hitler and Goebbels took their own lives.

THURSDAY – 3.5.45

Went for a bath, by way of Steinbeck and travelled some way on the Hamburg autobahn, the first I have seen, and a really marvellous motor road. At a camp beside the mobile baths, a column of liberated prisoners marched off after attending the burial of four of their comrades who had died of inflammation of the bowels, following their long starvation. For them, liberation came in a different way.

We return in time to hear that Hamburg has surrendered to our Division. We are on an hour's notice to move.

At 12.00 noon today, R.H.Q. gets word from "Main" that the complete surrender of Germany was offered at 7th Armoured Division H.Q.! Whether this is true or not, we don't know, but everyone in R.H.Q. is drunk! They have burst into the rum ration!

Fantastic though it seemed, we learned later that it was true that complete surrender was discussed at our Divisional Headquarters.

FRIDAY – 4.5.45

Move 3.00 p.m.. Route: Kakentorf, Trelde, Dibberson, Nenndorf, Totensen and stop at Hittfeld. At 8.30 p.m., a news flash says that the German Army has surrendered Denmark, North-West Germany, Heligoland and the Friesian Islands. This leaves them still holding Norway, Central Austria, a pocket near Brandenburg, Memel and the Channel Islands!

SATURDAY – 5.5.45

Many French soldiers, escaped or released, are going back in German camouflaged trucks and some even in trailers drawn by tractors, but many are still walking with packs on their backs. Why don't they take cycles from the Germans? They have suffered plenty at their hands. Some came to me this morning, asking if we could get them transport. I promptly told them where to get it but they shrugged and said, "The Germans will not!" Will not? They are going around on cycles with good tyres and all accessories, dressed in good clothes, while these fellows tramp. When they do get back to France and discover that their bicycles and their best clothes have been taken by the "Hun", they will say, "We were fools!"

Move 1.00 p.m. through Harburg, then over the Elbe by a fine big suspension bridge with very ornamental entrances in red stone. So into Hamburg, second city of Germany. It has been well bombed and wide areas are just hills and valleys of rubble and brick. I manage to get one photo as we enter the city but we keep moving afterwards and there is no chance of more until we are through at the other side. Here German troops are straggling on foot in an endless stream into Hamburg. I snap some of them, too. Their ages range from sixteen to sixty, the older men having a hopeless air about them. There are no guards and the German soldiers circulate freely amongst the British in the streets. I wonder what it would have been like in Britain if the Germans had been the victors?

We stop in the outskirts of the city and Joe and I manage to get eight eggs in exchange for two bars of chocolate, the children going wild with joy at seeing their first chocolate for five years.

The Nine o'clock News states that another part of Southern Germany has given in, including Berchtesgaden, Hitler's holiday haunt. British troops have been led into Denmark by the Desert Rats! The Russians have now linked up with us on the Elbe and the Baltic coast.

MONDAY – 7.5.45

Again the rumour of complete capitulation, this time said to come from Supreme H.Q. at Rheims. At six o'clock, the B.B.C. says the story came from correspondents at H.Q. but S.H.A.E.F. have not confirmed it. Still, I expect the journalists know something.

The next entry in my diary was in red ink, by way of emphasis!

9.00 p.m. It's True! Churchill, Truman and Stalin
will make a joint announcement at 3.00 p.m. tomorrow,
which will be V.E. Day.
THE WAR IS OVER!

The capitulation was signed by General Jodl for Germany.

It has been a long struggle, with Germany better prepared in the beginning, yet she has been defeated more decisively than ever before. And now, the Last All Clear – except, of course, for Japan!

In the midst of all the excitement and speculation, the official dispatch signed by General Eisenhower at Rheims seemed almost prosaic in its simplicity. It read:

"The mission of this Allied force was fulfilled at 02.41 local time, May 7, 1945."

With this masterpiece of understatement, "Ike" wrote *Finis* to the War in Europe.

TUESDAY – *8.5.45*

Move 9.00 a.m. Halstenbeck, Elmshorn, Horst, Steinburg, Itzehoe, Dageling, Edendorf. Stop at Hohenaspe. The countryside is lovely. Bright warm sunshine throws shadows from the fresh green trees and birds sing everywhere. Along the roads straggle the representatives of many nationalities. In a way it is tragic to see the fall of the German nation. Their people look with natural compassion on the soldiers of the broken German Army, many with wounds and more with Iron Crosses. But they asked for it – and they got it – and they still have to answer for their atrocities.

French shout "Vive les Allies!" and Russians, Poles, Belgians, Dutch, Yugoslavs, Czechs and Italians smile and salute. The Italians are here because some refused to fight against us and others were with Tito's Yugoslavs, fighting for us.

When we stop at Hohenaspe, a German general arrives at his H.Q., which is in a mansion. A lower officer opens the door to him and the first thing they do is raise their arms and say, "Heil Hitler!" That must be knocked out of them. It is the pagan worship of an arch murderer. We move into a field, where we fit up our radio and tune in to Hamburg. At 3.00 p.m. we hear the Prime Minister, speaking of peace in Europe and announcing two day's holiday (of course, not for us). He ends by saying, "Advance Brittania! Long live the cause of freedom! God save the King!"

All we have before us, however, is perhaps six months of regimentation, spit and polish, scrub and burnish, drill and parade in Germany.

That evening, after dark, the A.A. in the fields around us suddenly went crazy, in the only visible demonstration I saw our troops make to celebrate victory. The Bofors bumped and barked for the last time, red

Hochbrücke Grünenthal bei Albersdorf.
Spannweite 156,5m, Höhe 42m

High Grunenthal Bridge.

tracers soared up to burst in a continuous crackle, directly overhead, and such a hail of shrapnel came swishing down that we began to think we ought to look out our steel helmets and knock the dust off them!

WEDNESDAY – 9.5.45
While the folks at home have another day's holiday, we are on the road again. We travel by Schenefeld and Hademarschen, over the Kiel Canal by the high Grunenthal Bridge, then to Albersdorf, Arkebek, Osterwold and Nordhastedt, all picturesque places, and stop in Gaushorn.

British and German troops are on the roads together. Convoys of German vehicles move along slowly, mainly in the opposite direction to ours. There are many German soldiers in Gaushorn and one of their convoys goes down a lane beside our position, with girls in grey uniform seated on the wings of some of the trucks. They must be the equivalent of our A.T.S.

*We are now close to Main (Divisional) H.Q. and regimentation
begins. We have already been told to wear our battledress buttoned
to the chin when driving, though it is a sweltering day and the
engines run hot. However, we forget our troubles in the evening,
for we are invited to a celebration dance held by the Russians in
their prison camp. There are Russian and Polish girls and the music
is played by two Czechs on guitar and mandolin, typical Slavonic
music, fast and rhythmic. The dancers whirl into a sort of polka-
fox-trot mixture. Then we have solo dances of the Cossack type,
with much "frog-kicking", hand clapping and loud "Hoys!" Some
of their songs are very well harmonised.*

*Half-way through, one chap makes a speech and we have no idea
what he is talking about, until he finishes with a sudden sweeping
gesture towards us! There is a cheer and a rush by our hosts to our
half-dozen chairs. For the next five minutes we stand shaking hands
as they crowd past in procession! They are obviously very happy to
be free. The red flag, with its hammer and sickle, flies out in the
courtyard, above the barbed wire and, across the village green, the
German soldiers sit round the door of their quarters, singing to the
music of an accordion, so they also seem to be pleased that it's all
over.*

THURSDAY – *10.5.45*
*Victory has made little difference to us, for we just carry on with
our usual duties. Having unloaded everything for a stay of at least
a week, we are suddenly told to load up again, as we are moving
after all – and back! While we work, the "Jerries" are basking in
the sun or strolling beneath the trees of the gardens attached to their
H.Q.*

*Over the radio we hear the cheering of the crowds outside Bucking-
ham Palace. Lucky people at home who can celebrate while we
haven't even a bottle of beer. When the news of the surrender
eventually became official, we did not go crazy and dash around
patting each other on the back, as I had imagined we might. We
were thankful, that was all, just plain thankful.*

At various times I suddenly remind myself, with undiminished
astonishment – the war's over!

And all the time the radio keeps plugging all those silly old songs, sung by crowds of people who laugh and cheer foolishly at the end of each song.

As I bed down, camp fires are still flickering, for now there is no blackout and, across the way, where the Wehrmacht is, lights gleam through the long orange curtains of the french windows.

As we were to move back from Gaushorn, we thought this would be the most northerly point we would reach, so that I wrote in my diary, "From now on, our journeys will be ever back towards the West and, eventually, Home". But it was not to happen exactly like that.

FRIDAY – *11.5.45*
Move back to Itzehoe, re-crossing the Kiel Canal. We park in a big timber yard beside a muddy, tidal creek, which links with a larger river some way off. This will be our home for the next two weeks. There have been riots and murders here, and hand grenades have been thrown.

Well, we can play funny games too!

SATURDAY – *12.5.45*
We clean and grease the vehicles. We must wear belt, braces, pouches and anklets, all snow white, if we go out at night – so we don't go out. We have found a grand piano here, without legs, but we have set it up on trestles and Allan and I are having some practice.

In the evening, a few of us have a swim in the creek at full tide.

SUNDAY – *13.5.45*
Orders are changed and we need only wear belts now. The weather is glorious, so we go out in the afternoon for a swim in the larger river. The town is very pretty, enhanced by the presence of trees, many of which are ablaze with blossom. The bank of the river is lined with brightly dressed – and undressed – civilians, mixed with German soldiers, Russians and Italians. In the town, the German troops salute us. German police, wearing white armbands supplied by us, direct the traffic, which occasionally includes camouflaged cars with German officers sitting bolt upright in them.

The Jerboa has already taken over a cinema and we see some revealing news pictures of Belsen and Buchenwald.

Afterwards, we walk round the pleasant public park. We pass three temporary hospitals, all full of German wounded, many with arms or legs off. This is what Hitler has brought them to. Back in our lines, we find some beer in our canteen issue. We have tried some of the German beer but it is even more watery than ours.

WEDNESDAY – *16.5.45*
Using the timber in the yard, the L.A.D. launch a home-made float like a raft, with one end pointed. R.H.Q. "next door", seeing it, declared war and began to send down depth charges in the shape of large boulders. Then a battle royal began. Our sea-borne troops attacked the enemy shore, armed with stirrup pumps, to be met with more stirrup pumps. Meanwhile, we sent an outflanking party along the fence on the landward side, with buckets of water which were successfully unloaded on the rear of the enemy, dispersing him in confusion! "Gillie", however, was soaked through by enemy action. He had stuck to his stirrup pump in the face of superior enemy fire from an elevated position!

THURSDAY – *17.5.45*
Going for a bath, we pass an old-fashioned but very picturesque column of German troops on horse-drawn vehicles, including field kitchens, water tanks, farm wagons and gigs. This was near Hademar-schen. There were young soldiers, smart officers and some old-timers, not so smart but with fierce Prussian moustaches. I should think they were in the First World War, if not in the Franco-Prussian one!

We may now send uncensored letters.

This evening, we had a stage show by a Russian party in the Jerboa Cinema. A party of our boys, under the direction of Joe Brown, have worked all day to widen the stage by adding an extension to the front. C., R.A. complimented the L.A.D. on the job.

Joe was a carpenter, an unusual trade to find in an L.A.D. but we now combined a wider variety of trades. Before the end of the campaign, the strength of the L.A.D. had risen to about forty men.

The rear half of the audience was made up of Poles and Russians. It was a good little show, including an acrobatic display, conjuring, juggling, dancing (both ballet and "Apache"), slapstick clowning and a girl who sang songs in Russian and in French.

FRIDAY – *18.5.45*

Regimentation continues. Although, as tradesmen, we are attached for the particular purpose of repairing the vehicles of the Regiment, we are now doing guards and sleeping with clothes and boots on.

SATURDAY – *19.5.45*

At three o'clock this morning, while still in the "guardroom", I heard the sergeants noisily going to bed, drunk as usual. Whisky and gin are issued to them (not to us) because they are supposed to be responsible persons.

After breakfast, we sit out on the river bank in the sun. Down-stream, the spring verdure of trees rises against a blue sky. Nearby, bells are ringing from a red brick tower with a green spire. Someone murmurs, "Peace!" Yes, it is difficult to realise we will hear no more the guns rumbling and thudding, or the Bofors crackling away. An endless procession of people, carts and bicycles, crosses the bridge just as if there had never been a war.

There is less work in now and some of the boys have been fitting a small motor-cycle engine on the L.A.D. barge, coupled to a radiator fan, which takes the place of a propeller. To everyone's astonish-ment, it moves off through the water at quite a fair speed, carrying five men, including "Admiral" Bromley, who is wearing a Nazi naval cap heavy with gold braid! They have a rudder fitted too, and go well up the creek, much to the amusement of other soldiers on the bridge. As they pass our wharf, there are yells of "Last trip to Southend!" – "All hands to the pumps!" and other derisive re-marks.

At 10.00 p.m. the intrepid crew ties up and the "Admiral" is piped ashore.

SUNDAY – *20.5.45*

On parade, we are asked if anyone wants to sign on for one, two, or three years! The atmosphere becomes like that at a bad auction sale. There are no bids. No one moves even his little finger! Who would want to be away any longer, especially those who are mar-ried? For those of us who are younger, it is time we learned some-thing about civilian life. Meanwhile, we amuse ourselves as well as we can. Even the R.S.M. laughed as we sailed along in our barge.

Having supplied various items for this mechanical wonder, from scrap in stores, I was allowed to book a passage for this trip. "Admiral" Bromley, "Rear Admiral" Ewers and "Captain" Sanders (of the River) were all dressed in full naval regalia, with gold braid on the cuffs and Iron Cross ribbons on the lapels. We had to wait for the tide, then away we went, at a roaring five knots, the "Admiral" standing at the stern – the blunter end of the two – with legs apart like Bligh of the Bounty. At R.H.Q. he is greeted with a Nazi salute, to which he responds with quiet dignity!

THURSDAY – *24.5.45*
Himmler, found in disguise, and taken to Second Army H.Q., commits suicide. Laval is interned in Barcelona. The net is spread.

FRIDAY – *25.5.45*
The Grand Mufti of Jerusalem, who carried out treacherous activities in Palestine, is now a prisoner in Paris. Hermann Goering is also a prisoner and Quisling, the Norwegian traitor, is facing trial in Oslo. The fate of most of the war criminals is now known, except for Tojo and the other "Japs".

SATURDAY – *26.5.45*
We are now running a British Bedford 15 cwt. truck which the Germans have used since Dunkirk!

SUNDAY – *27.5.45*
On parade along with R.H.Q., we are told that the 7th Armoured Division, formed during this war at Cairo, will be carried on as a regular division but, to do so, it must contain regular units so the Norfolk Yeomanry (65th Anti-Tank Regiment) is being replaced and will be broken up later. Meanwhile, as part of the Army of Occupation, we are joining 11th Armoured Division.

So we will no longer wear the sign of the Jerboa, the "Desert Rat" of undying fame!

Our new sign will be a charging bull. (I thought they were only used to wreck china shops!)

We now have two engines in our motorised barge, with an increase of speed to about ten knots. The wash from the propeller is quite prodigious! A good sense of balance is required by a passenger on this craft, as there is no rail to prevent him from sliding off the flat deck!

MONDAY – *28.5.45*
March to the cinema for a talk by the Divisional Commander, Major-General L. O. Lyne. He outlined the part played by the Division from the Rhine to Hamburg, and said at one time we pushed ahead so rapidly that we had 150 miles of lines of communication open and unprotected but the enemy could not take advantage of the position because he was completely disorganised himself.

Then we got the full story of how the war ended.

Before Hamburg, three men came to his H.Q. One was the owner of a rubber factory which "Jerry" was using as a hospital. The second was a doctor from the hospital and these two had come, ostensibly, to ask if we would stop shelling the hospital! The third was a Nazi officer who had come to see "fair play". H.Q. Staff looked at some aerial reconnaissance photos and said yes, we would stop shelling the hospital – if they would remove the eight large guns in the hospital grounds!

The Nazi officer went outside and the civilian said he would like a quiet word with the General, "Now that fellow's gone."

Then he said that he "believed" the German Commander would like to surrender Hamburg. Could it be arranged? The General said it could, but only if a staff officer came along.

Next day, the staff officer appeared and was given a letter stating that nothing less than unconditional surrender would be accepted and hinting that, if Hamburg held out, we had a very large air force which at the moment was doing nothing!

Meanwhile, the radio gave out that Hitler had committed suicide so, thinking this might have some effect on the staff officer, they told him. The effect was rather unexpected. He asked, should he commit suicide as well? The General said on no account must he commit suicide – at least, until he had delivered the letter!

Later, the German Commander himself came to Divisional H.Q. and said things were different now. Where previously he had been working alone, he now had permission from Doenitz, the new

Fuhrer, to surrender Hamburg and Doenitz would also like to discuss the unconditional surrender of all Germany and occupied territory as well! The General had to get a word in edgeways and asked for time to do a little telephoning, as he thought it was time that a Field Marshal at least was on the scene!

And so, eventually, the enemy representatives went to "Monty's" 21st Army Group H.Q. at Luneburg – but these events, leading to the end of the European war, began at the H.Q. of our (Seventh Armoured) Division and the first offer of complete surrender was made to this man addressing us, our Divisional Commander!

Before leaving us, the General said that when we go back to civil life, we must keep the best things of the Army: co-operation, comradeship and discipline. He was sorry to lose us and wished us all the best of luck.

When he had gone, Brigadier "Tiger" Smith, Commander of the Divisional Artillery, also said a few words. He congratulated us on keeping good order here in Itzehoe. Two Germans, he said, had murdered two Russians, so he had ordered the Germans to try the murderers and, if found guilty, to shoot them. If the German Commander did not care about it, he would try them himself. The thugs were duly tried, found guilty and shot, by their own people and, since then, we had had no trouble whatsoever.

He said, "I expect you will soon be taking it easy on the Norfolk Broads, or wherever you came from!" and added that he would be doing something the same in his own Somerset, for he was now an "old man", having served for thirty-one years. He hoped we would forgive his "rudeness" and "bad temper" in the past. He believed Itzehoe area was, for some reason, known as "The Tiger Country!"

He went on, "If any of you come to Somerset, I hope you will come and see me and we'll have a beer together, if the pubs are open!" Then he shook hands with the officers on the platform and said good-bye.

This, then, was the end of our connection with the "Seventh". It was just over three years since I had first worn the shoulder badge of the Division in Egypt. Although we were now leaving it to join another division, those of us who had been in Africa felt that we had a right still to call ourselves "Desert Rats".

TUESDAY – *29.5.45*
By this evening, we are all packed up again ready to move.

WEDNESDAY – *30.5.45*
Once again we cross the Grunenthal Bridge over the Kiel Canal and go to Albersdorf, where we are billeted in a gasthof, or inn. We have electric light in each room and a piano in what used to be the bar and which is now our recreation room. We are now under the command of 11th. Armoured Division.

THURSDAY – *31.5.45*
Convoys of German troops have been passing through all day, driving their own transport, mostly gas-driven trucks, the gas being carried in cylinders. They are going to mob centres to hand over equipment and be discharged. They organise and "police" themselves. Some travel in carts, each pulled by two horses, usually fine animals.

FRIDAY – *1.6.45*
Still more German troops going through. Now many are marching, singing as they go – but they are a mixed, dirty and unshaven lot. Many carry rough sticks as if they were hikers or yokels. Two, I notice, pull a small barrow, with all their kit in it, which is better than carrying it on their backs. Girls come out and give them sprigs of flower for their buttonholes. The trucks that pass are very much patched up. Our own trucks, going the other way, are carrying Poles, men and girls, to be repatriated. They wave happily to us.

SUNDAY – *3.6.45*
Day off for Thanksgiving. The time is twelve noon. The door opens (just like the ITMA *show). "Billy" Bennett pokes his head in.*

ME: Good morning, Billy!

B.B.:   Oh, hello, Nick! So you've got up for dinner?

ME: Oh, yes! Got to eat sometime, you know!

B.B.:   Why?

ME: What do you mean – why?

Door closes. Chuckles heard off stage.

WEDNESDAY – *6.6.45*
A year ago today, the invasion began. We have another day off in celebration.

FRIDAY – *8.6.45*

A concert party from 258 Battery gave a show called "Just the Job". Any trace of gravity remaining in the audience after the first few sketches was entirely removed by an impersonation of a schoolmistress waving a lorgnette and directing an imaginary class of schoolgirls doing their "gyms"!

As the days are long now, Allan and I go for a stroll after the performance. We go into the local Church and are amazed at the large number of memorial wreaths on the walls for soldiers killed in this war. They are of uniform design, with a white cross on which is marked the name of the man and where he was killed. We find that two out of every three were killed on the Russian front. The wreaths are two deep all round the Church and along the gallery – and Albersdorf is not a large place.

Later, we walk along some beautiful lanes and come out on a pathway beside a small lake, where we find a swimming pool, complete with boxes and diving boards.

A motto painted above the boxes read, "Every German a swimmer, every swimmer a life-saver!"

SATURDAY – *9.6.45*

The Russians announce the discovery of Hitler's charred body, under the ruins of the Reich Chancellery. The body is said to have been identified by the teeth, checked with dental charts. Goebbels' body was also found.

THURSDAY – *21.6.45*

Go to swimming pool with Allan and find a guard – a sergeant and three men – to keep soldiers away while the civilians are there. We are told we can swim only in the afternoon, but we work till 5.00 p.m. each day, which means we cannot have a swim at all, though the regiment can.

At the same time, we have no bath facilities and have not been to a mobile laundry since we came here.

Otherwise, they are regimental enough. We have to lay out our kit in a particular design each morning. We had to carry a lot of unnecessary kit: steel helmets, respirators, etc. from the trucks 200 yards away, just to put it on show for officers who have nothing better to do.

We had been swimming in the pool, of course, until the regiment "discovered" the place and began to "regulate" it.

The days were less eventful now and entries in my diary were less frequent.

Wednesday – *4.7.45*
Walking through the woods, came upon a lookout tower, from which we had a fine view of the Kiel Canal, including four of the bridges.

Thursday – *5.7.45*
Polling Day. Troops in the field are enabled to mark their ballot papers and so take part in the General Election like the folks at home.

Monday – *9.7.45*
Half eclipse of the sun. I watched it through a welding glass. The birds suddenly stopped singing and remained quiet until the full brilliance of the sun returned.

Albersdorf awakes! The army authorities have discovered there are a thousand troops here with little entertainment, so a film or theatre show will be put on each week now.

Tuesday – *10.7.45*
On the wall of another inn, where we dine with R.H.Q., was fastened a large enamel plate, advertising Holstein Beer. The regiment must have found out something about it, however, for today some of our boys tore it down and there, behind it, was a stone plaque inscribed with a swastika and the words:

"In diesem hause weilte Adolf Hitler am 11.3.1929."
("In this house Adolf Hitler sojourned, on 11th March, 1929.")

Thursday – *12.7.45*
Took a close-up photo of the Hitler plaque, just in time, it was chiselled out in pieces later!

Monday – *16.7.45*
Started another home-leave journey along with "Gillie". First we went through Rendsburg to Schleswig, where 11th Armoured Division have their H.Q. beside a lake, on which are many yachts and

launches. Then we returned by Rendsburg and Neumunster to a camp at Hamburg. There were no trains for Calais for twenty-four hours, so we went to the camp cinema, some distance away. During the show, the fine weather broke down and, when we came out, we were glad to find lorry transport laid on to take us back to our lines through the pelting rain. There were deep pools of water in our tent, in one of which my pack lay. However, we slept fairly well on our wooden litters, in spite of steady rain all night.

TUESDAY – 17.7.45
To keep us amused, we were taken in a party to Belli's Circus in Hamburg, a really big show. Our train was to leave Hamburg at 2.30 in the morning.

WEDNESDAY – 18.7.45
It was raining a little as we trudged to the barrier under electric floodlamps and queued for the trucks taking us to Altona Station. Passing through Hanover, we reached Minden at 8.00 a.m. and had breakfast. Our route lay through acres of brick rubble in many well-bombed towns: Osnabruck, Munster, Mecklenburg, Wesel and Emmerich, where we crossed the Rhine by a sapper's bridge built on low wooden piles which creaked and groaned all the way, as the train crawled slowly across.

We went into Holland at Gennep and, as we passed through Veghel, Oisterwijk and Tilburg, we got another wonderful reception from our old friends, the Dutch people. Bicycles were tossed into ditches and hedges as they dismounted, rushed over and lined the track for a long way, waving, smiling and trying to pick out the faces of anyone they knew. They still cannot get cigarettes and many were thrown to them from the train.

Then we passed once more into Belgium, by Turnhout, Mechelen and Brussels, where tea was served on the platform at 11.30 p.m. by British and Belgian women.

I believe the ladies who gave us the tea belonged to the British Women's Volunteer Service, with Belgian helpers. It must have been a weary job out there on the dim platform at that time of night. I only hope they realised how much that tea was appreciated in the circumstances, for we were too cramped and tired to be able to express adequately our gratitude! The journey from Hamburg, so far, had taken twenty-one hours.

On through the night again and we pull into Calais at 6.00 a.m.

THURSDAY – *19.7.45*
The boat does not leave until afternoon, so we spend the time in the camp cinema.

An officer, who stamped my papers, apparently had his eye on the two large swords I was carrying, for he tried to convince me that I would never get through the customs with them and hinted that it might be better if I left them with him! This I declined to do and, when I arrived at Dover and stepped ashore from the *Golden Lilly*, I carried them openly, hanging by my side and, although the Customs men were checking the baggage of perhaps one man in twenty, no one took any notice of the swords.

The special train, which contained a Naafi coach, took me all the way from Dover to Edinburgh and I reached Stirling on Friday morning, 20th July. The whole journey from Albersdorf had taken four days.

On Saturday, 21st July 1945, while I was at home in Scotland, a big victory parade of the Navy, Army and Air Force was being held in Berlin. Winston Churchill (later Sir Winston) took the salute in the Charlottenburger Chausée and, near him, stood Field Marshal Montgomery and Major-General L. O. Lyne, our former Commander, then G.O.C. in the British zone of Berlin.

The Desert Rats were there, so the divisional axis was finally laid into the heart of the German capital! In the Charlottenburger Chausée itself, the Military Police of the Division erected a large signboard which set out the route followed by the axis from El Alamein to Germany. A German civilian, after reading the place-names on it, is said to have commented bitterly, "And the Fuhrer told us these British would not fight! No army in the world could have stopped them."

After the parade, Winston Churchill, addressing the 7th Armoured Division, spoke these words:

"You were the first to begin. The 11th Hussars were in action in the desert in 1940 and, ever since, you have kept marching steadily forward on the long road to victory. Through so many countries and changing scenes, you have marched and fought your way.

"I am unable to speak without emotion. Dear Desert Rats, may

Desert Rats' honours board: In the Charlottenburger-Chaussee, Berlin, where
Mr Churchill took the salute from the Desert Rats, Sergeant J. Landridge, of
Gravesend, and Corporal C. Cattermole of Cockfosters, set up a sign that all
who pass may read ... A journey's end table setting out the route of the Desert
Rats from El Alamein to the heart of Germany.

your glory ever shine. May your laurels never fade. May the memory of this glorious pilgrimage which you have made from El Alamein to the Baltic and Berlin never die, a march – so far as my reading of history leads me to believe – unsurpassed throughout all the story of war."

There is not much more of my story to tell, except for the break-up of the unit after Japan capitulated and the protracted, dismal wait for demobilization.

THURSDAY – *2.8.45*

After a good leave, with an extension of three days owing to bad seas in the Channel, I return to Dover, where I spend the night at the Duke of York's School.

FRIDAY – *3.8.45*

We are taken by truck down the steep winding road past Dover Castle, through the town to the docks, where the Lady of Mann *awaits us. The crossing is perfect and we arrive in Calais about midday, but put our watches forward one hour from British Summer Time to European Time.*

The Naafi in Calais, one of the finest, is now decorated with shields on the walls, bearing the signs of the various Divisions and Brigades. Entrain 7.30 p.m., passing St. Omer, Hazebrouck, Bailleul and Armentières, names which will always be connected with the First World War but, where formerly there was devastation, now there are neat, modern villages and Mademoiselle from Armentières wears lipstick.

This is the worst part of the journey, an interminable run all through the night and the next day, while we sit more or less upright, stiff and sore, and try to snooze with our heads lolling forward or leaning into the corners of the wooden seats.

SATURDAY – *4.8.45*

Arrive in Hamburg about midnight and go to the "Holding Unit" camp at Eidelstedt, where we thankfully stretch out for the night, under canvas.

SUNDAY – *5.8.45*

Reach 11th Armoured Division H.Q. at Schleswig, where we have a good meal in the Yacht Club overlooking the lake. Then by Regimental transport to Albersdorf, where the L.A.D. still is.

Some of the boys have already gone on "PYTHON" leave and two have been posted to other units.

How PYTHON leave got its name I cannot remember (if I was ever told) but perhaps it was a code to replace some other official name, which would in any case be long and wriggly! PYTHON leave lasted about six weeks.

This same evening (Sunday), I enjoyed a very good stage show by an "international" party. A first-class tenor, Inar Christiansen, came from Iceland and sang in English and Italian. Another Italian and his wife, who was Swedish, kept the audience rocking with laughter at their eccentric dancing and clowning. A Latvian contortionist, dressed in a green outfit, gave a clever imitation of a frog. Three Russian ballet dancers, stars from Leningrad, completed a grand bill.

MONDAY – 6.8.45
This evening, an announcement came over the radio, telling of the most stupendous discovery of the war, and perhaps of the whole history of science – the Atomic Bomb!

Before the war, I read that experiments were being carried out to atomise uranium. Now they know how to release its power. A single bomb has been dropped on a Japanese city and the city is believed to be wiped out! So far, no air photos have been taken, as everything is still under a pall of smoke and dust.

WEDNESDAY – 8.8.45
Russia declares war on Japan.

As from tomorrow (the 9th), Russia will be at war with Japan, so we will now have bases close to the enemy homeland.

Reconnaissance shows that sixty per cent of Hiroshima is destroyed by the atomic bomb. Over four square miles is completely cleared without even a trace of wreckage left. The Japanese say that the bodies around the explosion are too numerous to be counted. People outside their houses were burned to death and those inside were killed by blast. The explosive part of the bomb weighed only eight pounds. *The population of Hiroshima was about a quarter of a million.*

THURSDAY – *9.8.45*
The Russians advance into Manchuria. The second atomic bomb is dropped on Nagasaki, another city with a quarter of a million inhabitants.

Every nation must now keep the peace, or all may perish. We must reach sanity or cease to exist!

FRIDAY – *10.8.45*
Japan offers to accept our terms, if the Mikado remains her ruler.

SATURDAY – *11.8.45*
The Allies agree to let the Mikado remain, subject to the orders of an Allied Military Government.

SUNDAY – *12.8.45*
Visit Schlaswig for the day, passing through Rendsburg, where there are two fine bits of engineering, a swing bridge which carries road traffic over the Kiel Canal and a railway viaduct, which spirals round on itself to gain height and then crosses the canal on a high level.

Both towns are picturesque and very clean, full of quaint old houses and winding streets. In the Yacht Club, run by 11th Armoured Division, we are served by German frauleins. *The price of admission is one mark but meals are free and cakes are supplied from a nearby centre where army cooks are undergoing "trade-testing"!*

As we left Schleswig in our truck, the scene over the lake was quite poetic. Lights shone over the placid waters, trees were silhouetted against the fading light of day and a crescent moon added the last touch of the brush to nature's painting.

TUESDAY – *14.8.45*
At midnight, it is announced that Japan has agreed to the terms of the Potsdam Declaration – the Mikado, speaking over the radio for the first time, giving the news of the surrender to his people. The Japanese are reported to have bowed to the loudspeakers.

So at last we return to a state of peace.

A two day holiday is announced in Britain.

WEDNESDAY – *15.8.45*

Final "V" Day. Warned of a coming inspection by C., R.A. (11th Armoured Division). We work like Trojans: painting trucks, shifting heavy boxes, springs, axles and gearboxes and generally clearing the area. Then we are told to scrub all our web equipment once more. That's the sort of holiday we get.

The best room of this inn, previously used as our "office", is now given to three of our chaps as a bedroom because they were sleeping on tables in the scullery – a thing which never troubled our superiors before. A large soft divan and an armchair suddenly appear in our "recreation" room, so that the General will be sure that we are well looked after.

Thank goodness, we had those indefatigable concert parties, still coming at regular intervals, to keep our minds off our rather meaningless existence. When one of the players appeared in flowing robes and wearing a turban, he was somewhat surprised to be greeted by a loud "SA-EEEDA!" followed by other expressions in Arabic, some extremely polite and some the very opposite! At another show, two little girls with accordions brought the house down.

MONDAY – *27.8.45*

The German civilians are absolutely desperate for cigarettes. They have sold cameras, binoculars and watches for the nicotine narcotic and one man even got a 200-base accordion for 200 cigarettes. Every day grown men are seen, walking with their eyes on the ground, looking for cigarette ends which, even if squashed flat, they pick up to get the tobacco for use in a pipe. And, down at our cookhouse, one old German soldier is glad to wash our plates for the priviledge of sorting out a meal from our leavings.

The 21st Army Group will now cease to exist and we will be part of the British Army of the Rhine (B.A.O.R.).

TUESDAY – *28.8.45*

Four more men posted away.

TUESDAY – *4.9.45*

The strength of the L.A.D. is now only fifteen, though we still occupy our usual tables in the dining hall.

THURSDAY – *6.9.45*
Every evening for the past week, the children here have been par-
ading with paper lanterns just after dark and they repeat a chant as
they go up and down the streets in procession. They call it the "Walk
of the Lanterns".

It is connected with the Harvest Festival and I am told it goes on
all through September, with increasing enthusiasm until, near the
end, the adults join in.

SATURDAY – *8.9.45*
One of the things I will always remember about Albersdorf is the
children's nightly sing-song in our recreation room. Tonight, as I go
out to R.H.Q. guardroom, they are singing Brahms Wiegenlied *to*
Allan's accompaniment on the piano.

The kiddies were obviously taught part-singing at school, for their
harmony was delightful. Their leader was a bright, attractive little girl
called Inga, who often played around our quarters at the *"Gasthof zur*
Linde".

SUNDAY – *9.9.45*
This is a lovely morning, cool and misty, with the sun peeping through,
just as it did on those mornings last year, when we swept across France.
It reminds me of the time when we slept in the market square of
Lyons la Forêt, to awake while all the houses were still silent and
shuttered. The people seemed oblivious to the history passing their
doors but they would waken to a town from which the last enemy
had passed and find instead the moving columns of their allies.

Now everything is very calm and the sun is shining more strongly,
while the chestnut trees at the entrance to the Albersdorf churchyard
are already mellowing into autumn tints. We too, though still young,
have grown older and we can see things a little more clearly in the
light of peace.

The Colonel of the Regiment (Colonel Goring) spoke briefly to us
in farewell today, as he is leaving us for home. He thanked us and
paid a special compliment to the L.A.D. for having kept the Regi-
ment mobile. This is the beginning of the break-up for, though the
Regiment will remain, the Colonel says, for about a year, most of
the original members will be gone when Group 26 is released (I am

in Group 24). Two "old-stagers", "Q" Joy and the one and only
Eddie Gamble have gone already. R.S.M. Wolgar goes with the
Colonel. Today, too, our advance party goes to Kappeln, on the
Baltic coast, where we follow on Tuesday.

R.S.M. Wolgar, though a tough and forceful sergeant-major, was well-
liked, for he was just and had a sense of humour, too often lacking in
those of his rank. A story was told of his treatment of a tough troublemaker in one of the batteries. This fellow had been bullying other men
and causing fights, which he usually won, because he certainly could
use his fists. The R.S.M., though twice his age, was said to have once
won an Army boxing championship. He took the troublemaker behind
some huts and gave him the thrashing of his life. For a long time afterwards, the tough one was very quiet indeed. Be that as it may, when we
said goodbye to R.S.M. Wolgar, I am certain he had a tear in the corner
of his eye.

Our heavy equipment was gone by this time. The self-propelled Mio's
had been loaded on to tank-transporters and the long-barrelled 17-
pounders and the armoured vehicles which towed them had also been
taken away. All we had left was our lorry transport and the L.A.D.
vehicles.

MONDAY – *10.9.45*
Spend the day packing up the stores, now much thinned out. How
many times have I taken part in this packing of vehicles? It seems
endless.

We have our last "choir" with little Inga and the other kiddies, in
the dusk.

TUESDAY – *11.9.45*
Leave Albersdorf and take the road through Wrohm, Elsdorf, Budels-
dorf, Wittensee, Eckernforde, Waabs, to Kappeln.

Kappeln is a bright little town on the Schlei, a narrow inlet of the
Baltic, which links up with the lake at Schleswig about twenty miles
inland. Approaching the town, we had a striking view of the stretch
of blue water, with many yachts and small trawlers on it and a
swing-bridge running over it to the town. The red and white houses
rose in a gentle slope from the quayside and a white windmill
dominated the town at the top. We reached this mill through twist-
ing, cobbled streets and parked the trucks beside it. Our billets are

across the road from the windmill. I have an iron spring bed in a room all to myself (so far) and electric light.

Strolled round the town and along the quayside, where the salt smell was quite refreshing.

Wednesday – *12.9.45*
Explored the windmill, which is set on top of a three-storied ware-house. The millstones, driven by the power of the great sails, are massive things. Amongst the grain fed in for grinding, I noticed a proportion of beans, so the flour was not pure. Out on the wooden gallery, high above the ground, I walked carefully, for the planking was old and appeared half rotten, with many cracks and gaps in it but the miller, pushing the sails round with a pole to get them under way, ran along the gallery. As I watched the planks bending under his feet, I expected to see him crash right through them! Narrow stairs took me up through another four floors in the windmill, then up into the dome bearing the hub of the sails. A smaller set of sails are geared to rotate the whole dome, so that it automatically keeps itself facing into the wind. A set of rungs are fixed to the beams, sloping up to the smaller sails, so the miller must be a bit of a steeplejack as well! As I came down, the whole structure was throb-bing to the action of the machinery and the sails swept past with a great swish, giving an impression of tremendous power.

In the afternoon, we move to another billet, above a cinema restau-rant, where we eat – the usual Army meals, of course. These are said to be our winter quarters and we also have the garage across the way, where the stores truck will be unloaded (even to the steel bins) into a fixed stores department.

However, my L.I.L.O.P. leave is now due, so I will be going home again for six weeks.

And what did the mysterious letters L.I.L.O.P. stand for? – Leave in Lieu of Python – whatever that meant!

Those of us who were in the earlier groups for demobilisation would have been happier if this leave had been added at the end of our service, so that we should be demobilised earlier, instead of making that miserable long journey home and back again, just once more than was necessary. However, as this apparently could not be done and no one was very sure when his "demob" would come, we were glad to go on leave, if only to get away from regimentation.

With the end of hostilities, the Army's biggest function was at an end – and surely that function must be the lowest to be found in any "civilised" community, namely, to kill or be killed!

This evening, another big procession of children passed along the street below, with a great variety of lanterns and singing exactly the same chant as we heard in Albersdorf.

WEDNESDAY – *19.9.45*
At a film show, we saw a news picture of the last fighting in Borneo, showing the "Aussies" spraying flame on the terrified "Japs", who stumbled about covered in fire. The "Aussies" were remembering many atrocities. Out of 2,550 Australian and British prisoners held by the "Japs" on Borneo, only six survived.

My uncle was one of the many who were buried in Borneo, having died only a short time before hostilities ended.

THURSDAY – *20.9.45*
Left Kappeln by truck for Hamburg. On the train same evening and travel all night via Luneburg, Celle, Buchenwald, Minden, Osnabruck, Munster, Antwerp, Ghent and Bruges, to Ostend. Buchenwald was, of course, one of the atrocity camps and, at Luneburg at this time, Josef Kramer, the "Beast of Belsen", is standing trial.

FRIDAY – *21.9.45*
Sail from Ostend to Tilbury. On the ship a bunch of us, Desert Rats, had a chin-wag about the old days in the desert and the "flaps" in particular. All agreed that the spirit of comradeship of those days is seldom seen now. The men of the later divisions have a cold, selfish attitude and some of them will hardly even speak to you. Many tales were told, some of danger but mostly of humour and even the most desperate situations were often treated as a huge joke.

At Purfleet Camp, we find the spirit of the peace-time army: cold, officious, intolerant, amidst rows of huts and tents, where everything is regimental.

SATURDAY – *22.9.45*
Reach Bulwell, Notts., where I spend the night in a Nissen hut.

I reached home by Sunday night and, after enjoying the longest leave

I ever had from the Army, I returned to Bulwell on Thursday, 8th November. There was nothing much to look forward to but I was pleased to find "Gillie" Potter at the same camp, though he returned home next day on compassionate leave. No one seemed to know what to do with us, or whether to send us back to Germany or not. We were kept at Bulwell for a fortnight and, though we had come on leave wearing our "best" battledress, we spent most of the time on particularly dirty fatigues.

FRIDAY – *9.11.45*
On guard, as N.C.O. marching relief – not that there is anything to guard!

SATURDAY – *10.11.45*
On fatigues.

SUNDAY – *11.11.45*
Cookhouse fatigues.

MONDAY – *12.11.45*
Move to "Sunrise Hill" camp near Bulwell. Miserable place.

WEDNESDAY – *14.11.45*
Still here. J– and S– are both broke, so I help them out. Those who "know" seem to think that nobody under Group 25 will go overseas again, so I may not see Kappeln or my unit again.

SATURDAY – *17.11.45*
Now working each day loading boxes on to lorries, then transferring them onto railway trucks, under the direction of civilians who have been in "Blighty" all through the war. After a full day's work, I am to be on guard again all night but, when I make a complaint about doing both duties, I am told by the sergeant not to make "silly" statements or he will take me before the O.C. and soon have my "tape" removed!

TUESDAY – *20.11.45*
Taken off the working party and put on cookhouse fatigues, which we find not so bad. The new working party refuse point blank to shovel coal and are taken off the job while their complaints are "investigated".

I have a bad cold.

WEDNESDAY – *21.11.45*
Issued with winter woollens – too late – at Hucknall. Had a bath, took some asprin and went to bed with a sore chest.

FRIDAY – *23.11.45*
Warned to move but told we will not go back to our units.

SATURDAY – *24.11.45*
Reach Kearsney, then go aboard the Princess Astrid, *sailing overnight, so we appear to be going back to our units after all.*

SUNDAY – *25.11.45*
Stop for the day in Ostend. In a club run by the Y.M.C.A., a film show was being given by means of a portable projector, but the air was so foggy with cigarette smoke that the operator asked the audience of troops to put out their cigarettes, as the light on the screen was rather dimmed. The only response he got was from a tough Canadian who growled, "Aw, git on wit' the show, an' quit beatin' y'gums!"

Left for Hamburg by train at 6.00 p.m.. No steam heat in the carriages. Feet frozen all night.

MONDAY – *26.11.45*
Pass through Hanover, where there is snow on the ground. The ruins look even more forlorn when covered with snow, the broken gables rising against a grey sky.

Arrive at Hamburg at eight o'clock in the evening.

CHAPTER 8

The End of the L.A.D.

TUESDAY – *27.11.45*

Rise 4.00 a.m., take train to Schleswig (via Neumunster and Rends-
burg) and truck to Kappeln, arriving 4.30 p.m. to find the unit in
the same place as before, but few of the L.A.D. left. Eddie Culhane
and Jim Bryant have been de-mobbed, our captain has been pro-
moted and has gone to another post and Sergeant Les Harman is
left in charge. All the stores have gone, so there is nothing to do.

FRIDAY – *30.11.45*

Harry Bromley (the "Admiral") and I go out for a spin in an
ex-German speedboat. We went out to where the Schlei reaches the
Baltic and everything looked very calm and peaceful. A mallard
flew past us and a steam ferryboat, crowded with passengers, moved
across the channel. We had a good turn of speed and left a heaving
wake behind us but there was plenty of weed about, near the surface
and one of the water-ports which cool the engine became blocked
so we had to slow down to prevent a seizure. As we did so, the bow
came gently down on to the water and we chugged back steadily on
an even keel, though steam was coming from the blocked pipe.

Several of these fast launches had been commandeered. They were
originally intended for use in destroying big ships. The idea was for the
launch to be loaded with high explosive, which could be detonated by
pressure on a bar fixed round the bows. The launch thus became a sort
of controlled torpedo, which would destroy itself and its prey when
driven against the hull of a ship. The seat at the stern could be tipped
back by pulling a lever, so allowing the steersman to escape while the
launch rushed on towards the target. Presumably the steersman was to
be picked up by some other vessel. The bar around the bows was still
in position when we used the launch but, of course, there was no explosive. Indeed, the hull was bare and empty except for the engine, which

was a "V8" made in the German Ford factory. The hull itself seemed to be made of very thin plywood.

SATURDAY – *1.12.45*
Have a medical inspection in preparation for release. Having cleared the water intake on the launch, Les, Harry and myself go out in it to the fishing village of Maasholm, which we explore, then further out to the lighthouse at the narrow mouth of the Schlei, where the tide comes racing in over the bar. The lighthouse (Schleimunds) is about five miles from Kappeln. As the water was rough, we did not approach the bar. As it was, we got a bit wet from spray.

On the return trip, we again landed to inspect a German one-man submarine, on the shore near a camp now occupied by Poles. The submarine was high and dry and had been rendered useless. A torpedo lay beside it.

MONDAY – *3.12.45*
Said good-bye to Allan Thornewell and Tommy Bedford, who have now been posted back to 7th Armoured Division. They are both fine chaps and special friends of mine. One keeps making friends and losing them to the Army but a few are always outstanding, as they have been.

TUESDAY – *4.12.45*
Remainder of the L.A.D. posted to various units. I, with several others, will go to Flensburg, on the Danish frontier.

So this is the end of the L.A.D., which formed at Tel-el-Kebir and joined the Regiment at Almaza.

We are sorry to leave old comrades but also glad to take one step nearer to leaving the Army.

SATURDAY – *8.12.45*
Still here, waiting for transport to come from Flensburg.

The town (Kappeln) is now covered with snow, the roads are ice-bound and a bitter wind is blowing, yet the sun is shining.

I wonder if I will be home for this New Year?

SUNDAY – *9.12.45*
As I look down from this window, the post-war life of Kappeln passes before me in the winter sunshine. Four-wheeled wagonettes

*go by, each pulled by two horses. Couples walk the street in their
Sunday best but too many of the men wear peaked caps, as if they
were all taxi-drivers. A Polish soldier, accompanied by a girl wearing slacks, goes into the cemetery. They are paying their respects to
a comrade who will never return to Poland. Two months ago, three
Poles, killed while clearing mines, were buried here.*

*A German officer moves painfully along the sidewalk, with a stick
in his right hand. His left side seems paralysed. The leg is stiff; the
left arm is bent across his stomach. He has given much for his
country – too much for an unworthy Fuhrer.*

MONDAY – *10.12.45*
*One thing I appreciate here is having this room to myself, so that I
can go to bed when I want to, instead of being kept awake till one
o'clock by the card-players.*

*From my bed I can see the bare branches of a tree across the way,
"floodlit" by the lamp at our front door. A radio sends forth the
noise of a hysterically screeching trumpet, but it is too far away to
bother me.*

*Peace ... There is too much noise in this world and people have lost
the habit of enjoying one of the greatest gifts of nature to strained
nerves – Golden Silence!*

TUESDAY – *11.12.45*
*"Titch", the bewildered little dog belonging to "Q" Joy is still here.
He has been miserable ever since "Q" was demobbed, but arrange-
ments are being made by the Sergeants' Mess to send Titch home to
"Blighty" and, after going through quarantine, he should see Fred
Joy again.*

I hope Titch got home. It seems so tremendously important that the
absolute faith and trust of a dog, the longing in his bursting heart, should
not be disappointed. I think Jerome K. Jerome epitomised the nature of
a dog very well in his *Idle Thoughts of an Idle Fellow*, when he wrote:

"He is very imprudent, the dog is. He never makes it his business
to inquire whether you are in the right or in the wrong, never
bothers as to whether you are going up or down life's ladder, never
asks whether you are rich or poor, silly or wise, sinner or saint.

"You are his pal. That is enough for him and, come luck or good

"I KILLED THE COUNT"

by

Alec Coppel

Characters

(in the order of their appearence)

Count Victor Mattoni	LEONARD, HARRIS
Polly	BETTY STUART
Divisional Inspector Davidson . .	VICTOR GORDON
Detective Raines	FREDERICK E. SMITH
Martin	LESLIE LABEAU
P. C. Clifton	JOSEPH LUCAS
Louise Rogers	RONA LANE
Renee La Lune	PHYLLIS HOPE-BELL
Samuel Diamond	DENIS NORDEN
Johnson	GORDON MURRAY
Mullet	JACK BUNING
Bernard K. Froy	PETER MITCHELL
Viscount Sorrington	BILL FRASER

The play produced by BILL FRASER

SYNOPSIS OF SCENES

The action of the play takes place in the living room of
Count Mattoni's flat, Oxley Court, Baker Street. A Friday
morning in October.

Prologue	10 a. m.
Act I	11.30 a. m.
Act II	The action is continuous.
Act III	The action is continuous.

Stage Director	DENIS NORDEN
Stage Manager	JOHN M. DONALD
Electrician	WALTER WILDEY
Property Master	C. F. BREARLEY
Scenery designed by .	CAPT. TOM HUDSON RASC of ENSA
Scenery Built at . . .	ENSA Production Centre Lübeck

The play was produced at the A. W. S. 8 Corps Repertory
Production Centre, NEUMÜNSTER under the direction of
ERNEST CLARK.

fortune, good repute or bad, honour or shame, he is going to stick to you, to comfort you, guard you, give his life for you if need be – foolish, brainless, soulless dog."

WEDNESDAY – *12.12.45*
Leave Kappeln and arrive at 29th Armoured Brigade Workshops in a barracks in Flensburg, formerly occupied by German Panzer troops. Flensburg is a much bigger town than Kappeln and the familiar little yellow trams run along its streets.

SUNDAY – *16.12.45*
We now sleep on shaky two-tiered bunks and there is less peace at night. Once a bugle blew "Lights Out" at midnight. We were already asleep, so the bugle woke us up again. In the early morning, while it was still dark, someone "revved" an engine till it was screaming, down in the barrack yard. Another time, at about 1.00 a.m., a party came in drunk and began breaking up their room. Crashes and thuds echoed through the building as chairs and beds were heaved out into the passage. The "charging bulls" had found another "china shop"!

There is a nice saloon run by Naafi in town. The tables are set around a small stage and there is a row of boxes at the back, making it like an old-time music-hall. A German orchestra plays on the stage but, at the interval, "the boys" take over. A pianist from the Rifle Brigade, who used to play in a dance orchestra, sits at the grand piano, while a sailor slaps the string bass and two more soldiers play accordion and drums. Between the "boogie numbers", the pianist gives renderings of pieces such as the "Warsaw Concerto" or Tchaikowsky's Concerto in B Minor, which are well received.

As usual, however, things are leavened by the drunks. One, with a hopeless voice, but sufficient opinion of himself to get up on the stage, tries to sing a song but cannot even remember the words. Others encourage him with just as foolish applause. Another two, one a sergeant, try to put on a dance – unquestionably eccentric – and slither all over the place, until one finally collapses. They slap his face but he is completely unconscious, so they carry him out. The beer, incidentally, is atrocious.

TUESDAY – *18.12.45*
Nine of us in one room have to stay in tonight because, on morning

inspection of billets, a book was found on top of the radio. Next door, all occupants are confined to barracks because an ashtray was left on the table. Others are similarly punished for paltry technical infringements.

The Sergeant-Major (acting orderly officer) who imposed these penalties is in Group 24, so he is nearly finished with the Army. We cannot understand the mentality of a man who can look for such childish faults when other orderly officers are satisfied if the general effect of orders is carried out. Perhaps he wants to leave an impression of hate behind him.

THURSDAY – *20.12.45*
On guard. Should be my last.

(It was!)

FRIDAY – *21.12.45*
Hand in all spare kit to Q.M. Stores. No more work.

SATURDAY – *22.12.45*
Saw Elizabeth, *a translation of the French play. There was a very fine performance by Beatrix Lehmann but it is always difficult to hear quiet passages with so much coughing amongst an audience of smokers.*

This took place in a small but very modern theatre in Flensburg.

MONDAY – *24.12.45*
Special Christmas Eve show in the Victory Club, which was a scene of great merriment. The busy waitresses (Danish girls) remained good-humoured, though every time one passed between the tables, someone would pull the strings of her apron.

TUESDAY – *25.12.45*
My seventh Christmas away from home since the war began, but my last in the Army. We had tea and rum brought in by the sergeants in the morning and later assembled for dinner in the long attic hall upstairs, where we were served by officers and warrant officers, according to custom and a tot of whisky was added to each mug of beer. Later, a party was given by the sergeants to a crowd of German kiddies in the same hall. We also threw chocolate and sweets to the children scrambling outside the barrack gates.

Flensburg.

N.A.A.F.I.

PRESENTS

E.N.S.A. ENTERTAINMENTS FOR **H.M.F**ORCES

ELIZABETH

LA FEMME SANS HOMME

●

Adapted into English by
YVETTE PIENNE

from the French of
ANDRE JOSSET

with

BEATRIX　LEHMANN
LAURENCE PAYNE
ROBERT CARTLAND
DENIS CAREY
MICHAEL SEARS
WALTER HUDD
DEREK PROUSE
YVONNE COULETTE

The Play Produced by
D E N N I S   A R U N D E L L

SOUVENIR PROGRAMME

SCENES

Act I. Scene I ...... (1594) A Room in the Palace of Whitehall. Night.

Act I. Scene II...... (1596) Eighteen Months Later. Essex
House. Afternoon.

Act II............. (1597) One Year Later. A Room in the
Palace of Whitehall. Night.

Act III. Scene I .... (1599) Two Years Later. Elizabeth's
Room in Whitehall. Early Morning in
September.

Act III. Scene II .... (1603) Four Years Later. Same Scene.
Night.

Manager and Stage Director

·EDMUND S. PHELPS

Stage Manager

REGINALD CORNISH

Someone must have had more than just a tot of whisky, however, for after the festivities we found that a perfectly good piano in the hall had a panel smashed and several of the wooden hammers torn out.

SATURDAY – *29.12.45*
Pack up, hand in blankets and get on a truck to the station. Here the R.T.O. says no "A" release men can go on today's train. "B" and "C" having priority. So we return to barracks, draw out our blankets again and settle down to wait.

My companion on this last journey was Len Moore who, like myself, had joined the L.A.D. at Tel-el-Kebir. The only other remaining member of the L.A.D. was George Saunders, who joined us before the landing in Normandy. His demobilisation group was much later than ours and he remained in Flensburg when we finally took leave of him.

SUNDAY – *30.12.45*
Leave Flensburg for Hamburg. Here we were again pleasantly surprised to meet "Gillie" Potter, that cheerful ex-member of "Wavell's 30,000", on his way to "C" release! It was a short reunion, for "Gillie" was leaving by an earlier train than ours.

On the white wall of the great dining hall at Hamburg, someone has painted a fine mural. It depicts life-sized figures of Elizabethan times, in a period setting.

We fill in time until ten o'clock at night, when we get a meal which is officially called "breakfast", in preparation for our departure in the early morning.

MONDAY – *31.12.45*
Leave Hamburg at 1.20 a.m. Stop at Minden before midday for dinner, then continue by Bielefeld, Hamm, Dortmund and Gelsenkirchen, crossing the Rhine at Duisburg and on through Krefeld to Roermond in Holland. We passed into 1946 while I was lying on the luggage rack, trying to sleep.

TUESDAY – *1.1.46*
Reach Tournai, in Belgium, at 4.30 a.m. Here we were separated into our respective zones and I said goodbye to Len, my last link with the unit in which I served for over three years.

For some reason our currency could not be changed in one

transaction. I queued to change my money into Belgian francs, then joined another queue to change the francs into sterling.

WEDNESDAY – *2.1.46*
Continue via Lille and Armentières to Calais, where I arrive at 2.00 p.m. Have dinner and off again, sailing at 3.30 on the T.S.S. "Canterbury". As usual, we were crowded down below and everyone began smoking and coughing. When we struck a bit of a swell, however, even the chain-smokers stopped smoking and the atmosphere cleared and improved.

Put our watches back an hour, so arrived in Dover at 4.00 p.m.

After tea, left Dover and travelled overnight to Carlisle.

THURSDAY – *3.1.46*
At Carlisle, handed over most of my remaining kit. The kit was placed on a board, which I pushed on a roller belt around a room. Each item was slung into its respective compartment, a form was checked and signed, and out I went once more.

Paraded later to take the night train for Edinburgh.

Epilogue

> *"Soldier, rest! thy warfare o'er,*
> *Sleep the sleep that knows not breaking!*
> *Dream of battled fields no more,*
> *Days of danger, nights of waking."*
>   Scott (*Lady of the Lake*)

I ARRIVED AT REDFORD BARRACKS at 6.00 a.m. on Friday, 4th January, my Day of Days. By 9.00 a.m., I had had breakfast, handed in my enamel mug and knife, fork and spoon (the last items of kit, except for the battledress I was wearing), was fitted with civilian clothes, which were parcelled up, and went to Waverley Station as a civilian citizen, though still in uniform.

But what memories flooded through my mind as I walked through the streets clutching my brown-paper parcel: the surf breaking on the beach at Durban; the "Beer-Barrel Polka" rolling out in the Rue de la Fosse in Nantes; the shuttered windows of Lyons la Forêt; the machine-gunning on the ship leaving from France and more machine-gunning on the ship returning to Normandy; Vesuvius splashing fire at night above the Bay of Naples; the Albersdorf "choir"; the Jeep on Normandy beach-head with its saucy "I go – I come back!"; the broad Nile and the Sphinx gazing down placidly as it has done for thousands of years; the flying fishes; the wonders of Leptis; the palms at Freetown; – and, of course, the desert – the implacable, endless desert – tyre marks in the sand ... sands of time?

Such were the pictures passing before my inner eye, but they faded as I settled in the train. These were the green fields of my homeland passing the window.

The last page of my diary reads :

In the first few days of mobilization, I was Private Nicol, without a uniform and now, at the end, I am Mr. Nicol, with a uniform; but now I am free, and I am alive. No more parades; no more guards; no more spit and polish; no more "going back" ...

But I think too, of those who will never be demobbed; who will never again be civilians; whose remains lie in many foreign lands.

And I am silent.